T0323465

Pockets of Effectiveness and the Politics of State-building and Development in Africa

Pockets of Effectiveness and the Politics of State-building and Development in Africa

Edited by
SAM HICKEY

With a Foreword by Merilee Grindle

OXFORD
UNIVERSITY PRESS

Great Clarendon Street, Oxford, OX2 6DP,
United Kingdom

Oxford University Press is a department of the University of Oxford.
It furthers the University's objective of excellence in research, scholarship,
and education by publishing worldwide. Oxford is a registered trade mark of
Oxford University Press in the UK and in certain other countries

Published in the United States of America by Oxford University Press
198 Madison Avenue, New York, NY 10016, United States of America

British Library Cataloguing in Publication Data
Data available

Library of Congress Control Number: 2022945379

ISBN 978–0–19–286496–3

DOI: 10.1093/oso/9780192864963.001.0001

Printed and bound by
CPI Group (UK) Ltd, Croydon, CR0 4YY

Foreword

The African state fares poorly in contemporary assessments of governance, capacity, and effectiveness. With a few exceptions, states in the region are considered to have failed to deliver on development—their citizens remain poor and disregarded by their governments, corruption reigns, and public services are dismally unreliable and ineffectual. Reform initiatives are legion, but they seem futile or unsustainable in the face of systemic national performance deficits. The African state, it seems, is a failure.

But dig beneath tropes of disappointment that nothing works, corruption is ubiquitous, governance capacity is minimal, institutions are weak. Under these generalizations and the cross-national indices that attest to the poor performance of public sectors in Africa, a very different reality exists. Even the most dystopian of states is not monolithic; rather, it is a web of organizations and institutions that vary in how they are managed and the quality of the goods and services they produce. The overall level of accomplishment may be very low, but not all bureaucratic performance seeks out the mean. While some organizations can be unmitigated disasters, others might do quite well in accomplishing the tasks they are assigned. Indeed, no matter how dysfunctional a public sector is deemed to be, some parts of it usually manage to perform better than others. Figuring out why and when this is true is the focus of this notable volume on pockets of effectiveness in African states.

Of course, that pockets of reasonably good performance—not perfect by any means, but better than the norm—exist within public bureaucracies is not a new insight. Many studies attest to their existence across historical time periods and countries of the world. Thus, for example, military organizations, central banks, finance ministries, and some technically focused agencies are often found to produce better outcomes than others in the same context. Explanations of a penchant for higher performance invoke a variety of factors—state survival, revenue imperatives, the need to negotiate with international actors, or the demands set by technological requirements. Some studies point to astute leadership in search of bureaucratic autonomy, others to the incentives offered to their staffs, others to mission-driven organizational cultures, and yet others to ongoing strategic reform initiatives and international support. Each explanation seeks to clarify why good performance happens even when state-level-capacity cards are clearly stacked against it.

In terms of its focus, then—pockets of effectiveness in public sectors in Africa— this volume is part of a larger universe of studies that asks how and when reasonably well-performing public-sector organizations are created, managed, and sustained when surrounded by environments of dysfunction, corruption, and failure. But the research reported in this book raises the bar for such studies by bringing together a unifying theory and study design for a significant comparative analysis of this important conundrum about performance. Among the volume's notable achievements is that contributors collaborated in developing a core theory and set of hypotheses that were then addressed systematically in clearly identified country and organizational contexts. The choice of study countries and organizations proceeded from a consistent logic about distinct types of national political arrangements and public-sector agencies, strengthening the opportunities for making comparisons and exploring hypotheses. This book provides a unified explanation of a well-observed phenomenon across countries; its findings have relevance for other countries and regions of the world. This is comparative case analysis at its best.

Most important in terms of the volume's contributions to understanding development, its theoretically and methodologically convergent chapters begin and end with an effort to relate organizational performance to a broader political economy analysis centred on the concept of 'political settlement'. All states, the authors contend, exhibit explicit or implicit agreements among elites about the existential purpose of the state and the scope and limits of competition over power and claims to domination within it. The political settlement can be broad or exclusive and can incorporate distinct levels of struggles over power, but it endures over time as long as elites find room to agree on its usefulness in pursuit of their distinct ends. Thus, the volume goes far beyond claiming that 'politics matters' to how government agencies function by providing a consistent explanation for the way particular political settlements are played out within a state bureaucracy and account for the stability and instability and the highs and lows of performance in public-sector organizations.

The chapters in this volume explore the link between political settlements and organizational performance in Rwanda, Uganda, Ghana, Kenya, and Zambia. The character of the political settlements in each country, identified through historical and contemporary conditions of elite commitment and competition, is the starting point for assessing how well particular organizations achieve their purposes. Two of the countries feature dominant ruling coalitions, two conform to constrained competition over power, and one demonstrates the dynamics of moving from one type of political settlement to another. In some cases, researchers found, self-conscious state-building at the organizational level can occur; in others, settlements result in more sporadic efforts to improve or sustain the performance of strategically important state agencies. Over time, the nature of these coalitions can change, a situation then replicated in the operation of finance ministries, central banks, and revenue authorities, the organizations targeted for study.

Good performance happens, the authors affirm, not because it is essential to abstract state-building imperatives or because some organizations have extraordinary leadership or responsibilities, but because it is a predictable part of the logic of political settlements in historical and contemporary states. Thus, this volume takes us beyond understanding that politics matters to link performance at the bureaucratic level to national power configurations. When public-sector organizations perform relatively well, it is because state elites agree that such outcomes support and sustain their positions of power; the more stable the political settlement, the more likely good performance can be sustained. Often, ideas about how to pursue development bolster efforts to ensure organizational accomplishment.

In introductory chapters and the volume's conclusion, researchers probe the foundations of their approach and the puzzles it addresses. They bring together analyses of state-building over the longer term with development interventions that are usually conceived and implemented at the organizational level. Elsewhere named the 'missing middle' in development studies, such an approach iterates the normal process of how states acquire and lose capacity in the real world—not in lock-step across the state as a whole but rather in disjointed ways and across significant periods of time in accord with specific configurations of power.

When states are successful in carrying out development-relevant tasks, the contributors to this volume affirm, it is because political and economic elites have agreed about goals, the costs and benefits of change, and how performance wins and losses are to be distributed. Turning the lens around, pockets of effectiveness illuminate fundamental characteristics of how states are built and development occurs, as well as why such efforts often encounter resistance, stall, or break down. Here, then, is a way to explain how change happens within a political economy analysis that is at once historically informed and relevant to everyday reform initiatives in bureaucratic settings. It encourages serious efforts to assess relationships of power among governing elites and their impact on public-sector performance. As such, it expands our understanding of how political arrangements at national levels affect the development of the state.

Merilee S. Grindle
Harvard University

Acknowledgements

The origins of this book lie within work undertaken by the Effective States and Inclusive Development research centre (ESID), which was based at the Global Development Institute, University of Manchester, from 2011 to 2020. ESID's early research into the politics of development had already identified pockets of effectiveness (PoEs) as critical to developmental success in Africa. With our first phase drawing to a close, I wanted to find ways of exploring this further and of continuing to work with at least some of ESID's excellent research team. Shortly after gaining a grant from the Economic and Social Research Council, to fund work on PoEs in Ghana, Rwanda, Uganda, and Zambia, ESID was awarded a funding extension that enabled us to include Kenya.

The team for this project picked itself and my first round of thanks is to Abdul-Gafaru Abdulai, Badru Bukenya, Caesar Cheelo, Benjamin Chemouni, Marja Hinfelaar, Giles Mohan, and Matt Tyce for being such great colleagues to work with over these past few years. You've made this my most enjoyable research project to date. We were privileged to be joined on this journey by some outstanding scholars. Merilee Grindle's (2012) *Jobs for the Boys* and Michael Roll's (2014) collection on *The Politics of Public Sector Performance: Pockets of Effectiveness in Developing Countries* were our foundational texts and we were genuinely thrilled that both Merilee and Michael agreed to join us as critical advisors and commentators and also, later, to contribute to this volume. Their insights and advice have been highly influential on our work from start to finish. We owe a particular debt to Merilee for interrupting her retirement to help show us the way, not only within the confines of our many workshops, from Manchester to Livingstone, but also in the occasionally more stimulating world beyond them ('what goes on the Zambezi, stays on the Zambezi', in her memorable words…!).

Many others also made telling contributions: Pritish Behuria pushed us to think harder about the ideological politics of PoEs and delivered a forensic case study of the central bank in Rwanda; Kate Pruce conducted the initial literature review that underpinned the project proposal; and Badru Bukenya provided further literature reviews on each of our agencies and data analysis support. Chris Lyon diligently ensured that all of our working papers were externally peer reviewed. David Hulme and Kunal Sen were strong supporters of the project from the outset, with David attending virtually every workshop and offering his usual brand of creative suggestions and collegial encouragement throughout. Tim Kelsall and Nicolai Schulz pushed us to be more rigorous in terms of our theoretical claims and use of performance indicators. Emily Jones joined the final workshop in Livingstone and significantly improved our understanding of how to understand high-performing agencies in relation to broader economic trends within Africa. Louise Umutoni Bower assisted with the research in Rwanda and Justine Sichone performed data analysis for the Zambia study. Erin McDonnell generously shared the survey instrument that she used to identify PoEs for her ground-breaking doctoral work in Ghana. We are grateful to you all.

Many other excellent scholars were generous in attending and organizing workshops through which our work got discussed and improved, including at the School of Advanced International Studies, Johns Hopkins University, the Cambridge Centre for Development Studies, and GDI's State–Society Relations Group at Manchester. Our thanks to Brian Levy, Daniel Honig, Peter Lewis, Helena Perez Nino, Jon Phillips, Ha Choon Chang, Heather Marquette, Pablo Yanguas Gil, Jennifer Widner, Nic Jepson, Charis Enns, Clare Cummings, Matt Tyce, Tom Lavers, Abdul-Gafaru Abdulai, Barnaby Dye, and Pritish Behuria. We also got helpful feedback when we presented at various academic conferences, including those held by the African Studies Association (2018), Development Studies Association (2019, 2020), and ESID (2019). Our panel at the 2020 American Political Science Association conference benefitted greatly from the discussant comments of Martha Johnson and Julia Strauss, and Julia has been kind enough to ensure that this book finishes with a strongly comparative perspective.

Detailed comments on our working papers were gratefully received from Michael Roll, Anne Mette Kjaer, Ole Therkildsen, Prince-Young Aboagye, Frank Ohemeng, David Booth, Susan Mueller, Erin McDonnell, Abel Fumey, Emily Jones, Alex Caramento, Mick Moore, Jalia Kangrave, Barnaby Dye, Benjamin Chemouni, Attiya Waris, Alan Whitworth, Fiona Davies, Nick Roberts, Grieve Chelwa, Florence Dafe, Alexandra Zeitz, Martin Brownbridge, Roger Tangri, Monica Skaten, Lyndsay Whitfield, Alan Nicol, Radha Upadhyaya, Karuti Kanyinga, Christopher Adam, Neo Simuntanyi, and Lise Rakner.

We held inception workshops in our initial case-study countries—Ghana, Rwanda, Uganda, and Zambia—and our thanks to the dozens of experts who generously offered their time, insights, and contacts. And, of course, we are grateful above all to the hundreds of anonymous experts who responded to our survey questions and agreed to be interviewed for this project. Your insights provide the core of our work and both these and the time you were prepared to offer to us are deeply appreciated.

Many colleagues at Manchester have assisted with the management of this project, organizing workshops, handling budgets, copy-editing papers, and doing all the other administrative work required to make collaborative research happen. The whole team and myself are very grateful to Kat Bethell, Julia Brunt, Clare Degenhardt, Julie Rafferty, and Anna Webster, and I'm particularly grateful to Kat for her last-minute assistance in collating and delivering this manuscript. Thanks also to Adam Swallow at Oxford University Press for supporting this project from the outset and to his colleagues for guiding it through contracting and production.

Finally, this project has incurred more debts on the home front than usual, from the half-day borrowed from a family holiday in Ireland to get the funding proposal submitted through multiple trips away. My thanks and love to Fiona, Michael, Jesse, and Noah.

Sam Hickey
Manchester, January 2022

This book is an output from two funded research projects: the ESRC-DFID Poverty Alleviation Research Programme (ES/N01443X/1) plus additional support from ESID, which was funded by the then UK Department for International Development. The views expressed and information contained therein are not necessarily those of, or endorsed by, the UK Government, which can accept no responsibility for them.

Contents

I. INTRODUCTION

II. CASE STUDIES

III. PATTERNS AND WAYS FORWARD

List of Figures

List of Tables

List of Abbreviations

AfDB	African Development Bank
ACFIM	Alliance for Campaign Finance Monitoring
BNR	Central Bank of Rwanda (Banque Nationale du Rwanda)
BoG	Bank of Ghana
BoU	Bank of Uganda
BoZ	Bank of Zambia
CBL	Crane Bank Limited (Uganda)
CBK	Central Bank of Kenya
CEPS	Customs Exercise and Preventive Services (Ghana)
CG	commissioner general
COMESA	Common Market for Eastern and Southern Africa
COSASE	Parliamentary Committee on Commissions, Statutory Authorities, and State Enterprises (Uganda)
CPIA	Country Policy and Institutional Assessment
CVC	Citizen's Vetting Committee (Ghana)
DASP	Administrative Department of Public Service (Brazil)
DFID	UK Department for International Development
DG	director general
EU	European Union
FSI	financial stability index
FY	fiscal year
GDP	gross domestic product
GRA	Ghana Revenue Authority
HIPC	heavily indebted poor countries
HPSA	high-performing state agencies
IIAG	Ibrahim Index of African Governance
IMF	International Monetary Fund
IFIs	international financial institutions
IRS	Internal Revenue Service
KCCA	Kampala Capital City Authority
KNBS	Kenya National Bureau of Statistics
KRA	Kenya Revenue Authority
KTDA	Kenya Tea Development Agency
LTO	Large Tax Office (Zambia)
MDAs	ministries, departments, and agencies
MFPED	Ministry of Finance, Planning and Economic Development (Uganda)
MINECOFIN	Ministry of Finance and Economic Planning (Rwanda)
MININFRA	Ministry of Infrastructure (Rwanda)

MMD	Movement for Multiparty Democracy (Zambia)
MoF	Ministry of Finance
MoFEP	minister of finance and economic planning (Ghana)
MPs	members of parliament
MTEF	Medium-Term Expenditure Framework (Kenya)
NARC	National Rainbow Coalition (Kenya)
NCDP	National Commission for Development Planning (Zambia)
NDC	National Democratic Congress (Ghana)
NEC	national executive committee
NoEs	networks of effectiveness
NPA	National Planning Authority (Uganda)
NPLs	non-performing loans
NPM	new public management
NPP	New Patriotic Party (Ghana)
NRM	National Resistance Movement (Uganda)
NRS	National Revenue Secretariat (Ghana)
NWSC	National Water and Sewerage Corporation (Uganda)
OAG	Office of Auditor General
PA	Provincial Administration (Kenya)
PEFA	Public Expenditure and Financial Accountability
PF	Patriotic Front (Zambia)
PFM	public finance management
PFMA	Public Financial Management Act
PNDC	Provisional National Defence Council (Ghana)
PoEs	pockets of effectiveness
PS	permanent secretary
RDB	Rwandan Development Board
RPF	Rwandan Patriotic Front
RRA	Rwanda Revenue Authority
Rwf	Rwandan Franc
SADC	Southern African Development Community
SAPs	structural adjustment programmes
SARA	semi-autonomous revenue authority
SCCI	Seed Control and Certification Institute (Zambia)
SSA	sub-Saharan Africa
UK	United Kingdom
UNCTAD	United Nations Conference on Trade and Development
UNDP	United Nations Development Programme
UNIP	United National Independence Party (Zambia)
UPND	United Party for National Development (Zambia)
URA	Uganda Revenue Authority
VAT	Value Added Tax
WGI	World Governance Indicators
ZRA	Zambia Revenue Authority

Notes on the Contributors

Abdul-Gafaru Abdulai is an associate professor of development politics at the University of Ghana. His research focuses on the intersection between politics and development, with a particular focus on social policy and social protection, natural resource governance, and public-sector reform. He is the co-author of *Governing Extractive Industries: Politics, Histories, Ideas* (OUP, 2018). He is a member of the editorial advisory boards of *African Affairs* and *Politics & Policy*, and is also co-editor of *Ghana Studies*. He holds a BA in political science from the University of Ghana, an MPhil in development studies from the University of Cambridge and a PhD in development policy and management from the University of Manchester.

Badru Bukenya is a senior lecturer in the Department of Social Work and Social Administration, Makerere University, Kampala. His research focuses on development policy, state–civil society engagement, service delivery, public-sector performance, and social protection. He has recently published in *Journal of Development Studies*, *Social Sciences and Medicine*, *Journal of Refugee Studies*, *Transactions of the Institute of British Geographers*, and *Development Policy Review* among other international journals.

Caesar Cheelo, an economist, is currently associate executive director and research fellow at the Southern African Institute for Policy and Research (SAIPAR), and research economist at the Common Market for Eastern and Southern Africa (COMESA) Secretariat. He is also a member of the Bank of Zambia and Rural Electrification Authority boards and an editor on two peer review journals at SAIPAR. Caesar previously served as senior research fellow at the Zambia Institute for Policy Analysis and Research and before that, as lecturer and researcher in the Economics Department, University of Zambia. He has spent nearly twenty years conducting applied and academic economics research and policy analysis and consultancies for various national, regional, and international bodies as well as teaching, training, supervising, and mentoring others in economics.

Benjamin Chemouni is an assistant professor in the Centre of Development Studies at the Catholic University of Louvain. His work focuses on dynamics of state formation and on the political economy of development policies, in particular public-sector reform, decentralization, and service delivery. His field research concentrates on the Great Lakes region of Africa, especially Burundi and Rwanda. Previously, he was a research associate at the Effective States and Inclusive Development (ESID) research centre at the University of Manchester and a Leverhulme fellow at the University of Cambridge.

Merilee S. Grindle is Edward S. Mason Professor of International Development, Harvard University, Emerita. She is a specialist on the comparative analysis of policymaking, implementation, and public management in developing countries, with particular reference to Latin America. Her most recent book is *Jobs for the Boys: Patronage and the State in Comparative Perspective* (Harvard University Press, 2012). She is also the author of *Going Local:*

Decentralization, Democratization, and the Promise of Good Governance; Despite the Odds: The Contentious Politics of Education Reform; Audacious Reforms; Challenging the State; State and Countryside; Searching for Rural Development; and *Bureaucrats, Politicians, and Peasants in Mexico*. She has written numerous articles about policy management and the politics of policy reform and is also co-author, with John Thomas, of *Public Choices and Policy Change*.

Sam Hickey is professor of politics and development at the Global Development Institute, University of Manchester. As research director of the Effective States and Inclusive Development (ESID) research centre (2011–2020), he worked with many colleagues on the links between politics and development, with particular reference to state capacity, natural resource governance, social protection, education, and gender equity. ESID's multiple open access books and papers on these topics are available at https://www.effective-states.org. He is currently deputy CEO for the African Cities Research Consortium at the University of Manchester and president of the Development Studies Association.

Marja Hinfelaar is the director of research and programs at Southern African Institute for Policy and Research (SAIPAR), Lusaka, Zambia. She received her PhD in history at Utrecht in 2001 and her work focuses on post-colonial political history in Zambia. She is the co-editor of *Democracy and Electoral Politics in Zambia* (Brill, 2020) and co-author of *Governing Extractive Industries: Politics, Histories, Ideas* (OUP, 2018). Marja is on the advisory board of the *Journal of Southern African Studies* and the *Zambia Social Science Journal*. She has been resident in Zambia since 1997.

Haggai Matsiko is an independent researcher and journalist based in Uganda. His research and journalistic work has over the last ten years focused on politics and development, extractives governance, and regional security. He holds an MA in media and development from the University of Westminster. Until recently, he was the investigations editor for *The Independent Magazine*, Uganda's major weekly current affairs magazine.

Giles Mohan is professor of international development at the Open University in the United Kingdom. He is particularly interested in 'new' actors in African development and the threats and opportunities they offer for the continent. This has led to work on structural adjustment, participatory development, diasporas and development, and most recently China's engagement with Africa. Funded by a series of grants from the Economic and Social Research Council his recent projects have looked at China's aid to Africa, Chinese business migrants in Africa, the impacts of China's oil investments in Africa, and migration's potential contributions to inclusive growth. Professor Mohan has also sought to engage with learning beyond universities and has worked with the BBC on television programmes about development, as well as working with African and international NGOs on various capacity-building and training initiatives.

Kate Pruce is a postdoctoral research fellow with the Developmental Leadership Program (DLP) at the University of Birmingham. Kate's work focuses on the politics of development, in particular social protection, global health policy and policy transfer, with other research interests including developmental leadership, gender, and social justice. Previously, Kate was a research associate with the Effective States and Inclusive Development (ESID) research centre and an ESRC postdoctoral research fellow at the University of Manchester.

Michael Roll is a researcher at the German Development Institute / Deutsches Institut für Entwicklungspolitik (DIE) and the editor of *The Politics of Public Sector Performance: Pockets of Effectiveness in Developing Countries* (Routledge, 2014). His research focuses on governance and institutional change, state performance, corruption, public-sector reform, and the governance of urban sustainability transformation. He has previously worked for the Friedrich-Ebert-Stiftung (FES) in Nigeria and South Africa and for the German Federal Ministry for Economic Cooperation and Development.

Julia C. Strauss is professor of Chinese politics at SOAS, University of London, where she served as editor of *The China Quarterly* from 2002 to 2011. She works on twentieth-century state-building and institution-building in China and Taiwan. Her monographs include *Strong Institutions in Weak Polities: State Building in Republican China, 1927–40* (Oxford University Press, 1998), and *State Formation in China and Taiwan: Bureaucracy, Campaign and Performance* (Cambridge University Press, 2020). She also publishes on performance in politics, China's Belt and Road Initiative (particularly with respect to Africa), and Chinese forestry.

Matthew Tyce is a postdoctoral research fellow and associate lecturer at the University of Manchester's Global Development Institute. Prior to this, he was a research associate with the Effective States and Inclusive Development (ESID) research centre. His research to date has examined the political economy of development, predominantly in Kenya, with an emphasis on state-building, state–business relations, industrial policy, natural resource governance, and—through his current British Academy-funded research project—clean energy transitions.

PART I
INTRODUCTION

1

Pockets of Effectiveness and the Politics of State-building and Development in Africa

Sam Hickey and Kate Pruce

Introduction

> A political sensibility requires that one consider the political actors that set agendas and prioritize among competing goals; that deploy particular state agencies to implement those agendas; that mobilize social forces to support these agendas ... In short, both state capacity and politics must be studied if we are to explain state performance—especially in the developing world.
>
> (Centeno et al. 2017: 3)

> (Pockets of effectiveness are) ... public organisations that are relatively effective in providing public goods and services that the organisation is officially mandated to provide, despite operating in an environment in which effective public service delivery is not the norm.
>
> (Roll 2014: 24)

The critical role of the state in shaping development prospects in the global South is no longer in question. Repeated economic and health crises over the past half-century have underlined the folly of leaving market forces to govern the economy or of undermining the capacity of the state to protect citizens. The decline of neoliberal hegemony during the early twenty-first century and the related rise of 'new' powers, whose developmental trajectories have generally involved a significant role for the state, have also shifted the terms of debate. Development theorists and policy actors alike have once more had to engage with the questions of how, when, and why states become capable of delivering development (Centeno et al. 2017, World Bank 2017).

This renewed focus on the capacity of states to deliver development has been closely informed by two important insights—both heralded in the above quotations—that provide the central focus of this volume. The first concerns the recognition that states are highly differentiated in terms of their ability to deliver

Sam Hickey and Kate Pruce, *Pockets of Effectiveness and the Politics of State-building and Development in Africa.*
In: *Pockets of Effectiveness and the Politics of State-building and Development in Africa.* Edited by Sam Hickey, Oxford University Press. © Oxford University Press (2023). DOI: 10.1093/oso/9780192864963.003.0001

on different policy goals. The variation in the capacity and quality of states can be as high *within* as *between* states: for example, 'The difference in corruption scores between Ghana's best- and worst-rated state agencies approximates the difference between Belgium and Mozambique, spanning the chasm of so-called developed and developing worlds' (McDonnell 2017: 478). Of particular interest here are those high-performing state agencies that have been referred to as 'islands of excellence' (Therlikdsen 2008), 'bureaucratic niches' (McDonnell 2020) or, the term we adopt here, 'pockets of effectiveness' (Roll 2014). As Mkandawire (2015) notes, such agencies seem to contradict the sweeping generalizations of the state in Africa as irredeemably 'failed' or 'neopatrimonial'. For some, they offer a glimpse of the Weberian forms of stateness that might emerge in Africa given the right kinds of incentives, investment, and leadership (McDonnell 2020). However, our aim here is to move away from this exceptionalist discourse that too often surrounds the state in Africa. Instead, we reframe these bureaucratic 'outliers' as being embedded within the long-term processes of state-formation that all states go through. As Grindle (2012) shows, the challenge that African rulers face in building state capacity amidst multiple threats to their political survival is remarkably similar to the challenge faced by earlier state-builders in countries such as Britain, France, Japan, and the United States, albeit from the very different starting point of colonialism and thereafter within a particular world historical moment that has contained particular challenges.

The second critical insight for this volume from current debates on state capacity concerns the recognition that both state capacity and state performance are primarily shaped by *political* factors. Whether states or particular state agencies are able to deliver effectively on their mandates is not just a function of hiring the best staff or being imbued with a bureaucratic ethos. Rather, it is because of the political support that they receive from those in power (Centeno et al. 2017), support which is in turn shaped by the incentives and ideas generated by the political and political economy context within which political rulers operate. This recognition—that politics and power relations lie behind the emergence and deployment of state capacity—has come to centre-stage within development theory and policy debates over the past decade (Acemoglu and Robinson 2019, Kelsall et al. 2022, Khan 2010, North et al. 2009,) and provides our entry point. Going further, we aim to identify the specific forms of politics and power relations that shape decisions by rulers to invest in building effective state agencies and offer them the support and space to deliver on their mandates. Our comparative analysis of similar types of pockets of effectiveness (PoEs) within countries that represent different types of 'political settlement' (Kelsall et al. 2022, Khan 2017), offers the first systematic examination of the political conditions under which such PoEs emerge and become sustained within developing-country contexts.

The challenge, however, is not only to identify how such high-performing agencies emerge in relation to the often competing logics of regime survival, political competition, and state formation that characterize political development at the national level, but to also locate this in the global context that the negotiation of statehood in Africa been embedded within for well over a century now (Hagmann and Peclard 2010). A creation of colonialism (Mamdani 1996), the post-colonial state in Africa has continued to be profoundly shaped by external forces and agendas. Over the past three decades that we focus on here, the lending and policy agendas of international development organizations, as located within the broader project of 'disciplinary neoliberalism' that defined much of this period (Gill 1995), have been particularly influential. Our case-study organizations—which include finance ministries, central banks, and revenue authorities—offer particularly clear evidence of the influence of disciplinary neoliberalism on the capacity of the state to deliver development in Africa (Harrison 2010, Mkandawire 2014). These cases also offer us the chance to explore the extent to which the apparent ruptures caused by the global financial crisis, the commodity boom, and the rising powers phenomenon during the early twenty-first century—which seemed to generate a new political economy of development and governance in Africa[1]—has indeed opened up space for alternative projects of state-building and development to emerge (Grabel 2017, Jepson 2020, Jessop 2015).

Reframed as such, we conducted in-depth investigations of PoEs in Ghana, Kenya, Rwanda, Uganda, and Zambia, with chapters on each forming the core of this book's contribution. We found that Africa's high-performing state agencies offer a fascinating window onto how the politics of state-building, democratization, and regime survival are currently unfolding in Africa, as shaped by broader processes of capitalist development and international intervention. Our overall argument is that the apparent anomaly that PoEs in Africa present—as high-performing state agencies in otherwise difficult governance contexts—needs to be understood in relation to the distribution of political power, or what we term the 'political settlement', and how this shapes the strategies of governing coalitions. PoEs tend to emerge and flourish when rulers stitch together technocratic coalitions that give politically savvy organizational leaders the space to build high-performing state agencies. As early state-builders found (Grindle 2012), securing such spaces becomes much harder when the level of factionalism amongst elites increases, both within governing coalitions and between different groups competing for power, particularly where this competition is weakly institutionalized. And for investments in PoEs to extend into a more general project of state-building requires even more demanding conditions, most notably a perception amongst rulers that certain social groups pose such a threat to the political settlement that investing in a wider state-building effort constitutes a logical response. International actors have offered essential support for the specific type of PoEs we investigate here but this has been both insufficient and problematic; their highly

---

[1] See several contributions to the special edition of *New Political Economy* (2013, 7(5)).

partial investments have profoundly shaped which parts of the state work in Africa, and as elsewhere (Jessop 2015), what kinds of economic and social project it is capable of delivering. This leads us to argue that state-capacity building in Africa in the future, and in relation to economic development in particular, must involve a more balanced approach that supports those state agencies required to pursue the forms of structural transformation required to generate lasting processes of poverty reduction. Going further, we identify two different routes to higher levels of state effectiveness and state-building in contemporary Africa, one associated with contexts where political power is concentrated and another where power is more dispersed between competing factions.

The remainder of the chapter begins by placing the resurgent interest in PoEs within the context of longer-running debates around high-performing state agencies. The following section then sets out what we currently know about the origins and drivers of PoEs, identifying some of the key gaps and oversights within the existing literature and how this volume seeks to address them. The most significant concern identified is the tendency to frame PoEs as aberrations from the norm, as 'islands' cast adrift within a broader sea of patronage, rather than as creatures of their political context.[2] Both this and the absence of comparative work has led to an under-specification of the types of politics that shape the emergence, performance, and continuity of PoEs. To address these problems, the chapter locates PoEs within broader debates on how to understand the nature of state and bureaucratic practices, both historically and at the current moment, with particular reference to sub-Saharan Africa. This involves putting PoEs into conversation with histories of state formation and bureaucratic development, contested debates around the role of patronage, ethnicity, and colonial heritage and the role of ideas and transnational influences. The aim is to identify alternative strands of thinking that can shed greater light on the phenomenon of PoEs, reframing them as windows that can enable us to explore broader questions about the state, politics, and development in Africa.

Contextualizing the debate over PoEs

The apparent conundrum that some parts of government in developing countries perform much better than others has been of longstanding but episodic concern within development theory and policy. In the 1980s and 1990s, the developmental-states literature identified elite bureaucratic agencies as critical to the transformations taking place in South East Asia, particularly those associated

---

[2] We prefer the 'pockets' to the 'islands' metaphor, as the latter implies a disconnection between such agencies and their political context, whereas we are specifically interested in exploring how this context actively shapes the functioning of such agencies.

with planning, trade, industry, and commerce (Evans 1995, Johnson 1982, Left-wich 1995). However, this statist focus struggled to gain traction amidst the rise of neoliberal thinking during this period (Mkandawire 2014, Wade 1996). The influential literature on 'failed' and 'neopatrimonial states' further undermined the sense that the state could be a progressive force by identifying political culture and corrupt elites as the central cause of under-development in Africa (e.g. Bratton and van de Walle 1997, cf. Mkandawire 2015). These perspectives helped catalyse a focus on 'good governance' within international development from the early 1990s onwards, a project that aimed to reduce the influence of centralized authority in favour of a stripped-back, decentralized state apparatus subjected to strict rules aimed at curbing corruption and the capacity of the state to play an active economic role (Grindle 2004). Interest in PoEs thereafter was largely sporadic, often coming either from those continuing to make the case that 'politics matters' for development (e.g. Grindle 1997), or in ways that reflected ideas from new public management around how the state should operate. Here, 'islands of excellence' were associated with certain organizational forms (e.g. semi-autonomous agencies), including of a non-state variety (Korten 1987, Leonard 1991). As Roll (2014) notes, the focus on PoEs was a 'marginal monologue' during this period.[3]

The recent flourishing of interest in state-based PoEs has been catalysed by a series of intellectual and institutional shifts within development theory and policy during the early twenty-first century, including the strong turn to politics (Left-wich 2005) and the resurgent interest in state capacity identified above. The role of state capacity in shaping development prospects has been a staple of social science research for decades (Evans 1995, Geddes 1990), and the renewed interest in this question has been led by earlier pioneers of the field (e.g. Centeno et al. 2017, Evans and Heller 2010) but also by scholars previously more occupied by the inclusive and democratic nature of the state rather than its capacity to deliver development (Acemoglu and Robinson 2019, Fukuyama 2016). A shared characteristic across this literature is the strong sense that state capacity and performance flows not simply from institutional legacies but also the forms of political authority and coalitions that guide states and encourage the deployment of state capacity for specific purposes (Centeno et al. 2017, Slater 2010, vom Hau 2012). This understanding resonates strongly with the approach of critical state theorists such as Bob Jessop (2008, 2015), who have long argued that the state is not an homogenous actor but rather a collection of power centres that each offers different opportunities for wider social and economic interests to advance their projects, we explore this convergence between critical political theory and political settlements analysis in Chapter 2 when mapping out the conceptual framework deployed here.

---

[3] The role of bureaucrats and bureaucratic agencies remains a strikingly understudied aspect of post-colonial African politics (Bierschenk 2010).

The interest in PoEs as a specific form of state capacity was further motivated by the growing sense, from around the turn of the millennium, that the 'good governance' agenda was failing to deliver positive outcomes (Grindle 2004, 2007, Khan 2005). This catalysed a series of major research efforts aimed at identifying the actual rather than idealized conditions under which development occurred in the global South (e.g. Houtzager and Moore 2003). Successive research programmes on the politics of development identified PoEs as critical to explaining what works, despite having not deliberately set out to examine them (Booth 2015, Hickey et al. 2020, Whitfield et al. 2015).[4] Meanwhile, this sub-field of development theory and practice has been greatly advanced by the more deliberate efforts to identify PoEs across the global South, particularly the mixture of original case-study work and field surveys offered by Michael Roll (2014) and Erin McDonnell (2017, 2020), along with specific studies of 'sub-state agencies' (Bersch et al. 2017) and the 'asymmetric capabilities' of government (Porter and Watts 2017). New insights into how state bureaucracies and bureaucrats actually work in Africa from the perspective of political anthropology have also helped revive an interest in the everyday politics of state performance (e.g. Bierschenk 2010, de Herdt and de Sardan 2015, de Sardan 2013).

There is also some evidence that perspectives on governance and state capacity within international development agencies have started to change (Levy and Kpundeh 2004), with alternative approaches steadily replacing the now tattered certainties of the good governance agenda (Grindle 2007). This includes explicit efforts to identify more realistic governance solutions for developing countries (Roll 2014, also Levy 2014), with tentative suggestions that PoEs might form part of the new 'doing-development-differently' vanguard on governance (de Gramont 2014, Porter and Watts 2017, World Bank 2017).

Within the context of these shifting debates over the capacity of the state to deliver development in Africa, this book aims to help fill what Merilee Grindle (2017, also Foreword) has identified as the 'missing middle' within new thinking on governance. This involves a profound gap between studies of how politics shapes institutional performance over relatively long-run periods of time (e.g. Acemoglu and Robinson 2012, 2019, North, Wallis, and Weingast 2009) and of the more immediate world of governance reforms and state practices (e.g. Andrews et al. 2017). Critical to addressing this 'missing middle' is our theorization of different types of political and political economy context. As set out in the next chapter, this draws on the concept of 'political settlements', which we locate within a critical understanding of the transnational context within which state-building

---

[4] These three references reflect the respective work of three research centres: Developmental Regimes in Africa (run jointly by the Overseas Development Institute and the University of Leiden: http://www.institutions-africa.org/page/about%2Bdra.html), the Elites, Production and Poverty project (based at the Danish Institute for International Studies 2008–2012: http://drp.dfcentre.com/project/elites-production-and-poverty-comparative-study) and the Effective States and Inclusive Development Research Centre (ESID, University of Manchester, 2011–2020: https://www.effective-states.org).

in sub-Saharan Africa has taken place since colonial times. This enables us to place questions of state capacity and performance into direct conversation with deeper explanations of how power and politics actually work in sub-Saharan Africa, and how processes of state-building and development unfold over longer periods of time. Linked to an analysis of how external interventions have shaped this process, this hopefully enables us to deliver insights into power, politics, and pubic-sector performance in Africa that can also inform strategic efforts to improve the capacity of states in Africa to deliver inclusive forms of development.

What do we know about pockets of effectiveness? Insights and gaps

The central findings of the PoE literature up until around 2012 was captured very effectively in Michael Roll's (2014) collection on *The Politics of Public Sector Performance*. This section therefore weaves together his main insights with those of several studies published in the decade since then, along with reflections from the more historical literature on the bureaucracy within African states. The structure follows the three 'mega-hypotheses' that Roll distils from the wider literature on the main drivers of PoEs, namely political economy, leadership and management, and organizational function. After also discussing the potential 'spillover' effects' of PoEs, the final sub-section identifies some of the key knowledge gaps that remain.

The political economy drivers of PoEs

> The underlying political economy in which an organization is placed ultimately will overcome and dominate all other causal factors and thus determine what effectiveness is possible.
>
> (Roll 2014: 34, with reference to Leonard 2008: 25)

There is now widespread agreement that politics constitutes the main driver of public-sector performance in developing countries, particularly in terms of the commitment of political elites to protecting agencies from the worst excesses of political interference (Geddes 1990, 1994). In a finding that resonates with the developmental-states literature, Whitfield et al's (2015: 20) study of industrial policy in Africa concludes that:

> State capabilities are the product of underlying political relationships and not independent from them. State bureaucrats in charge of industrial policy must have political backing from ruling elites and a significant degree of autonomy from political pressures stemming from within the ruling coalition.
>
> (Whitfield et al. 2015: 20)

Portes and Smith (2012) also argue that high performance often stems from deliberate, concentrated efforts by governments at the highest levels of authority assigning top priority to institutional changes, as with the Chilean internal revenue service. Different types of elite interests seem to be involved in offering protection to certain state agencies, including:

- Interests that are integral to regime survival and legitimacy, including those where critical national resources are involved (Hickey and Izama 2016, Hout 2013, Roll 2014, Whitfield et al. 2015, Whitfield and Buur 2014);
- Interests flowing from strategies of economic accumulation that are significant to ruling elites for sectional rather than national interests (see Kjaer et al. 2012 on elite protection for the dairy sector in Uganda), including for predatory purposes (Soares de Oliveira 2007 on oil-sector governance in Angola);
- Interests of a more personal or ad hoc character (e.g. state agencies in Nigeria established by a vice-president's wife, Simbine et al. 2014).

There is some case-study evidence that PoEs are more likely to be protected and sustained by rulers who don't face a significant or imminent political challenge (e.g. Hertog 2014, Hout 2013, Roll 2014). For Whitfield et al. (2015: 97):

> The degree of vulnerability of the ruling elites shapes whether a pocket of efficiency emerges ... A low degree of vulnerability means that ruling elites are better able to absorb social costs and conflict that come from changing the existing distribution of benefits or the allocation of state resources. In this situation, it is easier to create a pocket of efficiency.

In contrast, high levels of competition for political power can make it difficult to protect and sustain such PoEs. According to Whitfield et al. (2015: 247), symbiotic and long-term relationships between political rulers and senior bureaucrats are less likely to unfold in more competitive settings, 'where elite factionalism makes it unlikely that ruling elites will invest sufficient capital and resources in building effective bureaucratic units'. In Ghana, the Cocoa Board has only received protection from the successive ruling coalitions of different political parties because cocoa provides one of the state's key sources of foreign exchange for the state (Whitfield and Buur 2014), which makes it critical 'to the economy and therefore to the political survival strategies of all ruling elites' (Whitfield et al. 2015: 247). The mixed fortunes of the Ghana National Petroleum Corporation under different ruling coalitions reflects the sense that intense democratic competition can undermine high-performing agencies over time (Hickey et al. 2020, Mohan et al. 2018). Several observers of PoEs in Brazil describe how a number of high-performing agencies (with regards power, oil, statistics, development banking) emerged and found protection under the centralizing, developmentalist, and technocratic military regime of President Vargas (1937–1946), before then being undermined when civilian rulers and multi-party politics returned (Geddes 1990, Grindle 2012, Willis 2014).

A number of historical studies concur that the process of displacing patronage-based governance with 'meritocratic' civil-service systems is more protracted in contexts where processes of democratic competition emerge before significant levels of bureaucratic capacity have developed (Fukuyama 2014, Grindle 2012, Shefter 1994). State bureaucrats in Africa were arguably at their most influential when the initially democratic dispensation of post-colonial rule Africa gave way to single-party (and often military) rule in many countries from the late 1960s. As Abernethy notes, 'The Weberian attributes of hierarchy, impersonality, and discipline are even more strongly emphasized in the military than the bureaucracy' (1971: 94), a comment that resonates with the case of mid-twentieth-century Brazil noted above and also the contemporary return of apparently developmental forms of 'bureaucratic/quasi-military authoritarianism' in countries like Ethiopia and Rwanda today. This affinity between PoEs and authoritarian forms of governance raises concerns, and can to some extent be traced back to the 'strong antidemocratic and militaristic aspect to some presentations of the rational-legal Weberian framework' (Mkandawire 2015: 599).

However, focusing on the association between PoEs and regime types may be less useful than focusing on the configuration of elite power that underlies different institutional arrangements. Many studies of the politics of PoEs refer to issues of 'elite fragmentation' or 'cohesion' or 'the ways in which power over decisions was dispersed' (Geddes 1990, Grindle 2012, Hertog 2014, Roll 2014, Willis 2014), rather than to formal political institutions themselves. As discussed in Chapter 2, this encourages us to frame the politics of PoEs in relation to the underlying configuration of power that constitutes a 'political settlement'.

Leadership and management: Towards deeper organizational sociologies?

Leadership and management have also been identified as central to the high performance of bureaucratic agencies, particularly with regards to organizational culture and management practices, recruitment and promotion, resource mobilization, and organizational goals (Roll 2014: 34, Grindle 1997). The professionalism of staff—particularly managers—and a strong sense of mission are commonly identified as significant (Leonard 1991, Grindle 1997, Simbine with Attoh and Oladeji 2014, Strauss 2014, Tendler 1997, Therkildsen 2008, Therkildsen and Tidemand 2007). Therkildsen and Tidemand (2007) find a clear relationship between the principle of *merit* for hiring, firing, and promotions and the performance-based rating of an organization, although Whitfield and Therkildsen (2011) later qualify this to suggest that merit should be accompanied by *loyalty*. Staff motivation within high-performing public agencies has been linked to rewards for good performance and other benefits (training, equipment), but also to non-material aspects, including consultation and participation in decision-making and autonomy in undertaking their duties (Grindle 1997, Roll 2014).

This question of 'organizational culture' looms large in the PoE literature. For McDonnell (2017, 2020), it is the presence of a 'bureaucratic ethos' that defines PoEs and Grindle and Hilderbrand (1995) and Grindle (1997) argue that a sense of organizational mission is more important for good performance than rules, regulations, and even remuneration. It is less clear where this ethos comes from. Some studies suggest that a patriotic desire to deliver on an organizational mandate can emerge around a key historical moment of renewal within a country's political development, as with the strong esprit de corps established within Uganda's high-performing oil department during the late 1980s and early 1990s (Hickey et al. 2020, Hickey and Izama 2016). For others, the bureaucratic ethos that persuades finance ministry officials in Ghana to work late into the night comes from a sense of professional pride and commitment that is nurtured over time through social-psychological means within specific organizational settings (McDonnell 2020). Both Grindle (1997) and Roll (2014) stress that a strong organizational culture and high levels of staff motivation are more likely when bureaucrats are given the sense that they form an elite that is distinct from and superior to the rest of the bureaucracy. This echo of how bureaucratic enclaves emerged under colonial rule is a theme we return to below.

The challenge of leading and managing high-performing state agencies is a political as well as a technical challenge, and the term 'technopol', coined to describe the kind of leadership required here (Domínguez 1997, Joignant 2011), is one we found very useful. A technopol can be a politician with the technocratic bent and expertise required to identify and support highly-skilled bureaucratic cadres, as with former lawyers or economists turned leaders in countries like Zambia and Kenya (see Chapters 4 and 5). Or it can refer to technocrats with the political capacities to persuade other actors of the logic of their organizational agenda and to ensure that their organizations receive the right balance of political attention and protection, as with the leaders of central banks and revenue authorities in several of our cases. The most successful state agencies may need the support of both types of technopol, whereby rulers and senior bureaucrats become tied together by bonds of political loyalty as much as any commitment to meritocratic principles of governance (Grindle 2012), as exemplified by the National Sugar Institute in Mozambique (Whitfield et al. 2015: 189) and several of our case-study organizations. The nature of the relationships between political rulers and senior bureaucrats remains largely undocumented. Insider studies have tended to focus on front-line civil servants (Bierschenk 2010, De Herdt and de Sardan

2015) or the social-psychological processes involved in forming bureaucratic cultures (McDonnell 2017), rather than the ways in which politics reaches into such agencies.

Organizational function

Are PoEs more prevalent amongst public-sector organizations that perform particular types of role? The PoE literature generally focuses on state agencies mandated to deliver on functions that are specific and targeted in nature (e.g. regulatory authorities), rather than broad-based and diffused (e.g. ministries of health or education) (Roll 2014: 34). Organizational function determines the specific technology, workforce, and tasks involved, and a typical feature of PoEs is the high-level of technical expertise required amongst bureaucratic staff (de Gramont 2014) and the targeted nature of the governance task being undertaken. PoEs are more often associated with delivering tasks that are more 'logistical' than 'transactional' in nature, in the sense that logistical policy tasks can be delivered by skilled agents delivering a known technology as opposed to transactional policy tasks that are more 'implementation intensive' (Andrews et al. 2017). Transactional challenges, such as ensuring health-sector workers attend work and treat patients well, require more interactive and dispersed forms of governance than the more tightly focused and bounded state agencies found within the PoE literature (Pritchett and Woolcock 2004). Many of the state agencies we examine here perform tasks that are more logistical than transactional in nature, something that leads Michael Roll to explore how far the notion of PoE stretches across the public sector in the critical commentary chapter that closes this book (Chapter 10).

A further common (if not universal) feature is that the high-performing state agencies identified in the literature often benefit from a mandate that not only clearly sets out a relatively narrow set of responsibilities but which is also protected in legal terms. This often includes specific measures to ensure organizational autonomy in their given field of policy formulation and/or implementation, as with the central banks and, to a lesser extent, the revenue authorities we explore here. However, our cases show that this de jure insulation is never enough to fully protect agencies from political pressure; indeed, and as explored in Julia Strauss' commentary on our work in Chapter 9, high levels of organizational performance require that state agencies are embedded within rather than divorced from their political contexts.

Can PoEs have spillover effects?

Can PoEs help drive up bureaucratic quality and performance levels across the public sector more broadly, acting as the vanguard of modern state-building?

This is arguably the 'holy grail' question within scholarly and strategic debates on PoEs and there is historical evidence that modern state bureaucracies necessarily emerged from and were built on such enclaves. Some of these have continued to maintain a degree of insularity and apartness as a result of their early formation, specific mission, and critical role in maintaining a sense of stateness. Particular attention is drawn to the functioning of the military (Tilly 1975), revenue generation (Moore 2008), the treasury, and central banks (Grindle 2012). A good example here is the Treasury in Britain, which, with 14,000 of the country's 17,000 public officials working in the eighteenth century, was 'where Britain's professional civil service was eventually housed (and) also where it began' (Grindle 2012: 83). The Treasury introduced the use of examinations for its officials in the 1830s and would later play a key role in extending a merit-based system across Whitehall.

However, this trajectory seems to be more complicated in later-developing countries, within which rulers confront particular challenges. The case of Brazil suggests that a more complicated relationship emerged between PoEs and early efforts to establish a civil-service system through the Administrative Department of Public Service (DASP). One early high-performing state agency, namely the Bank of Brazil (Willis 2014), had 'instituted its own system of meritocratic recruitment even before the DASP began to operate' (Grindle 2012: 228–9). Once the initial efforts of DASP were thwarted by opponents elsewhere in the public sector, frustrated staff left to work in other agencies that would go on to be recognized as PoEs, including the economic data unit and the national development bank (Grindle 2012: 226, also Willis 2014), none of which were then credited with having spillover effects on the quality of the public sector more broadly.

Indeed, there is little evidence from the recent literature on PoEs in developing countries that they have positive externalities (McDonnell 2020: 193, Roll 2014), and even some evidence to the contrary. Negative spillovers can occur through PoEs capturing the most qualified staff and securing a protected share of limited budgets. Most staff within PoEs are so highly paid in comparison with their counterparts in the mainstream civil service that they are unlikely to consider career-moves that involve moving sideways (or downwards) to help raise standards elsewhere. This problem is exacerbated by the fact that many PoEs are increasingly connected to private and often global professional networks that provide alternative career opportunities, as with the links between revenue-authority staff and large accountancy and legal firms (Moore 2014). This negative finding may be truer of some forms of PoE than others, and perhaps applies in particular to those semi-autonomous agencies created by the new public-management-inspired wave of 'agencification' that washed over developing countries from the 1980s, and which recent research suggests has generally had a negative effect on public-sector performance (Overman and van Thiel 2016). This could leave open the possibility that those state agencies which perform core state functions and have remained firmly embedded within broader civil service systems can play important roles in establishing modern forms of statehood and meritocratic forms of recruitment. It could also mean that the historical specificity of state-building in sub-Saharan Africa requires that we adopt an alternative perspective on state capacity and performance, one that learns comparative lessons from earlier experiences of state-building whilst not seeing this as the basis for making teleological predictions.

From key knowledge gaps towards an alternative framing of PoEs

The episodic nature of research into high-performing state agencies within developing countries over the past three decades means that we lack an accumulated stock of knowledge on this phenomenon, despite the current resurgence of scholarly interest in PoEs. As Roll (2014) notes, evidence on how PoEs emerge and persist remains weak. Although the existing literature on PoEs is clear that politics is central to shaping the emergence, performance, and sustainability of PoEs over time it has so far failed to identify which specific political factors or contexts offer the most favourable conditions. However, this problem is only partly down to the limited scale of research on high-performing state agencies; much of it also flows from the conceptual and methodological basis of the existing literature. We identify three particular problems here, each of which we hope to address in this volume through offering an alternative reframing of the PoE phenomenon.

First, and in methodological terms, the PoE literature produced to date has been based on choosing cases on the basis of their performance (the dependent variable), rather than through a more systematic process of case selection that would enable the identification of which independent variables are shaping the performance of which type of PoE. This has made it difficult to identify the causal mechanisms and pathways through which PoEs emerge and are sustained in particular areas of governance and policy, including the role of different kinds of political and institutional contexts. The methodological approach adopted here, involving comparative analysis of similar types of PoE within country cases chosen from a typology, was devised to deliver an improved theoretical understanding of PoEs. We also hoped that this would help generate policy-relevant findings that can reach beyond the specifics of individual cases whilst remaining relevant to particular types of context (Chapter 2). The second problem we identify here concerns the methodological nationalism that pervades much political analysis, and which has involved an underplaying of the role played by transnational factors in shaping public-sector performance.

The final major conceptual obstacle to identifying the political drivers of PoEs concerns the tendency to stress the *sui generis* character of PoEs—as islands afloat in a sea of patronage—which suggests that they are somehow disconnected from their political and institutional context, rather than embedded within it. We argue below that this framing offers a highly partial and ahistorical perspective on PoEs in Africa and that a more fruitful approach is to view such 'bureaucratic enclaves' not as some form of *deux ex machina* arriving from beyond to save Africa from neopatrimonial disaster (Mkandawire 2015), but as both reflecting and reproducing the deeper logics of how politics and state power in particular operate within sub-Saharan Africa.

Reframing the politics of PoEs

There is a widespread tendency within the literature on PoEs in developing countries to frame them as aberrations from the norm, cast adrift within a broader sea of patronage rather than creatures of their political context. This is problematic in several respects. Although McDonnell (2020) argues for giving greater recognition to the 'embedded' nature of PoEs within African politics and society, her work frames PoEs as 'a systematic organizational response to their common position' within 'neopatrimonial environments' (McDonnell 2017: 477), without defining this broad-brush term or distinguishing between different types of 'neopatrimonial' contexts. This tendency not only discourages a focus on the links between such state agencies and their specific political context; it also undermines our ability to develop a more contextualized and historicized understanding of what shapes its development and performance. The main issues we discuss here concern the problematic concept of neopatrimonialism and the difficulties that this leads to, including the misrepresentation of PoEs in relation to the distinction between meritocracy and patronage; overlooking the influence of colonial rule on both the post-colonial state in general and on elite bureaucratic agencies in particular; proposing a uniformly negative view of the role of ethnicity on public-sector performance; and underplaying the role of both ideas and transnational actors in shaping politics and governance in Africa. In setting out an alternative perspective, we draw particular inspiration from Merilee Grindle's seminal (2012) study of the struggle between patronage and civil-service systems in countries from across the Global North and South.

State-building and PoEs: Between patronage and meritocracy

> Contenders for power have at times sought to use patronage to create and maintain both administrative capacity and loyalty. As such, patronage is important in the consolidation of royal power, the creation of modern states, and the construction of competence in government.
>
> (Grindle 2012: 6–7)

The rise of bureaucracies that operate according to a largely non-patrimonial logic is often identified as a definitive dimension of modern state formation (Fukuyama 2014, 2016, Mann 1988). To frame PoEs in developing countries as rational-legal forms amidst a sea of patronage reflects a Weberian ideal that rests on a particular set of assumptions about what the state *should* look like in Africa. For Hagmann and Peclard (2010: 541), 'Underlying this "pathological" approach to state institutions in Africa are essentialist, teleological and instrumentalist conceptions of state and political authority.' Such readings of the state tend to draw attention to the gap between Western states and African states, with PoEs apparently signalling a route through which this gap might be closed.

Although this tendency is particularly prevalent in the Africanist literature (Bach 2012), some scholars of PoEs in Latin America also define them by their capacity to escape patronage politics (Geddes 1990). However, many of the agencies that would become known as PoEs in Brazil were 'set on a path toward technical decision-making and good performance through presidential patronage' (Grindle 2012: 183), and were also encouraged to employ patronage-based principles with their own internal hiring processes, in order to secure staff with the right mix of technical expertise and political loyalty (also Whitfield and Therkildsen 2011). In Mozambique, PoEs are characterized by their capacity to fuse political and technical functions, through a technocratic cadre with strong (embedded) links to both ruling elites (Whitfield and Buur 2014). Porter and Watts (2017) reveal a similar fusion in Nigeria, with rulers directly appointing lead agency staff and reaching over those elements of the bureaucracy loyal to previous incumbents. PoEs are in some ways uniquely suited to the logics of patronage, with their distinctive form in relation to the rest of the civil service enabling rulers greater discretion around appointments, governance arrangements, and organisational mandates. Grindle's (2012) *Jobs for the Boys* shows that patronage has been a highly persistent form of rule over time, not only because it offers rulers a means of maintaining order in fragmented polities, but because it can also help deliver progress in terms of government competence and the wider goal of state-building.

To argue that patronage seems to be a constitutive feature of why high-performing agencies are established and how they function in developing countries is not to overlook the inherent dangers involved in this mode of rule. Even if we accept that patronage can be compatible with developing high degrees of bureaucratic competence, it must be recognized that 'its weakness is its vulnerability to the caprice of those who manage such systems, not that it necessarily leads to corruption or incompetence' (Grindle 2012: 23). This is apparent not merely in relation to the use of patronage to undermine performance across large swathes of the public sector, but also within PoEs themselves. Longitudinal studies of PoEs reveal that their performance over time is shaped by this caprice, as political support and protection waxes and wanes (Geddes 1990, Hickey et al. 2020, Robinson 2006, Willis 2014), and outright capture for predatory aims a perennial danger (Soares de Oliveira 2007).

These reflections invite a discussion of whether different forms of patronage exist and the conditions under which they may enable developmental forms of state capacity to emerge and flourish. In an effort to fill the middle ground between Evans' (1995) depiction of the 'developmental state', on the one hand, and 'predatory patronage', on the other, Bach (2012) refers to the notion of 'regulated patrimonialism', to reflect the ways in which rulers use patronage to achieve multiple ends, some of which are developmental (Kelsall et al. 2010). As Mkandawire (2015: 595) notes in his searing critique of the overuse of neopatrimonialism in relation to development in Africa:

> One solution to the troublesome anomaly of neopatrimonial leaders presiding over high economic performance is the recourse to such *deus ex machina* as expatriates, 'oases of integrity', or 'pockets of reform/islands of alternative systems', that have inexplicably escaped the hold of neopatrimonialism. The possibility of enclaves of rationality in a universe of irrationality and self-serving behavior is then advanced to suggest that there might be such a thing as a 'neopatrimonial developmental state' or 'regulated neopatrimonialism'.

Even if the notion of 'regulated patrimonialism' were to provide a useful descriptor of the form that PoEs take, this tells us little about the conditions under which this form of patrimonialism might emerge, as compared to more predatory forms. Insofar as it may describe a style of rule, it does little to help identify the deeper ordering of power from which this mode of governance emerges. It is this deeper level of causality—along with other aspects of politics that PoEs represent and bring forth—that our adapted political settlements framework seeks to capture (Chapter 2).

Bureaucratic elitism: PoEs as echoes of colonial rule?

A further problem with viewing PoEs through the frame of neopatrimonialism is the implicit suggestion that African rulers were bequeathed rational-legal bureaucratic orders at independence and then set about subjecting them to patrimonial logics. Such a reading overlooks the strong sense in which the colonial state in Africa—primarily an instrument of political domination that operated through a network of local big men—bore closer resemblance to patrimonial rule than any rational-bureaucratic ideal type (Eriksen 2011, Mamdani 1996). Only at the very apex of the metropolitan centres of government was any effort made towards establishing a rational-bureaucratic order:

> Actual bureaucratic characteristics (specific training of the officials, documentary formality, the legality of administrative practice) were only found at the higher

levels of the administration. The people who displayed these characteristics had a privileged worldview, however; as expatriates, they expected an all-inclusive package with official residences, personnel, and foreign allowances.

(Bierschenk 2010: 6)

This depiction has a striking resonance with contemporary portrayals of PoEs in developing countries. Numerous studies emphasize that such agencies thrive on an elitist sense of otherness in relation to the rest of the civil service, a status under-written by higher rates of remuneration, better conditions of service, and parallel processes of hiring and promotion. Contemporary PoEs thus seem to reproduce the notion of an elite bureaucratic caste introduced under colonial rule as much as any commitment to building a rational-legal order.

Ethnicity, class, and gender: The political sociology of bureaucracy in Africa

The interpretation of politics in post-colonial Africa as neopatrimonial has often been preoccupied with the role of ethnicity, with a marked emphasis on critiquing the ways in which ethnic partiality has apparently undermined the emergence of more impersonal forms of rule and bureaucratic governance (Ekeh 1975, Berman 2004). However, scholars operating from alternative perspectives are alert to the role that ethnic identity may play in enhancing bureaucratic performance and accountability. One example is the state-building role played by the Kalangala, a minority ethnic group in Botswana whom Werbner (2004) argues have been critical to ensuring the quality of public service in the country amidst other contri-butions to the public realm. This commitment to public service flows not from the negation of ethnic identity in favour of the secular identity of career bureaucrats, but rather from a form of 'cosmopolitan ethnicity' (Werbner 2004) that carries echoes of John Lonsdale's (1994) earlier distinction between 'moral ethnicity' and 'ethnic tribalism'. The minority status of the Kalangala vis-a-vis the Tswana major-ity further incentivised efforts to ensure that the public sphere operated according to universal, rather than particularized, norms.

Similarly, recent scholarship on 'inclusive coalitions' has highlighted the extent to which top positions in the bureaucracy are allocated according to the poli-tics of ethno-regional balance in countries like Uganda and Zambia (Lindemann 2011a, 2011b), increasingly so in contexts where ruling elites felt increasingly vul-nerable to political threats from rival elites. However, the politics of balancing sub-national identities and power bases with a project of centralized state-building is not unique to post-colonial Africa. Similar difficulties faced earlier state-builders in now 'developed' countries, including the challenge of ensuring the loyalty as well as competence of bureaucrats amidst competing claims for state power amongst rival political elites. Grindle (2012: 7–8) shows how patronage appointments have historically been used to secure the stability and reach of the state through appointments from different regions (Prussia), to maintain class rule (the United Kingdom) or to change the basis of class rule and develop party-political support (e.g. the United States of America). Analysing this phenomenon therefore doesn't require the culturalist perspective embedded within neopatrimonial discourse but rather a perspective capable of understanding the political sociology of state-building, both on its own terms and as shaped by the politics of survival.

Ideas versus interests

> Policies are shaped not only by interests and structures but also by
> ideas ... ideas matter in African political affairs as much as elsewhere.
> (Mkandawire 2015: 598)

Instrumentalist approaches to African politics are reflected in the strong focus on how PoEs are tied to elite interests. This has meant that the current literature on PoEs tends to underplay the role of ideas in shaping elite commitment and bureaucratic performance. Although some work has examined the micro-foundations of building a 'bureaucratic ethos' within specific organizations (McDonnell 2020), there remains a significant gap in terms of the role that ideas play in shaping the commitment of political rulers to supporting state capacity and performance, including paradigmatic ideas around nation-building, patriotism, and development (Schmidt 2008). Observers of African bureaucracies have identified moments where rulers and bureaucrats alike have been imbued with the reformist zeal of nation-building, both at independence (Abernethy 1971) and later moments of liberation and/or post-conflict rebuilding (e.g. Peterson 2016). As we explore later, such moments in countries like Rwanda (Chapter 6) and Uganda (Chapter 7), offered a fresh opportunity for bureaucrats to be imbued with a new sense of mission under ideological rulers apparently keen to reinvigorate the state as a developmental force. Also largely absent are in-depth reflections on the role of transnational epistemic communities in shaping professional norms and capacities amongst state bureaucrats.

The transnationalized character of the state, governance, and PoEs in Africa

The final problem with the neopatrimonial framing of public-sector performance in Africa discussed here concerns the way in which this perspective overlooks the roles played by transnational factors in shaping public-sector performance. Such methodological nationalism characterizes much political analysis but is a particular hallmark of neopatrimonial scholarship, which sought to shift the analysis of under-development away from a structuralist frame and to render African political rulers as uniquely responsible for the fate of their countries' location within the global economic order (Mkandawire 2015). We argue here that the politics of PoEs in Africa needs to be reframed within an understanding of the modern state in Africa as a highly transnationalized phenomenon, from its colonial origins through to its entanglements with international development agencies and other global actors, ideas, and institutions (Eriksen 2011, Hagmann and Peclard 2010, Harrison 2010). Having already noted the relevance of colonialism to the bureaucratic elitism that PoEs seem to represent, the focus here falls on the influence that successive phases of international development lending and policy have had on the character of the state in post-colonial Africa in general, and in relation to PoEs in particular.

Given that many PoEs have been formed as solutions that enable rulers to 'reach around' the mainstream civil service (Geddes 1990, Grindle 1997), they have become strongly associated with the ambitions of the wave of 'new public management' (NPM) reforms that emerged as from the 1980s onwards (Turner et al. 2015). With their special status, emphasis on private-sector norms, performance-driven pay, distinct pay scales, and separation from the mainstream civil service, such agencies figure prominently in the PoE literature. International development actors had a significant influence in introducing this form of governance to sub-Saharan Africa, perhaps most obviously in the form of the Semi-Autonomous Revenue Agencies that became ubiquitous across (Anglophone) Africa from the early 1990s onwards (Fjeldstad and Moore 2009), and which we examine in our case-study chapters.

The promotion of NPM formed part of a wider effort by international financial institutions to radically reduce and reframe the role of the state during the era of 'disciplinary neoliberalism' (Gill 1995). The state in Africa (and elsewhere) was not only to be stripped back via programmes of structural adjustment and civil-service retrenchment but also to help embed a new market-led policy regime. As Mkandawire (1999) noted, this meant empowering the 'agencies of restraint' and disempowering the agencies of the activist and social-provisioning state, with ministries of finance and central banks granted the highest levels of support (Harrison 2010). These trends of state restructuring were also apparent in transitional countries (Phillips et al. 2006) and the Global North (Brenner 2004), particularly where the growth of financial capitalism within post-industrializing contexts helped secure the hegemony of treasuries and central banks vis-à-vis departments of planning and industry (Jessop 2013). In sub-Saharan Africa, this involved a battle over ideas as well as institutions, with IFIs inculcating a narrow form of economics within broader epistemic institutions and networks. This included universities and initiatives such as the African Economic Research Consortium that became geared towards producing the right sort of technocrats required to deliver on the reformed mandates of Africa's economic state agencies (Mkandawire 2014). Our case studies of finance ministries and central banks reveal the effects of this highly partial project of state-building on both organizational effectiveness and developmental trajectories. This is clear both in terms of the restricted mandate imposed on these agencies, such as the withdrawal of central banks from playing a more muscular role in directing finance towards developmental goals (Epstein 2006, 2013), and the removal of support from more productivist state agencies. The contrast between the PoEs of Africa's economic governance during this period and those associated with developmental statism (Evans 1995) is stark, and is discussed further in Chapter 8.

Importantly, the influence of external factors on politics and governance in Africa has varied over time and has always involved room for African political agency (Whitfield 2009). Responses include resistance but also partial engagement whereby rulers adopt various reforms either in order to fulfil their own objectives or as a means of signalling compliance with international norms and conditions, and whether or not these are being actively enforced. As de Waal (2015) notes, rulers may protect those elements of the state and governance required to retain legitimacy within the international order of sovereign states to secure access to the rents that this status generates. Within a neoliberal global economic order, the economic technocracy is particularly important in terms of sending signals of credibility and being open for business to international investors and credit agencies (Harrison 2010). In flagging a sufficient degree of stateness to external actors, PoEs may form part of the politics of 'extraversion' (Bayart 2000), helping rulers to attract transnational flows of recognition, legitimacy, and resources, which in turn enable them to pursue their political projects.

Importantly, the global grip of disciplinary neoliberalism identified here began to slip from the mid-2000s onwards. Tensions between governments and IFIs increased as countries graduated from debt, reduced their dependence on aid and started to benefit from both rising commodity prices and new financial flows from China, even before the global financial crisis of 2007–8 dealt a further blow to the neoliberal model. These trends, along with ongoing processes of democratization, have altered the political and political economy context within which the relationship between rulers and different parts of the state in Africa are embedded. Without positing the emergence of a fully post-neoliberal order, it is important to acknowledge that what Ilene Grabel terms the 'productive incoherence' of this interregnum period may have provided 'developing countries with more room to maneuver than they enjoyed in the stultifying neoliberal era' (2017: xv). In some contexts, a nascent cadre of 'new productivist' officials, keen to re-establish industrial policy in pursuit of structural transformation through national planning, do regular battle with stalwarts of fiscal responsibility in the entrenched bastions of the treasury and central banks (Chimhowu et al. 2019, Hickey 2013).

Our case-study chapters, which cover the period from the early 1990s through until the late 2010s, help us explore whether or not there has been a power shift between different state agencies in sub-Saharan Africa as a result of this changing global political economy of development.

Conclusion: Towards an alternative framing of PoEs in Africa

To understand the African bureaucracy is to understand a great deal about African politics.

(Abernethy 1971: 93)

Reframing PoEs as being firmly embedded *within* rather than somehow divorced from their 'dysfunctional' political contexts, and situating them within longer-run processes of state-building and bureaucratic development both within Africa and more broadly, enables a new perspective to emerge. Usually characterized as islands of Weberian-style governance, we argue that PoEs often reflect the logics of patronage as well as merit-based civil-service systems (Grindle 2012). They seem to carry with them echoes of the elitist bifurcation introduced into African bureaucracies by colonial rule, a period that did more to embed the logics of patronage within post-colonial polities than any notion of rational-legal orders (Mamdani 1996). By moving beyond instrumentalist, statist, and methodologically national-ist readings of the state in Africa, it becomes possible to gain a clearer sense of how ideas, political sociology, and external actors all shape the politics of public-sector performance. This is most apparent through the significant influence of inter-national development actors within the era of disciplinary neoliberalism, which profoundly restructured the state in Africa, particularly within the realm of eco-nomic governance (Harrison 2010, Mkandawire 2014). The analysis of PoEs in contemporary Africa therefore needs to be located at the intersection of transna-tional forces and the ideas and incentives that shape political elite behaviour within domestic political and organizational contexts. The next chapter outlines a new conceptual and methodological framework that can help capture this sense of PoEs as the outcomes of broader political projects and political economy contexts.

References

Abernethy, D. B. (1971). 'Bureaucracy and Economic Development in Africa', *African Review*, 1(1): 93–107.

Acemoglu, D. and Robinson, J. (2012). *Why Nations Fail: The Origins of Power, Prosperity and Poverty*. London: Profile Books.

Acemoglu, D. and Robinson, J. (2019). *The Narrow Corridor: States, Societies and the Fate of Liberty*. New York and London: Penguin Random House.

Andrews, M., Pritchett, L., and Woolcock, M. (2017). *Building State Capability: Evidence, Analysis, Action*. Oxford: Oxford University Press.

Bach, D. C. (2012). 'Patrimonialism and Neopatrimonialism: Comparative Receptions and Transcriptions'. In D. Bach and M. Gazibo (eds), *Neopatrimonialism in Africa and Beyond*. Abingdon: Routledge. 25–45.

Bayart, J. F., translated by Ellis, S. (2000). 'Africa in the World: A History of Extraversion', *African Affairs*, 99(395): 217–67.

Berman, B. (2004). 'Ethnicity, Bureaucracy and Democracy: The Politics of Trust'. In B. Berman, D. Eyoh, and W. Kymlicka (eds), *Ethnicity and Democracy in Africa*: Oxford: James Currey. 39–53.

Bersch, K., Praça, S., and Taylor, M. M. (2017). 'Bureaucratic Capacity and Political Autonomy within National States: Mapping the Archipelago of Excellence in Brazil'. In M. A. Centeno, A. Kohli, and D. J. Yashar (eds), *States in the Developing World*. Cambridge: Cambridge University Press. 157–83.

Bierschenk, T. (2010). 'States at Work in West Africa: Sedimentation, Fragmentation and Normative Double-binds'. Working Paper 113. Mainz: Department of Anthropology and African Studies, Johannes Gutenberg-Universität.

Booth, D. (ed.) (2015). Developmental Regimes in Africa: Synthesis Report. Africa Power and Politics Project. Available online: http://www.institutions-africa.org/filestream/20150216-developmental-regimes-in-africa-synthesis-report (accessed 6 June 2019). London: ODI.

Bratton, M. and van de Walle, N. (1997). *Democratic Experiments in Africa: Regime Transitions in Comparative Perspective*. Cambridge: Cambridge University Press.

Brenner, N. (2004) *New State Spaces: Urban Governance and the Rescaling of Statehood*. New York and Oxford: Oxford University Press.

Centeno, M. A., Kohli, A., and Yashar, D. J. (2017). *States in the Developing World*. Cambridge: Cambridge University Press.

Chimhowu, A., Hulme, D., and Munro, L. (2019). 'The "New" National Development Planning and Global Development Goals: Processes and Partnerships', *World Development*, 120: 76–89.

Domínguez, J. I. (1997). *Technopols: Freeing Politics and Markets in Latin America in the 1990s*. University Park, PA: Penn State Press.

Ekeh, P. P. (1975). 'Colonialism and the Two Publics in Africa: A Theoretical Statement', *Comparative Studies in Society and History*, 17(1): 91–112.

Epstein, G. (2006). 'Central Banks as Agents of Economic Development'. WIDER Research Paper No. 2006/54. Helsinki: United Nations University.

Epstein, G. (2013). 'Developmental Central Banking: Winning the Future by Updating a Page from the Past', *Review of Keynesian Economics*, 1(3): 273–87.

Eriksen, S. S. (2011). '"State Failure" in Theory and Practice: The Idea of the State and the Contradictions of State Formation', *Review of International Studies*, 37(1): 229–47.

Evans, P. (1995). *Embedded Autonomy: States and Industrial Transformation*. Princeton, NJ: Princeton University Press.

Evans, P. and Heller, P. (2010). 'Constructing the 21st-century Developmental State: Potentialities and Pitfalls.' In O. Edigheji (ed.), *Constructing a Democratic Developmental State in South Africa: Potentials and Challenges*. Cape Town: HSRC Press. 37–58.

Fjeldstad, O.-H. and Moore, M. (2009). 'Revenue Authorities and Public Authority in Sub-Saharan Africa', *The Journal of Modern African Studies*, 47(1): 1–18.

Fukuyama, F. (2014). *The Origins of Political Order: From Prehuman Times to the French Revolution*. New York: Farrar, Straus and Giroux.

Fukuyama, F. (2016). *Political Order and Political Decay: From the Industrial Revolution to the Globalization of Democracy*. New York: Farrar, Straus and Giroux.

Geddes, B. (1990). 'Building "State" Autonomy in Brazil, 1930–1964', *Comparative Politics*, 22(2): 217–35.

Geddes, B. (1994). *Politician's Dilemma: Building State Capacity in Latin America*. Berkeley, CA: University of California Press.

Gill, S. (1995). 'Globalisation, Market Civilisation and Disciplinary Neoliberalism', *Millennium: Journal of International Studies*, 24(3): 339–423.

de Gramont, D. (2014). 'Beyond Magic Bullets in Governance Reform', 4 November. Washington, DC: Carnegie Endowment for International Peace.

Grabel, I. (2017). *When Things Don't Fall Apart: Global Financial Governance and Developmental Finance in an Age of Productive Incoherence*. Cambridge, MA: MIT Press.

Grindle, M. (1997). 'Divergent Cultures? When Public Organisations Perform Well in Developing Countries', *World Development*, 25(4): 481–95.

Grindle, M. S. (2004). 'Good Enough Governance: Poverty Reduction and Reform in Developing Countries', *Governance: An International Journal of Policy, Administration and Institutions*, 17(4): 525–48.

Grindle, M. S. (2007). 'Good Enough Governance Revisited', *Development Policy Review*, 25(5): 553–74.

Grindle, M. S. (2012). *Jobs for the Boys: Patronage and the State in Comparative Perspective*. Cambridge, MA: Harvard University Press.

Grindle, M. S. (2017). 'Good Governance, RIP: A Critique and an Alternative', *Governance*, 30(1): 17–22.

Grindle, M.S and M. Hilderbrand. (1995) 'Building Sustainable Capacity in the Public Sector: What Can be Done?', Public Administration and Development, 15(5): 441–463.

Hagmann, T. and Peclard, D. (2010). 'Negotiating Statehood: Dynamics of Power and Domination in Africa', *Development and Change* 41(4): 539–62.

Harrison, G. (2010). *Neoliberal Africa: The Impact of Global Social Engineering*. London: Zed Books.

De Herdt, T. and de Sardan, J. P. O. (eds) (2015). *Real Governance and Practical Norms in Sub-Saharan Africa: The Game of the Rules*. Oxford: Routledge.

Hertog, S. (2014). 'Defying the Resource Curse: Explaining Successful State-owned Enterprises in Rentier States'. In M. Roll (ed.), *The Politics of Public Sector Performance: Pockets of Effectiveness in Developing Countries*. Oxford: Routledge. 173–93.

Hickey, S. (2013). 'Beyond "Poverty Reduction through Good Governance": The New Political Economy of Development in Africa', *New Political Economy*, 17(5): 683–90.

Hickey, S., Abdulai, A. G., Izama, A., and Mohan, G. (2020). 'Responding to the Commodity Boom with Varieties of Resource Nationalism: A Political Economy Explanation for the Different Routes Taken by Africa's New Oil Producers', *The Extractive Industries and Society*, 7(4): 1246–56.

Hickey, S. and Izama, A. (2016). 'The Politics of Governing Oil in Uganda: Going against the Grain?' *African Affairs*, 116(463): 163–85.

Hout, W. (2013). 'Neopatrimonialism and Development: Pockets of Effectiveness as Drivers of Change', *Revue Internationale de Politique Comparée*, 20(3): 79–96.

Houtzager, P. P. and Moore, M. (2003). *Changing Paths: International Development and the New Politics of Inclusion*. Ann Arbor, MI: University of Michigan Press.

Jepson, N. (2020). *In China's Wake: How the Commodity Boom Transformed Development Strategies in the Global South*. New York: Columbia University Press.

Jessop, B. (2008). *State Power: A Strategic and Relational Approach*. Cambridge: Polity Press.

Jessop, B. (2013). 'Finance-dominated Accumulation and Post-democratic Capitalism'. In S. Fadda and P. Tridico (eds), *Institutions and Economic Development after the Financial Crisis*. London: Routledge. 83–105.

Jessop, B. (2015). *The State: Past, Present, Future*. Cambridge: Polity Press.

Johnson, C. (1982). *MITI and the Japanese Miracle*. Stanford, CA: Stanford University Press.

Joignant, A. (2011). 'The Politics of Technopols: Resources, Political Competence and Collective Leadership in Chile, 1990–2010', *Journal of Latin American Studies*, 43(3): 517 46.

Kelsall, T., Booth, D., Cammack, D., and Golooba-Mutebi, F. (2010). 'Developmental Patrimonialism? Questioning the Orthodoxy on Political Governance and Economic Progress in Africa'. London: Africa Power and Politics Working Paper 9.

Khan, M. H. (2005). 'The Capitalist Transformation'. In K. S. Jomoand and E. S. Reinert (eds), *The Origins of Development Economics: How Schools of Economic Thought Have Addressed Development*. London: Zed Press. 69–80.

Khan, M. (2010). 'Political Settlements and the Governance of Growth-enhancing Institutions'. Draft Paper, Research Paper Series on 'Growth-Enhancing Governance'. London: SOAS, University of London.

Khan, M. H. (2017). 'Political Settlements and the Analysis of Institutions', *African Affairs*, 117(469): 636–55.

Kjær, A. M., Katusiimeh, M., Mwebaze, T., and Muhumuza, F. (2012). 'When Do Ruling Elites Support Productive Sectors? Explaining Policy Initiatives in the Fisheries and Dairy Sectors in Uganda'. DIIS Working Paper 2012: 05. Copenhagen: Danish Institute for International Studies.

Korten, D. C. (1987). 'Third-generation NGO Strategies: A Key to People-centred Development', *World Development*, 15 (Supplement): 145–59.

Leftwich, A. (1995). 'Bringing Politics back in: Towards a Model of the Developmental State', *Journal of Development Studies* 31: 400–27.

Leftwich, A. (2005). 'Politics in Command: Development Studies and the Rediscovery of Social Science', *New Political Economy* 10: 573–607.

Leonard, D. (1991). *African Successes: Four Public Managers of Kenyan Rural Development*. Berkeley, CA: University of California Press.

Leonard, D. (2008). 'Where Are the "Pockets" of Effective Agencies Likely in Weak Governance States and Why?' IDS Working Paper 306. Brighton: Institute of Development Studies, University of Sussex.

Levy, B. (2014). *Working with the Grain: Integrating Governance and Growth in Development Strategies*. New York: Oxford University Press.

Levy, B. and Kpundeh, J. S. (2004). *Building State Capacity in Africa: New Approaches, Emerging Lessons*. Washington, DC: World Bank.

Lindemann, S. (2011a). 'Just Another Change of Guard? Broad-based Politics and Civil War in Museveni's Uganda', *African Affairs*, 110(440): 387–416.

Lindemann, S. (2011b). 'Inclusive Elite Bargains and the Dilemma of Unproductive Peace: A Zambian Case Study', *Third World Quarterly*, 32(10): 1843–69.

Lonsdale, J. (1994). 'Moral Ethnicity and Political Tribalism'. In P. Kaarsholm and J. Hultin (eds), *Inventions and Boundaries: Historical and Anthropological Approaches to the Study of Ethnicity*. Copenhagen: Roskilde University.

Mamdani, M. (1996). *Citizen and Subject: Contemporary Africa and the Legacy of Late Colonialism*. Princeton, NJ: Princeton University Press.

Mann, M. (1988). *States, War and Capitalism: Studies in Political Sociology*. Oxford: Basil Blackwell.

McDonnell, E. M. (2017). 'The Patchwork Leviathan: How Pockets of Bureaucratic Governance Flourish within Institutionally Diverse Developing States', *American Sociological Review*, 82(3): 476–510.

McDonnell, E. M. (2020). *Patchwork Leviathan: Pockets of Bureaucratic Effectiveness in Developing States*. Princeton, NJ: Princeton University Press.

Mkandawire, T. (1999). 'The Political Economy of Financial Sector Reform', *Journal of International Development*, 11(3): 321–42.

Mkandawire, T. (2014). 'The Spread of Economic Doctrines and Policymaking in Postcolonial Africa', *African Studies Review*, 57(1): 171–98.

Mkandawire, T. (2015). 'Neopatrimonialism and the Political Economy of Economic Performance in Africa: Critical Reflections', *World Politics*, 67(3): 563–612.

Mohan, G., Asante, K. P., and Abdulai, A.-G. (2018). 'Party Politics and the Political Economy of Ghana's New Oil', *New Political Economy*, 23(3): 274–89.

Moore, M. (2008). 'Between Coercion and Contract: Competing Narratives on Taxation and Governance'. In D. Brautigam, O. Fjeldstad, and M. Moore (eds), *Taxation and State-building in Developing Countries: Capacity and Consent*. Cambridge: Cambridge University Press. 34–63.

Moore, M. (2014). 'Revenue Reform and Statebuilding in Anglophone Africa', *World Development*, 60: 99–112.

North, D. C., Wallis, J. J., Webb, S. B., and Weingast, B. R. (2009). *In the Shadow of Violence: Politics, Economics, and the Problems of Development*. New York: Cambridge University Press.

Overman, S. and Van Thiel, S. (2016). 'Agencification and Public Sector Performance: A Systematic Comparison in 20 Countries', *Public Management Review*, 18(4): 611–35.

Peterson, D. R. (2016). 'A History of the Heritage Economy in Yoweri Museveni's Uganda', *Journal of Eastern African Studies*, 10(4): 789–806.

Phillips, R., Henderson, J., Andor, L., and Hulme, D. (2006). 'Usurping Social Policy: Neoliberalism and Economic Governance in Hungary', *Journal of Social Policy*, 35(4): 585–606.

Porter, D. and Watts, M. (2017). 'Righting the Resource Curse: Institutional Politics and State Capabilities in Edo State, Nigeria', *Journal of Development Studies*, (53)2: 249–63.

Portes, A. and Smith, L. D. (2012). *Institutions Count: Their Role and Significance in Latin American Development*. Berkeley, CA: University of California Press.

Pritchett, L. and M. Woolcock. (2004). 'Solutions When the Solution Is the Problem: Arraying the Disarray in Development', *World Development*, 32(2): 191–212.

Robinson, M. (2006). 'The Political Economy of Governance Reforms in Uganda'. Institute for Development Studies Discussion Paper 386. Brighton: Institute for Development Studies.

Roll, M. (ed.) (2014). *The Politics of Public Sector Performance: Pockets of Effectiveness in Developing Countries*. Oxford: Routledge.

de Sardan, J. P. O. (2013). 'The Bureaucratic Mode of Governance and Practical Norms in West Africa and beyond'. In M. Bouziane, C. Harders, and A. Hoffman (eds), *Local Politics and Contemporary Transformations in the Arab World*. London: Palgrave Macmillan. 43–64.

Schmidt, V. A. (2008). 'Discursive Institutionalism: The Explanatory Power of Ideas and Discourse', *Annual Review of Political Science*, 11(1): 303–26.

Shefter, M. (1994). *Political Parties and the State: The American Historical Experience*. Princeton, NJ: Princeton University Press.

Simbine, A. T. with Attoh, F. C. and Oladeji, A. O. (2014). 'Taming the Menace of Human Trafficking: Nigeria's National Agency for the Prohibition of Traffic in Persons and Other Related Matters (NAPTIP)'. In M. Roll (ed.), *The Politics of Public Sector Performance: Pockets of Effectiveness in Developing Countries*. Oxford: Routledge. 128–146.

Slater, D. (2010). *Ordering Power: Contentious Politics and Authoritarian Leviathans in Southeast Asia*. New York: Cambridge University Press.

Soares De Oliveira, R. (2007). 'Business Success, Angola-style: Postcolonial Politics and the Rise and Rise of Sonangol', *The Journal of Modern African Studies*, 45(4): 595–619.

Strauss, J. C. (2014). 'Pockets of Effectiveness: Lessons from the Long Twentieth Century in China and Taiwan'. In M. Roll (ed.), *The Politics of Public Sector Performance: Pockets of Effectiveness in Developing Countries*. Oxford: Routledge. 43–73.

Tendler, J. (1997). *Good Government in the Tropics*. Baltimore, MD: Johns Hopkins University Press.

Therkildsen, O. (2008). 'Public Sector Reforms and the Development of Productive Capacities in LDCs'. Background Paper 1, UNCTAD Least Developed Countries Report 2009.

Therkildsen, O. and Tidemand, P. (2007). 'Staff Management and Organizational Performance in Tanzania and Uganda: Public Servants Perspectives'. Copenhagen: Danish Institute for International Studies.

Tilly, C. (ed.) (1975). *The Formation of National States in Western Europe*. Princeton, NJ: Princeton University Press.

Turner, M., Hulme, D., and McCourt, W. (2015). *Governance, Management and Development: Making the State Work*. London: Palgrave Macmillan. Second edition.

Vom Hau, M. (2012). 'State Capacity and Inclusive Development: New Challenges and Directions'. Effective States and Inclusive Development Research Centre Working Paper No. 2. Manchester: Effective States and Inclusive Development.

de Waal, A. (2015). *The Real Politics of the Horn of Africa: Money, War and the Business of Power*. Cambridge: Polity Press.

Wade, R. (1996). 'Japan, the World Bank, and the Art of Paradigm Maintenance: The East Asian Miracle in Political Perspective', *New Left Review*, I/217: 3–37.

Werbner, R. (2004). *Reasonable Radicals and Citizenship in Botswana: The Public Anthropology of Kalanga Elites*. Bloomington, IN: Indiana University Press.

Whitfield, L. (2009). *The Politics of Aid: African Strategies for Dealing with Donors*. Oxford: Oxford University Press.

Whitfield, L. and Buur, L. (2014). 'The Politics of Industrial Policy: Ruling Elites and their Alliances', *Third World Quarterly*, 35(1): 126–44.

Whitfield, L. and Therkildsen, O. (2011). 'What Drives State to Support the Development of Productive Sectors? Strategies Ruling Elites Pursue for Political Survival and their Policy Implications'. DIIS Working Paper 2011: 15. Copenhagen: Danish Institute of International Studies.

Whitfield, L., Therkildsen, O., Buur, L., and Kjær, A. M. (2015). *The Politics of African Industrial Policy: A Comparative Perspective*. Cambridge: Cambridge University Press.

Willis, E. J. (2014). 'An Enduring Pocket of Effectiveness: The Case of the National Development Bank of Brazil (BNDE)'. In M. Roll (ed.). *The Politics of Public Sector Performance: Pockets of Effectiveness in Developing Countries*. Oxford: Routledge. 74–96.

World Bank (2017). *World Development Report 2017: Governance and the Law*. Washington, DC: World Bank. Available online: http://www.worldbank.org/en/publication/wdr2017 (accessed 6 June 2019).

2

Reconceptualizing the Politics of Pockets of Effectiveness

A Power Domains Approach

Sam Hickey and Giles Mohan

Introduction

If dominant framings of pockets of effectiveness (PoEs) within the existing literature risk obscuring the origins and character of high-performing state agencies, as
argued in Chapter 1, what alternative approaches might be required? This chapter
establishes a conceptual and methodological framework for exploring the politics
of PoEs that aims to address current shortcomings and provide a basis on which
to advance this field of enquiry. It begins by introducing perspectives from critical theories of politics and the state, both in general (Jessop 2008, 2016) and in
particular relation to Africa (Hagmann and Peclard 2010, Mamdani 1996), which
go beyond the limits of neopatrimonial discourses.[1] This offers a 'relational' framing that resituates the state within the deeper forms of politics and power that are
increasingly emphasized within new thinking around the politics of development,
whilst incorporating a stronger focus on transnational- as well as national-level
factors. We argue here that one variant of this new thinking—namely political
settlements analysis—can offer an insightful framework for understanding the
conditions under which elites become committed to developing the state capacity required to deliver development effectively. To further nuance the analysis,
we suggest that PoEs are also shaped by the nature of the 'policy domain' that
they are located within, with different policy domains playing specific political
roles within given political settlements and being characterized by different actors,
ideas, and governance arrangements. The capacity and commitment to promote
PoEs is thus shaped by the interaction between two key domains of power, the
political settlement and specific policy domains.[2]

---

[1] See Mohan (2019) for a fuller discussion of the relevance of critical political theory to the
investigation of PoEs in Africa.

[2] See Hickey and Sen (2023) for a fuller overview of the power-domains approach, and both Hickey
and Hossain (2019) and Nazneen et al. (2019) for its application to the domains of education and
women's interests, respectively.

Sam Hickey and Giles Mohan, *Reconceptualizing the Politics of Pockets of Effectiveness*. In: *Pockets of Effectiveness and the
Politics of State-building and Development in Africa*. Edited by Sam Hickey, Oxford University Press. © Oxford University
Press (2023). DOI: 10.1093/oso/9780192864963.003.0002

The chapter then discusses the methodological approach that we used to generate new knowledge on PoEs in Africa. Methodologically, most existing research on PoEs eschews one of the 'golden rules' of rigorous political analysis, which urges against selecting on the dependent variable, by choosing case-study organizations on the basis of their performance level. This means that we lack a clear sense of which independent variables (and combination thereof) offer more or less conducive conditions for PoEs to emerge and perform well, including in terms of which different types of political context. This is particularly true in a comparative sense across different contexts but is also often true across time within the same contexts, as the field has relatively few long-term historical studies that trace public-sector performance across different political periods.[3] The approach deployed here involved (1) choosing five countries that represent different types of political settlement; (2) undertaking an expert survey to help identify high-performing public-sector organizations in each country; (3) conducting in-depth qualitative investigations of at least three such organizations in each country across a period of three decades (from the early 1990s until the late 2010s); (4) followed by both within-case process tracing and across-case comparative analysis. This chapter now sets out both the conceptual and methodological approach in more detail. This will include a brief summary of our expert survey results, which led us to focus on three particular types of state agency in each country (finance ministries, central banks, and revenue authorities), and of the indicators used to measure performance in each case.

Reframing PoEs within alternative forms of state theory

The association of high-performing state agencies with rational-legal bureaucratic orders was critiqued in Chapter 1 for offering a pathological and teleological interpretation of the state in Africa, and, more specifically, for misreading the origins and character of state effectiveness. In a bid to move studies of African politics away from this kind of 'history by analogy' towards 'history by process' (Mamdani 1996), alternative approaches to post-colonial state formation interpret African states as a category of practice (Painter 2006), rather than as a category of analysis. This involves a 'focus on how states are shaped by the practices of various actors and by their interrelationships and interactions' (Eriksen 2011: 238) and tracing 'the ways that states have become related to domestic society on the one hand and their relations with the external world on the other' (Eriksen 2011: 239).

---

[3] Exceptions here include Geddes (1994) and Strauss (1998).

This relational and transnational framing of the state has been articulated most clearly within critical readings of the state both in general and in relation to Africa. For Bob Jessop (2016: 58), the state is:

> an ensemble of power centres and capacities that offer unequal chances to different forces within and outside the state … its powers (plural) are activated by changing sets of politicians and state officials located in specific parts of the state, in specific conjectures. Although these 'insiders' are key players in the exercise of state powers, they always act in relation to a wider balance of forces within and beyond a given state.

This depiction of the necessarily uneven nature of state power helps bring 'bureaucratic outliers' more sharply into view, and the sense that state power is always asymmetric in character has already been deployed to examine PoEs within Africa to good effect (Porter and Watts 2017). A critical interpretation of the state as representing a particular coming together of statist and social logics, with 'state managers' (Block 1981) arriving at bargains through which the projects of both political and economic actors can be realized, establishes PoEs as more of an integral than accidental feature of state power. Whereas some scholarship on the state tends to view the bureaucracy as embodying the fullest expression of modern stateness, Jessop argues that there will always be a gap between what bureaucracies are capable of offering and what rulers require state power to deliver with regards to their wider projects and the relational demands made upon them:

> Although bureaucratic forms are appropriate to the execution of general laws and policies in accordance with the rule of law, they are less suited to ad hoc, discretionary forms of intervention … Indeed, the bureaucratic preconditions for the formal unity of the state system may limit the substantive efficacy of policies oriented to accumulation, legitimacy and social cohesion. This is reflected in the coexistence of formal bureaucracy governed by clear procedures and more informal, flexible, or ad hoc modes of intervention.
>
> (Jessop 2016: 68)

From this perspective, PoEs may represent less the fullest expression of Weberian bureaucratic orders than discretionary vehicles required for ruling elites to realize their ambitions.

This relational perspective resonates with recent framings of the state in Africa as a 'negotiated' and deeply embedded social phenomenon (e.g. Hagmann and Peclard 2010). For Hagmann and Peclard (2010: 552), 'the state is the product of complex processes of negotiation that occur at the interface between the public and the private, the informal and the formal, the illegal and the legal'. This can only be apprehended through adopting a relational concept of power

(Hagmann and Peclard 2010: 543), one that encompasses ideas as well as interests, the transnational as well the national, and popular as well as elite agency. Critical state theory is particularly alive to how 'political power in Africa is increasingly "internationalized"' (Schlichte 2008, cited in Hagmannn and Peclard 2010: 556, also Eriksen 2011). For Jessop (2008: 114; citing Gramsci 1971: 182), state theory must look beyond the national frame to explore how 'international relations intertwine with these internal relations of nation-states, creating new, unique, and historically concrete combinations'.

This critical approach, then, insists on viewing the state as a relational form of power that brings together statist and social logics within a transnational context. This resonates strongly with the political settlements approach that we set out below, which we argue can offer a useful framework for capturing the interplay of political power and institutional form that PoEs seem to represent.

Rethinking development politics: Political settlements and the power domains approach

The turn from an institutional to a relational reading of the politics of development has been one of the defining intellectual shifts of the past decade of development theory. Institutionalist scholars now emphasize how politics and elite bargaining shapes which institutions emerge and how conducive they are to political and economic development (Acemoglu and Robinson 2012, North, Wallis, and Weingast 2009). Approaching this question from a critical political economy perspective, Mushtaq Khan argues that the decision by ruling coalitions to invest in building and protecting 'growth-enhancing institutions' is determined by the underlying balance of power between organized groups, or what he terms the 'political settlement' (Khan 2010, 2017. From the mid-2010s, political settlements analysis, which we define in more detail in the next section, has gone beyond the earlier generation of governance research, as informed by new institutionalist economics, to offer compelling insights into the political conditions under which state capacity and elite commitment to deliver development emerge and can be sustained. Political settlement analysis has helped push forward our understanding of the politics of development across several different policy domains, including economic development (Behuria 2020, Gray 2018, Pritchett et al. 2018, Whitfield et al. 2015), natural resource governance (e.g. Bebbington et al. 2018, Macuane et al. 2018), social provisioning (Hickey and Hossain 2019, Hickey et al. 2019), and gender equity (Nazneen et al. 2019).

Some of this work has extended early political settlements analysis in two directions that are relevant here. The first is to move beyond a rational-actor emphasis on the 'incentives' that drive ruling coalitions to invest in institution building and development (or not), to include the role of paradigmatic elite ideas that underpin political settlements and help shape elite commitment to certain goals (Lavers 2018, Lavers and Hickey 2016). The second is to move beyond the realm of the national to incorporate a stronger sense of how politics and governance are shaped by transnational-level actors and processes, which are not simply contextual but which may form a constituent element of a 'national' political settlement (e.g. in the form of the rents required to maintain a ruling coalition in power, as per Behuria et al. 2017).

We take these moves further here by exploiting the synergy between political settlements analysis and the forms of critical political theory discussed above and in Chapter 1. Critical political theorists have long adopted a relational perspective on power and politics and viewed the state as a sphere within which broader social struggles take place and become articulated. In Jessop's strategic-relational approach, 'state power is an institutionally and discursively mediated condensation (a reflection and a refraction) of a changing balance of forces that seek to influence the forms, purposes, and content of polity, politics, and policy' (2016: 10). Note that Jessop goes further than standard political settlements analysis in introducing the significance of ideas, whilst also being alert to the transnational features of state power. Building on the observation that 'the state is an ensemble of power centres that offer unequal chances to different forces within and outside the state to act for different political purposes' (Jessop 2008: 37), recent work on PoEs has suggested that 'institutions at all scales, from the global to the local, are best understood as "ensembles of power", that is as the sites of, and the product of intra-elite and elite-citizen contest' (Porter and Watts 2016: 2). This approach opens up a more agential view of 'leadership, networks of connectors and convenors, entrepreneurs and activists' than standard political settlements analysis, and highlights the 'intersection of agency and structural conditions to show how "asymmetric capabilities" can emerge to create, constrain, and make possible particular reform options' (Porter and Watts 2017: 249). In line with Watts' (2004) earlier work on oil governance, this multi-levelled and transnationalized optic stretches PoE analysis beyond the public bureaucracy, to include the role of international capital and local economic interests in shaping the fields of power relations within which politicians and bureaucrats operate.

There are good reasons to expect that this extended form of political settlements analysis will be relevant to the analysis of PoEs (Mohan 2019). The existing literature on the politics of PoEs reviewed in Chapter 1 tends to emphasize the important role played by the kinds of political factors that form key categories within political settlements analysis—elite cohesion and interests, executive powers, political-bureaucratic relationships, concerns with political survival and legitimacy, the balance between rules and deals. And political settlements analysis has already been deployed to help uncover and explain the critical role played by PoEs in achieving developmental outcomes in Africa, including in relation to industrial policy (Whitfield et al. 2015) and natural resource governance (e.g. Hickey et al. 2020, Pedersen et al. 2020, Porter and Watts 2017, Salimo et al. 2020, Tyce 2020). This is arguably because it has certain advantages over other conceptual approaches that have been deployed to grasp the politics of public-sector performance. For example, Grindle's (2012) highly insightful study of how civil-service systems emerge blends the structural tendencies of historical institutionalism with an agential focus on how reform champions and policy coalitions drive through change at particular moments in time. However, this approach arguably has a 'missing middle' in that it does not theorize the forms of power and politics that lie between historical institutions and reform actors. A political settlements perspective addresses this missing middle by operating in between these levels of analysis. It aims to reveal how deep-seated institutional endowments (including colonial inheritance, the level of ethnic diversity, etc.) are refracted through shifting configurations of power that operate over mid-range timeframes and which in turn provide the immediate context within which political actors operate. Long-run theories of change are poorly equipped to explain when state capacity endowments are actually *deployed* and states effectively implement desired policies within specific timeframes, whilst the politics of policy reform literature draws attention only to how reformers take advantage of windows of opportunity, rather than theorizing how these windows emerge in relation to shifting configurations of power.

Political settlements analysis, as set out below, offers a mid-range theory that can help grasp the variations that emerge amongst otherwise similar types of state in terms of the broad overall level of development progress and as a means of understanding and explaining what happens *within* periods of relative equilibrium. The distinction between state capacity and state performance is particularly important here (Centeno et al. 2017). Whilst levels of state capacity may well be inherited from long-run processes of institutional development, the willingness of rulers to develop and/or activate these capacities is shaped by ideas and incentives generated by the contemporary political settlement within which they manoeuvre. The remainder of this section sets out how the political settlements approach elaborated here can provide the basis for a more systematic investigation of the politics of PoEs in Africa, particularly when joined by a further level of analysis that can capture the politics of the particular domain within which the relevant state agency operates.

The power domains approach: Linking political settlements to the policy domain

Uneven capabilities ... are not best explained merely as artefacts of "low capacity" or variable commitment by policymakers. Nor are episodes of capability and efficacy merely the product of heroic leaders or serendipity. Rather, it is more promising to see asymmetries as the product of dynamic interaction between political settlements and the institutional arenas through which economic and political elites combine, contest or make durable agreements. It follows that, even within so-called dysfunctional states, there are pockets of effectiveness amidst state deficits.

(Porter and Watts 2017: 254)

The above quotation reflects the sense that the commitment and capacity of states to deliver development—as represented in the form of PoEs—are directly shaped by the interaction of political settlements and specific institutional arenas, or what we term 'policy domains'. Whilst the dominant concept here is that of political settlements, it is important not to read off organizational performance from the nature of a political context alone. As discussed in Chapter 1, PoEs may be mainly shaped by political economy factors but other things matter too, particularly organizational-level factors and the nature of the organizational mandate (Roll 2014). Here we capture these factors in the notion of a 'policy domain', which refers to the broader policy arena within which specific types of PoE operate and their organisational contexts. This helps recognize that the conditions for PoEs to emerge in relation to, say, economic governance, may differ from those that shape organizational performance in relation to social or infrastructural sectors. These differences flow not only from the different organizational mandates involved but also the involvement of different types of actors, ideas and the relative political importance of different domains in different political contexts (Batley and Mcloughlin 2015). This sub-section defines both political settlements and policy domains in more detail and discusses how they can be brought together within a power domains approach to offer insights into how politics shapes organizational performance in specific ways (Hickey and Sen 2023). It also sets out some hypotheses that flow from this approach in relation to identifying the conditions under which PoEs are most likely to emerge and be sustained.

Political settlements analysis and PoEs

Under what conditions is organizational capacity deployed? What inputs are required for state capacity to translate into a range of outcomes? We highlight here two critical inputs: political coalitions (including leadership, classes, and parties) and the balance of social forces.

(Centeno et al. 2017: 17)

The term 'political settlement' refers to: *'an ongoing agreement among a society's most powerful groups over a set of political and economic institutions expected to generate for them a minimally acceptable level of benefits, which thereby ends or prevents generalized civil war and/or political and economic disorder'* (Kelsall et al. 2022: 21). The achievement of this basic settlement is a pre-requisite for processes of political and economic development to emerge. However, the form that these processes take and the distribution of resources and status that they generate is shaped by the type of political settlement that emerges in terms of 'the balance or distribution of power between contending social groups and social classes, on which any state is based' (di John and Putzel 2009: 4). In its original form, political settlements analysis focuses on how the configuration of power involving the ruling coalition shapes the incentives of elites to develop growth-enhancing institutions and the capacity to enforce these (Khan 2010, 2017). In particular, Khan argues that if a ruling coalition perceives that the threat to its hold on power is weak, it may feel confident enough to adopt a longer-term horizon towards questions of institution-building and development, with its relative dominance vis-à-vis other elites and organized social groups also enabling enforcement capabilities. Where the level of competition for political power is much higher, the threat of losing power means that the incentives for ruling coalitions to use public office and resources to maintain political loyalty through clientelistic means can be overwhelming. In such contexts, we may expect to see highly personalized forms of governance and elite capture of institutions and resources (Levy 2014). The presence of strong excluded coalitions is likely to reduce the time horizons of the ruling coalition and incentivize short-term moves to retain power. In theory, then, the highest levels of state capacity for development should be found within dominant rather than competitive settlements, a position that aligns closely with general tilt of the PoE literature on this topic, as discussed in Chapter 1. As such, some propositions on PoEs from the point of view of how political power is configured within a political settlement would be:

- **Proposition 1a**: PoEs are more likely to emerge, perform well and be sustained in political settlements where power is *concentrated*, as this can lengthen the time horizons of elites and enable clear principal–agent relationships to develop between rulers and bureaucrats over time.
- **Proposition 1b**: higher levels of power *dispersion* will reduce the possibility of PoEs being formed and undermine the performance of existing PoEs, as this will tend to incentivize rulers to undertake more short-term actions and multiplies the number of principals involved in directing bureaucratic behaviour.

However, history is clear that a concentration of political power around a ruling coalition is insufficient, in and of itself, to secure a long-term commitment to state-building and development, with many dominant leaders instead adopting predatory and personalized forms of rule. Other conditions are necessary for dominance to result in a commitment to either state-building or development, and we suggest here that these are likely to come from two sources that can also be theorized as endogenous to political settlements: the social foundations of power and paradigmatic ideas.

A key contribution of Tim Kelsall and his collaborators is to insist that the configuration of power within a political settlement extends beyond inter-elite relationships to encompass wider forms of state–society relations (Kelsall 2018, Kelsall et al. 2022). By including the *social foundations* of power as a key dimension of a political settlement, this formulation brings into focus the *type* of social groups that ruling coalitions rely on for support and to which they are likely to respond with regards to distributive demands. Influential groups can include external actors who supply the finance and legitimacy that ruling coalitions rely on to maintain themselves in power (Behuria et al. 2017), including international donors.

This focus on the political sociology of state-building resonates with some wider literature, particularly in terms of recognizing the significance of social groups that possess the resources and capacities to disrupt the coalition or even the settlement itself. Slater (2010) argues that ruling elites will only invest in state-building when they perceive themselves to be vulnerable to overthrow from below, as this perception of 'systemic vulnerability' can incentivize them to devise means of distributing public goods to offset this risk. This can involve forming 'protectionist pacts' build on strong and durable institutions as opposed to maintaining power through the easier world of 'provisioning pacts', whereby rulers distribute public goods in return for political loyalty and stability. Resting on the premise that the power of groups in society is likely to be a good predictor of who will benefit from government policy, ruling coalitions can be deemed to be either 'broad' or 'narrow' in relation to the broader social composition. Integrating this sociological dimension of political settlements analysis should advance its causal powers, and is suggestive of the following propositions:

- **Proposition 2a**: where power is concentrated *and* elites perceive themselves to be subject to 'systemic vulnerability', PoEs may emerge and be sustained as part of a broader state-building strategy.

However, it is plausible that the establishment and maintenance of PoEs may take place within the context of a provisioning rather than a protection pact, and therefore be associated with projects of elite survival and accumulation rather than state-building (as with Sonangol, Soares De Oliveira 2007):

- **Proposition 2b**: where elites are dominant but not subject to 'systemic vulnerability', PoEs may emerge and be sustained as part of a strategy of patronage-based regime survival.

Finally, there have been growing calls for political settlements analysis to move beyond the limits of a rational-actor perspective to acknowledging the role that ideas as well as incentives play in shaping elite behaviour (Behuria et al. 2017, Gray 2019, Hickey et al. 2015). We agree that ideas need to be theorized as constitutive elements of political settlements, being critical to the configuration of power, the perceptions of ruling elites and their commitment to particular forms of state-building and development (Lavers 2018). Here we align with a broader body of work, including critical political theory, that has shown how institutional change is profoundly shaped by ideational factors and that 'interests' are perceived constructs and therefore ideational in nature (Hay 2011, Schmidt 2008). Ideas are central to how political settlements function and are maintained, in that these provide 'a relatively coherent set of assumptions about the functioning of economic, social, and political institutions' (Béland 2005: 8). These overarching ideas not only shape elite interests, but 'can also be actively used by actors to achieve their perceived interests, for example, with elites securing the support of lower level factions through appeals to ideas such as nationalism, social justice, or religion' (Lavers 2018). For some political settlement theorists, 'political commitments to particular political ideologies are a potentially significant force that structures institutions' (Gray 2019: 9), including those institutions of the state.

As indicated in Figure 2.1, both domains of power that we deal with here—the political settlement and specific policy domains—are shaped by ideas. Schmidt's (2008) schema helps show the different but interrelated levels at which ideas operate, with paradigmatic ideas critical to the realm of political settlements, whilst problem definitions and policy solutions operate primarily within the policy domain. In relation to PoEs, the above review suggests that, whilst paradigmatic ideas tend to operate primarily at the level of political rulers, leading bureaucrats may also adhere to wider projects of nation-building and certain forms of development, as well as being experts in the arts of problem-framing and the delivery of policy solutions. These ideas may have their origins in the transnational arena, including via the promotion of various models of governance and development by donors and broader epistemic communities (Stone 2012); what matters here is that they form the dominant frames that powerful members of governing coalitions use to organize and justify their actions. This suggested that our approach would need to track carefully the role that different levels and types of idea play in shaping elite commitment to building PoEs in certain areas of governance and development policy, in shaping bureaucratic commitment to effective performance, and in identifying the ideational basis of particular forms of organizational practice within certain PoEs.

From this ideational version of political settlements analysis, then, we would suggest that:

Proposition 3: PoEs are more likely to emerge where there is an alignment between the paradigmatic ideas of elites and the policy ideas that are central to the policy domain within which the organization operates and the specific functions it discharges.

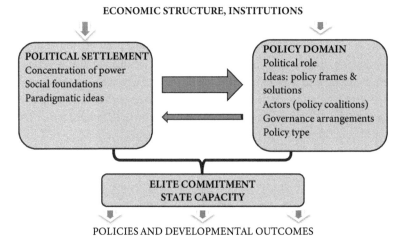

Figure 2.1 The power domains framework
Source: Editor.

The policy domain

> A state's effectiveness in a given sector can be judged only in the
> context of a political decision to make that sector a priority.
>
> (Centeno et al. 2017: 11)

It is increasingly clear that the influence of political settlements on elite commitment to state-building and development is highly uneven across different
policy domains and tasks. Adding to the strong sense that state capacity is
highly differentiated across different parts of the state (see Chapter 1), comparative studies across different types of policy domain have shown that the
ideas and incentives generated by the same political settlement play out differently in different policy domains.[4] This suggests that we need to understand
the specific arena within which a given public-sector organization operates
rather than simply reading off its performance from the more general political
settlement.

A policy domain can be defined as a meso-level field of power relations associated with specific fields of interest or concern, and as denoting a more politicized
realm than that called forth by the term 'sector'. Policy domains are constituted by
those actors, ideas, and institutions that directly govern and shape the negotiation
of agendas within a specific field, akin to the concept of the 'oil assemblage' that

---

[4] See, for example, Bebbington et al. (2018), Gray (2018), Hickey and Hossain (2019), Nazneen et al.
(2019), and Pritchett et al. (2018)

Michael Watts (2004) uses to capture the field of natural resource governance. Policy domains are both integral to the broader political settlement and possess their own logics and characteristics. As indicated in Figure 2.1, it is particularly important to grasp the political role that different policy domains play in ensuring the survival of the ruling coalition and the delivery of its ideological projects, through their contribution of either rents and/or legitimacy. This will directly shape the extent of elite interest in the domain, and the degree of politicization and/or protection to which it is subjected. Other key features of policy domains include:

- Ideas: as discussed above, the ideas that predominate within policy domains concern the identification of policy problems and solutions (Schmidt 2008). Such ideas may gain greater traction the more strongly they are aligned with the broader paradigmatic ideas (or ideologies) that underpin the political settlement, and can provide bureaucrats, bureaucratic organizations, and the policy coalitions that underpin them with shared frames of reference around which to cohere.
- Actors: the influential players within a given policy domain in developing countries are likely to include a mixture of politicians and bureaucrats at multiple levels, private sector actors (firms and individual capitalists), civil-society actors (e.g. unions, business associations, advocacy organizations, social movements), international development agencies and transnational epistemic communities (including professional associations), and other 'politically salient stakeholders' (Levy and Walton 2013). The incentives and ideas of these actors, their capacity to form coalitions across different interest groups and around particular ideas (Leftwich 2010), and to exert their demands on government, are likely to shape the possibilities for PoEs to emerge within a given domain. Some of the PoE literature suggests that transnational actors play a particularly important role in shaping the capacity of specific public-sector organizations in Africa to perform effectively (Roll 2014).
- Governance arrangements: these include the processes through which policies are formulated and implemented, the mechanisms in place to ensure accountability and the specific public-sector entities responsible for delivering these functions, namely ministries, departments, and agencies (MDAs).
- Organizational factors: how these MDAs are managed, and how they function internally, has already been identified as critical by the PoE literature (e.g. Roll 2014). As discussed in Chapter 1, of particular importance here are issues of organizational leadership and management, processes of recruitment and promotion, and also less formalized norms through which bureaucratic behaviour is governed, including organizational culture (Grindle 1997).

- Policy type: an important distinction to be drawn here is between policy challenges that are primarily 'logistical' in nature, whereby the problem is largely one that can be solved through technical means (e.g. employing more staff, delivering more resources, building more infrastructure); and challenges that are 'transactional', which may require shifts in behaviour and multiple forms of human interaction and multiple levels before progress can occur (Andrews et al. 2017). This resonates with Roll's (2014) suggestion that organizational 'function' is a defining feature of PoEs, which are more likely to emerge around policy challenges that are logistical rather than transactional in character.

By placing this concept of a policy domain into conversation with the PoE literature on organizational-level factors, the following propositions can be suggested:

- **Proposition 4a**: PoEs are more likely to emerge within policy domains and organizations that are critical to basic state functioning and/or the survival of political rulers.
- **Proposition 4b**: PoEs require the presence of organizational leaders that are both politically and technically capable, and who are able to protect their organization from political pressure and develop organizational cultures geared towards performance.
- **Proposition 4c**: state agencies are more likely to become PoEs when their main policy functions are logistical rather than transactional in nature.

The policy domain element of our framework also responds to Jessop's argument that the uneven powers of any given state is defined in part by the capacity of social actors to shape the incentives of ruling elites (Jessop 2016). These social actors within a given policy domain may be domestic, such as different types of capitalists that place often competing demands on various parts of the state, but can also be transnational (Eriksen 2011, Hagmann and Peclard 2010, Jessop 2008). This is particularly apparent in the context of the economic policy domain in Africa, from where we draw our organizational case studies. Following Ferguson's (2006) analysis of how Africa has become inserted into the global economy in a highly selective and often 'enclaved' form, it seems logical to assume:

a bifurcated governance model, in which the increasingly unusable formal state structures are 'hollowed out' fiscally and in terms of authority and personnel, while the usable enclaves are governed efficiently as private entities in a similar vein to pre-colonial mercantilist entrepots.

(Mohan 2019: 13)

It is also this economic domain that has been most fully opened up to the logics of international reform agendas (Harrison 2010). With this in mind, and given that governments in low-income-country contexts are unlikely to be able to fully resource the high costs associated with running elite bureaucratic organizations, it seems likely that external actors will also play an important role in shaping the emergence and performance of PoEs in sub-Saharan Africa, hence our final proposition:

> **Proposition 5**: PoEs are more likely to emerge within policy domains and organizations that benefit from external financial support and are aligned to international policy agendas.

Researching PoEs: Methodological issues and approaches

Researching the politics of PoEs involves a number of methodological challenges, particularly in terms of how to select cases at both country and organizational level and how to define and measure organizational performance over time. Having already noted that most existing studies of PoEs have not tended to choose cases in a systematic way, whether through identifying country cases that represent different types of political context or controlling for the type of public-sector organization and policy domain involved, we first discuss how we chose our countries and then our case-study organizations.

Country case-study selection

The fact that so few PoE studies have sought to systematically compare across different types of political context (cf. Hout 2013) has undermined theory-building around PoEs and also reduced the policy relevance of research in this field. Single-shot case studies abound, and even where a comparative approach has been attempted (e.g. Grindle 1997), country cases were not selected in ways that would enable theory testing in relation to the different political economy conditions under which PoEs might emerge and be sustained. A comparative case-study approach arguably offers the most appropriate research design for generating a more systematic body of knowledge which can both advance theory and produce findings that have policy relevance within and across different contexts (George and Bennett 2005). This is the approach adopted here, with country cases having been chosen to reflect the two main forms of political settlement identified in the literature, with two countries where power is relatively 'concentrated'—namely Rwanda and Uganda—and three cases where power is more 'dispersed'—namely Ghana, Kenya, and Zambia.

Our cases also offer variation within this continuum, with the configuration of power becoming less concentrated in Uganda and more concentrated in Zambia during the period under study, which stretches from the early 1990s until the late 2010s. The cases also offer variation in terms of the social foundations dimension of the political settlement, particularly in terms of how the ethno-regional calculus of coalition-building plays out in relation to cases where there are clear minority and majority groupings (e.g. Rwanda) and much more multi-ethnic settings (e.g. Uganda) and where ethnic concerns are either dominant in these concerns (e.g. Kenya) as opposed to contexts where political coalitions are also formed around programmatic agendas (e.g. Ghana).

The choice of five (largely Anglophone) countries from sub-Saharan Africa limits our range but has methodological advantages in that it enabled us to hold certain important factors at least somewhat constant across the cases—including colonial histories of state formation and the insertion of these countries into a particular mode of global economic governance (e.g. all countries experienced structural adjustment reforms during the 1980s and early 1990s)—in order to focus on the more specific political factors of interest. However, this does make it difficult to make representative claims that stretch beyond the kinds of countries and time period identified here.

This variation both across and within country cases over time enabled us to test the framework from multiple angles, with the strengths of these two methodological approaches helping us to both build contingent explanations through comparative analysis whilst also reducing the risk of mistaken inferences through within-case analysis (George and Bennett 2005). This typological approach to case selection and comparative analysis also has policy pay-offs, in that it offers the prospect of generating policy implications across different *types* of context (George and Bennett 2005). We hoped this would offer a coherent way of exploring the propositions generated here, and to arrive at a more relevant theory of PoEs in relation to deeper processes of regime survival and state-building in Africa.

Identifying performance patterns and choosing organizational case studies

Studies of PoEs have struggled to overcome the lack of a clear identification strategy. Simply put, how can we know—objectively—that some organizations are systematically performing at a higher level than most other organizations in the same governance context? General indexes of state capacity, such as the World Bank's World Governance Indicators, are of little value here, as they operate at an aggregate country level rather than offering a more disaggregated view of how capacities are distributed across public-sector organizations within specific countries. As Bersch et al. (2017) note, we do not currently have a reliable means of comparing the capacities of bureaucratic agencies within the same context. Whilst they go on to construct such an index for Brazil, they acknowledge that the data required for this task is simply not available for most countries in the developing world, including sub-Saharan Africa. Although some efforts are under way to achieve a much more fine-grained perspective on within-state levels of bureaucratic capacity,[5] we are currently left with the challenge of identifying high-performing agencies via alternative means.

Following other research into PoEs (McDonnell 2017), we therefore decided to undertake an expert survey within each country context, whereby key informants were invited to identify what they saw as being the highest-performing public-sector agencies. Given the absence of easily quantifiable and 'objective' metrics on governance, expert surveys have become commonplace within governance research and underpin many leading indexes, including the World Governance Indicators, and indexes produced by the Varieties of Democracy and the Quality of Government projects. Expert surveys are obviously subjective in nature, although given the intangible nature of many dimensions of governance, they may have greater validity than objective measures that are unable to properly reflect the nature of what is being measured. Obvious problems include the nature of the experts consulted and their depth and range of knowledge of the subject area, the difficulties of including the views of end-users of public-sector organizations, and problems of reputational bias, whereby higher-profile organizations (including those with public relations operations) may receive higher rankings than less visible or media-savvy organizations.

Given these potential problems, we identified experts who had either working and/or academic expertise on public-sector organizations. These included public-sector professionals, politicians, officials within international development agencies, researchers and consultants, and representatives of both the private sector and civil society. We sought to interview between twenty and thirty experts per country, in person wherever possible, although a few surveys were completed via email. The survey (see Appendix) included a range of questions, the most important of which required respondents to identify (a) the spread of performance levels across the public sector and (b) particularly high-performing state agencies. The results of each country survey will be discussed in the subsequent chapters on Ghana, Kenya, Rwanda, Uganda, and Zambia; here we briefly discuss the responses to these key questions in order to identify some broad performance patterns and to show how these findings shaped our choice of which organizations to subject to in-depth case-study investigations. We also discuss how we sought to overcome concerns with the subjective nature of expert surveys by triangulating the findings with more objective sources of performance data.

[5] See the World Bank's Bureaucracy Lab: https://www.worldbank.org/en/research/dime/brief/Bureaucracy-Lab (accessed 13 December 2021).

To capture the spread of performance across the public sector, we asked our experts to identify the proportion of ministries, departments, or agencies (MDAs) that regularly delivered on their mandate. A comparative analysis of the responses to this question across our countries revealed some patterns of theoretical interest. For Kenya, Uganda, and Zambia, the patterns that emerged were very similar: around three-quarters of respondents judged that 'Only a few ministries/departments/agencies regularly deliver on their mandate, whilst the majority generally fail to do so', with only two respondents in total across all countries claiming that most did so. This pattern was still apparent in Ghana, albeit to a lesser extent, with respondents split more evenly across those who suggested that 'all', 'some', or 'only a few' performed well. Most strikingly, a clear majority of our respondents in Rwanda agreed that 'Most ministries/departments/agencies regularly deliver on their mandate, with only a few failing to do so'. This suggested that it was actually very difficult to identify PoEs at all in this context, and that there instead seemed to have been a more generalized effort to improve state performance across the board, rather than only in selective agencies.

This pattern of public-sector performance largely aligns with figures from the Mo Ibrahim Foundation (IIAG 2016; Figure 2.2), which judges that Ghana and Rwanda currently outperform Kenya, Uganda, and Zambia on measures of 'government effectiveness'. This suggested that the PoE phenomenon was prominent in these three countries, in line with Roll's (2014) definition of PoEs as 'high-performing agencies in otherwise dysfunctional governance contexts'. In terms of Ghana and Rwanda, it is notable that the composition of each country's aggregate score is very different: whereas Rwanda scores highly on 'public management', Ghana's scores have declined in this area whilst remaining strong in terms of participation and human rights, safety, and rule of law. The possibility that these findings are suggestive of two different routes to state-building in contemporary Africa, one in concentrated settlements and the other in more dispersed settlements (Propositions 1 and 2), is taken up in Chapter 8.

In terms of which state agencies were identified as delivering on their mandates most effectively, the most striking finding was that respondents in every country tended to identify organizations that operated within the 'economic technocracy' as being amongst the highest performers. This was particularly in terms of ministries of finance (usually the budget department), central banks, and revenue authorities. Other relatively highly ranked organizations included national development boards, investment authorities, passport offices, and the occasional utility company, but none were identified from within the social sector. This tends to support Propositions 4a and 4c, with regards to PoEs being most likely to emerge in relation to core state functions and within organizations charged with delivering largely logistical policy tasks. In addition, the economic policy domain is characterized by both high levels of financial support and disciplinary oversight from international actors (Proposition 5).

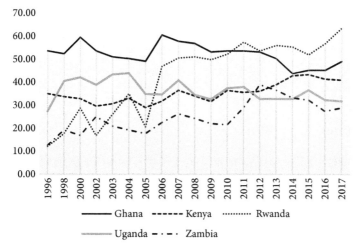

Figure 2.2 Government effectiveness in our five countries
Source: World Governance Indicators.

However, and although this is consistent with other PoE studies that have also found higher levels of performance in the domain of economic governance (Grindle 1997, Johnson 2015), it was not entirely predictable from the outset. As McDonnell (2017: 482), has noted:

> Empirical patterns do not support this intuition: finance ministries are regarded as among the most corrupt state agencies in Benin, Ecuador, Madagascar, and Zambia, although their central banks are well regarded. The opposite is true in Burundi, Guinea, Indonesia, and Slovakia, where central banks are among the worst-reputed public agencies; in Thailand, both organizations are poorly regarded (World Bank 1999–2007).

Importantly, our survey results also suggested that these economic agencies had not performed uniformly well over time: for example, some respondents also placed the top-ranked organizations as being amongst those whose performance had deteriorated over the past five years. Choosing organizations whose performance had been deemed to fluctuate over time also offered the possibility of undertaking within-case comparisons, particularly in relation to changing political settlement dynamics over time. Although this focus on the economic technocracy limited our range in terms of the policy domains being covered, it offered a good range of the different *types* of public-sector organization, ranging from standard governmental departments through semi—to fully autonomous agencies (see Table 2.1). It also works well in terms of offering a strong basis for comparing how similar types of organization performed across different political contexts.

Table 2.1 Organizational case-study selection

Organizational type➜ Type of political settlement ⬇	Traditional Department (Finance ministry budget departments)	Semi-autonomous agencies (Revenue authorities)	Autonomous agency /regulatory body (Central banks)
Concentrated: Rwanda	MINECOFIN	RRA	BNR
Concentrated: Uganda	MFPED	URA	BoU
Dispersed: Ghana	MFNEP	GRA	BoG
Dispersed: Kenya	MoF	KRA	CBK
Dispersed: Zambia	MoF	ZRA	BoZ

Our surveys did identify some high-performing agencies that lay beyond the economic technocracy, as with the cases of the National Water and Sewerage Corporation in Uganda and the Seed Control and Certification Institute in Zambia, both of which could be verified as high performers with reference to international performance indexes and awards. The absence of an obvious explanation for these agencies to be such high performers, including with reference to core state functions and regime survival, encouraged us to conduct in-depth studies of these organizations also, although these findings are reported elsewhere (e.g. Bukenya 2020).

Before embarking on the in-depth organizational case studies, we first needed to verify the expert survey responses observations by triangulating our survey findings with more 'objective' forms of performance data. We were also mindful of Michael Roll's (2014) four criteria required for an agency to be considered as a pocket of effectiveness, namely:

1. Relative effectiveness (which we took to mean 'performance against mandate' relative to other organizations in the same political context, rather than by some 'global' standard)
2. Capacity to deliver nationally
3. Delivery in line with human rights and laws, in the sense of not using illegal means or violating human rights, particularly in relation to law enforcement
4. Persists for at least five years.

For example, this meant that we did not look at either the military (given the association with human rights abuses) or municipal authorities (lack of national scope), despite these being ranked highly in some of our surveys. Our focus on specific entities may also have meant that we missed out on high-performing networks or broader governance systems, a challenge that Michael Roll expands on in his closing commentary (Chapter 10).[6] The trickier task was to identify levels of performance over time, including for the qualifying periods of at least five years, given the absence of objective performance data on most specific MDAs. This process involved choosing the major dimensions of a given organization's mandate and looking for the most credible forms of data on which to track performance over time. This included internal governmental assessments of particular sectors and agencies, international evaluations of particular aspects of performance, and also macro-level data on outcome indicators, where these could be plausibly tied to the performance of specific organizations (e.g. on fiscal and monetary discipline or revenue generation). The ones we used are summarized in Table 2.2, which includes reference to the qualitative as well as the quantitative dimensions of tracking organizational performance over time.

For *finance ministries*, the department most frequently identified as high performing within our expert survey was the budget department. According to Simson and Welham (2014), 'The most well-established international measures of budget credibility are the PFM (public financial management) performance

Table 2.2 Performance indicators for case-study PoEs

Organizational type	Indicators	Data sources	Critical episodes
MoF budget departments	Public expenditure patterns over time (e.g. supplementaries)	Annual budget reports Also PEFA, CPIA	Spikes in public expenditure Reforms (e.g. PFM)
Central banks: price stability	Inflation rates over time	IMF	Spikes in inflation
Central banks: financial stability	Financial stability data (e.g. % of non-performing loans)	IMF financial stability reports	Bank closures
Revenue Authorities	Tax effort	Youhou and Goujon 2017	Trends in data

[6] For example, some of the most interesting recent work on PoEs has focused on networks or channels of effectiveness, rather than agencies per se. This includes studies of a high-performing strategic team within Edo state in Nigeria (Porter and Watts 2017), which delivered impressive results within infrastructure and revenue generation, through building coalitions, connections, and networks across political/bureaucratic/commercial boundaries and different levels, and the 'channel of effectiveness' identified in Cambodia's health sector by Kelsall and Seiha (2014).

measurement framework indicators' used within the Public Expenditure and Financial Accountability (PEFA) assessment framework. Within this, key indicators include those on 'Aggregate expenditure outturn compared to original approved budget' and the 'Composition of expenditure outturn compared to original approved budget with two sub-indicators'. The African Development Bank's Country Policy and Institutional Assessment (CPIA) also has relevant indicators on the quality of budgetary and financial management. These provided useful reference points but both are limited in terms of the time periods that they cover, with CPIA running from 2004 and PEFA from 2006, whereas we were interested in a longer time period. Both also tend to focus more on processes than actual outcomes and we were keen to look more at how budgets were actually delivered and less at how they were constructed. To achieve this, we used the budget performance reports produced by national ministries of finance to track patterns of actual versus planned expenditure over longer periods of time. This included a particular focus on periods or moments of fiscal ill-discipline, as indicated (for example) by the number, size, and timing of supplementary budgets and any significant divergence between predicted and actual expenditures that lacked clear explanations.

Central banks in developing countries have been charged with two major mandates in the past few decades: securing price stability through controlling inflation and securing financial stability, largely through banking supervision. Price stability over time can be tracked via data from the International Monetary Fund (IMF) data on inflation, although further analysis is required to identify the extent to which changes in inflation rates are due to exogenous factors (e.g. oil price rises, droughts) rather than the failure of central banks to set and implement effective monetary policy. What is more controversial is drawing out a normative judgement that being 'effective' in maintaining inflation at a particular level, usually a low one, is necessarily the 'right' thing from a developmental perspective. Most observers agree that both significant macroeconomic instability and very high rates of inflation are objectively 'bad' in that they damage the prospects for economic growth and undermine the confidence of investors. Achieving macroeconomic stability was seen as critical to the success of developmental states in South East Asia (Gore 2000) before it became a shibboleth of the structural adjustment agenda of the IFIs. However, there are major disagreements with regards to what the ideal level of inflation should be, with some advocating a more expansive approach as compared to the hawkish position of the IMF and whether the role of central banks should be restricted to this particular policy agenda. This is an important debate and one we re-engage with in some of the fieldwork chapters and in Chapter 8. Viewed from the narrower perspective of organizational performance, our immediate job here was to identify whether a given central bank was proving itself capable of delivering on the mandate that it had been tasked with, including the target rate of inflation. The fact that this varied across our countries (e.g. with the East African countries largely bound to single-digit targets as opposed to the often looser approach adopted in Ghana and, in particular, Zambia) meant that we could not apply a universal standard here but rather tracked performance against national policy targets over time.

On financial stability, the IMF's Financial Stability Index enabled us to get a sense of how committed and capable our central banks were to the effective regulation and supervision of banks, although again this needed to be triangulated with national policy guidance. For example, the non-performing loan to total loan ratio and the liquid asset to deposit ratio are both important indicators of the viability of a private bank and the sector more broadly, and are indicators that central banks monitor closely. However, the rules on these indicators, such as the statutory liquidity requirement, varies between countries; again, and shaped by Roll's definition of the 'relative effectiveness'of PoEs, we judged each central bank against nationally relevant targets and policy contexts. Bank closures also offered us a rich source of data, although not in a straightforward sense. Given that political interference in the banking sector could lead to banks being either closed or maintained, the overall level of bank closures is less significant than either non-closures of 'failing banks' or of the ways in which specific closures were handled by central banks, both in terms of the effectiveness of the action (e.g. were closures undertaken without depositors suffering losses or causing financial instability within the wider sector?) and in terms of whether central banks observed due process whilst closing a given bank.

The central mandate of *revenue authorities* is clear enough; however, measuring how successful a given revenue authority is at generating tax revenues is far from straightforward. First, the most frequently used indicator of performance, namely the ratio of tax to GDP, is limited by the fact that this is strongly shaped by the structure of the economy, with the size and nature of the informal economy a critical determinant of a country's capacity to generate domestic revenue. We instead used the 'tax effort' metric, which accounts for the structure of the economy and offers a ratio of the actual tax collection to the predicted tax revenue. However, the second challenge here is that this metric captures the effect of *tax policy* as well as *tax administration*, whereas revenue authorities are only directly responsible for administration, with tax policy usually set by the parent ministry of finance. This meant that we also needed to track the nature of the tax regime over time, in an effort to identify whether shifts in revenue generation performance could be most plausibly linked to either the policy and/or administrative function respectively.

Importantly, we were also keen to go beyond a purely statistical approach to identifying performance trajectories over time and sought to identify other indicators that could alert us to whether our organizations were being nurtured as PoEs and/or interfered with. This involved in-depth organizational biographies with a particular focus on critical junctures and on how organizations responded to crisis points, particularly where these seemed to be of a political nature (e.g. fiscal indiscipline resulting from electoral pressures).

Organizational biographies and the importance of crises

The next stage was to subject each organizational case to an in-depth qualitative investigation, using literature reviews and documentary analysis, key informant interviews and field visits to gain insider accounts of how organizations functioned in practice. We focused on examining the interface of organizations with their policy domain and political context and on more internal aspects. Drawing on the conceptual framework set out above and the PoE literature discussed in Chapter 1, this guided us towards looking at both the formal and informal aspects of organizational autonomy; the political and technical competence of organizational leaders and of how long they were allowed to remain in office; efforts to generate positive organizational cultures, including through formal (e.g. salary incentives, training budgets) and informal means (e.g. awards, leadership-by-example, inculcation of professional norms); various indicators of staff capacity and organizational strength and also processes of recruitment and promotion (see Table 2.3).

Table 2.3 Organizational-level factors

Indicators	Sub-indicators	Sources
Organizational autonomy	De jure: legal status and governing rules De facto: examples of direct interference with mandate	Indexes for specific agencies (e.g. IMF's Central Bank Legislation Database Institutional Profiles Database A310 Case-study research
Capacity and character of leadership	Educational and professional backgrounds Political connections with incumbents Length of tenure of senior leaders Political management skills	Public record, media, key informant interviews
Organizational culture	Perceptions of staff that they are empowered to perform their role effectively Budgets for training, allowances for travel Recruitment and promotion processes Number/scale of corruption cases directly involving our agencies	Key informant interviews Organizational documentation (e.g. funding levels, training budgets) Media, interviews, public reports on recruitment (e.g. Inspectorate of government, Hansard)

Organizational *strength*	Number of staff with post-graduate training/criteria for entry Percentage of senior posts filled Organizational structure: how coherent? Does it provide incentives for staff to seek advancement?	Key informant interviews Organizational documentation (e.g. funding levels, training budgets)

Table 2.4 Within-country analysis via process tracing (key headings)

Performance period	Political settlement dynamics	Organizational leadership	Organizational culture and capacity	Transnational factors	Other factors

Analysing performance patterns over time

By integrating our reading of objective performance indicators with our in-depth qualitative research we were able to identify the level of performance achieved by each state agency across time. Identifying these 'performance periods' enabled us to confirm whether or not the organization could be considered to be a PoE, in accordance with Roll's five-year time period, and to start tracing performance patterns to their underlying drivers. A process-tracing approach was used to track back from key moments (e.g. particular spikes in inflation, loss of fiscal discipline) to produce detailed narratives of institutional performance over time. These performance trajectories were then mapped onto political settlement dynamics over time within each case, whilst also tracking other potential drivers of performance (e.g. leadership and management, international support). As depicted in Table 2.4, this offered a means of testing whether any of the main variables from our power domains framework could help explain performance levels over time, whilst also tracking the role of factors beyond our framework.

Given our focus on state agencies that perform economic functions, an important challenge here was to control as far as possible for 'reverse causation', whereby favourable economic conditions can enable (say) central banks to achieve their mandate relatively easily. We sought to overcome this tricky question of attribution through our choice of performance indicators and process-tracing approach. For example, most of our performance indicators are either not directly susceptible to being influenced by shifting patterns of economic growth (e.g. budgetary performance) or directly account for these factors (e.g. tax effort). In tracing back particular episodes of both high and low performance over a lengthy period to a wide range of contextual conditions, as, for example, with sudden spikes in inflation, we have tried to identify the relative weight of economic and political factors in explaining particular outcomes, as with the different origins of inflation spikes within countries like Ghana, Uganda, and Rwanda (both over time and between them). After our country-level work was complete, the material was then subjected to comparative analysis across political settlement type, as presented inss Chapter 8.

Conclusion

Researching the politics of PoEs presents several conceptual and methodological challenges. This includes overcoming a tendency to see 'islands' of effectiveness as divorced from their wider political context and the general lack of comparative research required to start identifying the types of political conditions under which PoEs emerge and become sustained. This chapter has proposed a conceptual and methodological approach that can start to address this challenge. It has argued that an alignment of political settlements analysis with critical theories of state power can help reveal the ways in which PoEs are both shaped by, and help to reproduce, particular institutional forms in developing countries, with particular reference to the competing logics of regime survival, state-building, and democratization within a transnational context. This in turn needs to be explored in relation to the particular policy domains within which specific PoEs are located through a power domains analysis.

Operationalizing this conceptual approach through a comparative case-study research design, involving systematic process of within- and across-case analysis, should produce relevant and verifiable causal stories on the politics of public-sector performance. This in turn should enable theoretical development concerning the conditions under which PoEs emerge and also help inform policy actors keen to understand how to align interventions with different types of political context. Identifying indicators through which the performance of public-sector organizations can be tracked over time remains a challenge, and although we have made at least some progress on this, more remains to be done. However, we would advocate that this cannot be resolved through metrics alone; using qualitative methods to gain insider perspectives on how public-sector organizations actually function and on their relationship with political actors and events is essential. Moments of 'organizational crisis' and the critical junctures that organizations go through within their lifecycle can, as with individual biographies, offer important insights into how capable and resilient they are at dealing with 'external' pressures. The book now goes on to demonstrate this approach through its five country case studies, each of which looks at the three public-sector organizations, before offering a comparative analysis of the over-arching findings and implications.

References

Acemoglu, D. and Robinson, J. (2012). *Why Nations Fail: The Origins of Power, Prosperity and Poverty.* London: Profile Books.

Andrews, M., Pritchett, L., and Woolcock, M. (2017). *Building State Capability: Evidence, Analysis, Action.* Oxford: Oxford University Press.

Batley, R. and Mcloughlin, C. (2015). 'The Politics of Public Services: A Service Characteristics Approach', *World Development,* 74: 275–85.

Bebbington, A., Abdulai, A.-G., Humphreys Bebbington, D., Hinfelaar, M., and Sandborn, C. (2018). *Governing Extractive Industries: Politics, Histories, Ideas.* Oxford: Oxford University Press.

Behuria, P. (2020). 'The Domestic Political Economy of Upgrading in Global Value Chains: How Politics Shapes Pathways for Upgrading in Rwanda's Coffee Sector', *Review of International Political Economy,* 27(2): 348–76.

Behuria, P., Buur, L., and Gray, H. (2017). 'Research Note: Studying Political Settlements in Africa', *African Affairs,* 116(464): 508–25.

Béland, D. (2005). 'Ideas and Social Policy: An Institutionalist Perspective', *Social Policy and Administration,* 39(1): 1–18.

Bersch, K., Praça, S., and Taylor, M. M. (2017). 'Bureaucratic Capacity and Political Autonomy within National States: Mapping the Archipelago of Excellence in Brazil'. In M. A. Centeno, A. Kohli, and D. J. Yashar (eds), *States in the Developing World.* Cambridge, MA: Cambridge University Press. 157–83.

Block, F. (1981). 'Beyond Relative Autonomy: State Managers as Historical Subjects', *New Political Science,* 2(3): 33–49.

Bukenya, B. (2020). 'The Politics of Building Effective Water Utilities in the Global South: A Case of NWSC Uganda'. ESID Working Paper 152. Manchester: Effective States and Inclusive Development Research Centre.

Centeno, M. A. Kohli, A., and Yashar D. J. (eds) (2017). *States in the Developing World.* Cambridge, MA: Cambridge University Press.

Di John, J. and Putzel J. (2009). 'Political Settlements: Issues Paper'. Governance and Social Development Resource Centre, University of Birmingham.

Eriksen, S. S. (2011). '"State Failure" in Theory and Practice: The Idea of the State and the Contradictions of State Formation', *Review of International Studies,* 37(1): 229–47.

Ferguson, J. (2006). *Global Shadows: Africa in the Neoliberal World Order.* Durham, NC: Duke University Press.

Geddes, B. (1994). *Politician's Dilemma: Building State Capacity in Latin America.* Berkeley, CA: University of California Press.

George, A. L. and Bennett, A. (2005). *Case Studies and Theory Development in the Social Sciences.* Cambridge, MA: MIT Press.

Gore, C. (2000). 'The Rise and Fall of the Washington Consensus as a Paradigm for Developing Countries', *World Development,* 28(5): 789–804.

Gray, H. (2018). *Turbulence and Order in Economic Development: Institutions and Economic Transformation in Tanzania and Vietnam.* Oxford: Oxford University Press.

Gray, H. (2019). 'Understanding and Deploying the Political Settlements Framework'. In N. Cheeseman, E. Bertrand, S. Husaini (eds), *The Oxford Encyclopedia of African Politics.* Oxford: Oxford University Press.

Grindle, M. (1997). 'Divergent Cultures? When Public Organisations Perform Well in Developing Countries', *World Development*, 25(4): 481–95.

Grindle, M. S. (2012). *Jobs for the Boys: Patronage and the State in Comparative Perspective*. Cambridge, MA: Harvard University Press.

Hagmann, T. and Peclard, D. (2010). 'Negotiating Statehood: Dynamics of Power and Domination in Africa'. *Development and Change* 41(4): 539–562.

Harrison, G. (2010). *Neoliberal Africa: The Impact of Global Social Engineering*. London: Zed Books.

Hay, C. (2011). 'Ideas and the Construction of Interests'. In D. Béland and R. H. Cox (eds), *Ideas and Politics in Social Science Research*. Oxford: Oxford University Press, 65–82.

Hickey, S., Sen, K. and Bukenya, B. (eds) (2015) *The Politics of Inclusive Development: Interrogating the Evidence*. Oxford: Oxford University Press.

Hickey, S., Abdulai, A.-G., Izama, A., and Mohan, G. (2020). 'Responding to the Commodity Boom with Varieties of Resource Nationalism: A Political Economy Explanation for the Different Routes Taken by Africa's New Oil Producers', *The Extractive Industries and Society*, 7(4): 1246–56.

Hickey, S. Lavers, T. Niño-Zarazúa, M. and Seekings, J. (eds.) (2019). *The Politics of Social Protection in Eastern and Southern Africa*. Oxford: Oxford University Press.

Hickey, S. and Hossain, N. (eds) (2019). *The Politics of Education in Developing Countries: From Schooling to Learning*. Oxford: Oxford University Press.

Hickey, S. and Sen, K. (2023). *Pathways to Development: From Politics to Power*. Oxford: Oxford University Press.

Hout, W. (2013). 'Neopatrimonialism and Development: Pockets of Effectiveness as Drivers of Change', *Revue Internationale de Politique Comparée* 20(3): 79–96.

IIAG (2016). *A Decade of African Governance: 2006–2016*. Ibrahim Index of African Governance.

Jessop, B. (2008). *State Power: A Strategic and Relational Approach*. Cambridge: Polity Press.

Jessop, B. (2016). *The State: Past, Present, Future*. Cambridge: Polity Press.

Johnson, M. C. (2015). 'Donor Requirements and Pockets of Effectiveness in Senegal's Bureaucracy', *Development Policy Review*, 33(6): 783–804.

Kelsall, T. (2018). 'Towards a Universal Political Settlement Concept: A Response to Mushtaq Khan', *African Affairs*, 117(469): 656–69.

Kelsall, T. et al. (2022). *Political Settlements and Development: Theory, Evidence, Implications*. Oxford: Oxford University Press.

Kelsall, T. and Seiha, H. (2014). 'The Political Economy of Inclusive Health Care in Cambodia'. ESID Working Paper 43. Manchester: Effective States and Inclusive Development Research Centre, University of Manchester.

Khan, M. (2010). 'Political Settlements and the Governance of Growth-enhancing Institutions. Draft Paper', Research Paper Series on 'Growth-Enhancing Governance. London: SOAS, University of London.

Khan, M., H. (2017). 'Political Settlements and the Analysis of Institutions', *African Affairs*, 117(469): 636–55.

Lavers, T. (2018). 'Taking Ideas Seriously within Political Settlements Analysis', ESID Working Paper No. 95. Manchester: University of Manchester.

Lavers, T. and Hickey, S. (2016). 'Conceptualising the Politics of Social Protection Expansion in Low Income Countries: The Intersection of Transnational Ideas and Domestic Politics', *International Journal of Social Welfare*, 25(4): 388–98.

Leftwich, A. (2010). 'Beyond Institutions: Rethinking the Role of Leaders, Elites and Coalitions in the Industrial Formation of Developmental States and Strategies', *Forum for Development Studies*, 37(1): 93–111.

Levy, B. and Walton, M. (2013). 'Institutions, Incentives and Service Provision: Bringing Politics back in'. ESID Working Paper No. 18. Manchester: Effective States and Inclusive Development Research Centre, University of Manchester.

Levy, B. (2014). *Working with the Grain: Integrating governance and growth in development strategies*. New York: Oxford University Press.

Macuane, J. J., Buur, L., and Monjane, C. M. (2018). 'Power, Conflict and Natural Resources: The Mozambican Crisis Revisited', *African Affairs*, 117(468): 415–38.

Mamdani, M. (1996). *Citizen and Subject: Contemporary Africa and the Legacy of Late Colonialism*. Princeton, NJ: Princeton University Press.

McDonnell, E. M. (2017). 'The Patchwork Leviathan: How Pockets of Bureaucratic Governance Flourish within Institutionally Diverse Developing States', *American Sociological Review*, 82(3): 476–510.

Mohan, G. (2019). 'Pockets of Effectiveness: The Contributions of Critical Political Economy and State Theory'. ESID Working Paper No. 118. Manchester: University of Manchester.

Nazneen, S., Hickey, S., and Sifaki, E. (eds) (2019). *Negotiating Gender Equity in the Global South: The Politics of Domestic Violence Policy*. Oxford: Routledge.

North, D. C., Wallis, J. J., Webb, S. B., and Weingast, B. R. (2009). *In the Shadow of Violence: Politics, Economics, and the Problems of Development*. New York: Cambridge University Press.

Painter J. (2006). 'Prosaic Geographies of Stateness', *Political Geography*, 25(7): 752–74.

Pedersen, R. H., Jacob T., and Bofin P. (2020). 'From Moderate to Radical Resource Nationalism in the Boom Era: Pockets of Effectiveness under Stress in "New Oil" Tanzania', *The Extractive Industries and Society*, 7(4): 1211–18.

Porter, D. and Watts, M. (2016). 'Multi-Scalar Governance and Institutions: Intentional Development and the Conditions of Possibility in the Extractive Sector'. Background Paper for the *World Development Report 2017*. Washington, DC: The World Bank.

Porter, D. and Watts, M. (2017). 'Righting the Resource Curse: Institutional Politics and State Capabilities in Edo State, Nigeria', *Journal of Development Studies* (53)2: 249–63.

Pritchett, L., Sen, K., and Werker, E. (eds) (2018). *Deals and Development: The Political Dynamics of Growth Episodes*. Oxford: Oxford University Press.

Roll, M. (ed.) (2014). *The Politics of Public Sector Performance: Pockets of Effectiveness in Developing Countries*. Oxford: Routledge.

Salimo, P., Buur, L., and Macuane, J. (2020). 'The Politics of Domestic Gas: The Sasol Natural Gas Deals in Mozambique', *The Extractive Industries and Society*, 7(4): 1219–29.

Schmidt, V. A. (2008). 'Discursive Institutionalism: The Explanatory Power of Ideas and Discourse', *Annual Review of Political Science* 11: 303–26.

Simson, R. and Welham, B. (2014). 'Incredible Budgets: Budget Credibility in Theory and Practice'. London: Overseas Development Institute.

Slater, D. (2010). *Ordering Power: Contentious Politics and Authoritarian Leviathans in Southeast Asia*. New York: Cambridge University Press.

Soares De Oliveira, R. (2007). 'Business Success, Angola-style: Postcolonial Politics and the Rise and Rise of Sonangol', *The Journal of Modern African Studies*, 45(4): 595–619.

Stone, D. (2012). 'Transfer and Translation of Policy', *Policy Studies*, 33(6): 483–99.

Strauss, J. C. (1998). *Strong Institutions in Weak Polities: State Building in Republican China, 1927–1940*. Oxford: Oxford University Press.

Tyce, M. (2020). 'Unrealistic Expectations, Frustrated Progress and an Uncertain Future? The Political Economy of Oil in Kenya', *The Extractive Industries and Society*, 7(2): 729–37.

Watts, M. (2004). 'Resource Curse? Governmentality, Oil and Power in the Niger Delta, Nigeria', *Geopolitics*, 9(1): 50–80.

Whitfield, L., Therkildsen, O., Buur, L., and Kjær, A. M. (2015). *The Politics of African Industrial Policy: A Comparative Perspective*. Cambridge: Cambridge University Press.

Youhou, D. H. and Goujon, M. (2017). 'Reassessing Tax Effort in Developing Countries: A Proposal of a Vulnerability-adjusted Tax Effort Index'. Working Paper. Clermont-Ferrand, France: FERDI.

PART II
CASE STUDIES

3

Political Settlement Dynamics and the Emergence and Decline of Bureaucratic Pockets of Effectiveness in Ghana

Abdul-Gafaru Abdulai

Introduction

Although Ghana is justifiably hailed as a democratic success story in Africa, it is widely perceived that the country's public organizations are generally ineffective in performing their mandated functions (Ansu 2013, Resnick 2016).[1] Observers have characterized public administration in Ghana as a system which 'does not work' (Whitfield 2010: 735), and which severely reduces governments' ability to implement reforms and programmes (IMANI 2018, (Killick 2008). However, amidst this broader image of a dysfunctional public sector, there is recognition that 'Ghana possesses a range of state agencies that work far more effectively than the stereotypical image of a "third world" civil service' (McDonnell 2017: 483).

Studies on these bureaucratic pockets of effectiveness (PoEs) in Ghana are scarce, as most scholarship has focused on identifying constraints to strengthening the capacity of public organizations (Appiah and Abdulai 2017, Ayee 2013, Ohemeng and Ayee 2016). The few existing studies on PoEs have concentrated on identifying broad characteristics that separate relatively effective public organizations from dysfunctional ones, with a particular focus on organizational sociology and culture (McDonnell 2017, Owusu 2006a, 2006b,). Whilst important, these studies have generally overlooked the political economy conditions that shape the emergence and persistence of PoEs in Ghana, and there is virtually no research that explains variations in the performance of such agencies over time.

This chapter contributes to filling these gaps by explaining the performance trajectories of three PoEs in Ghana, namely, the Ministry of Finance (MoF), the Bank of Ghana (BoG), and the Ghana Revenue Authority (GRA). Drawing on the conceptual framework elaborated in Chapter 2, particular attention is paid to

[1] The author gratefully acknowledges the role that Giles Mohan played in the study of Ghana's Finance Ministry (Abdulai and Mohan 2019).

Abdul-Gafaru Abdulai, *Political Settlement Dynamics and the Emergence and Decline of Bureaucratic Pockets of Effectiveness in Ghana*. In: *Pockets of Effectiveness and the Politics of State-building and Development in Africa.* Edited by Sam Hickey, Oxford University Press. © Oxford University Press (2023). DOI: 10.1093/oso/9780192864963.003.0003

exploring the roles of political settlement dynamics in shaping the performance trajectories of these organizations, as well as organizational-level factors and the role of international support. Briefly, our framework hypothesizes that the capacity and commitment of ruling elites to invest in high-performing public-sector organizations will be strongly shaped by the degree to which power is either *concentrated* or *dispersed* in a given political settlement. Where power is dispersed, ruling elites will most likely focus on accommodating powerful factions by redistributing resources and creating opportunities for rent-seeking. In contrast:

> a low degree of contestation means that ruling elites have greater control over factional and individual demands within the ruling coalition, which in turn means they are better able to fend off distributional demands ... that could undermine economic objectives.
>
> (Whitfield et al. 2015: 100)

Ghana is a particularly suitable case for testing this framework, given the extent to which the configuration of power has changed between different types of political settlement over its post-colonial period. Although power has been widely dispersed during much of Ghana's post-colonial history, particularly since the return to multi-party democracy in 1992, the 1980s witnessed a period when power was concentrated largely around the head of state (Hutchful 1997, Whitfield et al. 2015). Our findings show that although PoEs can emerge under different political settlement types, such agencies are more likely to endure in concentrated political settlements than in contexts characterized by dispersed configurations of power. The main mechanism that links Ghana's shifting political settlement and organizational performance is the quality of organizational leaders and their relationship to political leaders. High levels of support from international development organizations and their privileged status as key nodes of economic governance have undoubtedly helped these organizations attain impressive levels of performance. Nevertheless, the fact that their performance has waxed and waned over time, despite international support and mandates being largely constant, suggests that the key to understanding their performance lies with political economy factors.

The rest of the chapter proceeds thus: the next section offers a brief history of Ghana's political settlements since independence and then explores the impact of contemporary political settlement dynamics on public-sector performance. It then uses the extant literature and an expert survey to identify PoEs within Ghana's public sector, before the section following presents summarized versions of the case-study findings. The chapter goes on to discuss the factors that explain the performance of these organizations over time with reference to the conceptual framework summarized above, before concluding and highlighting some policy implications.

Political settlement dynamics and public-sector performance in Ghana

In the early post-colonial period, Ghana's political history was characterized by constant power struggles between elite factions for control over the state. The initial concentration of power around Kwame Nkrumah, Ghana's first president, soon dissipated, with various ethnic- and regional-based parties demonstrating their growing electoral strength (Austin 1964: 353). In the 1970s a series of military coups ensured that the settlement became unstable and power even more dispersed, with state power shifting from one ethno-regional group to the other (Chazan 1982), but with no ruling coalition able to maintain power for long (Whitfield et al. 2015). Most ruling coalitions were very short lived, with their performance undermined by significant internal rivalries and the pursuit of personal ambition (Berry 2008: 39).

These dynamics changed significantly in the 1980s, when Ghana's political settlement became characterized by a high degree of elite cohesion and power concentration after the Jerry Rawlings-led Provisional National Defence Council (PNDC) took power for the second time. Under the PNDC, power was centralized around Rawlings and a few economic technocrats, most of whom had no independent power base of their own, and instead owed their positions to the president. Excluded political factions were weakened by a legitimacy crisis given their association with political instability and economic decline (Whitfield 2018). Autonomy was a key feature of the PNDC ruling coalition (Chazan 1991), with Rawlings able 'to centralize power progressively around himself and to establish his personal preeminence and his autonomy vis-à-vis social movements, state institutions, and the PNDC itself' (Hutchful 1997: 26). In terms of undertaking difficult reforms, and as discussed below, this 'insulation' allowed the PNDC to 'do more than other more constrained regimes' (Callaghy 1990: 277).

However, by the early 1990s rival political groupings and civil-society actors had successfully lobbied for the return of multi-party elections (Abdulai 2011, Whitfield 2018). Ahead of presidential and parliamentary elections in November and December 1992, Rawlings converted the PNDC into a political party, the National Democratic Congress (NDC), which included a larger group of political elites and patronage networks at the constituency level (Whitfield 2018: 100). In this context, power became more dispersed both within the ruling coalition and between it and excluded factions. Since December 1992, Ghana has conducted eight rounds of highly competitive presidential elections, three of which resulted in power alternations between two dominant political parties, the New Patriotic Party (NPP) and the NDC. In addition, both the NDC and NPP are characterized by a high degree of *internal* elite factionalism and strong lower-level groups who render ruling elites vulnerable through various distributional demands (Whitfield 2018). In this environment, winning and maintaining political power is an expensive endeavour and party financing is typically done through kickbacks on state contracts and awarding state contracts to party members (Bob-Milliar 2012).

How have these political settlement dynamics shaped the capacity of the Ghanaian bureaucracy to deliver on its mandated functions? Evidence from the World Governance Indicators suggests that, within the context of sub-Saharan Africa, Ghana has long been an above-average performer across most dimensions of governance, ranging from the quality of regulatory institutions to overall government effectiveness (see Figures 3.1 to 3.5). However, this comparative picture masks significant unevenness between different dimensions of Ghana's state bureaucracy. Between 2007 and 2017, Ghana's average score on overall government effectiveness was just 51 per cent. During this period, marginal improvements were recorded in indicators relating to the rule of law, and voice and accountability, whilst those on overall government effectiveness, regulatory quality, and control of corruption deteriorated. Across all indicators, Ghana now lags behind Rwanda but still performs better than the other case-study countries for this project (Figures 3.6 to 3.8).

Observers have increasingly attributed the difficulties Ghana has faced in achieving improvements across all dimensions of governance to the political settlement dynamics described above. First, the dispersed nature of power means that ruling elites are perennially vulnerable to being removed from office. Consequently, there are 'strong incentives for ruling elites across both parties to focus on short-term objectives of political survival' (Whitfield et al. 2015: 157). Thus, and irrespective of which of the two dominant parties is in power, there is often 'a premium on visible, quick-fix actions', as opposed to investing in the long-term task of building bureaucratic capability (Killick 2008: 29). Here, short-term political survival strategies involve several actions that undermine the capacity of the state

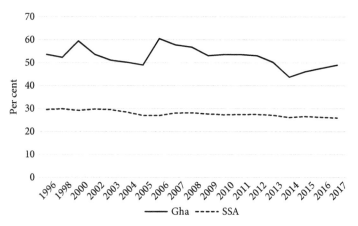

Figure 3.1 Government effectiveness in Ghana, 1996–2017
Source: World Governance Indicators.

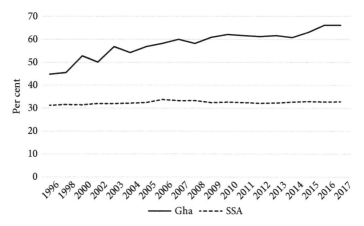

Figure 3.2 Voice and accountability in Ghana, 1996–2017
Source: World Governance Indicators.

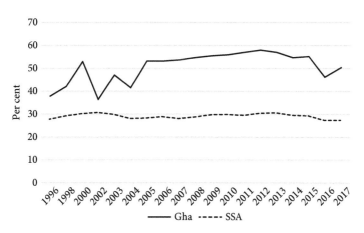

Figure 3.3 Regulatory quality in Ghana, 1996–2017
Source: World Governance Indicators.

bureaucracy, including politically motivated changes in senior bureaucrats during electoral turnovers. As Yaw Ansu observes:

> State capacity in Ghana is weak. The main reason for this is not the lack of competent Ghanaians or poor remuneration. In large part, it is due to a partisan political environment that produces a large turnover of senior staff and technocrats whenever governments change, as they do in Ghana. This undermines professionalism, continuity, long-term planning orientation, learning and innovation in the public service.
>
> (Ansu 2013: 512)

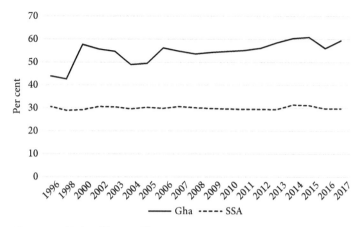

Figure 3.4 Rule of law in Ghana, 1996–2017

Source: World Governance Indicators.

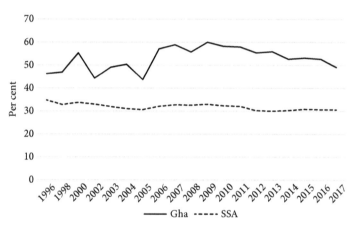

Figure 3.5 Control of corruption in Ghana, 1996–2017

Source: World Governance Indicators.

As a result of excessive partisanship, each ruling party tends to govern mainly on the basis of its election campaign promises, rather than on the basis of a broad national development agenda. The result has been 'a perpetual discontinuity in plans, policy direction, and projects following party turnovers in government' (Gyimah-Boadi and Prempeh 2012: 102, see also Mills 2018). Thus, as Kaye-Essien (2020: 1) has recently put it, 'any time a new government comes to power, programs set by predecessors are abandoned and replaced with new ones, sometimes without regard for the wider national implications'. Opportunities for party

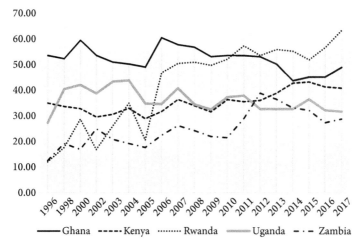

Figure 3.6 Government effectiveness in our five countries, 1996–2017

Source: World Governance Indicators.

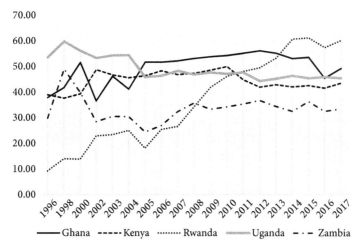

Figure 3.7 Regulatory quality in our five countries, 1996–2017
Source: World Governance Indicators.

financing have also given rise to a 'tradition of Ghanaian presidents asserting control over strategic state agencies' (Gyimah-Boadi and Prempeh 2012: 100) and undermining the operational autonomy of bureaucrats in the performance of their functions.

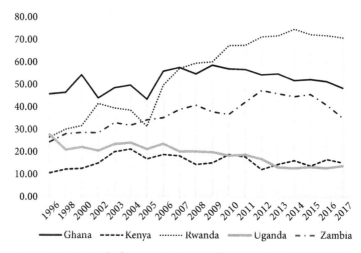

Figure 3.8 Control of corruption in our five countries, 1996–2017
Source: World Governance Indicators.

Pockets of effective organizations in Ghana

This section moves beyond aggregate public-sector performance trends to examine the role of specific public-sector organizations in Ghana's development processes. At the beginning of the comparative research project that this study forms part of, we conducted a mini-survey with twenty-four experts in Ghana[2] in order to identify the most effective government ministries, departments, and agencies for further in-depth research. In a reflection of the generally weak state of bureaucratic capacity in Ghana, nearly half of the survey respondents reported that *only a few* government ministries are able to deliver their mandated functions effectively, whilst the majority generally fail to do so (Figure 3.9).

When respondents were further asked to specify the ministries that they considered to be more effective in the Ghanaian context, the MoF topped the list (Figure 3.10). The BoG emerged as the most effective regulatory authority (Figure 3.11), while the GRA topped the list of government agencies perceived to be relatively effective in the performance of its core function. All of these three organizations, or at least some specific units within them, have long been identified as high-performing public organizations in previous studies (see Joshi and Ayee 2009, McDonnell 2017, Owusu 2006a, 2006b,), and we were also able to identify independent sources of objective performance data to support this view. We therefore selected these organizations for further in-depth investigation.

---

[2] These were drawn from academia, the public sector, civil society, donors, and an independent consultant.

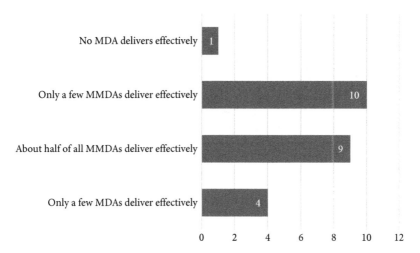

Figure 3.9 Expert survey on public-sector performance in Ghana
Source: Author's survey results, January 2018.

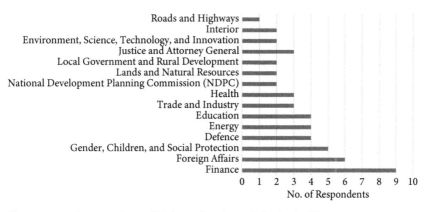

Figure 3.10 Expert ratings of high-performing ministries in Ghana
Source: Author's survey results, January 2018.

In terms of the existing literature on PoEs in Ghana, Owusu (2006a, 2006b) found that higher-performing organizations were observed to be paying higher salaries and using merit-based recruitment strategies, while their poor-performing counterparts were more likely to hire employees based on their personal connections and pay them less. Following Grindle (1997), McDonnell goes beyond a focus on salaries to emphasize the significance of 'organizational culture' in shaping higher levels of performance in Ghana's public service, including within the MoF and BoG. Whitfield et al.'s (2015) in-depth account of the state-run Cocoa Board (Cocobod) applies a political settlements perspective to explain why and how Cocobod emerged and remained a PoE for a prolonged period. Following

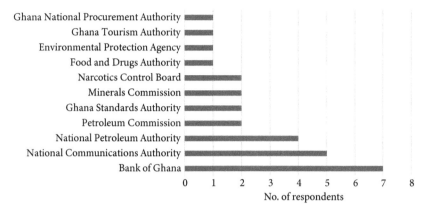

Figure 3.11 Expert ratings of high-performing regulatory agencies in Ghana
Source: Author's survey results, January 2018.

reforms that started in the 1980s, Cocobod is widely noted to have consistently 'performed impressively' (Williams 2009: 3), partly because political elites consider the 800,000 plus cocoa-farm households in Ghana as an important voting bloc to win over (Whitfield et al. 2015). In this research, we follow a similar political settlements approach, whilst also taking due account of policy domain and organizational-level factors in explaining the varied performance of our case-study organizations over time.

The political economy of PoEs within Ghana's economic technocracy

This section summarizes how each of the three case-study organizations have performed, relative to their mandates and related performance indicators, since the 1970s (for the full case-study papers, see Abdulai 2022a, 2022b, Abdulai and Mohan 2019,). Each section draws on secondary and grey literature, quantitative performance indicators, and qualitative data generated through a total of sixty-four in-depth key informant interviews with those directly acquainted with the workings of our case-study organizations.

Ministry of Finance

The main mission of Ghana's MoF is to ensure macroeconomic stability and promote sustainable economic growth through formulating and implementing sound macroeconomic policies; preparing and implementing the annual budget; reducing and restructuring domestic debt and ensuring the sustainability of public

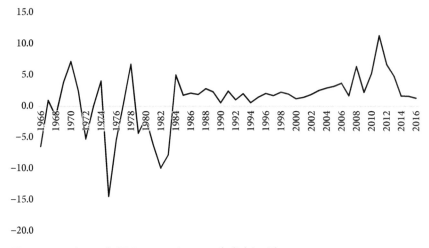

Figure 3.12 Annual GDP per capita growth (%) in Ghana, 1966–2016
Source: World Development Indicators.

debt; and improving public expenditure management. Three broad trends can be discerned in the MoF's performance of these core functions in Ghana's post-colonial history (see Figures 3.12 to 3.14). The first is the weak and declining performance from the 1960s to the early 1980s. Second, the 1980s and the first half of the 2000s witnessed an almost across-the-board improvement in performance (Figure 3.14). Third, the MoF is relatively inefficient in the tasks of public expenditure management and budget controls, with relatively high budget deficits in election years (Figure 3.14).[3]

The weak and declining performance of the MoF in the early post-colonial period was principally the result of the power initially concentrated around the Nkrumah presidency becoming dispersed and the strategies adopted by various ruling coalitions thereafter to manage their vulnerability in the face of strong excluded elite factions. Having initially supported the MoF to deliver on its mandate, Nkrumah and subsequent rulers undermined attempts at development planning, as budgets and technocratic advice were routinely ignored (Killick 2010). Nkrumah took over responsibility for preparing the national budget himself, sacking Ghana's first finance minister and appointing a series of more amenable finance ministers (Killick 2010: 167). Nkrumah's chief economic adviser, the eminent development economist Arthur Lewis, advised against these practices and ultimately resigned over concerns about Nkrumah's politically expedient spending (Tignor 2006: 192). In the last three years of Nkrumah's rule, annual per

---

[3] Relative to the immediate preceding year, budget deficits were especially high in the 1992, 1996, 2000, 2008, and 2012 election years (see Figure 3.14).

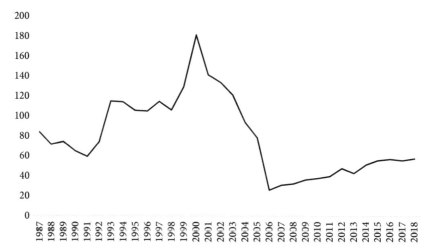

Figure 3.13 Debt-to-GDP ratio in Ghana, 1987–2018
Source: Budget Unit, Ministry of Finance, Accra.

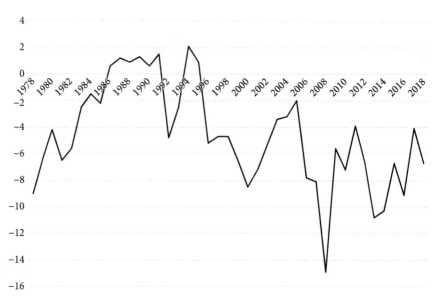

Figure 3.14 Budget deficits in Ghana (% of GDP), 1978–2018
Source: Budget Unit, Ministry of Finance, Accra.

capita growth rates were consistently negative, reaching minus 6.4 per cent in 1966 (Figure 3.12):

> None of the seven short-lived military and civilian regimes that governed in the next decade-and-a-half was able to turn the economy around, as macroeconomic

reforms continued to be undermined by political imperatives. Bureaucratic autonomy was curtailed and macro-economic reforms informed by technocratic advice ignored by politicians beholden to 'public opinion and special interests'.

(Hutchful 1997: 7)

The coups mounted by Flight Lieutenant Jerry Rawlings in 1979, and more decisively in 1981, enabled a consolidation of power that would eventually see the MoF succeed in reversing the decades-long experience of economic instability. The severity of the twin economic and political crises of the 1970s created a window of opportunity for changing the political settlement and the emergence of a new and cohesive group of ruling elites led by Rawlings under the PNDC (Whitfield 2018). With excluded elite factions weakened by a legitimacy crisis and wider social groups 'fragmented and dispersed' (Chazan 1991: 30), the PNDC had the opportunity to undertake difficult macroeconomic reforms with the longer-term national interest in mind. Importantly, Ghana's parlous economic condition meant that it had little choice but to accept the implementation of the donor-led structural adjustment reforms during this period, reforms that included high levels of support for economic governance institutions, most notably the MoF.

The design and implementation of macroeconomic policies was left in the hands of a technocratically competent set of political appointees who enjoyed bureaucratic autonomy and received the protection of the head of state (Chazan 1991). The key players were Kwesi Botchwey, then minister of finance and economic planning (MoFEP),[4] his deputy, Amissaph-Arthur, and Joseph Abbey, who held various influential positions during this period (Hutchful 1997: 7). Whitfield (2011: 15) refers to these three technocratic managers as technopols, to capture the sense in which they combined technical expertise with political influence. As Hutchful (1997) comments, 'it was rare for the PNDC to contradict the Ministry of Finance and Economic Planning position on policy' (pp. 9–10), a significant departure from previous practice.

With the return to multi-party electoral competition in the early 1990s, most of the MoFEP's performance indicators either stagnated (e.g. economic growth) or worsened, especially with regards to debt management and fiscal balance (Figures 3.13 and 3.14). The MoF's capacity to ensure fiscal discipline was undermined by the growing vulnerability of the ruling coalition, both to powerful excluded political factions that accompanied the return to competitive elections and to growing factionalism within the ruling coalition (Abdulai and Mohan 2019). Amidst a row over who controlled the state-owned oil company, whose borrowing imbalanced the government's money supply, relations between Botchwey and Rawlings deteriorated (Green 1995: 583). In August 1995, Botchwey resigned

---

[4] MoFEP was renamed Ministry of Finance (MoF) following the regime change that accompanied the 2016 elections.

in protest against his inability to restrain the excessive budgetary demands of the public sector (Hutchful 2002, Jeong 1998,), including 'a plan for a spending splurge to win the 1996 elections' (Africa Confidential 2016). A purge of the MoF then swept away much of the technical team that had underpinned this period of macroeconomic stability (Hutchful 1997: 39).

The widely dispersed nature of power has meant that 'from day one, politicians here are trying to figure out how they win the next election, not how to get growth going—that is a second order thing'.[5] With increased electoral competition, political business cycles became a feature of the Ghanaian economy (Mosely and Chiripanhura 2016), periodically undermining the MoF's performance. The only notable exception was in 2004, when a combination of HIPC loan conditionalities, effective leadership at the MoF, and fairly benign economic conditions contributed to fiscal discipline and macroeconomic stability despite a tightly fought election that year (see Figures 3.12 to 3.14). Under Osafo Maafo, whose achievements were recognized internationally,[6] even the Office of Government Machinery, of which the presidency is part, rarely spent more than its budgeted sum, underscoring the relative fiscal discipline during this period (Abdulai and Mohan 2019).

However, immediately after the December 2004 elections, Osafo Marfo was reshuffled out of the MoF—a decision that observers noted resulted in 'weakening the administrative capacity of the Kufuor government to deliver' (Ayee 2008: 32). Commentators expressed shock that President Kufuor had replaced someone who, 'for the first time ... was able to resolve the cyclical problem of loose fiscal and monetary policies, characteristic of election years'.[7] Some accounts suggest that Osafo Marfo was removed due to his refusal to pursue lax fiscal policies ahead of the 2004 elections in ways that denied the ruling NPP campaign funds.[8] Unsurprisingly, the government's budget deficit, which stood at a moderate 3.2 per cent in 2004 (an election year) had more than quadrupled to reach 14.9 per cent by the 2008 election year (see Figure 3.13).

Despite reforms aimed at enhancing budget credibility, large in-year budget deviations have continued to occur, leading to higher budget deficits around election years. By the close of 2016, an unplanned $1.6 billion budget gap emerged, due to 'significant public spending commitments that bypassed public financial management systems'.[9] This led to an increase in the fiscal deficit to 9.1 per cent

---

[5] Donor official, 18 November 2017.

[6] He was also named joint Finance Minister of the Year in November 2001 by the World Economic Forum in Davos.

[7] Public Agenda, 17 January 2005, 'Asaga shocked by Osafo Maafo's removal'. Available at: https://www.ghanaweb.com/GhanaHomePage/NewsArchive/Asaga-Shocked-By-OsafoMaafo-s-Removal-73678 (accessed 3 June 2019).

[8] Public Agenda, 17 January 2005, 'Asaga shocked by Osafo Maafo's removal'.

[9] http://www.imf.org/en/News/Articles/2017/02/10/pr1743-IMF-Staff-Concludes-Visit-to-Ghana.

of GDP.[10] Overall, this case study shows that the capacity of MoF bureaucrats to deliver on their mandate has remained limited, not because of insufficient technocratic expertise within the ministry, but because of politicians' limited commitment to heeding technocratic advice in the context of mounting electoral pressures.

Bank of Ghana

Formed at independence in 1957, the core mandate of Ghana's central bank centres on the maintenance of price and financial-sector stability (BoG 2018). The BoG has long been considered one of Ghana's topmost public-sector organizations (Jones 2020, McDonnell 2017, Mensah et al. 2018, Owusu 2006a, 2006b), although its performance has varied substantially over time. In the period prior to the reforms of the 1980s, the BoG performed poorly in maintaining both price and financial stability. In particular, the period from the mid-1970s to the early 1980s was characterized by high and growing levels of inflation, which peaked at 123 per cent in 1983 (Figure 3.15). Meanwhile, the financial system was characterized by large non-performing bank loans, excessive intermediation costs, and inefficient credit allocation (World Bank 1997: 9–10, Figure 3.16).

From the mid-1980s, however, indicators for both price and financial-sector stability began to improve steadily, until major spikes in inflation were recorded in 1995 and 1996. Following the adoption of an inflation-targeting regime in the early

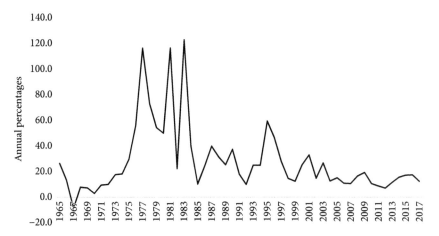

Figure 3.15 Inflation trends in Ghana, 1965–2017
Source: Word Development Indicators.

[10] my joy online, https://www.myjoyonline.com/business/2017/February-12th/ghanas-fiscal-deficit-deteriorated-to-an-estimated-9-of-gdp-imf.php.

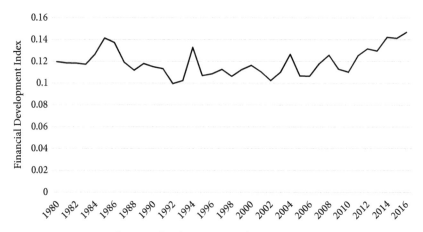

Figure 3.16 Financial-sector development in Ghana, 1980–2016
Source: https://www.imf.org/external/datamapper/datasets.

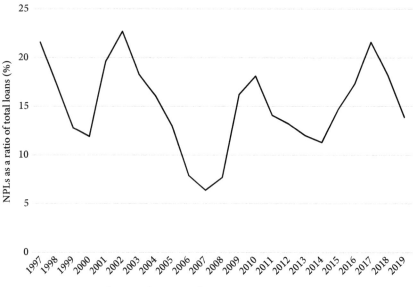

Figure 3.17 Non-performing loans in Ghana, 1997–2019
Source: Bank of Ghana data.

2000s, further improvements in price stability were recorded from 2004 onwards.
As the BoG was granted greater formal autonomy in 2002, financial-sector stability
also witnessed further improvements, especially with regards to the proportion of
non-performing loans (Figures 3.16 and 3.17). The BoG entered its third performance period from around 2008 until 2019, during which inflation has remained

more stable while financial stability deteriorated somewhat, especially between 2011 and 2017.

In the period from independence up to 1983, the BoG's poor performance in ensuring price stability was caused largely by growing political interference in its operations and the near complete erosion of the bank's operational autonomy. In 1963, the Nkrumah-led ruling coalition passed a new BoG Act, which vested the power to determine both interest and exchange rates in the government through the minister of finance. The new law empowered President Nkrumah himself to determine how much the government could borrow from the central bank in any given year, with the governor now requiring the prior approval of the finance minister in deciding monetary policies (Abdulai 2022a).

As power became more widely dispersed during the frequent military coup d'états of the 1970s, inflation rates of above 100 per cent were recorded in 1977, 1981, and 1983. This deterioration was enabled by the continuous erosion of the central bank's autonomy, as BoG governors 'constantly had to look over their shoulders (sometimes literally at the barrel of a gun) with concern with regard to the reaction of political authorities' (Bawumia 2015: 330). These factors, together with the BoG's weak regulatory capacity, also undermined its capacity to maintain financial-sector stability, given its reliance on government-owned banks to provide finance for government investments.

From 1984, the BoG's performance benefitted from the PNDC's political commitment to monetary and fiscal discipline and international support. The central bank kept tight reins on the supply of money, both by refusing to print new money and by increasing the rate of interest on commercial lending. However, with the political pressures that accompanied the return to multi-party democracy in 1992, the 1990s witnessed more erratic and worsening trends in price stability, especially during the 1996 elections. Here, election-driven expenditures led to high fiscal deficits, and governments' recourse to the BoG's financing of the deficits led to an increase in broad money supply, which in turn contributed to undermining price stability around election years (Abdulai 2022a).

In the early 2000s, and following significant donor pressure, attempts were made to address the recurring problem of fiscal dominance through the passage of a new BoG Act in 2002. This Act strengthened BoG's operational autonomy by requiring it to operate 'independent of instructions from the Government or any other authority'. Under the law, government's borrowing from the central bank and other banking institutions was capped at 10 per cent of the total revenue for the fiscal year in which the advances were made. Despite these rules, the BoG's financing of the budget deficits continued to follow a clear political business cycle, with borrowing levels often far exceeding the 10 per cent cap during election years. This was especially the case in 2008, when the BoG's financing of the fiscal deficit amounted to 38.7 per cent of the previous year's tax revenue, compared to 0 per cent financing in the three previous consecutive years (Abdulai 2022a).

The BoG entered its third performance period from around 2007 until 2019, during which inflation remained fairly stable while financial stability deteriorated, due primarily to growing levels of non-performing loans (NPLs). The deterioration in financial stability resulted from a combination of the impact of the global financial crisis, which contributed to a deterioration in the quality of banks' assets (IMF 2011), and growing deficiencies in banking supervision, driven in large part by compromises between political elites and central bank leaders. BoG officials felt incapacitated to deal with the emerging threats in the banking sector, due to the government's role in creating the conditions that undermined financial stability and the dominant role of political elites in determining bank closures. As the government's fiscal situation deteriorated, state-owned and politically connected banks were used to finance extra budgetary expenditures and the poor performance of these banks created contingent liabilities for the government. High and growing fiscal deficits compounded the NPL situation, as government arrears undermined the capacity of contractors to service their obligations to banks, resulting in substantial impairment of banks' asset quality (Akosah et al. 2018, IMF 2011).

Moreover, the stability of the financial sector was undermined by a nationwide power crisis that began in 2012 and persisted until the end of 2015. Amidst the crisis, government was unable to pay for the supply of gas from Nigeria, and a number of banks stepped in to fund the importation of crude oil, gas, and the procurement of power plants on behalf of the government. Ruling NDC political elites were apparently unwilling to close down struggling banks and the BoG instead resorted to providing them with liquidity support. Leading members of the BoG's banking supervision department indicated that their work ended with the submission of reports, and that any decision to act on them was determined by the minister of finance and the president (Abdulai 2022a). It was not until major changes in the BoG's leadership, which accompanied the transfer of political power to the NPP in January 2017, that decisive measures were taken to restore financial stability, including by revoking the licences of some nine banks deemed to be insolvent.

Ghana Revenue Authority

The GRA started operations in 2010, following the amalgamation of the then three existing revenue agencies under the leadership of one commissioner general. Prior to this, Ghana had experimented with the semi-autonomous revenue authorities model in the 1980s, with a significant degree of success. In the period from 1970 to 1983, the overall performance of revenue agencies was poor, as tax revenues took a downward trend, both in absolute terms and in relation to GDP (Figure 3.18). Following reforms in both tax policy and administration, significant and sustained improvements were recorded during 1984–1991. With a loss of the

Figure 3.18 Tax revenue-to-GDP ratio in Ghana, 1973–2018
Source: Revenue Statistics in Africa 2018 oe.cd/revenue-statistics-in-africa

reformist zeal from the mid-1990s onwards, however, overall performance became highly erratic, as reflected in the tax-to-GDP ratio and in Ghana's tax effort scores (Figure 3.19). However, and as reflected in data on tax-to-GDP ratios, the period from 2001 to 2004 witnessed unprecedented levels of improvements in revenue mobilization, and remains the period of Ghana's most impressive performance in domestic revenue mobilization to date. Performance began to decline from 2005, and has stagnated somewhat since the formation of the GRA in 2010.

In the period 1970–1983, an increasingly overvalued exchange rate led to reduced prices for exporters and sharply declining exports, depriving governments not only of large foreign exchange earnings, but also revenue in the form of export duty as well as income and sales taxes (Kusi 1991: 184). Yet, various ruling coalitions were reluctant to adjust the exchange rate to realistic levels because of what Kusi (1991: 188) refers to as 'the fragile political base of all ... governments' during the period. Direct weaknesses in tax administration also contributed to poor performance during this period (Chand and Moene 1999). Widespread tax evasion and low tax effort meant that government failed to collect more than 5 per cent of taxable GDP in income taxes in 1978, compared with a 15 per cent average in countries at similar levels of development at the time. The decline in

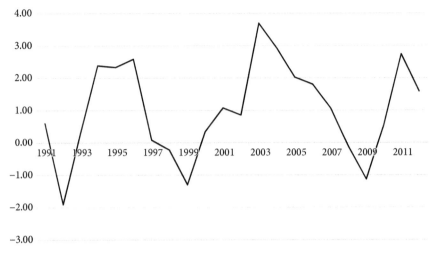

Figure 3.19 Ghana's tax effort, 1991–2012
Source: Yohou and Goujon (2017).

tax revenues was also associated with an increasingly disorganized tax administration system. The central revenue department was grossly understaffed, while the salary of tax officials 'hardly sufficed for a minimal standard of living', which in turn created an environment that encouraged malfeasance among tax officials (IMF 1986: 37).

The period from 1984 to 1991 marked significant improvements in tax revenue mobilization. Unlike previous ruling coalitions, the PNDC 'intentionally used devaluations to raise government revenue during 1983–1986' (Kapur et al. 1991: 27), undertook reforms to broaden the tax base to the informal sector, and improved tax compliance through the establishment of a Citizens Vetting Committee (CVC) that investigated and penalized tax evaders (Asibuo 1991: 258). A number of measures were adopted to help create and sustain a performance-based organizational culture within the revenue agencies. This included the adoption and monitoring of performance targets linked to staff incentives, improved conditions of service, and the dismissal of corrupt and non-performing staff. Some twenty-eight revenue officials were dismissed, while an additional 230 personnel were retired (Dia 1996: 89). The basic salaries of all tax and customs officials were raised to comparable levels in the private and banking sectors and generous annual bonuses were paid to staff who exceeded agreed revenue targets. These measures enabled revenue agencies to attract more qualified professionals, and to boost staff morale (Chand and Moene 1999, Hutchful 1995, Terkper 1994,). The Internal Revenue Service (IRS) and the Customs Exercise and Preventive Services (CEPS) were allowed to meet their own operational expenses by withholding 3.5 per cent and 2.5 per cent of the revenues collected, respectively (Dia 1996). This incentive-based mechanism allowed them to provide more training for staff as well as contributing to supervising and monitoring both tax officials and corporate bodies. These initiatives succeeded largely because of the 'dynamic leadership' of Ato Ahwoi, a technopol in charge of National Revenue Secretariat (NRS) who had the full backing of the head of state and 'the right blend of personal leadership characteristics: charisma, a flair for innovation, ability to motivate, and organizational acumen' (Dia 1996: 90).

Ghana's erratic performance in revenue generation during much of the 1990s can be explained mainly by the power dispersals that accompanied the return to multi-party electoral competition in 1992. Tax policy became increasingly lax: major tax reductions were announced during election years and exemptions for politically connected individuals and businesses became much more widespread, as competitive elections increased the financing requirements for winning presidential and parliamentary elections. An initial attempt to introduce a Value Added Tax failed, due to widespread opposition from organized labour and leading political opponents. Tax administration began to suffer from 'bureaucratic frictions' and 'turf wars' among the various tax agencies and between the MoF and the NRS (Chand and Moene 1999, Dia 1996). Consequently, the NRS was abolished and the system that allowed revenue agencies to retain part of their collections was discontinued at the beginning of 1993.

The improved performance of Ghana's revenue agencies during the early 2000s is explained mainly by substantial donor support to a political leader who had formed a strong relationship with highly capable bureaucrats to (re)build high-performing organizations within the economic technocracy. Donor support took the form of both technical and financial resources, the influence of HIPC conditions and temporary waivers of conditions by the IMF around the 2004 elections. Citizens' unprecedented 'good will' to the new ruling political elites who assumed office in January 2001 translated into minimal resistance to taxes and enabled government to adjust existing taxes and raise new ones without fears of a political backlash. Political commitment to tax administration was signalled by the appointment of Janet Opoku-Akyeampong—a close relative of President Kuffour who had worked with the country's revenue agencies for over thirty years—as commissioner of the IRS. Under her leadership, the IRS implemented several administrative reforms that contributed to improved revenue generation, including the establishment of a Large Taxpayer Unit, and a mandatory tax stamp for all small-scale self-employed businesses was also introduced.

However, by 2005, these reforms had begun to falter, due partly to leadership changes within the IRS and the Ministry of Finance, where internal party struggles led to the replacement of the minister (see above). The IRS commissioner who had championed most of the revenue administration reforms retired in March 2005 and was replaced with a technocrat with no direct working experience with any of the three revenue agencies at the time. Meanwhile, donor pressure for reforms also appeared to ease as Ghana reached the HIPC Completion Point in 2005. The politicization of taxation deepened, with the NDC criticizing the ruling NPP for subjecting Ghanaians to 'excessive taxation' (NDC 2008: 42).

Since its formation a decade ago, the GRA's performance has been modest. Amidst the rising costs of winning elections the GRA's efforts to mobilize domestic revenues are undermined as the two dominant parties both resort to discretionary tax exemptions linked to campaign financing (Abdulai 2022b). Moreover, several state agencies are able to grant tax exemptions, and coordination among these agencies remains weak (Prichard and Bentum 2009: 23). Tax administration remains heavily politicized, with GRA's top management changed as a matter of course during political transitions.

Analysing the political economy of PoEs in Ghana

Five broad performance periods have been identified across Ghana's key agencies of economic governance during the past five decades: a period of poor and deteriorating performance during 1970–1983; a period of improved performance during the 1980s, before a period of decline in the 1990s; a period of mostly improved performance during 2001–2006; and a period of average and often stagnating performance since 2008. This section discusses the three most crucial drivers of these performance trajectories, namely, political settlement dynamics, organizational-level factors, and the role of international organizations.

Political settlement types and dynamics

Ghana's political settlement has changed significantly over time. While power has been widely dispersed during much of the country's post-colonial history, the 1980s saw power concentrated largely around the head of state. These shifting power configurations have played a central role in shaping the performance trajectories of all the three organizations under study. In particular, our overall findings provide support for the hypothesis that PoEs are more likely to emerge and endure in political settlements where power is concentrated than under dispersed power configurations. This is because power concentration allows leaders to pursue state-building projects under longer time horizons and also makes it relatively 'easier for state leaders to insulate particular state agencies from political pressures' (Kelsall and vom Hau 2020: 19).

During much of the 1980s, the PNDC ruling coalition governed in a context where both excluded elites and lower-level factions of the ruling coalition were weakened. In this context, the MoF and BoG enjoyed significant operational autonomy and received the protection of the head of state. This enabled them to implement several difficult but important reforms that succeeded in reversing the decades-long economic decline. The PNDC was also able to broaden the tax base to previously untaxed informal-sector operators and improve tax compliance through the coercive powers of the state.

With the power dispersion that accompanied the return to multi-party democratic competition and subsequent need to use public spending to offset electoral challenges from powerful political opponents, the performance of the BoG and MoF now fluctuated in line with the electoral cycle, and also the level of factionalism within each main political party. The autonomy and capacity of the BoG and GRA in particular have been undermined by the rapid turnover of organizational leaders during political transitions and higher levels of political interference in technical operations.

One period in which difficult political settlement dynamics did little to undermine the effectiveness of the BoG and MoF was during the first term of John Kuffour's presidency (2001–2004)—a period which marked the second episode of high performance amongst all our three case-study organizations. Operating within relatively benign economic conditions, and with strong support from international financial institutions, President Kuffour was able to put in place and protect a highly capable economic governance team that managed to maintain both fiscal and monetary discipline over a period that spanned a competitive election in 2004. However, this technocratic coalition was short lived, with intra-party factional politics leading to the removal of the finance minister in ways that undermined the performance of both the MoF and revenue mobilization agencies.

Although the MoF was again led by a renowned technopol from 2013, with Seth Terkper managing to implement several politically difficult reforms, including the removal of subsidies and a new Public Financial Management Act, this period did not witness significant improvements in macroeconomic stability, partly because of the debilitating energy crisis but also because the minister was removed from office following the NDC's defeat at the December 2016 elections. Party footsoldiers and leading ruling party members had become concerned that the minister's fiscal discipline would undermine their bid to retain power at the 2016 elections, making his position untenable. Political settlement dynamics can, then, explain why the main shifts in organizational performance have taken place in Ghana.

Organizational factors

Organizational-level factors have also shaped the performance trajectories of our case-study organizations, even if factors such as the longevity with which leaders stay in office and operate with autonomy are themselves subject to political settlement dynamics. In a finding that underlines how personalized forms of governance remain pervasive in Ghana, every period of good performance identified here involved leaders who combined technocratic expertise with political loyalty. This earned them the political protection required to adopt often unconventional organizational practices (see also McDonnell 2017: 498) and to push through difficult reforms.

The technopols identified within our case-study organizations were often allowed to stay in office for relatively lengthy periods of time. This was especially the case during the PNDC ruling coalition, when Kwesi Botchwey remained finance minister for a ten-year period, while Dr. G. K. Agama served as governor of the BoG for nine years. In contrast, between independence in 1957 and 1982, finance ministers in Ghana served for an average of less than three years, while BoG governors also had very short tenures in office. Such longevity allowed for continuity, credibility with donors, and a consolidated process of organizational learning. It enabled leaders to build performance-based organizational cultures, including through using their political influence to negotiate greater funding for staff training and improved working conditions, as in the case of NRS discussed above. These findings confirm the observation that PoEs gain organizational autonomy not by isolating themselves from politics, but instead by cultivating 'strong political relations' and engaging in 'political bargaining' with ruling elites (Roll 2014: 213, Leonard 2010).

Finally, although many scholars have highlighted the importance of a good remuneration system for facilitating the emergence and persistence of PoEs (Owusu 2012, Roll 2014), our findings suggest that improved salaries are neither a necessary nor a sufficient condition for building effective public-sector organizations. Although GRA staff enjoy amongst the highest salaries in Ghana's public sector, staff morale is low, due in large part to a promotions system that remains opaque. In contrast, the MoF which has been able to build and maintain a more positive organizational culture that drives up staff performance in a context where salaries are relatively low. Here, most staff remain motivated, due to the prestige associated with working with the ministry and some indirect benefits like training and international networking opportunities. Together, these experiences suggest that creating capable public organizations may have little to do with higher remunerations, and 'more to do with establishing social and moral reward systems that make it possible for government agencies to tap the creativity, sense of duty, and public-spiritedness of their workers' (Dilulio 1994: 315, see also Grindle 1997, McDonnell 2017).

Transnational factors

Although to varying degrees, all the three case-study organizations emerged as PoEs in part because of the disproportionate support they receive from donors, both in terms of funding and technical assistance. This was especially so during the

1980s and the period of HIPC debt relief during the first half of the 2000s. Since the 1980s, most major reforms that facilitated the effectiveness of the MoF and BoG in performing their mandated functions have been driven by donor conditions. Conditions associated with the HIPC completion point and the IMF ESAF programme played crucial roles in the passage of a new Banking Act that enhanced the operational autonomy of the BoG in 2002. The recent bank closures that enhanced the stability of the financial sector were also clearly triggered by the IMF's loan condition that required the BoG to undertake asset quality reviews of all banks using a more stringent approach to loan classifications than had been done in the past.

However, our findings also reveal that it is neither the quantum of aid nor the strength of aid conditionality per se that matters in shaping the impact of external development assistance, but instead the extent to which the interests and ideas of domestic and transnational elites are aligned. Not surprisingly, while domestic revenue mobilization efforts have sometimes far 'exceeded that required by conditionality' (World Bank 1992: 20–1), apparently because of the importance of tax revenue for the maintenance of ruling coalitions, donors have largely failed to help MoF to avoid political budget cycles. In a highly competitive context, donor reforms continue to be trumped by the imperative of winning elections.

It is also precisely for these reasons that donor conditionalities have been unable to prevent the central bank's financing of budget deficits, which remains a major source of inflationary pressures during election years. As discussed elsewhere (Abdulai 2022a), a bipartisan parliamentary committee successfully resisted IMF conditions that aimed at strengthening the autonomy of the central bank through eliminating central bank financing of budget deficits. MPs felt that this measure could tie the hands of governments during presidential elections and national crisis, leading the IMF to concede that broad-based elite support for a zero central bank financing arrangement was 'not politically feasible at this juncture' (IMF 2018: 16). Together, these analyses provide support for recent observations that donor requirements can encourage African leaders to create and sustain PoEs only when donor incentives are congruent with domestic political calculations (Johnson 2015: 784).

Conclusions and implications

This chapter set out to explore the conditions under which relatively effective public-sector agencies may emerge and endure in Ghana, with a particular emphasis on the potential roles of political settlement dynamics and organizational-level factors. The analysis focused on the experiences of the MoF, the BoG, and the GRA—three public-sector organizations that have long been acknowledged to have maintained relatively good levels of performance for long enough to be classified as PoEs (Roll 2014), but which have also experienced significant dips in performance over time.

The findings show that PoEs can emerge under different political settlement types and dynamics, from the concentrated political settlements of Ghana during the 1980s to its dispersed counterpart in the 2000s. However, improvements in performance were sustained for longer in the 1980s than the 2000s, due to the concentrated nature of power and the relatively cohesive nature of the ruling elites during that period. In line with others, our findings show that PoEs are more difficult to create under dispersed power configurations (Whitfield et al. 2015), and that, even when high performance is established, this can be easily undermined by factional politics both within and across ruling coalitions.

Paradoxically, while PoEs are more difficult to nurture in countries characterized by dispersed power configurations, it is in such contexts that a strategy of building PoEs represents a more realistic way of improving the performance of public-sector organizations (see Levy 2014). This is because as ruling elites face a credible threat of losing power, both to excluded elite factions and to other powerful elites within the ruling coalition, the imperative of short-term political survival will always take precedence over the long-term task of building bureaucratic capability across the board. In such contexts, reformers are likely to make a better impact if attention is targeted on building PoEs within the state bureaucracy, rather than trying to engage in wholesale reforms of the public sector. Together with other research on high-performing state agencies in Ghana (McDonnell 2017), actionable measures here could include efforts to identify and support organizational leaders to develop the mix of both technocratic skills and effective political management skills required to strike a good balance between the pursuit of organizational objectives and the political survival of ruling elites.

Contrary to recent research that identifies improved salaries as a prerequisite for improved organizational performance in Ghana (Owusu 2012: 148), our findings suggest that higher salaries are neither a necessary nor a sufficient condition for building effective public-sector organizations. Rather, more effort should be placed on organizational leaders using innovative measures to develop a widely held sense of purpose within their organizations, or what Grindle (1997) terms 'organizational mystique', which can help foster staff commitment to organizational and political goals.

References

Abdulai, A.-G. (2011). 'The Political Context of Human Rights Promotion in Ghana'. Working Paper No. 4, Human Rights, Power and Civic Action in Developing Societies research project. Oslo: The Norwegian Centre for Human Rights, University of Oslo, Norway.

Abdulai, A.-G. (2022a). 'Beyond "Institutions Matter"? A Political Settlement Analysis of Central Bank Performance in Ghana'. ESID Working Paper, forthcoming.

Abdulai, A.-G. (2022b). 'The Political Economy of Taxation in Ghana: The Centrality of Political Settlement Dynamics'. ESID Working Paper, forthcoming.

Abdulai, A.-G. and Mohan, G. (2019). 'The Politics of Bureaucratic "Pockets of Effectiveness": Insights from Ghana's Ministry of Finance'. ESID Working Paper No. 119, Manchester: Effective States and Inclusive Development Research Centre, University of Manchester.

Africa Confidential (2016). 'It's the Contract Election', *African Confidential*, 57(5): 4 March. Available online at: https://www.africa-confidential.com/article/id/11540/ (accessed 29 June 2021).

Akosah, N., Loloh, F., Lawson, N., and Kumah, C. (2018). 'Measuring Financial Stability in Ghana: A New Index-based Approach'. MPRA Paper No. 86634, Munich.

Ansu, Y. (2013). 'Industrial Policy and Economic Transformation in Africa: Strategies for Development and a Research Agenda'. In J. E. Stiglitz, J. L. Yifu, and E. Patel (eds), *The Industrial Policy Revolution II: African in the Twenty-first Century*. Basingstoke: Palgrave Macmillan. 492–528.

Appiah, D. and Abdulai, A.-G. (2017). 'Competitive Clientelism and the Politics of Core Public Sector Reform in Ghana'. ESID Working Paper No. 82. Manchester: Effective States and Inclusive Development Research Centre, University of Manchester.

Asibuo, S. K. (1991). 'The Revolutionary Administration of Justice and Public Accountability in Ghana', *Philippine Journal of Public Administration*, 35(3): 253–63.

Austin, D. (1964). *Politics in Ghana, 1946–1960*. London: Oxford University Press.

Ayee, J. (2013). 'Public Administrators under Democratic Governance in Ghana', *International Journal of Public Administration*, 36(6): 440–52.

Ayee, J. R. A. (2008). 'Some Thoughts on Ministerial Reshuffles in Ghana'. Paper delivered at the Ghana Academy of Arts and Sciences. British Council, Accra, 8 May.

Bawumia, M. (2015). 'The Role of the Central Bank in Reforming the Financial Sector: The Case of Ghana'. In K. Appiah-Adu and M. Bawumia (eds), *Key Determinants of National Development: Historical Perspectives and Implications for Development*. Aldershot: Gower Publishing. 303–4.

Berry, S. (2008). 'Ancestral Property: Land, Politics and "the Deeds of the Ancestors" in Ghana and Côte d'Ivoire'. In J. M. Ubink and K. S. Amanor (eds), *Contesting Land and Custom in Ghana: State, Chief and the Citizen*. Leiden: Leiden University Press. 27–53.

Bob-Milliar, G. (2012). 'Party Factions and Power Blocs in Ghana: A Case Study of Power Politics in the National Democratic Congress', *Journal of Modern African Studies*, 50(4): 573–601.

BoG (2018). *Banking Sector Report, July 2018*. Accra: Bank of Ghana.

Callaghy, T. (1990). 'Lost between State and Market: The Politics of Economic Adjustment in Ghana, Zambia, and Nigeria'. In J. Nelson (ed.), *Economic Crisis and Policy Choice: The Politics of Adjustment in the Third World*. Princeton, NJ: Princeton University Press. 257–319.

Chand, S. K. and Moene, K. O. (1999). 'Controlling Fiscal Corruption', *World Development*, 27(7): 1129–40.

Chazan, N. (1982). 'Ethnicity and Politics in Ghana', *Political Science Quarterly*, 97(3): 461–85.

Chazan, N. (1991). 'The Political Transformation of Ghana under the PNDC'. In D. Rothchild (ed.), *Ghana: The Political Economy of Recovery*. Boulder and London: Lynne Rienner Publishers. 21–47.

Dia, M. (1996). 'Africa's Management in the 1990s and Beyond: Reconciling Indige-nous and Transplanted Institutions'. Washington, DC: World Bank.

Dilulio, J. D. (1994). 'Principal Agents: The Cultural Bases of Behavior in Federal Government Bureaucracy', *Journal of Public Administration Research and Theory* 4: 277–318.

Green, D. (1995). 'Ghana's "Adjusted" Democracy', *Review of African Political Econ-omy*, 22(66): 577–85.

Grindle, M. S. (1997). 'Divergent Cultures? When Public Organisations Perform Well in Developing Countries', *World Development*, 25(4): 481–95.

Gyimah-Boadi, E. and Prempeh, H. K. (2012). 'Oil, Politics, and Ghana's Democracy', *Journal of Democracy*, 23(3): 94–107.

Hutchful, E. (1995). 'Why Regimes Adjust: The World Bank Ponders its "Star Pupil"', *Canadian Journal of African Studies*, 29(2): 303–17.

Hutchful, E. (1997). 'The Institutional and Political Framework of Macro-economic Management in Ghana'. UNRISD Discussion Paper 82. Geneva: UNRISD.

Hutchful, E. (2002). *Ghana's Adjustment Experience: The Paradox of Reform*. Melton, United Kingdom: James Currey.

IMANI Center for Policy and Education (2018). 'Assessing Ghana's Performance on Governance Using the Mo Ibrahim Index of African Governance (IIAG)'. Accra: IMANI.

IMF (1986). 'Ghana: Promoting Economic Growth Tax Reform'. IMF Staff Working Paper. Washington, DC: IMF.

IMF (2011). 'Ghana: Financial System Stability Assessment Update'. Washington, DC: IMF.

IMF (2018). 'Ghana Fifth and Sixth Reviews under the Extended Credit Facility, Request for Waivers for Nonobservance of Performance Criteria, and Request for Modification of Performance Criteria'. IMF Country Report No. 18/113. Washing-ton, DC: IMF.

Jeong, H.-W. (1998). 'Economic Reform and Democratic Transition in Ghana', *World Affairs*, 160(4): 218–30.

Johnson, M. C. (2015). 'Donor Requirements and Pockets of Effectiveness in Senegal's Bureaucracy', *Development Policy Review*, 33(6): 783–804.

Jones, E. (2020). *The Political Economy of Bank Regulation in Developing Countries: Risk and Reputation*. Oxford: Oxford University Press.

Joshi, A. and Ayee, J. (2009). 'Autonomy or Organization? Reforms in the Ghanaian Internal Revenue Service', *Public Administration and Development*, 29: 289–302.

Kapur, I., Hadjimichael, M. T., Hilbers, P., Schiff, J., and Szymczak, P. (1991). 'Ghana: Adjustment and Growth, 1983–1991'. Washington, DC: IMF.

Kaye-Essien, C. W. (2020). 'The Politics of Discontinuity and its Medium-term Policy Outcomes: Evidence from Ghana', *International Journal of Public Administration*, 43(7): 599–610.

Kelsall, T. and vom Hau, M. (2020). 'Beyond Institutions: Political Settlements Analysis and Development'. Working Paper 2020/56. Barcelona: Institut Barcelona d'Estudis Internacionals.

Killick, T. (2008). 'What Drives Change in Ghana? A Political-economy View of Eco-nomic Prospects'. In E. Aryeetey and R. Kanbur (eds), *Economy of Ghana: Analytical Perspectives on Stability, Growth and Poverty*. Oxford: James Currey. 20–34.

Killick, T. (2010). *Development Economics in Action: A Study of Economic Policies in Ghana*. Second edition. London: Routledge.

Kusi, N. K. (1991). 'Ghana: Can the Adjustment Reforms Be Sustained?' *Africa Development*, 16(3/4): 181–206.

Leonard, D. K. (2010). '"Pockets" of Effective Agencies in Weak Governance States: Where Are They Likely and Why Does It Matter?' *Public Administration and Development*, 30: 91–101.

Levy, B. (2014). *Working with the Grain: Integrating Governance and Growth in Development Strategies.* New York: Oxford University Press.

McDonnell, E. M. (2017). 'Patchwork Leviathan: How Pockets of Bureaucratic Governance Flourish within Institutionally Diverse Developing States', *American Sociological Review*, 82(3): 476–510.

Mensah, S., BeInye, F., Anane-Antwi, A., Seddoh, D., and Aboagye, A. (2018). 'A Comprehensive Financial Sector Regulatory Framework Study for Ghana'. Final Report, August. London: Department for International Development/SEM International Associates Limited.

Mills, C. A. (2018). *Politics, policy, and implementation: The 'Ghanaian Paradox': Africa in Focus.* Washington, DC: Brookings Institutions.

Mosley, P. and Chiripanhura, B. (2016). 'The African Political Business Cycle: Varieties of Experience', *Journal of Development Studies*, 52(27): 917–32.

NDC (2008). *Manifesto for a Better Ghana 2008.* Accra: National Democratic Congress.

Ohemeng, F. L. K. and Ayee, J. R. A. (2016). 'The "New Approach" to Public Sector Reforms in Ghana: A Case of Politics as Usual or a Genuine Attempt at Reform?', *Development Policy Review*, 34(2): 277–300.

Owusu, F. (2006a). 'Differences in the Performance of Public Organisations in Ghana: Implications for Public-sector Reform Policy', *Development Policy Review*, 24(6): 693–705.

Owusu, F. (2006b). 'On Public Organizations in Ghana: What Differentiates Good Performers from Poor Performers?' *African Development Review*, 18(3): 471–85.

Owusu, F. Y. (2012). 'Organizational Culture and Public Sector Reforms in a Post-Washington Consensus Era: Lessons from Ghana's Good Reformers', *Progress in Development Studies*, 12(2–3): 135–51.

Prichard, W. and Bentum, I. (2009). *Taxation and Development in Ghana: Finance, Equity and Accountability.* London: Tax Justice Network.

Resnick, D. (2016). 'Strong Democracy, Weak State: The Political Economy of Ghana's Stalled Structural Transformation'. IFPRI Discussion Paper 01574. Washington, DC: International Food Policy Research Institute.

Roll, M. (ed.) (2014). *The Politics of Public Sector Performance: Pockets of Effectiveness in Developing Countries.* New York: Routledge.

Terkper, S. E. (1994). 'Ghana's Tax Administration Reforms (1985–93)', *Tax Notes International*, 23: 1393–400.

Tignor, R. (2006). *W. Arthur Lewis and the Birth of Development Economics.* Princeton, NJ: Princeton University Press.

Whitfield, L. (2010). 'The State Elite, PRSPs and Policy Implementation in Aid-dependent Ghana', *Third World Quarterly*, 31(5): 721–37.

Whitfield, L. (2011). 'Competitive Clientelism, Easy Financing and Weak Capitalists: The Contemporary Political Settlement in Ghana'. DIIS Working Paper 2011:27. Copenhagen: Danish Institute of International Studies.

Whitfield, L. (2018). *Economies after Colonialism: Ghana and the Struggle for Power.* Cambridge: Cambridge University Press.

Whitfield, L., Therkildsen, O., Buur, L., and Kjær, A. M. (2015). *The Politics of African Industrial Policy: A Comparative Perspective.* Cambridge: Cambridge University Press.

Williams, T. (2009). 'An African Success Story: The Case of Ghana's Cocoa Marketing Industry'. IDS Working Paper 318. Brighton: Institute of Development Studies.

World Bank (1992). 'First and Second Structural Adjustment Credits'. Report No. 10686-Gh. Washington, DC: World Bank.

World Bank (1997). 'Implementation Completion Report Republic of Ghana Second Financial Sector Adjustment Credit (FINSAC II), (CR. 2318-GH)'. Washington, DC: World Bank.

Yohou, D. and Goujon, M. (2017). 'Reassessing Tax Effort in Developing Countries: A Proposal of a Vulnerability-adjusted Tax Effort Index'. Working Paper 186. Clermont-Ferrand, France: FERDI.

4

'Holding against the Tide'

The Varying Fortunes of Bureaucratic Pockets of Effectiveness in Kenya

Matthew Tyce

Introduction

Existing literature on the capacity and performance of the Kenyan state has not engaged extensively with the PoE concept, but nonetheless suggests the phenomenon has become increasingly prevalent since the 1980s. This was as a combination of external and domestic pressures around elite fragmentation, state informalization, and political and economic liberalization eroded the previously broad-based capacities of the Kenyan state (Barkan and Chege 1989, Branch and Cheeseman 2008, Leonard 1991, Mueller 2011, Opalo 2019). Today, scholars observe that distribution of capacity within the Kenyan state is 'not uniform' (Porisky 2020: 4) and that there is significant 'variability' in its performance, both 'over space' and 'across agencies' (Hassan 2020: 14). However, beyond Kenya's coercive apparatus—and, particularly, the Provincial (or, since 2013, the National) Administration—there is little sense of where the higher levels of capacity and performance might actually be observed.

This chapter seeks to help fill that gap. It introduces three examples of current or recent pockets of effectiveness (PoEs) within the Kenyan context—the Central Bank of Kenya (CBK), Kenya Revenue Authority (KRA), and National Treasury—and tracks the drivers of their performance since the 1990s, utilizing the expanded, multi-scalar version of political settlement analysis outlined in Chapter 2. As predicted by the framework and already borne out in the case of Ghana (Chapter 3), Kenya's 'dispersed' political settlement (which also moved from a 'narrow' to 'broad' social foundation during the period of analysis) creates an environment that is generally unconducive to the emergence—and, certainly, sustenance—of PoEs. This is because political leaders tend to be preoccupied with shorter-term efforts to maintain power, rather than longer-term state-building, and lack sufficient enforcement powers to discipline and centralize rent-seeking or protect state organizations from these pressures. Nonetheless, the case-study

Matthew Tyce, *'Holding against the Tide'*. In: *Pockets of Effectiveness and the Politics of State-building and Development in Africa*. Edited by Sam Hickey, Oxford University Press. © Oxford University Press (2023).
DOI: 10.1093/oso/9780192864963.003.0004

organizations have all—to varying degrees, at different points, and for differing lengths of time—functioned as PoEs, conceived of here as being relatively effective in undertaking their formally mandated tasks. This is because countervailing factors have mitigated the pressures emanating from Kenya's political settlement. These include organizational-level factors, especially the extent of each organization's formal autonomy, as well as, more informally and contingently, the political embeddedness of their leadership. Transnational factors have also been important, notably the levels of technical assistance provided to these organizations and the varying extents to which they have been supported by the disciplinary logics of global neoliberalism (though these logics have, at the same time, confined them to mandates and functions that reflect a neoliberal development agenda). Finally, ideational factors have helped to buttress the performance of these organizations during certain periods, as policy coalitions comprising politicians and technocrats—drawing on, but not beholden to, external support—have come together around shared ideas to try and protect them from the more corrosive pressures generated by Kenya's political settlement.

The chapter now offers a history of Kenya's political settlement before moving on to an overview of public-sector performance since the 1990s. Subsequent sections offer: the results of a literature review and survey that, together, identified the three case-study organizations; condensed histories of how the three organizations have performed over time; an analysis of the factors that explain their performance; and, finally, some implications for policy and research.

Kenya's political settlement

Since independence in 1963, Kenya has moved through all four of the political settlement-types identified in Chapter 2. Until the early-1990s, Kenya possessed a *concentrated* political settlement, with power centralized around the presidency and an executive bureaucracy—including the Provincial Administration (PA)—that did the president's bidding. This was the case under both presidents during this period—Jomo Kenyatta (1963–1978) and Daniel arap Moi (1978–2002). However, there was significant variation in terms of the settlement's social foundation. Under Kenyatta, it was *broad-concentrated*, as he hailed from one of Kenya's largest and most powerful ethnic groups and enjoyed broad-based legitimacy because of his role in Kenya's independence movement. Kenyatta's status as 'father' of the nation gave him sufficient assurances not just to tolerate competitive one-party elections, but to delegate significant autonomy to regional 'barons' who commanded sizeable ethnic bases beyond his own, thereby expanding the political settlement's reach (Cheeseman 2009: 95). By contrast, Kenya moved towards a *narrow-concentrated* settlement under Moi, as he not only came from a smaller and more fragmented ethnic group, but entered office as the global economy was entering a downturn, undermining his ability to sustain the extensive clientelist networks that Kenyatta built (Barkan and Chege 1989). Following an attempted coup in 1982, Moi adopted an 'increasingly exclusionary form of governance' that relied less on co-opting rival factions and more on outwardly repressing them (Branch et al. 2010: 251).

Another shift in Kenya's settlement occurred in the early 1990s, as democratization pressures led to a *narrow-dispersed* configuration. Political liberalization allowed politicians to defect freely from the ruling party while economic liberalization unravelled Moi's ability to prevent business elites from providing them with political financing (Arriola 2013). However, the settlement remained narrow because the costs of repressing and intimidating rival groups were still less than co-opting them. Moi's allies financed ethnic militia to suppress opposition supporters and encouraged rival presidential candidates to fragment the opposition (Kajwanja 2009). The continued narrowness of the settlement was, perhaps, best illustrated by the fact that Moi secured re-election in 1992 and 1997 with around a third of the votes. In 2002, with Moi constitutionally barred from standing again, the social foundation of Kenya's settlement appeared to be broadening again, as an inclusive National Rainbow Coalition (NARC) led by Mwai Kibaki came to power promising different forms of politics. However, NARC soon disintegrated, leaving Kibaki, by 2005, in charge of a narrow coalition dominated by co-ethnics, and his ex-NARC principals back in opposition, claiming they were once again being 'excluded from the political process' (Cheeseman 2009: 170).

These historical grievances, and feelings of exclusion from the settlement, formed the backdrop to Kenya's 2007 elections, and the violence that followed. Yet they also informed debates around a new constitution, which was the overriding objective of a unity government, led by Kibaki, that brought together (in unwieldy and fragmented fashion) all major factions. The passage of this constitution, in 2010, offers a formal manifestation of what has been a broader shift, since 2008, to a *broad-dispersed* political settlement. This is because there have been explicit attempts, through the constitution, to broaden the foundations of Kenya's settlement. For example, there are new electoral rules, including that presidential candidates must secure over 50 per cent of votes and at least 25 per cent in half of Kenya's forty-seven counties, to incentivize them to appeal more programmatically to voters and construct broader coalitions. Within the state, there have been moves towards 'representative bureaucracy', with rules mandating ethnic, gender, and regional diversity in public-sector appointments while presidential influence over senior appointments has also (nominally) been reduced (Hassan and O'Mealia 2020). The constitution also introduced an extensive form of devolution that 'was not merely a central government gimmick to control peripheral elites', but a genuine attempt to 'improve service delivery, ensure geographically equitable public spending, and curtail presidential powers' (Opalo 2020: 852). It remains a work-in-progress, but devolution has been, and will continue to be, 'a game changer in Kenya's politics of development', securing greater buy-in to the political settlement (Kanyinga 2016: 163).

The corollary of these attempts to expand the foundation of Kenya's political settlement is that they have entailed even greater dispersions of power within it. Devolution was framed as a way of unravelling Kenya's winner-takes-all political system and all-powerful presidency and has produced an even more dispersed configuration of power, whereby extensive numbers of 'veto players' at different political and administrative levels restrain the enforcement powers of executive authorities (Boone et al. 2018). Kibaki experienced some of these realities during his second term (2008–2013), as Kenya began shifting towards a *broad-dispersed* settlement. However, as discussed in the following sections, they have been even greater for Kibaki's successor, President Uhuru Kenyatta, the son of Kenya's founding president Jomo Kenyatta, whose election as the leader of the Jubilee Alliance coincided with the full implementation of devolution from 2013.

Public-sector performance

The literature offers a somewhat sobering assessment of public-sector management in Kenya. There are regular discussions of 'state failure' (Branch and Cheeseman 2008) and 'state capture' (Maina 2019: vii) and claims that the Kenyan state has been 'repurposed into a zone for personalized appropriation' and 'gut[ting] state resources for electioneering' (2019). The Kenyan state has variously been depicted as 'grabbed' (Manji 2012), 'criminal' (Kajwanja and Southall 2009), or, most often, simply as 'weak' (Hassan 2020: 15). These realities are often linked to the transition to multi-party politics, which accelerated pre-existing processes of elite fragmentation and state informalization and saw a 'slide into corruption and financial scandal, ineffective governance, [and] the crumbling of institutions' (Kajwanja 2009: 366). During Moi's latter presidency, the looting of state coffers and use of ethnic militias eroded the state's monopoly over the legitimate use of force and led to 'oversight institutions' being weakened to enable 'pervasive corruption' (Mueller 2011: 104).

Yet similar dynamics have been observed under Moi's successors, suggesting a story of 'continuity rather than change' (Murunga and Nasong'o 2006: 22). For Cheeseman (2009: 94), Kenyan elites have 'displayed a remarkable ability to re-invent the status quo'. To some extent, this has been the case with Kenya's much-heralded new constitution, which does not appear to have fundamentally improved the nature of public-sector performance, despite an array of provisions seeking to incentivize technocratic rather than politicized decision-making. According to Maina (2019: 8), deep-rooted processes of state capture have remained remarkably 'stable' under Kenya's new constitutional dispensation.

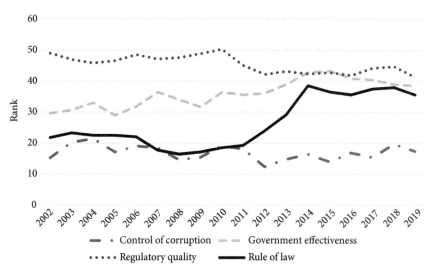

Figure 4.1 Kenya's governance metrics, 2002–2019
Source: World Governance Indicators.

The World Governance Indicators (WGI) do not provide clear evidence of improved public-sector performance in Kenya since the unveiling of its new constitution either (Figure 4.1). The country's scores for government effectiveness and, particularly, rule of law, have improved overall. However, since 2014 there are signs of reversing outcomes across both these metrics, or at least a sense of stagnation. Kenya's government effectiveness scores had also been increasing prior to the introduction of Kenya's new constitution. By contrast, Kenya's scores for regulatory quality have declined, while control of corruption—in the clearest echoes of the literature—continues to be Kenya's lowest area of performance by quite some margin, with few signs of improvement under the new constitutional dispensation. Indeed, Kenya's scores for control of corruption fall well below the sub-Saharan African (SSA) average.

PoEs in Kenya: Past and present

While the WGI offers high-level insights into aggregate public-sector performance, it says little about the extent to which performance varies *within* the state—and, thus, whether there are PoEs that might be bucking broader trends. Indeed, there is evidence that the PoE phenomenon has become increasingly pronounced in Kenya since the mid-1980s, though the terminology has rarely been used. Previously, Kenya had a relatively 'strong state' (Opalo 2019: 12) and 'autonomous administrative apparatus' (Leys 1975: 122). This was inherited from the colonial regime and preserved by President Kenyatta within the context of a *broad-concentrated* settlement. Nonetheless, certain parts of the state were particularly effective. These included the coercive apparatus—and particularly the PA—which had a disciplined and well-remunerated workforce (Barkan and Chege 1989). Within the economic technocracy, the CBK and Finance Ministry were highly capable, led by trained economists from Kenyatta's ethnic group and supported by technical assistance from donors. Reflecting the fact that Kenyatta and many of his allies were invested in commercial agriculture, particularly tea, and derived support from regions producing key commodities, the state also maintained effective agricultural authorities like Kenya Tea Development Agency (KTDA). In all cases, Kenyatta's recruitment policy combined 'an element of personal loyalty with a preponderance of objective merit' (Leonard 1991: 134).

Yet the performance of these organizations—and the state generally—declined through the 1980s, as processes of elite fragmentation and state informalization took root. These emerged during the tail-end of Kenyatta's presidency, as his worsening health saw factional conflict within the ruling coalition, but escalated throughout Moi's, as Kenya shifted towards a *narrow-concentrated* settlement. Across the state, but particularly within the economic technocracy, long-standing, capable technocrats were removed because they hailed from Kenyatta's ethnic group—or, indeed, from any group outside the narrowing social foundations of Moi's coalition. In their place, Moi appointed individuals he trusted, but who lacked the capacity or experience to run such entities (O'Brien and Ryan 2001). Agricultural agencies like KTDA were also hobbled as Moi re-routed state support from cash crops like tea and coffee, grown in areas populated by rival factions, towards cereal crops produced in his own social heartlands. In turn, 'this switch meant reduced earnings from exports' and a 'reduction in the state's capacity to deliver basic services' (Kanyinga 2016: 161). The 'exception was the security apparatus', where 'Moi was careful to maintain the [PA's] capacity and professionalism' because of its role in coercing opponents and ensuring basic political settlement stability (Branch and Cheeseman 2008: 11).

Compounding this situation, Kenya's structural adjustment reforms from the 1980s, 'further undermined the state's capacity' (Murunga and Nasong'o 2006: 197). In sectors ranging from health and education to energy and water, external pressures around liberalization led state organizations to disengage—often 'too rapidly' (2006: 23)—from administrative processes, creating a 'regulatory and monitoring vacuum' that often only heightened corruption further (Tyce 2019: 563).

These domestically rooted pressures around state informalization and elite fragmentation, coupled with more external pressures around economic and political liberalization, have continued to restrain the state's effectiveness and capacity. Nonetheless, Hassan (2020: 15) argues that some entities remain 'very capable'. These include the PA, which continues to deliver on its formal (and informal) mandate, even if it would not meet Roll's (2014) criteria for a PoE because of its human-rights infringements. 'Strategic variation of capacity' within the state (Hassan 2020: 15) is also apparent with Kenya's Export Processing Zones Authority (Tyce 2019) and energy-sector entities like the Geothermal Development Company, which have been effective at fostering renewable energy 'niches' with foreign investors (Newell and Phillips 2016). Similarly, Upadhyaya (2020) suggests CBK is a relatively effective organization within the Kenyan context, while Moore and Prichard (2017: 11) claim that the 'Kenya Revenue Authority is one of the most effective tax administrations in sub-Saharan Africa'. Thus, PoEs do appear to be a salient feature within Kenya's political economy, even if their status may be fragile and reflective of a 'disciplinary neoliberalism' (Gill 1995, Newell and Phillips 2016) that encourages investment in particular organizations and functions over others.

Expert survey

To identify potential examples of contemporary PoEs, the researcher surveyed twenty-one respondents with expertise on Kenya's public sector. Despite the pitfalls of this method (see Chapter 2), the survey offered interesting insights—even if only a snapshot in time—about the nature of the Kenyan state, particularly once triangulated with secondary literature and statistical data. The survey corroborated the sense that PoEs are a relevant phenomenon. Most respondents claimed that a minority of state organizations regularly deliver on their mandates (Figure 4.2). Regarding the identity of these potential PoEs, CBK emerged as the clearest contender, receiving nearly twice as many nominations

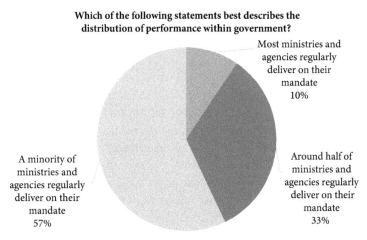

Figure 4.2 Expert survey on public sector performance in Kenya
Source: Author's expert survey.

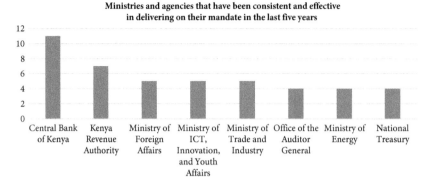

Figure 4.3 Expert ratings of high-performing ministries in Kenya
Source: Author's expert survey.

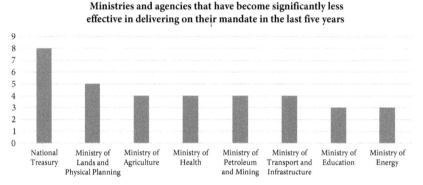

Figure 4.4 Expert ratings of low-performing ministries in Kenya
Source: Author's expert survey.

as KRA, the second-ranked organization (Figure 4.3). The sense that these organizations were PoEs was supported by the literature cited above, which had identified them—albeit often only in passing—as being relatively effective organizations.

An interesting point of divergence between Kenya and the other countries discussed in this book was that the Kenyan Ministry of Finance (or what, since 2013, has been called the National Treasury) was not generally regarded as a high performer. Instead, it was identified as an organization whose performance had declined significantly (Figure 4.4), perhaps because the survey was conducted amidst widespread reporting of Kenya's 'ghost dams' scandal, within which the Treasury was accused of paying out hundreds of millions of dollars for dams before feasibility studies were conducted (Maina 2019). That said, many survey respondents—and, to some extent, the statistical indicators—suggested that the

Treasury had previously been a relatively high-performing organization, so a decision was taken to use it as a potentially revealing case of a PoE that had been undermined.

Investigating PoEs in Kenya: Case-study findings

The following sections summarize how each of the organizations have performed, relative to their mandates and related performance indicators, since the 1990s. The summaries represent condensed versions of the case-study papers (Tyce 2020a, 2020b, 2020c). The section begins with the organization that offers the clearest and most consistent example of a PoE—CBK—then turns to KRA, which offers a more partial example. Finally, it discusses the Treasury, whose performance has been most variable and inconsistent, to the extent that it may only have briefly met the PoE criteria during the early/mid-2000s. Each section draws on secondary and grey literature, quantitative performance indicators, and qualitative data generated through key informant interviews.

Central Bank of Kenya

CBK is a long-standing PoE within the Kenyan context, as it has been broadly effective at delivering on its core mandate of maintaining price and financial-sector stability since 1993, when the organization was overhauled after the 1992 elections. That said, there have been periods when outcomes have been *relatively* high or low, across both aspects of its mandate. Beginning with price stability, inflation rates fell rapidly during the early 1990s, then remained mostly in single digits for that decade (Figure 4.5). Inflation then 'accelerated substantially' from around

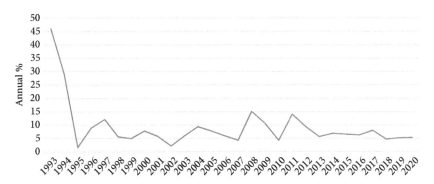

Figure 4.5 Annual inflation in Kenya, 1992–2020
Source: https://www.imf.org/external/datamapper/datasets.

2002, hitting a series of peaks in 2004, 2008, and 2011 (IMF 2009: 18). Since 2013, inflation has been remarkably stable, almost always coming within CBK's formal target of 5 per cent with a tolerance of +/−2 per cent.

Intriguingly, indicators for financial-sector stability reveal similar periodizations, though the headline outcomes—in crude terms—appear to contrast with those for price stability. In the 1990s, when inflation was consistently low, financial-sector indicators were more erratic (Figures 4.6 to 4.8). By contrast, from 2002, when inflation was itself becoming more erratic, financial-sector indicators improved markedly, especially the number of bank failures and prevalence of non-performing loans (NPLs). Finally, there have been signs of increased financial-sector instability since around 2012/13, just as inflation rates were entering their most stable period. The drivers of these performance patterns are explored below.

The 1993–2002 period saw strong price stability outcomes because there was commitment, inside and outside of CBK, to an inflation-targeting framework. Internally, CBK was led by a reformist governor, Micah Cheserem, appointed

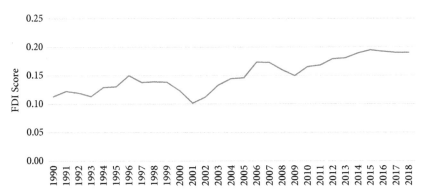

Figure 4.6 Financial sector development in Kenya, 1992–2018
Source: https://www.imf.org/external/datamapper/datasets.

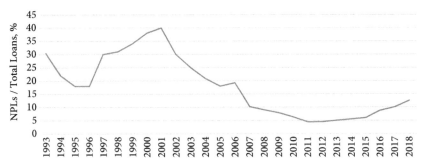

Figure 4.7 Non-performing loans in Kenya, 1992–2018
Source: https://data.worldbank.org.

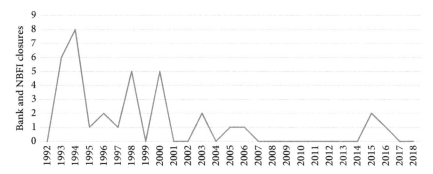

Figure 4.8 Bank closures in Kenya, 1992–2018

Source: Author's calculations, based on data in Brownbridge and Harvey (1998), Upadhyaya (2011), and media reports.

in 1993. As an ex-corporate accountant, Cheserem had ideational proclivities for installing 'discipline' and 'balancing the books'[1] and, in his own words, 'readily agreed' with donor prescriptions (Cheserem 2006: 123). Externally, Cheserem received support from influential domestic capitalists and investors, whose ventures had suffered because of spiralling inflation and exchange rates after the 1992 elections (Dafe 2019). The interests of a range of powerful actors therefore converged around a policy framework prioritizing low inflation. This shift was reflected in a change to the CBK Act in 1996 that narrowed CBK's monetary policy mandate to maintaining price stability and even, initially, allowed it to set its own inflation targets. These developments help to explain why inflation remained in single figures for much of this period, save for a blip during the 1997 election cycle.

CBK was less obviously successful in its financial-sector stability mandate, where Cheserem performed a delicate 'juggling act'.[2] Overall, Cheserem had to restore confidence in Kenya's financial sector by clamping down on political banks licensed by his predecessor which 'were no more than officially sanctioned money laundering operations' (Mueller 2011: 104), but while also allowing Moi's inner circle sufficient leeway to generate political finance. Thus, Cheserem adopted a more flexible approach than with monetary policy, easing the pace of reform during election periods, then entering 'clean-up mode' thereafter, as reflected in Figures 4.6 to 4.8.[3] Cheserem also accepted that some banks, like Moi's own Transnational Bank, had to remain 'off limits'.[4] Cheserem's relative success with this sensitive side of CBK's mandate owed to him being the brother-in-law of Moi's

[1] Interview, ex-CBK official, Nairobi, 3 April 2019.
[2] Interview, journalist, Nairobi, 28 April 2019.
[3] Interview, journalist, Nairobi, 5 May 2017.
[4] Interview, ex-CBK official, Nairobi, 3 April 2019.

closest advisor, which gave him 'access to State House'.[5] Cheserem had an ability to 'read the mood of politics', and to 'give and take', which is 'so important for a position like that'.[6]

In the 2002–2013 period, Figures 4.5 to 4.8 suggest that CBK's performance may have been a near-inverse of the preceding period, as inflation increased while financial stability indicators improved. However, the data presents a somewhat misleading picture of CBK's performance across both tasks. Much of the heightened inflation—particularly the 2008 and 2011 spikes—was associated with exogenous factors like the global financial crisis, region-wide droughts and oil price shocks. During this period there was also reputedly an agreement between CBK and Kibaki, a trained economist whose presidency (2003–2013) spanned the period, that CBK did not need to be so single-minded in maintaining ultra-low inflation. This development was reflected in a change to CBK's mandate in 2007. Price stability remained CBK's primary objective, but a secondary objective of 'support[ing] the economic policy of the Government, including the objectives of growth and employment', was added. More moderate levels of inflation—and periodic criticism from the IMF (2009: 18)—were tolerated if CBK was contributing to other policy goals, notably to drive financial inclusion and increase private-sector credit.

CBK had success with these other, less formal, organizational objectives, particularly under Governor Njuguna Ndung'u (2006–2015) (Upadhyaya 2020). However, CBK under Ndung'u arguably became more consumed with deepening than regulating the financial sector, allowing some banks to continue operating despite serious governance issues. Nonetheless, CBK was, overall, a high-performing PoE. In contrast to KRA and the Treasury, Kenya's shift from a *narrow-* to *broad-concentrated* political settlement from 2008 did not significantly undermine its functioning. If anything, CBK became more effective, as it was led by a governor who was deeply embedded with the private sector and social networks around Kibaki.

Moving to CBK's third performance period, which began in around 2013, a weakening of CBK's embeddedness has contributed to the increased financial-sector instability observed. Significantly, this weakening resulted from the electoral victory, in 2013, of President Kenyatta's Jubilee coalition, who—along with his vice-president, William Ruto—has demonstrated less interest than the 'technocratic' economist Kibaki in protecting CBK, and Kenya's economic technocracy generally, from political encroachments. However, CBK's embeddedness was also weakened by the appointment of a new governor, in 2015, who was unable, or unwilling, to demonstrate similar political sensitivities to his predecessors. A career IMF executive, informants described Patrick Njoroge as 'the Teflon man'

---

[5] Interview, ex-CBK official, Nairobi, 26 March 2019.
[6] Interview, ex-CBK official, Nairobi, 3 April 2019.

(because he 'has no political allegiances or soft spots that can be exploited'),[7] 'a bull terrier',[8] 'monk',[9] and 'a theorist'.[10] Taken together, these personality traits do not appear to have made him especially well suited to the transactional and politically delicate task of regulating banks.

Instead of his predecessor's incremental reforms, Njoroge came in 'all guns blazing', putting three banks in receivership and declaring this was the beginning of a 'deep cleaning'.[11] Even CBK (2017: 9) reports acknowledge that these moves caused 'liquidity stress' for small and medium banks, 'panic withdrawal of deposits', and 'overall instability' and 'uncertainty in the market'. Additionally, the closures, conducted without warning, led the Treasury to pass a measure forcing CBK to 'consult' with it before putting banks into receivership, drawing fire from the IMF for curtailing CBK's independence. However, informants also criticized Njoroge for his 'lack of political judgement', which they argued has been a general feature of his tenure. As a 'stickler for the rules',[12] Njoroge has demanded '100 per cent compliance with regulations, no matter who your owners are'.[13] As such, Njoroge spent much of his first term consumed by fighting spurious lawsuits, parliamentary committee hearings, and corruption investigations designed to force him from office.

CBK has, however, performed strongly in its price-stability mandate, which is a task that plays to Njoroge's strengths as a 'very sharp macroeconomist'.[14] Inflation has remained within single figures, despite combined pressures of interest-rate caps and fiscal dominance leading to 'an extremely difficult environment in which to conduct monetary policy'.[15] Internally, Njoroge enhanced the analytical capacities of CBK's research department and strengthened its linkages with the Monetary Policy Committee, which he has chaired effectively. Externally, he has benefitted from Kenya's new constitution, which enhanced CBK's independence with respect to its price stability mandate. Informally, there also seems to be some acceptance amongst Jubilee's leadership that CBK needs leeway in undertaking this function to avoid jeopardizing Kenya's ability to borrow from international capital markets. Jubilee's leaders have made heavy recourse to external financing, which has given CBK some space in its monetary-policy functions. CBK's performance, then, while remaining at a broadly high level throughout, has fluctuated across its dual mandate in line with political dynamics, transnational factors, and organizational leadership.

---

[7] Interview, commercial bank executive, Nairobi, 8 November 2016.
[8] Interview, financial sector analyst, Nairobi, 3 November 2016.
[9] Interview, economic analyst, Nairobi, 6 March 2019.
[10] Interview, commercial bank executive, Nairobi, 13 March 2019.
[11] Interview, economic analyst, Nairobi, 6 March 2019.
[12] Interview, ex-CBK official, Nairobi, 21 March 2019.
[13] Interview, banking executive, Nairobi, 12 November 2016.
[14] Interview, journalist, Nairobi, 28 April 2019.
[15] Interview, financial sector analyst, Nairobi, 3 November 2016.

Kenya Revenue Authority

KRA was established in 1995, as Kenya followed other (predominantly anglo-phone) African countries in hiving off its Tax Office from the Treasury to create a Semi-Autonomous Revenue Authority (SARA). Informed by the new public management (NPM) agenda, donors hoped a SARA would insulate tax adminis-tration from political pressures and increase revenues. Yet, initially, KRA's creation had the opposite effect. Revenues, relative to GDP, declined between 1995 and 2002, as did 'tax effort' (Figures 4.9 and 4.10). There was, though, a period of

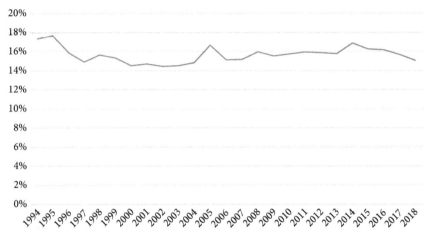

Figure 4.9 Tax-to-GDP in Kenya, 1994–2018
Source: https://www.wider.unu.edu/data.

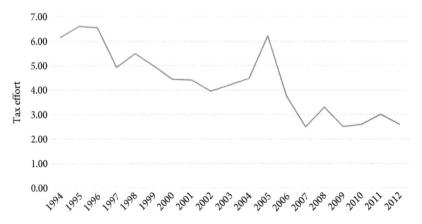

Figure 4.10 Tax effort in Kenya, 1991–2012
Source: Yohou and Goujon (2017).

improved performance from 2002 to 2014—especially up to 2006. Since 2014, revenue metrics have fallen again.

As to the period of poor performance between 1995 and 2002, much explanation can be found in factors outside of KRA's control. Pervasive political corruption during the 1990s caused many Kenyans to withhold their taxes—indeed, this was even an 'informal opposition strategy', designed to weaken the fiscal basis of Moi's regime (Prichard 2015: 132). KRA was also undermined by the Treasury's inconsistent tax policies and widespread issuance of tax exemptions to secure allegiances during the period of political jockeying that surrounded Kenya's transition to a dispersed settlement.

However, organizational factors also contributed. Prior to KRA's establishment, various deals were cut—reflecting fears that a powerful tax authority could become a political weapon—that constrained KRA's operational autonomy. These included the creation of a strong board with a mostly ministerial composition. Board members 'intervened a lot' in KRA's affairs, shielding particular firms from scrutiny and influencing internal appointments to well-remunerated posts.[16] Board meddling also caused constant turnover in KRA's management, undermining internal coherency and morale at all levels. Commissioner general (CG) and commissioner positions received no legal security of tenure.

KRA enjoyed a period of improved performance between 2003 and 2013, when it emerged as a PoE. As with CBK, this period was linked to the presidency and ideas of Kibaki, whose inner circle identified revenue mobilization as critical to their developmental vision, since it would create fiscal space for investing in infrastructure, education, and health, while restoring Kenya's sovereignty by diluting donor influence over the budget. Kibaki appointed a friend, Michael Waweru, as KRA's CG in 2003. Critically, Waweru enjoyed significant stability in his tenure, such that he not only became the first CG to serve one full term, but three. This gave him sufficient assurances to undertake 'deep reforms'.[17] Internally, he cultivated a more unified organizational culture through salary increments, performance management tools, organization-wide bonuses, and enhanced training. KRA also invested in transfer-pricing and digital-tax-collection capacities, becoming an 'acknowledged leader' in these areas (Moore and Prichard 2017: 11, Waris 2017). An external rebranding emphasized KRA's new customer-friendly approach and the linkages between paying taxes and Kenya achieving aid independence.

Initially, KRA's reforms were supported by relatively conducive tax policies, as the Treasury, led by another Kibaki ally, revised outdated VAT and income-tax legislation and introduced transfer-pricing regulations. With tax administration and policy pulling in similar directions, revenue metrics improved strongly between

---

[16] Interview, ex-KRA official, Nairobi, 27 March 2019.
[17] Interview, PFM specialist, Nairobi, 12 April 2019.

2003 and 2005. However, political developments from 2005 halted this momentum. In 2005, Kibaki's NARC coalition collapsed, as Odinga's allies decamped back to the opposition. To offset this loss, Kibaki co-opted politicians loyal to ex-President Moi, luring them with tax exemptions and favourable fiscal policies that ate into KRA's revenue base. From 2008, Kenya's transition to a *broad-dispersed* political settlement generated further challenges. KRA broadly remained a PoE, as Waweru was 'not someone that you could bully', and he enjoyed Kibaki's unflinching support.[18] However, as explained further in the following section, infighting within Kibaki's unity coalition over control of the Treasury—combined with the emergence of new centres of power outside the executive, especially the legislature—undermined his government's ability to devise new tax legislation. Kibaki had 'the least legislative success of Kenya's three presidents at the time—with only 56.5% of bills getting passed'—and so-called 'money bills' regarding taxation and spending were a particular victim (Opalo 2019: 195). This hobbled KRA's ability to tap new revenue streams. Thus, while KRA remained a broadly functional organization, it increasingly became marooned within a dysfunctional policy environment, helping to explain why revenues tailed off from 2006.

In around 2013, KRA entered an apparent third performance period, within which its own status as a PoE is being eroded. Defining features have been the arrival of a new ruling coalition and a shift away from any ideological project that could bind it together. Unlike Kibaki's inner circle, Kenyatta's advisors have placed little emphasis on revenue mobilization, especially when borrowing—particularly from China and international capital markets—offers a faster and politically less-onerous route to financing deficits and lucrative opportunities for siphoning off funds (Maina 2019, Ndii 2020). As a result, support for KRA has waned. Indeed, Kenyatta has sought to use KRA as a political weapon for hounding enemies and shielding allies in his power struggles with Deputy President Ruto. Additionally, the lack of interest amongst either of Jubilee's leaders for fiscal discipline has led the Treasury, trying to make its budgets look credible, to set increasingly unrealistic revenue targets, while giving KRA ever-fewer funds to achieve them. This has caused morale loss at all levels within KRA, as unrealistic targets have cascaded down, and training schemes and performance bonuses have been slashed.

KRA has also experienced an even more difficult tax-policy environment during this period. In the first months of his presidency, Kenyatta passed a new VAT Act that, along with the launch of KRA's digital I-Tax platform in 2013, drove a spike in Kenya's tax-to-GDP ratio in 2014, as KRA tapped new revenues and enhanced the efficiency of collections. However, since then, various provisions within the Act (and other pieces of tax legislation) have been reversed, weakened, or stalled. Numerous goods and services have returned to concessionary rates, either because they are widely consumed, and serve as easy vote-winners, or because they are

---

[18] Interview, ex-KRA director, Nairobi, 10 April 2019.

produced by businesses linked to Jubilee elites (Wawire 2020). This has deprived KRA of new revenue sources, forcing it to keep on 'milking the same people dry'.[19] The continued (but growing) failings of tax policy, then, combined with an erosion of KRA's status as a PoE, help to explain why Kenya's tax-to-GDP ratios have been falling since 2014.[20]

The Treasury

The Treasury's core functions include maintaining macroeconomic stability; devising revenue and expenditure policies that finance the budgetary requirements of national and county governments; and sustaining an appropriate portfolio of debt. Figures 4.11 to 4.14 offer a sense of its performance across these tasks. They point to similar performance periods to those identified for CBK and KRA. Between 1993 and 2002, the indicators fluctuate significantly, often in tandem with election cycles, in a period of variable performance. By contrast, from 2003, Figures 4.11 to 4.14 suggest a period of improved and more stable performance, though, similar to KRA, outcomes were more impressive before 2007 than after. Finally, from around 2012/13, there are signs of a third period, marked by deteriorations across most indicators, offering further echoes of KRA's experiences in particular.

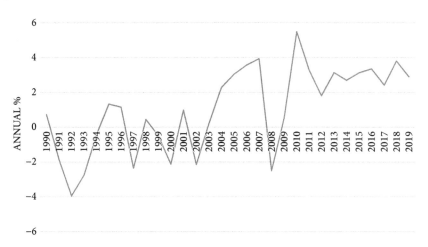

Figure 4.11 GDP per capita growth in Kenya, 1990–2018
Source: https://data.worldbank.org/.

---

[19] Interview, economic analyst, Nairobi, 12 March 2019.
[20] It should, however, be stressed that it is still too early to confirm for certain whether this is indeed a wholly new performance period, characterized by worsening outcomes, given the lack of data points post-2013.

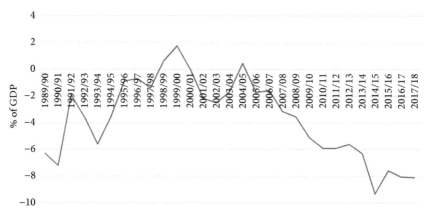

Figure 4.12 Fiscal balance in Kenya, 1990–2017
Source: KNBS annual surveys.

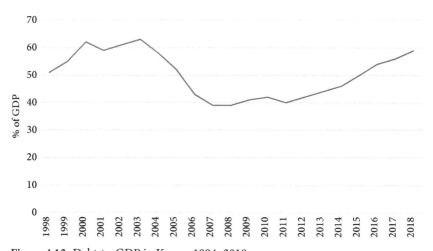

Figure 4.13 Debt-to-GDP in Kenya, 1994–2018
Source: https://ieakenya.shinyapps.io/public-debt-kenya/.

The 1993–2002 period saw variable outcomes as the Treasury's reform efforts waxed and waned. Between 1993 and 1996, the Treasury made strong progress in reducing budgetary deficits and debt as new reformist leadership (appointed at the same time as CBK's) tried to restore economic credibility after the 1992 elections. However, as with CBK's attempts to stabilize the financial sector, there was a 'slackening of reform efforts' as the 1997 elections approached and the Treasury struggled to contain 'a pre-election spending spree' orchestrated by the President's Office (O'Brien and Ryan 2001: 509). Following the 1997 elections, the cycle started again. Another reform-minded minister, Simeon Nyachae, was

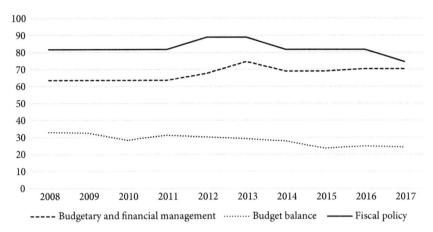

Figure 4.14 Selected IIAG scores for Kenya, 2008–2017
Source: https://mo.ibrahim.foundation/iiag.

appointed and entered 'clean up mode'.[21] Nyachae slashed spending, unveiled donor-appeasing taxes, and implemented a Medium-Term Expenditure Framework (MTEF). However, he was sacked two years later, once renewed donor support was secured, as his reformist zeal had caused him to be identified as a potential rival to Moi's favoured successor, Uhuru Kenyatta. The Treasury then cycled through two more ministers between 2000 and 2002, undermining its coherency and performance. Indeed, it required countervailing forces to prevent an even greater unravelling: the first were donors who, upon resuming aid in late-1999, negotiated strict conditions that subjected almost all spending to approval; the second came from CBK which, in 1997, capped government overdrafts at 5 per cent of revenues. Together, this provided a 'restraining influence on expenditure ... and budgetary expansion' (Mosley and Chiripanhura 2016: 923).

The Treasury entered its second performance period in 2003, with the onset of Kibaki's presidency. Kibaki saw the Treasury, along with CBK and KRA, as core enablers of his developmental vision, the tenets of which were enshrined in NARC's Economic Recovery Strategy (2003–2007). Mirroring his approach with CBK and KRA, Kibaki appointed David Mwiraria—another like-minded economist and friend—as finance minister. Mwiraria, like Kibaki's other 'technopols', enjoyed significant autonomy and discretion when leading his organization, even when policies challenged donor orthodoxy. Similar to how CBK pushed back against rigid inflation targets, the Treasury resisted pressure for 'austerity'.[22] Instead of reducing spending, officials channelled significantly expanded allocations towards sectors like infrastructure, health, and education, but kept

---

[21] Interview, journalist, Nairobi, 28 April 2019.
[22] Interview, ex-Treasury official, Nairobi, 29 March 2019.

deficits in check by enhancing budget financing and execution (Chege 2008). These efforts led to strong outcomes across most indicators during Kibaki's first term, as the Treasury slashed debt levels and interest payments, kept deficits within targeted bounds, and generally contributed to 'the only episode of five-year consecutive growth acceleration in the country's history' (Kimenyi et al. 2016: 2).

As with KRA, performance indicators appear to tail off from around 2007, especially with regards to fiscal balance. However, to some extent, these outcomes reflected more difficult external conditions outside Treasury control. In 2008, the Treasury faced the combined effects of Kenya's electoral crisis and the global financial crisis. These crises required a reconstruction exercise and the Treasury, cooperating with CBK, helped to revive Kenya's economy with a counter-cyclical fiscal stimulus equivalent to 2 per cent of GDP. That said, there was some deterioration in the Treasury's performance, as it experienced less stability and coherency in its leadership. This started in 2006, when Minister Mwiraria was caught up in Kenya's Anglo-Leasing scandal, forcing him to resign. But it escalated throughout Kibaki's second term, as factions comprising Kenya's unity coalition jockeyed for influence, and control over the Treasury, within the context of Kenya's shift to a *broad-dispersed* political settlement. The longest-serving finance minister during these years was Uhuru Kenyatta, between 2009 and 2012, who Kibaki appointed not because of any relevant experience or technical expertise, but to cater to factional interests around ensuring Kenyatta as successor. One informant described Kenyatta as a mere 'figurehead', as 'Kibaki and [Joseph] Kinyua [the Treasury PS] were running the show',[23] though Kibaki 'could only do so much with everything else he had going on'.[24] In particular, without a strong minister to champion Kibaki's legislative agenda within an increasingly assertive legislature, the Treasury struggled passing 'money bills' around taxation and spending, at least not without making significant concessions to powerful interests that went 'against the publicly stated preferences of the president' (Opalo 2019: 195).

However, the full implications of Kenya's shift to a *broad-dispersed* political settlement did not materialize until 2013, partly because this was when devolution was fully implemented. Devolution has created significant fiscal pressures for the Treasury to accommodate, while exacerbating pre-existing coordination issues within the budgeting process, as national and county governments have fought over responsibility for different policy functions and their corresponding budget lines. Kenya's constitution has also engendered 'arguably Africa's strongest legislature' (2019: 238), leading to a growing trend of budget statements and finance bills being held 'hostage' by legislators—many of whom are, because of the competitive and expensive nature of Kenyan politics, highly indebted, which makes

---

[23] Interview, economic analyst, Nairobi, 6 March 2019.
[24] Interview, parastatal chairperson, Nairobi, 5 March 2019.

them susceptible to lobbying and rent-seeking (Wawire 2020). At the same time, Kenya's constitution states that ministers can no longer be elected politicians, which has reduced the Treasury's influence within parliament. As one official lamented, 'when our minister was a politician, we could make deals with MPs to get policies through ... Those deals can still be made, but it is much more difficult now.'[25]

Yet the Treasury has also been facing increased pressures since 2013 because that was when President Kenyatta's fragmented Jubilee coalition was elected. As with KRA, Kenyatta has made little attempt to protect the Treasury, and shares no real ideational affinity with its technocrats, particularly around commitment to fiscal discipline. Instead, Kenyatta and Vice-President Ruto have pressured the Treasury to accommodate all their development projects and policy whims—which have rarely been coordinated, as Jubilee essentially contains 'two governments in one'—while publicly accusing its technocrats of conspiring with donors to restrain Jubilee's development agenda through calls for fiscal caution.[26] Jubilee's leaders have also forced senior Treasury officials to 'bend over backwards'[27] in accommodating (and disguising) increasingly egregious forms of 'budgeted corruption' (Ndii 2020). To a significant extent, these problems flow from the incentives generated by Kenya's new *broad-dispersed* settlement, which requires politicians to build and maintain broader coalitions. Not only have these imperatives heightened the incentives for politicized patterns of spending, as part of the formal budget process, but they have also increased the importance of informal transfers to politicians who command sizeable voting blocs. Equally, though, Jubilee's leaders have made little or no attempt to try and resist these pressures—or even to moderate their impact on key organizations like the Treasury. They have often done the opposite, fuelling factional power struggles across the state bureaucracy.

Analysing the politics of Kenya's PoEs

Bringing these summaries together, there are three overarching performance periods that cut across the organizations. These are: a period of variable, and often poor, outcomes between 1993–2002; a period of improved, and certainly more consistent, performance between 2003–2013; and a period of mostly declining outcomes since around 2013. This section discusses the role that the factors comprising the project's conceptual framework have played in these outcomes.

[25] Interview, Treasury official, Nairobi, 22 November 2016.
[26] Interview, PFM specialist, Nairobi, 12 April 2019.
[27] Interview, ex-Treasury official, Nairobi, 11 March 2019.

Political settlements

The case studies support the project's hypothesis that dispersed power configurations deprive ruling elites of the enforcement capacities required for pursuing longer-term state-building and institutional reform (Chapter 2). Instead, what often prevails are short-term fixes and more targeted (and, often as a result, more reversible) investments in capacities and functions that serve more immediate interests. These realities are readily observed at the Treasury whose performance has fluctuated constantly in line with political cycles. However, KRA and, to a lesser extent, CBK have faced similar pressures.

That said, there is a sense that ruling elites must strike some kind of balance between political survival and bureaucratic autonomy with all three organizations. This is because Kenya's economic technocracy plays such a key role in maintaining the broader functioning of the state, and the viability of the political settlement, that they need to be able to undertake their mandated functions to a minimally sufficient degree; or, at least, be given enough space to enter 'clean-up mode' when political survival efforts spiral out of control, particularly following elections.

One period in which the three organizations enjoyed more than a minimum of autonomy was during Kibaki's presidency, particularly his earlier years. This was as a techno-political alliance within the ruling coalition, bound by shared ideas and close connections to Kibaki, sought to protect these organizations from political pressures and (re)build their internal capacities and cultures. Strong upticks in performance were consequently observed across Kenya's economic technocracy between 2002 and 2005. However, these efforts faced increasingly adverse political headwinds, revealing the difficulties of maintaining concerted institutional reform within dispersed configurations of power. In 2005, Kibaki's coalition collapsed, forcing him to co-opt new coalition partners in ways that infringed on KRA's revenue-generating capacity and the Treasury's fiscal discipline. There was also an increasing turn to political financing schemes to help Kibaki assemble a winning coalition at the 2007 elections, against an increasingly strong and united opposition. The most illustrative was Kenya's Anglo-Leasing scandal, exposed in 2006, which led to the resignation of the Treasury's own technopol minister.

From 2008, Kibaki's ability to support and protect these organizations was eroded further, as Kenya shifted towards a broad (and, as a result, even more dispersed) settlement. Within this context, the Treasury's performance, in particular, was weakened, as factions comprising the unity government jostled for influence and sought to position themselves for the 2013 elections by securing control over key levers of patronage and rents. The emergence of an increasingly autonomous and assertive legislature also stymied the passage of new legislation and budgets that could have supported the activities of Kenya's economic technocracy.

However, the full effects of the transition to a *broad-dispersed* political settlement were only felt in 2013. Since then, Kenya's economic technocracy has experienced even greater pressures, related both to the expanded foundations of the settlement and a correspondingly increased dispersion of power within it. Regarding the enlarged social foundation, the most obvious set of pressures have been fiscal. These have come not only through devolution, which required the creation (and financing) of new political and administrative structures, but significant new forms of state provisioning, through social protection schemes in particular, that have been used to 'redraw the social contract between state and citizens since 2008' (Lavers and Hickey 2021: 20). New electoral rules have heightened these pressures, and in turn weakened the Treasury's ability to maintain budgetary discipline, as the need to construct and maintain broader electoral coalitions has ramped up incentives for politicized modes of spending as well as the 'budgeted corruption' that caters to the more informal dimensions of coalition building (Maina 2019, Wawire 2020). At the same time, the increased dispersion of power within Kenya's political settlement has further reduced the ability of political leaders or technocrats to manage these pressures in coordinated or consistent ways. As a result, Kenya's economic technocracy increasingly finds itself 'pushed and pulled' between an array of conflicting interests and demands, from within and outside the ruling coalition.[28] This reality was captured by an ex-KRA commissioner who declared that 'I would not want to be a CG under the current arrangements. Now you get calls from the president, his deputy, MPs, governors, senators. Anyone can push you around.'[29]

Organizational factors

However, at an organizational level, CBK, KRA, and the Treasury have been exposed to these political pressures to differing degrees. An obvious factor explaining such variations is the degree of each organization's formal autonomy. Of the three, CBK has the strongest protections, codified both within its own Act and in Kenya's new constitution. Various provisions within nominally 'semi-autonomous' KRA's Act, by contrast, leave it as a 'virtual appendage of the Treasury', while the Treasury has fewer protections still.[30] These variations offer part of the explanation for why, of the three cases, CBK has offered the most consistent example of a PoE, while the Treasury has offered the least.

However, while formal autonomy is a significant factor in explaining performance, it is not sufficient. Even CBK's autonomy is 'not set in stone', as seen in the

---

[28] Interview, journalist, Nairobi, 19 March 2019.
[29] Interview, ex-KRA commissioner, Nairobi, 9 May 2019.
[30] Interview, journalist, Nairobi, 28 April 2019.

backlash to Governor Njoroge's bank closures in 2015, which 'clipped CBK's independence' as a measure was passed forcing it to consult with the Treasury before closing banks.[31] Echoing Leonard's (1991: 258) work on Kenya's bureaucracy, 'the autonomy of an organization ... is not something that can be simply granted in a single constitutional act. It has to be earned and maintained through political connections.' What is especially critical, referencing Joignant's (2011) concept of a technopol, is for senior bureaucrats to possess both technical skills and political nous, the latter of which can help them to steer their organizations through shifting political contexts. Organizational leaders must be 'astute operatives'[32] and possess strong 'relationship management skills.'[33] They must also be able to 'give and take' with an array of actors—from the presidency to donors, the legislature to the private sector—while not being beholden to any of them.[34] Maintaining this multifaceted kind of 'embedded autonomy' (Evans 1995) is a high-wire act, requiring constant 'trade-offs' and an ability to transverse murky 'grey areas.'[35] However, each organization experienced its best periods of performance when leaders struck some kind of balance here.

It was also under such leaders that the organizations made most progress in developing cohesive internal cultures. Organizational leaders who are relationally and ideationally aligned with incumbent political networks are likely to have sufficient assurances regarding their positions to devote more time to achieving their mandates (Johnson 2015, McDonnell 2017). They are also likely to enjoy sufficient trust to be delegated with greater responsibility and be able to negotiate greater access to limited budgetary resources (Hassan 2020). Certainly, this is what happened at CBK and KRA during the second period, when both organizations had deeply embedded and long-serving leaders who experimented with performance management tools and reward/recognition schemes. The Treasury initially undertook similar efforts, but the loss of its minister in 2006, and subsequent instability in its leadership, caused these efforts to slow. Nonetheless, insiders at all three organizations often recalled feeling greater job satisfaction and motivation during the second period than before or after. This was not just because of the increased pecuniary and material incentives on offer, but because they simply felt more 'pride' to be working for organizations that were spearheading Kenya's development efforts.[36] These findings echo Roll's (2014) conclusion that a 'sense of mission' is an important internal feature of POEs (albeit a fragile and reversible one).

---

[31] Interview, journalist, Nairobi, 28 April 2019.
[32] Interview, KRA official, telephone, 12 April 2019.
[33] Interview, KRA official, Nairobi, 3 May 2019.
[34] Interview, ex-KRA director, Nairobi, 20 November 2018.
[35] Interview, ex-CBK official, Nairobi, 27 March 2019.
[36] Interview, Treasury official, Nairobi, 9 April 2019; interview, KRA official, Nairobi, 3 May 2019.

Transnational factors

Transnational factors have, to varying degrees, enhanced the performance of all three organizations, with Kenya's economic technocracy benefitting from higher levels of technical assistance and external oversight than other parts of the state. However, the political interference that the Treasury, in particular, has experienced throughout the period of analysis shows there are limits to the disciplinary powers of external actors—in the Treasury's case, it has helped to lessen the impact of political budget cycles, rather than prevent them.

The disciplinary powers of Kenya's (traditional) donors have also been weakening since the mid-2000s, in line with the increasing availability of alternative forms of external financing, especially from international capital markets and China (Chege 2020, Zeitz 2019). Intriguingly, though, these alternative financial flows have not lessened the strictures of 'disciplinary neoliberalism' (Gill 1995) with respect to economic governance. Partly, this is because access to Chinese financing has been accompanied by the rise of international capital markets. These markets favour low and stable inflationary environments, and thus Kenya's heavy recourse to them has reinforced incentives to focus on inflation-targeting monetary policies. In a study on the financial statecraft of African debtors, Zeitz (2019: 199) argues that the increasing availability of alternative forms of external financing has enhanced Kenya's negotiating position vis-à-vis traditional donors, particularly since 2013. However, Kenyatta's government has mostly used its increased leverage to push back on donor governance conditionalities and to 'mute their criticism' of his government's political and human rights record, in a period when, for much of it, both Kenyatta and his deputy faced ICC investigations for their alleged roles in Kenya's 2007/08 violence. By contrast, Kenya's traditional donors have doubled down on economic and financial management issues, as they have become wary of Jubilee's proclivity for politicized spending, which threatens to put 'repayments of their own development loans at risk' (2019: 51). As a result, Kenya's macroeconomic approach has 'remained broadly in line with donor interests', despite their waning influence more broadly (2019: 170). Kenya's continued adherence to the tenets of neoliberal economic governance is also driven by the country's status as— and strategy to be—a commercial and financial hub for East Africa, which requires continued alignment with internationally accepted 'best practices' and regulatory standards (Upadhyaya 2020).

Ideas

From the preceding discussion, it is clear that ideas and ideologies have played an important role in shaping the form and function of Kenya's economic technocracy—and, further, that these ideas have mostly been neoclassical and neoliberal in nature. Ever since independence, Kenya's economic technocrats have been exposed (and predisposed) to such ideas, with donors viewing Jomo Kenyatta's government as a poster child for market-led development. Donors offered significant technical assistance to, and embedded advisory teams within, Kenya's economic technocracy. This 'undoubtedly influenced the analytical capabilities of Kenyan technocrats ... and their approach to analysing economic issues' (O'Brien and Ryan 2001: 475).

However, while Kenya's technocrats have been—and continue to be—broadly amenable to such ideas, this does not mean that they have not also tried to ensure greater degrees of what Lavers and Hickey (2021: 8) call 'ideational fit' between the overarching, paradigmatic ideas of global neoliberalism and the political economic realities of the Kenyan context. Between 2003 and 2013, for example, Kibaki's inner circle needed no convincing of the merits of particular economic policies, as many of them were, like Kibaki, trained economists who had risen through Kenya's economic technocracy. In many respects, their ideas aligned with neoclassical economics, reflecting the fact that many had studied at Western universities and worked for Western donors (O'Brien and Ryan 2001, Upadhyaya 2020). However, in others, their vision diverged somewhat from orthodoxy, especially in the way that it pushed back against more rigid forms of inflation-targeting and deficit reduction. This was encapsulated by a senior ex-CBK official, who recalled spending a lot of time 'reassuring the IMF that we wanted the same outcomes ... it was just a slightly different way of getting there'.[37]

The nature of Kibaki's presidency offers wider insights into the role of ideas, and not just interests, in motivating political behaviour. Kibaki became president when Kenya possessed a *narrow-dispersed* political settlement that, according to the conceptual framework, appears to hold least promise for PoEs because of the perverse incentives it generates. These hypotheses certainly held for Moi's presidency but, under Kibaki, shared ideas around national sovereignty, fiscal discipline, NPM, and the productive potential of public investment motivated Kibaki and his technopols to try and protect Kenya's economic technocracy from the more corrosive pressures associated with its political settlement. As a result, Kenya witnessed higher and more inclusive socio-economic outcomes during the 2000s, even though these were not matched by political advancements, as Kibaki resisted demands for a new constitution and more inclusive politics. Indeed, according to many informants, Kibaki partly resisted these demands precisely because he felt that unravelling the powers of the executive would undermine the ability to enact his development agenda. This did happen after Kenya's 2007/08 crisis, as the social foundations of Kenya's political settlement expanded and the dispersion of power within it increased. Kibaki continued to try and support the economic technocracy but struggled to centralize rent-seeking pressures, control bureaucratic

[37] Interview, ex-CBK official, Nairobi, 27 March 2019.

appointments, or overcome coordination issues as before. Nonetheless, the ideas of his inner circle continued to play a restraining role on the pressures generated by Kenya's shifting political settlement. This became clear when Kibaki was replaced by President Kenyatta in 2013, whose lack of interest in similar ideas, especially around fiscal discipline and having a 'respect for institutions', has subjected Kenya's economic technocracy to an even greater set of challenges.[38]

PoEs and state-building in Kenya: Policy and research implications

Can a strategy of supporting PoEs be an important part of a more realistic 'with-the-grain' governance agenda? The dispersion of power within Kenya's political settlement means that political leaders will often be so preoccupied with fending off challenges from rival factions, both inside and outside of the ruling coalition, and so lacking in the enforcement powers required to centralize rent-seeking, that protecting even a handful of organizations at any one time will be a politically consuming task—let alone the kinds of state-wide reforms that the Good Governance agenda promoted (Grindle 2017).

As to where efforts to promote PoEs could be directed, this research has found clear justifications for a continued focus on the economic technocracy, which has, and always will, play a central role in driving any country's development (Besley and Persson 2011, Bräutigam et al. 2008). Indeed, the Covid-19 pandemic is only affirming the necessity of having capable economic technocracies, as the limited fiscal basis of the state in many African countries—and, recently in Kenya, its shrinking fiscal basis—has left political leaders with 'very blunt tools' for navigating such crises.[39]

Yet this research also suggests the need to rethink how economic technocracies like Kenya's are configured, and with what tasks they should (or should not) be mandated. For example, there are questions about whether central banks should be so narrowly confined to inflation-targeting when this can come at the expense of more active, productivist forms of directed lending that East Asian developmental states used in their development strategies (Amsden 1989) and which may be critical for steering sustainable economic transformations in the face of climate change (Volz 2017). Similarly, there are questions about whether KRA should be so closely modelled on a Western tax authority, and whether external actors have placed too much emphasis on capacities to collect particular taxes, like VAT, which are not only potentially regressive, but also have less revenue-generating potential in countries with large informal sectors (Wawire 2020). According to KRA insiders, informal and micro businesses have been largely 'ignored', when bringing

---

[38] Interview, ex-CBK official, 18 April 2019.
[39] https://kenopalo.com/2020/04/13/some-policy-lessons-from-covid-19/.

them into the tax net 'could eventually generate lots of revenue'[40] and potentially strengthen the state's social contract with citizens.

In addition to thinking about the mandates of these organizations, findings from this research suggest that more attention should be directed towards enhancing coordination between them. Informants stressed that the 'triangular relationship between a finance ministry, central bank, and revenue authority is so important.'[41] However, technical assistance—in Kenya and beyond—has often adopted a siloed approach, focusing more on building the internal effectiveness and technical capacities of organizations, rather than the kinds of external capabilities that allow them to coordinate and cooperate with one another. Indeed, the very logic of turning central banks and revenue authorities into autonomous/semi-autonomous authorities was to 'intentionally distance them from other branches of government', including line ministries like the Treasury (Moore et al. 2018: 200). In the process, though, they have become detached from each other, resulting in growing disconnects between fiscal and monetary policies. Practitioners and researchers, then, should not just be focused on building individual 'pockets' of effectiveness, but whole integrated 'networks' (Porter and Watts 2017: 249) or 'channels' of effectiveness (Kelsall and Seiha 2014: 11), across what Michael Roll terms the 'topography of state performance' in the closing chapter of this book.

Finally, it should be stressed that efforts to build PoEs, or networks of effectiveness (NoEs), should not be confined to the economic technocracy. There is a sense, in Kenya and beyond, that donors have focused their capacity-building efforts on economic technocracies, neglecting other parts of the state (Johnson 2015, O'Brien and Ryan 2001). Certainly, the economic technocracy is the only part of the Kenyan state in which donors have encouraged extensive use of special salary structures and recruitment practices. This has allowed CBK, KRA, and the Treasury to attract 'some of Kenya's best and smartest people'; but, equally, it has generated few spillovers for the rest of the bureaucracy, and perhaps even done the opposite, by drawing talented officials away from it. Indeed, the only real beneficiaries of spillovers have been donors and consultancy firms, who seek the skills (and connections) of Kenya's economic technocrats and are about the only employers who can offer comparable remuneration. It is beyond the remit of this chapter to specify where other PoEs, or NoEs, might usefully be promoted. However, it points to a need to be selective in identifying the areas where the greatest possible gains, and spillovers, can be achieved, and for this process to be guided by a contextualized understanding of Kenya's political economy, and its likely pathways to sustainable transformation, rather than impulses towards 'isomorphic mimicry' (Andrews et al. 2017). As early success unlocks new opportunities in related areas of activity, these efforts can then be scaled up over time, as part of a phased and

---

[40] Interview, ex-KRA official, Nairobi, 9 May 2019.
[41] Interview, parastatal chairperson, Nairobi, 5 March 2019.

more iterative approach to state-building than was promoted as part of the Good Governance agenda.

References

Amsden, A. (1989). *Asia's Next Giant: South Korea and Late Industrialization*. New York: Oxford University Press.

Andrews, M., Pritchett, L., and Woolcock, M. (2017). *Building State Capability: Evidence, Analysis, Action*. Oxford: Oxford University Press.

Arriola, L. (2013). *Multiethnic Coalitions in Africa: Business Financing of Opposition Election Campaigns*. Cambridge: Cambridge University Press.

Barkan, J. and Chege, M. (1989). 'Decentralising the State: District Focus and the Politics of Reallocation in Kenya', *Journal of Modern African Studies*, 27(3): 431–53.

Besley, T. and Persson, T. (2011). *Pillars of Prosperity: The Political Economics of Development Clusters*. Princeton, NJ: Princeton University Press.

Boone, C., Dyzenhaus, A., Manji, A., Gateri, C., Ouma, S., Owino, J., Gargule, A., and Klopp, J. (2018). 'Land Law Reform in Kenya: Devolution, Veto Players, and the Limits of an Institutional Fix', *African Affairs*, 118(471): 215–37.

Branch, D. and Cheeseman, N. (2008). 'Democratization, Sequencing, and State Failure in Africa: Lessons from Kenya', *African Affairs*, 108(430): 1–26.

Branch, D., Cheeseman, N., and Gardner, L. (2010). *Our Turn to Eat: Politics in Kenya since 1950*. Munster: Lit Verlag.

Bräutigam, D., Fjeldstad, O.-H., and Moore, M. (2008). *Taxation and State-building in Developing Countries*. Cambridge: Cambridge University Press.

Brownbridge, M. and Harvey, C. (1998). *Banking in Africa: The Impact of Financial Sector Reform since Independence*. Oxford: James Currey.

CBK (2017). 'Annual Financial Sector Stability Report'. Nairobi: CBK.

Cheeseman, N. (2009). 'Kenya since 2002: The More Things Change the More They Stay the Same'. In A. Mustapha and L. Whitfield (eds), *Turning Points in African Democracy*. London: James Currey. 94–113.

Chege, M. (2008). 'Kenya: Back from the Brink?' *Journal of Democracy*, 19(4): 125–39.

Chege, M. (2020). 'The Political Economy of Foreign Aid to Kenya'. In N. Cheeseman, K. Kanyinga, and G. Lynch (eds), *The Oxford Handbook of Kenyan Politics*. Oxford: Oxford University Press. 547–61.

Cheserem, M. (2006). *The Will to Succeed: An Autobiography*. Nairobi: Jomo Kenyatta Foundation.

Dafe, F. (2019). 'The Politics of Finance: How Capital Sways African Central Banks'. *The Journal of Development Studies*, 55(2): 311–27.

Evans, P. (1995). *Embedded Autonomy: States and Industrial Transformation*. Princeton, NJ: Princeton University Press.

Gill, S. (1995). 'Globalisation, Market Civilisation, and Disciplinary Neoliberalism', *Millennium*, 24(3): 399–423.

Grindle, M. S. (2017). 'Good Governance, RIP: A Critique and an Alternative', *Governance*, 30(1): 17–22.

Hassan, M. (2020). *Regime Threats and State Solutions: Bureaucratic Loyalty and Embeddedness in Kenya*. Cambridge: Cambridge University Press.

Hassan, M. and O'Mealia, T. (2020). 'Representative Bureaucracy, Role Congruence, and Kenya's Gender Quota', *Governance*, 33(4): 809–27.

IMF. (2009). Kenya: Selected Issues and Statistical Appendix. Country Report No. 09/192. Washington, DC: IMF.

Johnson, M. (2015). 'Donor Requirements and Pockets of Effectiveness in Senegal's Bureaucracy', *Development Policy Review*, 33(6): 783–804.

Joignant, A. (2011). 'The Politics of Technopols: Resources, Political Competence and Collective Leadership in Chile', *Journal of Latin American Studies*, 43(3): 517–46.

Kajwanja, P. (2009). 'Courting Genocide: Populism, Ethno-nationalism and the Informalisation of Violence in Kenya's 2008 post-election Crisis', *Journal of Contemporary African Studies*, 27(3): 365–87.

Kajwanja, P. and Southall, R. (2009). 'Kenya—A Democracy in Retreat?' *Journal of Contemporary African Studies*, 27(3): 259–77.

Kanyinga, K. (2016). 'Devolution and the New Politics of Development in Kenya', *African Studies Review*, 59(3): 155–67.

Kelsall, T. and Seiha, H. (2014). 'The Political Economy of Inclusive Health Care in Cambodia'. Working Paper 43. Manchester: Effective States and Inclusive Development Research Centre, University of Manchester.

Kimenyi, M., Mwega, F, and Ndung'u, N. (2016). *The African Lions: Kenya Country Case Study*. Washington, DC: Brookings Institution.

Lavers, T. and Hickey, S. (2021). 'Alternative Routes to the Institutionalisation of Social Transfers in Sub-Saharan Africa: Political Survival Strategies and Transnational Policy Coalitions', *World Development*, 146(2021): 105549.

Leonard, D. (1991). *African Successes: Four Public Managers of Kenyan Rural Development*. Berkeley, CA: University of California Press.

Leys, C. (1975). *Underdevelopment in Kenya: The Political Economy of Neo-colonialism*. London: Heinemann.

Maina, W. (2019). *State Capture: Inside Kenya's Inability to Fight Corruption*. Nairobi: AfriCOG.

Manji, A. (2012). 'The grabbed state: lawyers, politics and public land in Kenya'. *Journal of Modern African Studies*, 50(3): 467–492.

McDonnell, E. M. (2017). 'The Patchwork Leviathan: How Pockets of Bureaucratic Governance Flourish within Institutionally Diverse Developing States', *American Sociological Review*, 82(3): 476–510.

Moore, M. and Prichard, W. (2017). 'How Can Governments of Low-income Countries Collect More Tax Revenue?' Working paper 70. Brighton: ICTD.

Moore, M., Prichard, W. and Fjeldstad, O.-H. (2018). *Taxing Africa: Coercion, Reform and Development*. London: Zed Books.

Mosley, P. and Chiripanhura, B. (2016). 'The African Political Business Cycle: Varieties of Experience', *Journal of Development Studies*, 52(7): 917–32.

Mueller, S. (2011). 'Dying to Win: Elections, Political Violence, and Institutional Decay in Kenya', *Journal of Contemporary African Studies*, 29(1): 99–117.

Murunga, G. and Nasong'o, S. (2006). 'Bent on Self-destruction: The Kibaki Regime in Kenya', *Journal of Contemporary African Studies*, 24(1): 1–28.

Newell, P. and Phillips, J. (2016). 'Neoliberal Energy Transitions in the South: Kenyan Experiences', *Geoforum*, 74(2016): 39–48.

Ndii, D. (2020). *Highway Robbery: Budgeting for State Capture*. Nairobi: AfriCOG.

O'Brien, F. and Ryan, T. (2001). 'Kenya'. In Devarajan, S., Dollar, D., and Holmgren, T. (eds), *Aid and Reform in Africa: Lessons from Ten Case Studies*. Washington, DC: World Bank. 469–532.

Opalo, K. (2019). *Legislative Development in Africa: Politics and Postcolonial Legacies*. Cambridge: Cambridge University Press.

Opalo, K. (2020). 'Citizen Political Knowledge and Accountability: Survey Evidence on Devolution in Kenya', *Governance*, 33(4): 849–69.

Porisky, A. (2020). 'The Distributional Politics of Social Transfers in Kenya'. Working Paper 155. Manchester: Effective States and Inclusive Development Research Centre, University of Manchester.

Porter, D. and Watts, M. (2017). 'Righting the Resource Curse: Institutional Politics and State Capabilities in Edo State, Nigeria'. *The Journal of Development Studies*, 53(2): 249–63.

Prichard, W. (2015). *Taxation, Responsiveness and Accountability in Sub-Saharan Africa: The Dynamics of Tax Bargaining*. Cambridge: Cambridge University Press.

Roll, M. (2014). *The Politics of Public Sector Performance: Pockets of Effectiveness in Developing Countries*. Oxford: Routledge.

Tyce, M. (2019). 'The Politics of Industrial Policy in a Context of Competitive Clientelism: The Case of Kenya's Garment Export Sector', *African Affairs*, 118(472): 553–79.

Tyce, M. (2020a). 'The Politics of Central Banking in Kenya: Balancing Political and Developmental Interests'. Working Paper 130. Manchester: Effective States and Inclusive Development Research Centre, University of Manchester.

Tyce, M. (2020b). '"KRA Has the Capacity, But It Is Kept on a Tight Leash": The Politics of Tax Administration and Policy in Kenya'. Working Paper 159. Manchester: Effective States and Inclusive Development Research Centre, University of Manchester.

Tyce, M. (2020c). 'The Kenyan National Treasury: A "Pocket of Effectiveness" Curtailed'. Working Paper 150. Manchester: Effective States and Inclusive Development Research Centre, University of Manchester.

Upadhyaya, R. (2011). 'Analysing the Sources and Impact of Segmentation in the Banking Sector: A Case Study of Kenya'. PhD. London: School of Oriental and African Studies.

Upadhyaya, R. (2020). 'Kenya: "Dubai" in the Savannah'. In E. Jones (ed.), *The Political Economy of Bank Regulation in Developing Countries: Risk and Reputation*. Oxford: Oxford University Press. 218–38.

Volz, U. (2017). 'On the Role of Central Banks in Enhancing Green Finance'. Nairobi: UN Environment.

Waris, A. (2017). 'How Kenya Has Implemented and Adjusted to the Changes in International Transfer Pricing Regulations: 1920–2016'. Working Paper 69. Brighton: ICTD.

Wawire, N. (2020). 'Constraints to Enhanced Revenue Mobilization and Spending Quality in Kenya'. Policy Paper 163. Washington, DC: CGD.

Yohou, D. and Goujon, M. (2017). 'Reassessing Tax Effort in Developing Countries'. Working Paper 186. Clermont-Ferrand: FERDI.

Zeitz, A. (2019). 'Financial Statecraft of Debtors: The Political Economy of External Finance in Africa'. PhD. Oxford: University of Oxford.

5

State Capacity-building in Zambia amidst Shifting Political Coalitions and Ideologies

Caesar Cheelo and Marja Hinfelaar

Introduction

The shock expressed both within and beyond Zambia by the firing of Denny Kalyalya, a competent governor of the Bank of Zambia (BoZ), in 2020, revealed two things. First, that the BoZ had remained, unlike most of the public sector in Zambia, largely unscathed by the politicization of the bureaucracy that had been increasingly apparent since 2011. Until recently, the BoZ had remained an island of professional effectiveness, delivering on its mandate amidst overall bureaucratic decline. Second, and whilst the move was directly linked to the fiscal pressures catalysed by Zambia's populist mode of politics ahead of the 2021 elections, the resulting plunge in Zambia's currency and Eurobonds also reflected the key role that the BoZ had played in maintaining Zambia's fiscal credibility amidst disruptive relations with international financial institutions (IFIs). The sharp decline of Zambia's economic institutions stands in contrast to the gains that were made in the 2000s, when a technocratic consensus resulted in relatively high levels of performance amongst economic agencies that included but also stretched well beyond the central bank.

In this chapter, we trace the trajectory of the three main public-sector organizations that have achieved the status of 'pockets of effectiveness' (PoEs) in Zambia, namely the Ministry of Finance (MoF), the BoZ, and Zambia Revenue Authority (ZRA). These economic organizations only fully blossomed during the 'technocratic era' of neoliberalism (2001–2008), before then struggling to fulfil their mandates during the Patriotic Front (PF) era, from 2011 to 2021. All three PoEs emerged during a period when state capacity was undermined by structural adjustment programmes (Mkandawire 2017). During this period, economic policies were prescribed by the IFIs and bilateral donors and then carried out by a small political and technocratic elite at the national level. The reforms that led to the 'modernization' and emergence of these PoEs were largely driven by the need to integrate Zambia's economy into the global capitalist order, which meant a clean break from the country's previous state-led economy. While the PoEs become highly functional in a narrow organizational sense, they turned out over

Caesar Cheelo and Marja Hinfelaar, *State Capacity-building in Zambia amidst Shifting Political Coalitions and Ideologies*. In: *Pockets of Effectiveness and the Politics of State-building and Development in Africa*. Edited by Sam Hickey, Oxford University Press. © Oxford University Press (2023). DOI: 10.1093/oso/9780192864963.003.0005

time to be politically unsustainable in the face of developmental failures, alternative ideological commitments and, above all, elite fragmentation and political populism.

This study fills an important gap in the literature, as there are limited studies on Zambia's organizations of economic governance, with the partial exception of the revenue authority. This void is partially caused by characterizations of the state in Africa as being '(neo)patrimonial' in character and the related tendency to understudy the actual role of bureaucracy and bureaucrats (Chapter 1). Employing the conceptual and methodological approach set out in Chapter 2, this chapter is based on documentary analysis and in-depth case studies of each organization based on over sixty-five key informant interviews with representatives of all key stakeholders (senior bureaucrats, politicians, ministers, governors, corporate lawyers, civil society, embassies) and participant observation.[1] These case-study investigations tracked the performance of each organization from 1991 to date, including quantitative analysis of available performance data. This approach revealed two distinct performance periods, the first of which ran from around 2001 to 2008, when all three organizations delivered relatively effectively on their mandate. This was followed by a period of decline from around 2011 to 2021, with the exception of the BoZ, which was able to maintain strong organizational leadership and resist political pressures for longer than its fiscal counterparts.

The chapter continues with an overview of Zambia's political settlement and general patterns of governance and public-sector performance over time. It then describes how we identified our three organizations, before first setting out and then analysing their performance trajectories. We conclude with a discussion of the strategic and policy implications that flow from this analysis, and some broader reflections on the future of state-building and development in Zambia.

Zambia's political settlement and the technocracy

Economic governance in Zambia has been affected by the country's rapidly shifting political settlements over the past three decades. In particular, the bureaucracy has struggled to fulfil its mandate under the pressures arising from a heightened political competition and the short-term goals that accompany the interplay of multi-partyism with an enduring politics of clientelism. However, the continued functioning of the BoZ until very recently suggests that 'dispersed' political settlements do not automatically undermine bureaucratic autonomy (cf. Khan 2010). The prospects for an institution to emerge as a PoE are also shaped by organizational factors, namely the scope and clarity of its mandate; the strength and political linkages of its leadership; and its internal culture and cohesiveness

---

[1] One author has cooperated with all three organizations over the last five years.

(Grindle 2012, Roll 2014). Transnational actors and regional epistemic com-munities also play important roles in shaping the incentives, ideas, and relative autonomy of bureaucratic actors.

Since independence, Zambia has had a highly centralized and presidential-ized system of governance. In Kaunda's era (1964–1990) the concentration of power was helpful in terms of offering a longer-term vision and the capacity to deliver. Yet, the broad social foundations of Zambia's settlement required that inclusive coalitions needed to be forged through elite-level bargaining across mul-tiple ethnic-linguistic groups. This led to a settlement that was good for stability but less conducive to development, with the elitist bargain incentivizing rulers to buy-off different constituencies with public-sector resources and jobs (Lindemann 2011). The strategy of building inclusive coalitions and pursuing state-driven development was only sustainable when the country's natural resource base was valued highly within global commodity markets (Cheelo, Hinfelaar, and Ndulo 2020). The economic decline from the mid-1970s onward, caused by the oil cri-sis and plummeting copper prices, resulted in severe food shortages in the late 1980s, which in turn undermined Kaunda's political dominance. This helped catalyse the re-introduction of multi-party democracy in 1991, with Frederick Chiluba's Movement for Multiparty Democracy (MMD) taking power. The transi-tion was accompanied by an ideological shift from state- to market-led economics that required a restructuring and repositioning of Zambia's economic gover-nance and the civil service more broadly. Liberalization led to ruptures between those in power and major socio-economic interest groups like the trade unions (Rakner 2003), whilst structural adjustment undermined previously high levels of investment in social sectors, notably health and education.

The reintroduction of multi-party rule in 1991 saw Zambia's political settlement shift from a broad-concentrated to a broad-dispersed form of political settlement,[2] which has seen two electoral turnovers (United National Independence Party [UNIP] to MMD in 1991, and MMD to PF in 2011). The coalitional basis of both the MMD and PF has shifted over time and the privatization of state companies like the mines—the traditional mode of patronage—made State House, political parties, and political actors more susceptible to the interests of politico-economic entrepreneurs. This in turn had a profound effect on public finances, as alterna-tive rents were sought elsewhere within government entities, including through government contracts, procurement, and pension funds. In the process, it under-mined the relatively formal structures that previously guided accountability and oversight of the business lobby and associated deal-making processes (Mosley 2017).

From 2015 onwards, Zambia has been showing signs of becoming increasingly authoritarian in character, as President Lungu has sought to re-concentrate power,

---

[2] See Chapter 2 on political settlements.

place limits on oppositional politics, and undermine certain accepted modes of inclusive incorporation with regards to the broad social foundations of Zambia's political settlement. The shift to multi-party democracy in 1991 did little to change the wide powers conferred on the office of the president by the Independence constitution, which mean that the president is not obliged to followed advice tendered by any person or authority. The lack of institutionalization of political parties and their lack of ideological coherence has also undermined state capacity-building and policy coherence over time. Like the UNIP in 1991, the MMD dissipated after it lost power in 2011. By 2014, the party had split, with many members moving to either the PF or United Party for National Development (UPND). In the 2016 elections, MMD did not even field a presidential candidate. President Lungu's second term has been full of controversy and he faces significant challenges to his hold on power, from those within his own party who oppose his bid to contest for a third time in 2021, and from opposition parties, particularly UPND.

On the back of sustained economic growth caused by the commodity supercycle from 2004, and also Zambia's graduation from the enhanced heavily indebted poor countries (HIPC) initiative in 2005, the role of donors in Zambia has greatly diminished. Their contribution to government revenue dropped from around 40 per cent in the 1990s to less than 2 per cent by 2018.[3] This has weakened their leverage vis-à-vis the government, but has also put civil-society organizations under financial pressure, leaving them more susceptible to political co-optation. Zambia has always lacked a strong domestic capitalist class capable of supporting other export-led earnings or local manufacturing (Caramento forthcoming, Craig 1999) and the ruling coalition has few positive links to productive capitalists, making it very difficult to develop and implement a proactive economic development strategy. International capital, most notably in the form of mining companies that benefitted from the privatization of Zambia's mines at the end of the 1990s, is influential and impacts on the direction of taxation and monetary policy. The International Monetary Fund (IMF), which had been further sidelined from the mid-2000s by Zambia's capacity to borrow on the private markets (Eurobonds) and attract concessional loans from China, has been re-established as an important player since 2018. Amidst growing indebtedness and fiscal indiscipline, Zambia has applied for funding from the IMF, but seen negotiations fail due to its apparent inability and unwillingness to impose discipline within its realm of economic governance. In November 2020, Zambia defaulted on its first Eurobond repayment.[4]

The British-style civil-service system that Zambia inherited after Independence was reformed through a process of 'Zambianization' that saw the civil service

---

[3] National Budget Speeches, 2005–2018. See https://www.mof.gov.zm/?page_id=5248 (accessed 29 June 2021).

[4] See https://jubileedebt.org.uk/blog/zambias-debt-default (accessed 29 June 2021).

expand massively in terms of numbers and functions (Tordoff 1980). Following the economic crisis in the 1970s, the pay, skills, and also the professionalized culture of the civil service started to erode. In the 1980s, many professionals left Zambia and moved overseas. Weak supervision and accountability mechanisms eventually resulted in few incentives for civil servants to implement formal rules, and the allocation of resources became gradually more determined by the relative bargaining power of civil servants vis-à-vis their bureaucratic and political peers and local 'strongmen' (Simutanyi and Hinfelaar 2018). Repeated efforts to reform the public service have been undertaken in the wake of structural adjustment programmes during the 1980s, including the 1993 Public Service Reform Programme that greatly reduced the number of civil servants and dismantled most state-owned enterprises. A further round of civil-service reform was catalysed by Zambia's Public-Sector Capacity Building Project from 2000, although various evaluation reports suggest these reforms have yielded no great improvement as compared to some other countries (see Figure 5.1).

Political will is cited as one major hindrance for these reforms, but Zambia's continued dependence on copper, a commodity subject to volatile and unpredictable pricing shifts, also helped place the country under constant fiscal stress. The boom in commodity prices from the mid-2000s enabled government to steadily increase the number of ministries and civil servants, reversing the earlier lean period for the civil service. With PF taking power in 2011, public-sector wages were increased by 35 per cent in 2012, contributing to an enormous wage bill that grew by 20.1 per cent per year on average over 2012 to 2014 compared to 9.1 per cent per

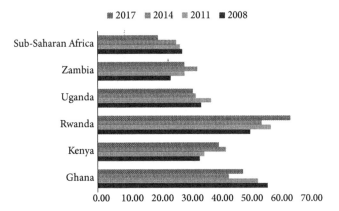

Figure 5.1 Government effectiveness in Africa and our five countries, 2008–2017

Source: World Governance Indicators (https://databank.worldbank.org/source/worldwide-governance-indicators).

annum during 2009–2011, despite falling levels of real GDP growth).[5] Because of fluctuating revenues, Zambia has a long history of cash budgets replacing appropriated budgets, which has undermined budget predictability. The flip side is that a public sector career is now seen as an attractive option, offering better wages and more long-term security than the private sector or civil society and has helped to reverse the earlier brain drain. Ideas around fiscal responsibility, debt levels, and macroeconomic stability became quite firmly settled within the economic technocracy during the 1990s and 2000s and, although controversial in terms of the implications for Zambia's development trajectory, this shared ideological perspective arguably helped organizations like the MoF, the BoZ, and ZRA to gain greater coherence and develop a shared organizational culture.

The literature on state capacity and public-sector performance in Zambia is very limited. Many research outputs are linked to evaluations of IMF reform programmes, meaning that the discussion of state capacity 'has been within a highly normative framework so that only capacities to do what is deemed desirable by particular individuals or institutions are considered' (Mkandawire 2017: 184). Di John finds that while Zambian economic policies might have been weak, the state had been resilient 'against all odds' (2010: 6) in terms of maintaining a centralized patronage system. The pressures on state resilience seemed to mount from the late 2000s onwards with the de-institutionalization of the political parties, as the result of growing factionalism along regional and ethnic lines (Cheeseman and Hinfelaar 2010). This in turn started to affect political stability and state resilience, and the functioning of the state as whole. As discussed below, the rapid turnover of presidents, parties, and factions has had a negative effect on the bureaucracy, as changeovers were constant, ranging from State House staff all the way down to the level of departmental directors in ministries and also embassy staff. Ministries were variously added, removed, and renamed and the boards of regulatory bodies overhauled by every new government (2011, 2015, 2016). Appointments are now widely seen to be based more on party-political affiliation and being representative of a particular social identity, rather than on competence.[6] By positioning itself as a vanguard party, PF had increased political interference in the running of the technocracy and overseen an influx of political cadres, without the required qualifications and experience, into ministries, regulatory bodies, and state-owned enterprises.

---

[5] Complied and computed from Central Government Operations tables in (various) MoF Annual Economic Reports for 2006 to 2016.

[6] This observation on appointments was taken from the expert survey discussed in the next section.

Identifying PoEs in Zambia

In the absence of secondary data on the performance of specific ministries, departments, and agencies within Zambia, we undertook an expert survey to try and identify high-performing parts of the public sector (see Chapter 2 for the methodology). From July to October 2017, twenty interviews were held with public-sector experts, derived from the private sector, international organizations, think tanks, academia, and civil service. Despite its methodological limitations, the survey revealed some interesting insights.

All but one informant observed that most ministries in Zambia had become less effective over the past decade. All point to this decline being caused by political factors, namely the increased political interference within the civil service since PF came into power, even more so since Lungu's election in 2015. Respondents noted that political appointments now reached beyond ministers and permanent secretaries to director level within ministries, introducing a sense of insecurity amongst officials that incentivized them to be risk averse. The same decline was identified with regulatory authorities, with many of our experts arguing that they have become a threat to the growth of the economy.

The consensus was that the financial and economic ministries performed better than average, particularly parts of the MoF, the BoZ, and ZRA.[7] Survey respondents noted that this was largely because of their mandates, the political incentives to ensure that they functioned effectively, and international pressure and superior working conditions. Nonetheless, as revealed below, the performance of these key nodes of economic governance has fluctuated significantly over time, often in line with shifting political settlement dynamics.

The ups and downs of Zambia's PoEs

This section sets out the performance trajectories of Zambia's MoF, revenue authority, and central bank in turn. The summaries represent condensed versions of the more detailed case-study papers, respectively Hinfelaar and Sichone (2019) and Cheelo and Hinfelaar (2020a, 2020b).

Zambia's Ministry of Finance

The MoF was established in 1959 during the colonial period. Although the Ministry of Finance (Incorporation) Act invested the MoF with the legal authority to discharge the mandate of the finance ministry, this autonomy soon clashed

---

[7] Another organisation singled out for praise was the Seed Certification and Control Institute.

with Kaunda's ambitions after Zambia's shift to one-party rule in 1973. Before the reforms of the 1990s, policymaking was determined by the influential and left-leaning National Commission for Development Planning (NCDP), many of whose staff had been trained in the Eastern Bloc. In the 1990s, this unit was dismantled and integrated back into the MoF, creating a perennial tension:

> We, as classic economists, looked down upon them. They were utopian in their planning, whereas we at Budget were interested in realism and balancing the books.[8]

These changes had far-reaching consequences for the MoF, as it led to the decline of planning capacity and a fragmentation of functions with available staff resources spread thinly (Bird 2009: 9).

The MoF was now mandated to maintain a stable macroeconomic environment, formulate revenue and expenditure policies to finance the national budget, and manage a sustainable level of debt. Between 1991 and 2002, Zambia's growth rates and fiscal balance fluctuated significantly. In 2002, Zambia improved its performance, especially from 2006 onwards after graduating from HIPC and benefitting from historically high copper prices. From 2015, the third performance period, there has been deterioration across most indicators. Overall, we distilled three distinct periods of performance since the 1991 reforms:

- A period of mixed performance, especially under Minister of Finance Ronald Penza (1991 to 1998)
- A period of economic growth and strong performance, especially during Ng'andu Magande's ministerial tenure (2003–2008)
- A period from 2011 to 2021 that has seen bureaucratic and economic decline, especially under Alexander Chikwanda.

Performance Indicators

The Budget Office was identified as one of the more effective departments within MoF. While budget discipline has been a constant problem in Zambia, and has led to regular supplementary and excess budget expenditures, there is variety in performance over the years. In Figure 5.2, we see the fluctuations over time in terms of fiscal deficits from 1994 to 2017. Fiscal deficit trends show that deviations before 2000 were much wider and then became narrow up to 2010, which our interviewees traced to adherence to fiscal and budgetary discipline on the part of the president and minister of finance. The main exception during this period involved an episode of deviation around the closely fought 2006 elections. From 2012, fiscal

---

[8] Interview with retired senior MoF official, 2 March 2018 quoted in Hinfelaar and Sichone (2019).

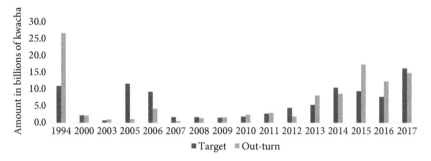

Figure 5.2 Fiscal deficit trends in Zambia, 1994–2017

Source: Ministry of Finance and budget speeches, Zambia (https://www.parliament.gov.zm/taxonomy/term/54 (accessed 29 June 2021)).

Table 5.1 Trends in selected Public Expenditure and Financial Accountability (PEFA) indicators in Zambia, 2005–2016

Indicator	2005	2008	2012	2016
Aggregate revenue out-turn compared to original approved budget	A	A	C	C+
Classification of the budget	C	A	B	B
Extent of unreported government operations	D+	B+	NR	
Transparency of intergovernmental fiscal relations	D+	D+	C	
Oversight of aggregate fiscal risk from other public-sector entities	C	C	C	
Public access to key fiscal information	B	A	B	D
Orderliness and participation in the annual budget process	B	C+	B+	
Multi-year perspective in fiscal planning, expenditure policy, and budgeting	C+	B	B	

Source: PEFA 2017.

deficits have fuelled a rise in public debt (i.e. both external and domestic), pushing debt to levels of over 75 per cent of GDP (IMF 2019).

Table 5.1 also shows an improvement in budget performance in the 2003–2008 era. The Public Expenditure and Financial Accountability (PEFA) table sets out the MoF performance in relation to four points in time between 2005 and 2016. To cover the pre-PEFA period of the 1990s we picked up information from auditor general reports, the economic annual reports and a World Bank report on cash budgets. Overall, these reports reveal low levels of budgetary performance, specifically in the late 1990s when unconstitutional supplementary budget expenditures led to a number of budget crises (Economics and Statistics Analysis 2004).[9] According to the auditor general reports, the election year of 1996 not only saw 14.74 per cent of under-expenditure, which was attributed to the non-release of funds by the MoF and Economic Development, it also contained unauthorized expenditure amounting to 11.09 per cent of the actual expenditure (Auditor General reports 1996–1998). After an improvement of the budget performance in the 2000s under Mwanawasa, the period we defined as 'effective', the budget performance goes into decline, particularly after 2012.

PEFA indicators show a decline of budget discipline: whereas pre-2015 arrears were less than 2 per cent of total expenditure, the latest report for 2016 indicates a sharp increase of more than 10 per cent of total expenditure (PEFA 2017). It shows a relatively poor performance by almost all indicators for management of assets and liabilities, and predictability and control in budget execution, but budget reliability, transparency of public finances, and accounting/reporting have mixed results (PEFA 2017).

Zambia experienced a decade of strong economic growth from 2004 to 2014, averaging 7.4 per cent a year. This growth has been linked, first and foremost, to the rise of copper prices and international debt relief, but also to the relatively high bureaucratic performance under President Mwanawasa. This era was preceded by sweeping and controversial reforms that led to the privatization of state-owned companies and the mining industry and the reduction and reform of the civil service. Both periods saw strong-minded leaders in the MoF, who enjoyed support from State House, a prerequisite for the functioning of the ministry, and also a shared commitment to a technocratic mode of governance aimed at embedding neoliberal economic policies.

Counterintuitively, from the perspective of political settlements theory, this period of effective performance by MoF (against its mandate at least), was also marked by high levels of political competition and power dispersal. We identify a coalition of political and technocratic actors able to hold out against the short-termism usually associated with these pressures, inspired in part to react against the economic and political mismanagement of the 1990s. An unusually consultative president, the lawyerly Mwanawasa deliberately chose a technocratic cabinet, many of whom were political outsiders, including the minister of finance. Good working relationships between the minister, secretary to the treasury, permanent secretaries, and State House (including a key economic advisor as well as the president) established the grounds for policy consistency and implementation.[10]

---

[9] World Bank (1999) and interview, senior official, MoF, 17 January 2019.

[10] This group had all been part of Office of National Development and Planning, which housed the Central Planning Unit under the Director of Planning, under UNIP. Those coming from NCDP carried 'a badge of honour'. They also had a strong academic background and has been active in the Economic Association of Zambia, which became critical of UNIP in the late 1980s.

Wanting to break from donor conditionality and dependency and having the fiscal space to do so due to high copper prices and debt relief, the government sought to chart its own course albeit without significant deviance from the prevailing neoliberal orthodoxy of the time (Jepson 2019). Despite the decline of donor influence, international standards remained consequential, ensuring some adherence to economic conventions, such as macroeconomic stability, single-digit inflation rates, and a liberal foreign exchange regime.

However, the productive cooperation between the executive and technocrats did not outlive the individuals involved, with Mwanawasa dying in office in 2008 and Minister of Finance Magande leaving in the same year. The neoliberal settlement they had established would soon become politically unsustainable in the face of continued impoverishment in society and the populist challenge of the PF. Once in power, the PF's haphazard attempts to chart an alternative development course led to a weakening of professionalism and loss of a sense of direction within the MoF. It also resulted in a decrease in economic growth, despite sustained copper prices, and a growing debt crisis, with the MoF deviating from earlier norms regarding fiscal discipline and debt management.

Zambia Revenue Authority

The ZRA was established in 1994 against the context of falling revenue earnings in Zambia. By the early 1990s, Zambia's tax earnings had dropped from average highs of around 30 per cent of GDP per year in the early 1970s, on the back of high copper prices and a highly formalized economy, to an average of only 13 per cent of GDP per annum.[11] Tax policy in Zambia is guided by the MoF and approved by parliament, while ZRA administers tax policies and laws. ZRA is headed by a commissioner general (CG), who is appointed by the president, without the need for approval from parliament. International actors have long been closely involved in Zambia's tax administration: the IMF, World Bank, and the UK Department for International Development (DFID) supported what was then a fiscal affairs department within the MoF from the early 1990s and ZRA's leadership was in expatriate hands until 2001.

The ZRA is regarded as a relatively high performer in both national and international terms. Zambia's overall tax effort in 2017 was slightly above the average held by the rest of the African Tax Administration Forum's thirty-seven member states and ZRA ranked fourth for revenue productivity (revenue per tax employee), making it one of the most efficient authorities on the continent (African Tax Outlook 2019: 136). However, ZRA's performance has been uneven over time, with

---

[11] External ZRA website: https://www.zra.org.zm/about-us/ (accessed February 2020).

our review suggesting that ZRA has gone through the following performance periods (Cheelo and Hinfelaar 2020b):

- 1994 to 2005: relatively low tax revenue and uneven performance. Strong political and external support for ZRA is undermined by a weak tax policy regime and trade liberalization (IMF 2005); tax-to-GDP ratio varied from 17.2 (1994) to 13.7 (2005).
- 2006 to 2014: relatively good performance in an era of technocratic consensus, economic growth, and organizational reform. Strong political backing for domestic revenue mobilization to counterbalance reduced levels of donor support. Tax policy increasingly fragmented after 2011 although boosted by a windfall tax on natural resources that saw the tax-to-GDP ratio reach 18.2 per cent in FY2013/14, up from 14.08 per cent in 2006.
- 2015 to 2019: relatively weak performance. ZRA receives financial incentives but is undermined by the politically motivated appointments of unqualified staff and a controversial commissioner general plus an incoherent tax policy regime. Tax-to-GDP ratio drops to an average of 15 per cent of GDP.

Indicators

Tax effort can offer a more useful indicator of revenue performance than tax-to-GDP, as it takes into account the level of taxation that a country might be expected to generate given the structure of its economy. Figure 5.3 reveals the positive effects of a far-reaching tax-policy reform programme introduced in 1992 before the establishment of ZRA (Di John 2010). Established by Finance Minister Ronald Penza, the reforms had the political backing of President Chiluba, as well as the support of the IMF. The ongoing privatization process and low copper prices meant that mining contributed very little tax revenue during the 1990s. The graph also reveals shows a high effort shortly after the formation of ZRA in 1994, followed by decline; from 1997 to 2008, Zambia's tax-to-GDP ratio largely flat-lined at around 17–18 per cent per year on average, arguably because expenditure was fairly flat over the period, which meant that there was little pressure being exerted to raise taxes.

From the mid-2000s, revenue collection remained relatively low despite the rapid rise in copper production and high copper prices. Mining tax reforms were urged by civil society, the media, opposition parties, and also donors, all of whom rallied around the 'Windfall Tax'. The new tax regime had the support of all cabinet ministers,[12] but was met with some resistance by some MoF technocrats, who argued that it would stifle the profits of the mining companies. In any event, the Windfall Tax was never fully implemented, as the passing of President Mwanawasa

---

[12] Interview, former Minister of Mines, April 2018.

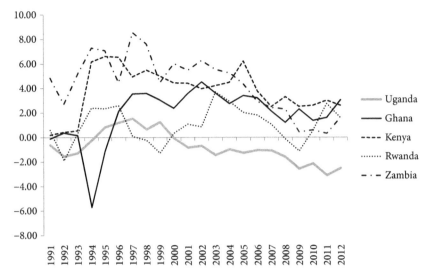

Figure 5.3 Zambia's tax effort 1991–2012 in comparative perspective
Source: Yohou and Goujon (2017).

led not only to an intraparty power struggle but also to the departure of many cabinet ministers championing the Windfall Tax, notably the Minister of Finance Magande. Crucially, the global financial crisis of 2008 led to mining companies lobbying hard against the reforms. In 2009, the Windfall Tax was replaced by a Variable Tax that was less ambitious but which still marked an improvement (Fjeldstad and Heggstad 2011: 73), ensuring that higher tax revenues were sustained until 2014.

The World Bank reflected on this period as follows:

> After ten years of rapid growth and a doubling in size of the economy from 2004 to 2014, Zambia emerged from being a country with a high aid dependency to one where, in 2015, grants provided a meagre 1.4% of revenue compared to 98.6% domestic revenue earned largely through taxation. Revenues increased in real terms as the economy grew from the early 2000s and by 2013, with domestic revenue reaching 16.9% of GDP. It rose further to 18.2% of GDP in 2014 and 18.5% in 2015.
>
> (World Bank 2016: 25)

With our tax effort data ending in 2012, other indicators help us to assess the period from 2012 to 2019, notably: the *expenditure-to-GDP ratio*, a proxy for the amount of fiscal pressure that public spending places on revenue authorities to raise tax revenue; the *non-tax revenue-to-GDP ratio*, a proxy for the amount of fiscal relief in terms of an alternative fiscal revenue source aside from taxes; the

ZRA grant-to-GDP ratio, a proxy for the amount of aggregate financial incentive for the Authority to raise tax revenue; and the *public debt-to-GDP*, also a proxy for the amount of fiscal relief through alternative fiscal revenue source aside from taxes. The main points are that ZRA performance was significantly influenced by expenditure policy, public-debt position, non-tax revenue performance, and grant rewards going to ZRA.[13]

In 2011, PF came into power with expansionary fiscal policies to support its more populist and statist policy agenda. Now able to borrow commercially as a lower-middle-income country, Zambia's increased spending was initially financed out of borrowing (including 2012, 2013, and 2015 Eurobonds) and non-tax revenue adjustments (2013–2016), so relatively little pressure was placed on ZRA to increase performance. In 2015, as President Lungu came into office, an economic crisis hit Zambia and commercial debt service payments also started to escalate, further eroding the fiscal space that PF had inherited in 2011. This started to exert pressure on tax revenue performance, hence reflecting a marginal increase in tax-to-GDP over 2016–2018, in an attempt to keep pace with a massive and growing expenditure appetite. Figure 5.4 incorporates the debt-to-GDP ratio, and this offers part of the explanation for the divergence between the (declining) tax revenue and (increasing) expenditure.

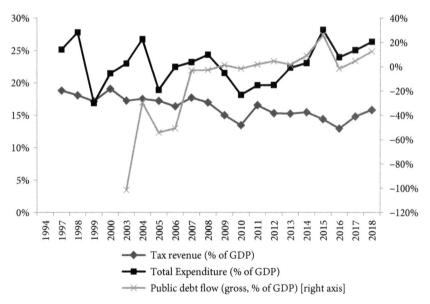

Figure 5.4 Fiscal expenditure and revenue ratios (% of GDP) in Zambia, 1994–2018

Source: Constructed by the authors from data in Annual Economic Reports and Fiscal Tables.

---

[13] Interview, former MoF senior official, 8 March 2020.

Figure 5.5 Variance between targeted and actual tax revenue in Zambia, 1994–2018 (% of target)

Source: Constructed by the authors from data in Annual Economic Reports and Fiscal Tables.

Moreover, as seen in Figure 5.5, the considerable over-expenditure on ZRA (8.7 per cent above target per year on average) was coupled with significantly higher over-expenditures relative to budget targets than in any other sub-period. Therefore, the Lungu period saw the largest expenditure effort and reward effort to ZRA coupled with the second weakest tax revenue collection efforts among the three sub-periods.

ZRA's tax performance is strongly linked to Zambia's shifting political settlements. The tax revenue policy function lies mostly within MoF, which in turn is dependent on the functioning of its minister and his/her relationship with State House. With rapidly changing ruling coalitions from 1990s onward, and the varying influence of the international organizations, Zambia's taxation regimes have veered from fiscal prudence, a policy direction that ultimately undermined MMD's ruling coalition in 2011, to the PF's platform of populist resource nationalism (Caramento 2019). As a result of Zambia's particular political settlements, tax efforts have gone into collecting tax from the large and formal sector, with an uneven effort to tax either the elites (notably on properties and procurement) or the informal sector. At all stages, taxation has remained closely linked to the politics of copper (Bebbington et al. 2018). Because of the emphasis on mining companies, the Large Tax Office (LTO) is where most capacity within ZRA was built, with varying results. Beyond a brief five-year period of effectiveness in the mid-2000s, ZRA has been heavily undermined by both the country's political economy (reliance on mining and associated rents) and politics (personalized forms of competitive clientelism and, under Lungu, vulnerable authoritarianism). The political interference was not cushioned by autonomous leadership either, as we see with the case of the BoZ below. Although all CGs have had the technical competence to perform their roles effectively, and have often received strong support to develop a professionalized cadre within ZRA, the direct appointment of the CG by the president amidst an increasingly dispersed political settlement has rendered the office increasingly vulnerable to patronage and political interference.

Bank of Zambia

Central banking in Zambia started with the establishment of the Bank of Northern Rhodesia in 1938. The Bank was heavily dominated by expatriate staff until Independence in 1964, after which a process of Zambianization was put in place and banking policy was realigned with national interests. Before 1991, the BoZ had a very narrow mandate and limited capacity:

> The Bank was like a government department. When I joined [in the mid-1980s] there were only a minority of graduates. The conditions were better in government than BoZ at the time, so people moved from BoZ to the ministries.[14]

One of the aims of the post-1991 economic reforms was to secure the independence of the BoZ. The 1996 Bank Act reduced the MoF's role in monetary policymaking and, in the words of former BoZ Governor Jacob Mwanza, 'provided (BoZ) more autonomy on matters of monetary policy, financial stability, and macroeconomic policy' (Mwanza, quoted in Bank of Zambia 2014: 93). In the process, the BoZ lost the developmental function it had performed during the 1980s, when it was able to extend credit guarantees to the small and medium enterprise sector. Its mandate was narrowed to focus on achieving and maintaining price and financial-system stability, in order to foster 'sustainable economic development',[15] including through ensuring appropriate monetary policy formulation and implementation and licensing, regulating, and supervising banks and financial service institutions.

From the 2000s onward, the BoZ has been regarded as Zambia's most consistently high-performing public-sector organization, albeit within the narrow confines of neoliberal orthodoxy (Cheelo and Hinfelaar 2020a). During the 1990s, it transformed from an organization that existed primarily to service a state-led command economy to a 'modern' central bank geared towards accommodating the requirements of an IMF-led economic policy reform programme and which operated with relative autonomy, from political pressures at least. Although never entirely free from domestic political pressures, the BoZ has remained remarkably immune to even the increased politicization of the bureaucracy that took place from 2011 onward, both because of its legal autonomy and critical role in 'signalling' credit-worthiness to international financial markets. Aided by the need

---

[14] Former BoZ official, 14 January 2019.
[15] BoZ website: https://www.boz.zm/about-us.htm (accessed 28 June 2021).

to abide by international central banking standards, successive governors were largely able to defend the Bank's mandate vis-à-vis the Executive, although this became more difficult once the PF took power and sought to break away from the neoliberal conventions that the BoZ saw itself as working to uphold.

The effectiveness of the BoZ in delivering on its dual mandate of helping to ensure price and financial stability between 1991 and 2018 can be characterized as follows:

- 1991–2001. Weak performance, involving high inflation and bank failures, in a period of economic decline and high levels of corruption; independence and increased professionalism of staff in 1996 enables the building of a strong economic team.
- 2001–2011. Strong performance on both price and financial stability, during a period of economic growth and technocratic consensus on economic policies.
- 2011–2019. Mixed performance: relatively weak BoZ leadership from 2011 to 2015 and pressures on BoZ policies (effects seen in 2015–2016), followed by strong leadership. But, overall, price and financial stability were maintained. The firing of Governor Kalyaya in 2020 creates uncertainty around the autonomy of the BoZ (Cheelo and Hinfelaar 2020c).

The BoZ's performance over time, 1991–2019

Zambia's inflation rate, which had risen to a peak of 183 per cent in 1993, gradually declined to 26 per cent by 2000 (Figure 5.6). The price instability that emerged in the late 1980s escalated in the early-to-mid-1990s, partially because of the de-control of consumer prices as the then Prices and Income Commission was abolished under structural adjustment. It would only fall to stable single-digit figures for the first time in 2010, when Zambia recorded a rate of 8.5 per cent. The very high commercial-lending interest rates and exchange rate volatility of the 1990s had also significantly dissipated by 2000, setting up a stable macroeconomic environment that allowed the establishment of sustained real GDP growth from 1999 onward.

Improvements in building and maintaining financial stability, particularly sound commercial bank performance, took rather longer for the BoZ to achieve and only came in the late-1990s. The closure of Meridien BIAO Zambia in 1995, after it had risen to become the third largest commercial bank by 1994, placed considerable strain on Zambia's financial system and significantly eroded confidence in the BoZ's capacity to effectively supervise commercial banks (McPherson 2004, Mwape 2014). An upward trend in overall financial stability was only established by around 2002 (Figure 5.7). With the support of the United Nations Development Programme (UNDP), the BoZ also undertook a number of capacity-building activities to improve the efficiency of the financial system (Maimbo 2000: 8).

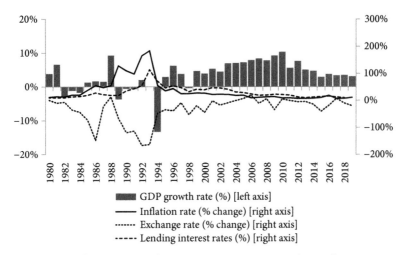

Figure 5.6 Inflation rate, exchange rate, interest rates, and growth in Zambia, 1980–2019

Source: Constructed from World Bank WDI database (accessed Oct 2019).
Note: This was constructed from World Bank World Development Indicators (WDI) data (accessed October 2019). The BOZ data start around 1996, and do not go into the 1980s and early 1990s, so we miss the opportunity of showing the high price (inflation) and exchange rate instabilities in the later 1980s and early 1990s.

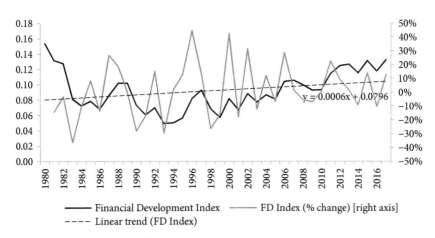

Figure 5.7 Financial stability in Zambia, 1980–2016
Source: https://data.imf.org/?sk=F8032E80-B36C-43B1-AC26-493C5B1CD33B.

Besides training, the BoZ also responded to these failures by prolifically issuing new banking regulations and improving its off-site supervisory and monitoring techniques.

Historically, the BoZ governor plays an important role in defending the BoZ's mandate vis-à-vis the Executive. The Bank's era of high performance in the mid-2000s was underpinned by technocratic cooperation between BoZ Governor Fundanga and Minister of Finance Magande, with the political backing of President Mwanawasa. This helped to stabilize monetary headwinds by establishing a favourable financial system in terms of fiscal deficit, inflation, economic growth, and financial reserves, and a responsive monetary policy stance. While Mwanawasa's economic team did not counter the dominant IMF orthodoxy, they agreed that the economic reforms in Zambia had been too hasty and had to be moderated (Magande 2018). The BoZ's autonomy was briefly under threat in 2011, via PF's short-lived attempt to confront conventional central-banking policies through the appointment of Governor Gondwe. This appointment led to internal divisions that our respondents report were only overcome when Gondwe was replaced by Denny Kalyalya in 2015, who managed to strengthen the BoZ's autonomy until his removal in 2020.

Analysing the politics of PoEs in Zambia

Bringing all three case studies together, three broad performance periods can be discerned in terms of the capacity of Zambia's core economic agencies to deliver on their mandates, as largely circumscribed by the neoliberal orthodoxy that has dominated the period under study. A period of rapid reforms, but generally poor outcomes between 1991 and 2001 was followed from 2002 to 2011 by a period of improved, and focused performance in an era of economic growth and fiscal space, after which, from 2012 to date, the PoEs examined here have been significantly undermined. These periods largely overlap with the tenures of some of Zambia's presidents, Chiluba, Mwanawasa, and Sata/Lungu, respectively. However, as was noted in all three studies, notably the BoZ case, other factors were at play.

Interestingly, the most effective performance period for economic governance across all three of our case-study organizations is situated in an era of intense political competition, which seems to contradict predictions that such conditions are often associated with short-term policymaking and the politicization of the bureaucracy (Khan 2010). The high performance was mostly determined by leaders who reacted against the economic and political mismanagement of the 1990s and who had the fiscal space to chart their own course amidst favourable structural economic conditions. Mwanawasa, a lawyer who resigned from MMD in 1994 when corruption crept in, deliberately chose a technocratic cabinet and forged a critical axis with a powerful minister of finance. Despite the decline of donor influence, international standards remained consequential, influencing the appointment of the minister of finance and other high-level technocrats and embedding technical assistance within the MoF, the BoZ, and ZRA. They also ensured some adherence to economic conventions, such as macroeconomic stability, single-digit inflation rates, and a liberal foreign exchange regime. The investment in ZRA during this period, most notably the establishment of specialized units and a drastic change of the mining tax regime in 2008, saw ZRA's performance improve from 2006 onwards.

This drive was informed by the need for a renewed mandate after a period of upheaval in the late 1990s, consisting of high levels of corruption, questionable privatization deals, and economic decline. It informed Mwanawasa's anti-corruption drive and moderation of privatization plans, albeit still disciplined by HIPC conditionalities. Nonetheless, this technocratic coalition was unsuccessful in securing popular support for its project, not least because the neoliberal model that they were embedding was failing to deliver inclusive patterns of growth: levels of poverty and unemployment remained high, despite impressive GDP figures. Mwanawasa's technocratic mode of governance and narrow ruling coalition actually helped engender a shift within the political settlement, heralding a more populist, somewhat economic nationalist approach. PF, a populist urban-based party, was able to create an opposition coalition with independent media, civil society, trade unions and the informal sector. Mwanawasa's anti-corruption drive was perceived to be narrowly focused on the Bemba-speaking politicians, which also played into PF's hands. The increasingly fragmentary nature of intra- as well as inter-elite relations made it very difficult to sustain ruling coalitions and their links to bureaucrats over time. The untimely death of Mwanawasa in 2008 was part of the story, but the larger one involved the fragmentation of the MMD as a political force and the country's more general absence of coherent and programmatic political parties.

Ideas were important here: the PF's displacement of MMD introduced a challenge to the neoliberal orthodoxy that in turn made it more difficult for the MoF, the BoZ, and (to a lesser extent) ZRA, to deliver on their mandates of maintaining a neoliberal economic order. With a more coherent ideology and higher levels of elite cohesion within the PF, this may have led to a new era of state restructuring in support of the kind of alternative development agenda that many were calling for in Zambia at the time. However, PF's governing coalition was neither committed to nor capable of reversing the imbalanced neoliberal approach to state-building by restoring the capacity of the relevant ministries of planning, trade, and mines. The Office of National Development Planning was revived as the Ministry of National Development Planning in 2011, but remained in a marginal position. The prospects of a more productivist economic development strategy emerging were further undermined by the continued absence of a strong domestic capitalist class capable of supporting other export-led earnings or local manufacturing (see Zambia chapter in Bebbington et al. 2018).

Zambia's changing and heavily transnationalized political settlement therefore offers a partial explanation for the findings discussed here, particularly for the MoF and ZRA, if less so for the more autonomous BoZ, which has been more insulated from political pressures. However, the social foundation of Zambia's political settlement may offer a better explanation for the politicization of Zambia's civil service than the concentration of power dimension. The social foundations of Zambia's settlement has always required that an inclusive coalition be forged through an elite-level bargain across multiple ethnic-linguistic groups and associations (trade unions, civil society, church bodies). In Kaunda's era, the concentration of power around an inclusive coalition was helpful in terms of offering a longer-term developmental vision and at least some capacity to deliver. This has tended to deliver a stable political settlement but not one that is geared towards delivering either state-building or development. By the late 2010s, even the stability of the settlement seemed to be weakening. Under PF, power had been concentrated around a president with increasingly authoritarian tendencies, who lacked a commitment to forging an inclusive coalition. The perception and reality of exclusion of ethnic groupings (Beardsworth and Mutuna forthcoming) rendered Zambia's political settlement increasingly vulnerable to instability and further undermined the possibility of merit-based appointments to key bureaucratic positions.

Policy implications

Our analysis of Zambia's pre-eminent PoEs reveals that the performance of these apex economic institutions has varied, both between them and over time, largely depending on structural forces underpinning the country's historical trajectory (the character of Zambia's political settlement, the structure of the economy, and the far-reaching influence of global neoliberalism) and the incentives and ideas of different ruling coalitions seeking to navigate this terrain. This conclusion sets out some of the key policy and strategic implications that flow from this analysis.

The move to strengthen the respective legal frameworks of ZRA and the BoZ helped to protect these apex institutions from undue political interference, albeit it to varying degrees. The establishment and mandate of the BoZ, including the parliamentary ratification of the president's appointment of the governor, are all enshrined in the Republican Constitution, whereas ZRA is legally established as a subsidiary authority under the MoF, offering the institution relatively less protection from undue political interference. Efforts to strengthen the revenue authority's legal framework, giving it similar constitutional-level independence to the BoZ or, at least, subsidiary law-level autonomy similar to that accorded to the Auditor General's Office, could enhance institutional protection.

Although all three institutions have achieved high levels of organizational capacity and performance at various times, the extent to which this was an inherent part of a structured internal reform process was quite limited. Establishing internal processes of continuous human resource, business process, and financial programming reforms such as succession and continuity planning could help enhance the professionalism, operation efficiency, and continuity of all three organizations in relation to their policy formulation, policy implementation, and policy coordination functions.

In order to enhance the level and quality of incentives offered in autonomous economic institutions, it will be important to explore options for benchmarking conditions of service in these institutions against similar organizations in the sub-region. This sort of recognition will increase the chances of a culture of professionalism and resistance to political interference growing in these apex institutions. Further such measures could include the (re)establishment of national inter-organizational peer review and coordination mechanisms as well as regional peer exchange forums, platforms, or communities of practice, which domestically and regionally foster peer support, policy coordination, and professionalism.

The influence of neoliberal orthodoxy in building the power of the MoF, the BoZ and ZRA has created a hierarchy, in which other crucial economic ministries, such as the Ministry of Mines, Commerce and Trade and Development Planning, lost their influence and the BoZ was prevented from playing a more proactive developmental role. This helped to embed a neoliberal project that has so far proved unable to secure inclusive development whilst also undermining alternative development strategies from emerging. The Mineral Value Chain Monitoring Project of the 2010s, a Norwegian/EU/UNCTAD-funded project based at ZRA, exemplified the importance of building capacity *across* institutions. While ZRA was central to its project, the project aimed at developing a system to monitor the country's mineral value chain from exploration to export across all relevant institutions, including the Ministry of Mines and Mineral Development. It led to some successful interventions, most notably the mining audits. Although the prospects of such reforms being successful are limited under current political conditions, it is to this more broad-based project of state-building and development that Zambia should seek to return.

References

African Tax Outlook (2019). ATAF Publication https://www.scribd.com/document/436918331/African-Tax-Outlook-2019 (accessed 25 April 2021).

Bank of Zambia (2014). *50 years of Central Banking.* Commemoration of the Golden Jubilee. Lusaka: Bank of Zambia.

Beardsworth, N. and Mutuna, K. (forthcoming) 'Cabinet Appointments and Regional Balancing: How Do Recent Zambian Administrations Compare?' SAIPAR working paper. Lusaka: South African Institute for Policy and Research.

Bebbington, A., Bebbington, D. H., Hinfelaar, M., Sanborn, C., and Abdulai, A.-G. (2018). *Governing Extractive Industries: Politics, Histories, Ideas.* Oxford: Oxford University Press

Bird, A. (2009). 'Analysis of the Planning and Budget Process'. Background Paper for World Bank Public Expenditure Review, mimeo.

Caramento, A. (2019). 'Cultivating Backward Linkages to Zambia's Copper Mines: Debating the Design of, and Obstacles to, Local Content', *The Extractive Industries and Society* 7(2): 310–20.

Caramento, A. (forthcoming). 'Domestic Capital Formation in the 'Old' and 'New' Copperbelts: The Political Economy of Zambian Mine Suppliers and Service Providers'. PhD thesis, York University.

Cheelo, C. and Hinfelaar, M. (2020a). 'Bank of Zambia's Autonomy amongst Political Turnovers in Zambia'. ESID Working Paper No.153. Manchester: Effective States and Inclusive Development Research Centre, University of Manchester.

Cheelo, C. and Hinfelaar, M. (2020b). 'Zambia Revenue Authority professional performance amidst structural constraints, 1994–2019'. Pockets of Effectiveness Working Paper No. 13. Manchester: Effective States and Inclusive Development Research Centre, University of Manchester.

Cheelo, C. and Hinfelaar, M. (2020c). 'What's the Future of Zambia's Political Economy Following the Firing of the Governor?' ESID blog, https://www.effective-states.org/whats-the-future-of-zambias-political-economy-following-the-firing-of-the-governor/ (accessed 28 June 2021).

Cheelo, C., Hinfelaar, M., and Ndulo, M. (eds) (2020). 'The Developmental State in Zambia: Plausibility, Challenges and Lessons from South Korea'. Cornell Occasional Paper. Ithaca, NY: Cornell University.

Cheeseman, N. and Hinfelaar, M. (2010). 'Parties, Platforms, and Political Mobilization: The Zambian Presidential Election of 2008', *African Affairs*, 109(434): 51–76.

Craig, J. R. (1999). 'State Enterprise and Privatisation in Zambia, 1968–1998'. PhD thesis, University of Leeds.

Di John, J. (2010). 'The Political Economy of Taxation and State Resilience in Zambia since 1990'. Working Paper No. 78, Series 2. London: Crisis States Research Centre.

Economics and Statistics Analysis (2004). 'The Fiscal Effects of Aid in Zambia'. ESAU Working Paper 10. London: Overseas Development Institute.

Fjeldstad, O.-H. and Heggstad, K. K. (2011). 'The Tax Systems in Mozambique, Tanzania and Zambia: Capacity and Constraints'. CMI Brief, 3.

Grindle, M. S. (2012). *Jobs for the Boys: Patronage and the State in Comparative Perspective*. Cambridge, MA: Harvard University Press.

Hinfelaar, M. and Sichone, J. (2019). 'The Challenge of Sustaining a Professional Civil Service amidst Shifting Political Coalitions: The Case of the Ministry of Finance in Zambia, 1991–2018'. ESID Working Paper No. 122. Manchester: Effective States and Inclusive Development Research Centre, University of Manchester.

IMF (2005). *Analysis of Change in Zambia's Mining Fiscal Regime*. IMF Country Report No 15/153. Washington, DC: IMF. Available online: https://www.imf.org/en/News/Articles/2017/10/10/pr17394-imf-executive-board-concludes-2017-article-iv-consultation-with-zambia (accessed 12 October 2020).

International Monetary Fund (2019). 'IMF Staff Completes 2019 Article IV Visit to Zambia'. Press release, 30 April. Available online: https://www.imf.org/en/News/Articles/2019/04/30/pr19130-zambia-imf-staffcompletes-2019-article-iv-visit (accessed 13 June 2019).

Jepson, N. (2019). *In China's Wake: How the Commodity Boom Transformed Development Strategies in the Global South*. New York: Columbia University Press.

Khan, M. (2010). 'Political Settlements and the Governance of Growth-enhancing Institutions. Draft paper'. Research Paper Series on 'Growth-Enhancing Governance'. London: SOAS, University of London.

Lindemann, S. (2011). 'Inclusive Elite Bargains and the Dilemma of Unproductive Peace: A Zambian Case Study', *Third World Quarterly*, 32(10): 1843–69.

Magande, N. P. (2018). *The Depth of my Footprints: From the Hills of Namaila to the Global Stage*. Atlanta, GA: Maleenda.

Maimbo, S. (2000). 'The Prediction and Diagnosis of Bank Failures in Zambia'. Finance and Development Research Programme Working Paper Series, No. 13. Manchester: Institute for Development Policy and Management, University of Manchester.

McPherson, M. F. (2004). 'Monetary Policy, Exchange Rate Management, and Financial Reforms'. In C. B. Hill and M. F. McPherson (eds), *Promoting and Sustaining Economic Reform in Zambia*. Cambridge, MA: John F. Kennedy School of Government. 145–85.

Mkandawire, T. (2017). 'State Capacity, History, Structure, and Political Contestation in Africa'. In D. Mistree, M. Centeno, A. Kohli, and D. Yashar (eds), *States in the Developing World*. Cambridge: Cambridge University Press. 184–216.

Mosley, P. (2017). *Fiscal Policy and the Natural Resources Curse: How to Escape from the Poverty Trap*. London, New York: Routledge.

PEFA (2017). *Report on the Evaluation of the Public Finance Management System of Zambia*. Government of Zambia and World Bank Group. Available online: https://www.pefa.org/sites/default/files/ZM-Nov17-PFMPRPublic%20with%20PEFA%20Check.pdf (accessed 13 June 2019).

Rakner, L. (2003). *Political and Economic Liberalisation in Zambia 1991–2001*. Uppsala: Nordic Africa Institute.

Roll, M. (ed.) (2014). *The Politics of Public Sector Performance: Pockets of Effectiveness in Developing Countries*. London and New York: Routledge.

Simutanyi. N. and Hinfelaar, M. (2018). 'Understanding Zambia's Black Box'. SAIPAR, Discussion Paper, No. 3. Lusaka: Southern African Institute for Policy and Research.

Tordoff, W. (ed.) (1980). *Administration in Zambia*. Manchester: Manchester University Press.

World Bank (1999). 'Cash Budgeting, Strengths, Weaknesses and Prospects: A Case Study'. Washington, DC: World Bank. Available online: www1.worldbank.org/publicsector/pe/befa05/executioncasestudy.doc (accessed 28 June 2021).

World Bank (2016). 'Zambia Economic Brief: Raising Revenue for Economic Recovery', Issue 8. Washington, DC: World Bank. Available online: https://documents1.worldbank.org/curated/en/166021480932290112/pdf/110728-WP-P157243-PUBLIC-ZambiaEBRaisingRevenueforEconomicRecoveryDecember.pdf (accessed 30 June 2021).

Yohou, H. D. and Goujon, M. (2017). 'Reassessing Tax Effort in Developing Countries: A Proposal of a Vulnerability-adjusted Tax Effort Index'. FERDI Working Paper. Clermont-Ferrand: FERDI.

6

The Politics of State Capacity in Post-genocide Rwanda

'Pockets of Effectiveness' as State-building Prioritizations?

Benjamin Chemouni

Introduction

Analysing pockets of effectiveness (PoEs) in Rwanda necessarily involves analysing a major project of state re-building after its near complete destruction around the 1994 genocide.[1] The Ministry of Finance and Economic Planning (MINECOFIN) is a case in point. After the genocide, the Ministry was a hollow shell. When it resumed its activity on 16 July 1994, only seven people reported to work. Most staff had fled or been killed. New hires were diaspora returnees with some level of education but no experience of the Rwandan context; returnees from Uganda and Kenya did not read French and were not familiar with the French accounting system. Staff were not paid for the first three months, and were only remunerated in kind, with rice and cooking oil for instance, until 1995. The Ministry's work in the following years was limited to the narrow task of managing scarcity, handling chaotic salary payments, scrambling to adapt legislation to the new context, and dealing with international financial institutions (IFIs) adamant about Rwanda repaying the debt left by the former regime.

Fast forward ten years, and the Ministry had become a clear outlier in relation to other parts of the state, with a better paid and skilled cadre of civil servants. It had been placed at the forefront of the ruling Rwanda Patrioic Front government's transformative project that aims, through rapid socio-economic development, to address the elite's vulnerability by shoring up its legitimacy, particularly amongst the majority Hutu population. MINECOFIN consequently gained unprecedented power over line ministries and, standing as the main entry gate to donor support, it even became seen as 'one of the more powerful finance ministries in the region' (World Bank 2013b: 67).

---

[1] The author acknowledges the significant contribution that research conducted by Pritish Behuria on the central bank in Rwanda makes to this chapter (Behuria 2020a).

Benjamin Chemouni, *The Politics of State Capacity in Post-genocide Rwanda*. In: *Pockets of Effectiveness and the Politics of State-building and Development in Africa*. Edited by Sam Hickey, Oxford University Press. © Oxford University Press (2023). DOI: 10.1093/oso/9780192864963.003.0006

The case of MINECOFIN epitomizes why and how PoEs matter in Rwanda, albeit in a particular way. Unlike the general depiction of PoEs as high-performing agencies operating within an otherwise dysfunctional state (Roll 2014), such state agencies in Rwanda should instead be regarded as the vanguard of a broader and systematic state-building project that is a response to the systemic vulnerability that Rwanda's rulers perceive themselves to be facing. As a result, what we will term here high-performing state agencies (HPSAs) emerge in Rwanda because of their priority in the regime's wider state-building project and because the ruling coalition has secured the level of power concentration required to enforce this project. However, whilst this combination of vulnerability and dominance provides the necessary structural condition for the creation of HPSAs, a range of more proximate factors were also critical, including organizational leadership and the nature of the task (specific, measurable, and not transaction intensive) being performed (Roll 2014).

To explore the origins and the role of HPSAs in Rwanda, this research adopts a qualitative approach that is best suited to understanding processes and causal changes over time. It relies on a comparative case study of three agencies: MINECOFIN, the Rwanda Revenue Authority (RRA) and the central bank, Banque Nationale du Rwanda (BNR). The identification of these cases results from an expert survey undertaken with twenty-three respondents based in Kigali between July and September 2017, as detailed in Chapter 2. The survey's assessment has been triangulated with data from statistical performance indicators for each organization, as well as standardized international assessment and rankings. The analysis draws on the existing literature, statistical data, technical reports, as well as 120 interviews conducted in Rwanda between July 2017 and December 2019 with politicians, current and former civil servants, journalists, consultants, and donors.

This chapter now sets out the nature of the state-building project in Rwanda since the genocide, the changing nature of the political settlement and the influence that this has had on public-sector performance. It then summarizes the performance trajectories of the three case-study organizations before analysing these in relation to three key drivers of performance: political, organizational, and transnational. The conclusion sets out the main findings and suggests some of the policy implications that flow from them.

The state-building project in Rwanda

The genocide created a critical juncture for the process of state formation in Rwanda. The four years of civil war that culminated in the 1994 genocide decimated the state (Kimonyo 2017). New civil servants were returnees from the diaspora with no experience of the Rwandan state's procedures. State collapse was paralleled with economic collapse. In 1994, GDP per capita had declined by one-half, and four out of five persons lived under the poverty line. Rwanda became the second poorest country in the world and the one where life expectancy was the shortest (World Bank 2019: 2).

Since the genocide, the evolution of the Rwandan political settlement has involved the concentration of power in the RPF and its chairman, Paul Kagame. Two main periods can be distinguished. The first, from 1994 to 2000, involved the RPF consolidating its power and centrality to the post-genocide settlement. The RPF was created in 1987 in Uganda by Tutsi refugees who fled the anti-Tutsi pogroms of the 1950s and 1960s. It was formed with the objective of allowing the return of refugees to Rwanda, which the two Hutu-dominated regimes since independence had constantly opposed. The RPF launched an attack from Uganda in 1990 and gained power in 1994 by stopping the genocide against the Tutsi ethnic group and achieving a clear victory over the government's army. However, the RPF's situation remained precarious: whilst waging war against the interahamwe in the Congo, the new regime had to restore security and, until 1999, fight a full-fledged insurgency in the north-west of the country.

The RPF became the ruling party while giving representation in government to other legal political parties. In the first post-genocide government, eight of seventeen ministerial seats were occupied by RPF members. Power was nominally divided along ethnic lines, with a balance of Tutsi and Hutu at ministerial level. This arrangement, aimed at demonstrating the RPF's commitment to unity and power-sharing, did not, however, reflect the reality of power. Helped by its control of the military, the RPF set about establishing its dominance over other parties by sidelining the most vocal opposition leaders and tightly monitoring other parties. It also disciplined civil society into accepting its rules for public engagement (Reyntjens 2013).

Power was also concentrated within the RPF itself. Prominent Hutu figures within the RPF who were critical of the leadership or sought to establish a power base for themselves were sidelined. In the early 2000s, a series of Tutsi members also fell out with the RPF leadership and fled the country. The party's cohesion has been tested by growing corruption, with growing tensions between members eager to enjoy the spoils of victory and those promoting discipline and restraint. This struggle was eventually resolved in 1999 in favour of those denouncing corruption when Kagame publicly sided with them and disciplined senior cadres and army officers (Kimonyo 2020). The episode both consolidated the pre-eminence of Kagame in the party and established the basis for higher levels of public-sector performance.

The second period, from 2000, is characterized by the undisputed dominance of the RPF in Rwanda's political settlement and the completion of Kagame's ascendency. Taking the presidency in 2000, Kagame reinforced his power in the party by sideling several senior RPF (Tutsi) members who fell out with him and encouraging a generational shift that saw senior 'historical' RPF members replaced by a new guard mostly composed of well-educated diasporic returnees fiercely loyal to Kagame. The change of constitution in 2017, allowing Kagame to remain president until 2034, was adopted without open resistance from the RPF or other parties.

The current political settlement is consequently characterized by an extraordinary concentration of power in the ruling party. The opposition is weak and located mainly outside Rwanda. Representatives of other parties occupy cabinet positions in accordance with the constitutional requirement that the dominant party in parliament cannot have more than 50 per cent of ministerial portfolios. However, non-RPF ministers are closely monitored and never challenge the RPF's line. The power of the ruling party is also reinforced by the informal role of the RPF in influencing policymaking and occasionally acting as an enforcer of the president's decisions on the bureaucracy (Chemouni and Dye 2020, Golooba-Mutebi and Habiyonizeye 2018: 26). The RPF has also concentrated power economically, curbing the emergence of any significant independent domestic economic force able to challenge it (Behuria 2016) and dominating the capitalistic sector though RPF-owned or military-owned companies and by opening the economy to foreign investors. The RPF's close links to the army helps consolidate its hold on power and a military ethos now infuses the state (Reyntjens 2020), helping the ruling party to impose change.

Power in the settlement is also concentrated vertically. The RPF enjoys significant autonomy from its followers and the wider population. It remains a cohesive party, despite regular high-level defections, and possesses strong enforcement capabilities (Khan 2010). Such capabilities are enhanced by its tight control of the local administration that penetrates deep into the countryside (Chemouni 2014).

Despite its hegemony, the ruling elite continues to perceive itself as highly vulnerable in relation to the social foundations of Rwanda's political settlement. After the genocide, the RPF suffered from a profound lack of legitimacy. Led by a small Tutsi minority, it had seized power by force and had to rule over a Hutu-dominated population previously mired in genocidal ideology. This lack of legitimacy was magnified by the weak links that some diasporic RPF members had with everyday Rwanda (Ansoms 2009: 295). In this respect, the situation echoes that of the systemic vulnerability of east Asian developmental states (Doner, Ritchie, and Slater 2005). Faced with extraordinary political, security, and economic challenges, building an effective state became a way for the elite to ensure its own survival while delivering 'side payments' to its potentially restive population.

Since the end of the genocide, the regime has rebuilt a state that seems to outperform countries of similar wealth. Even authors generally critical of Rwanda's trajectory recognize that 'the regime's achievements in this field are undisputable' (Reyntjens 2013: xv). This is well captured by Figure 6.1, which shows that in two decades, Rwanda switched from having the lowest to the highest score in the World Bank's government effectiveness indicators among the countries analysed in this project. The World Bank's Country Policy and Institutional Assessment (CPIA) also places Rwanda ahead of most competitors.

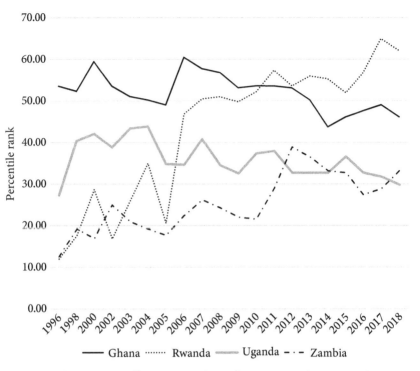

Figure 6.1 Government effectiveness in Rwanda in comparative perspective, 1996–2018

Source: World Bank's World Governance Indicators.

This evolution was supported by a rapid reduction of administrative corruption over the past two decades, with Rwanda rising to the rank of forty-eight out of 180 countries in 2018 for control of corruption in the Transparency International's Corruption Perception Index, from being ranked 121 in the 2006 ranking. State effectiveness has been built by frequent reforms of the core public sector (Chemouni 2017) and the heavy incentivization of the civil service through top-down performance indicators (*imihigo*). While this approach has enabled the RPF to deliver on several policy priorities it means that consultation with the lower rungs of the bureaucracy let alone the population is weak (Chemouni 2014). The bureaucracy has limited independence from the ruling party (Chemouni and Dye 2020), risks misunderstanding local contexts, and tends to adopt an aggressive approach to policy implementation by civil servants concerned with meeting their performance targets (Ansoms 2009, Chemouni 2018).

Pockets of effectiveness in Rwanda

MINECOFIN, the RRA, and the central bank (BNR) were selected as case studies here because they emerged as high performers within the expert survey conducted

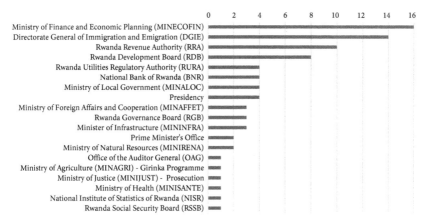

Figure 6.2 Expert ratings of the best-performing state agencies in Rwanda (number of mentions in the survey)

Source: Author's expert survey.

in Kigali in 2017 (Figure 6.2). MINECOFIN and RRA were respectively the most and the third-most cited high-performing state agencies, while the BNR was the joint fifth highest performing. These three were selected from the top five identified in Figure 6.2, both because of their significance to development in Rwanda and to enable comparisons with the other country case studies included in the project that this book is based on.

MINECOFIN

MINECOFIN's standing as the best-performing organization within Rwandan public service in the expert survey is supported by by international assessments.[2] The Public Expenditure and Financial Accountability (PEFA) evaluations reveal a continuous and widespread improvement of the organization in terms of financial management (Table 6.1). In 2010, Rwanda outperformed neighbouring countries on all dimensions of the PEFA framework bar one of the PEFA framework. In 2016, this performance had further improved across most categories, with declines apparent in only three of twenty-eight, two of which were due to circumstances beyond the control of MINECOFIN, namely the 2013 suspension of aid, which undermined the credibility of the budget.

The World Bank's Country Policy and Institutional Assessment (CPIA) also indicates the good performance of the Ministry in terms of economic and budget management in comparison to the other country case studies of this project (Chemouni 2019: 10) and to the rest of the continent (Figure 6.3).

---

[2] This section is mainly based on Chemouni (2019).

Table 6.1 Trends in selected Public Expenditure and Financial Accountability (PEFA) indicators in Rwanda, 2008–2016

Indicators	2008	2010	2016	Comments
Credibility of the budget				
Aggregate expenditure out-turn compared to original approved budget	B	A	B	Stable (probably due to the 2013 aid suspension that led to changes from the original budget)
Composition of expenditure out-turn compared to original approved budget	D	D	B+	Improvement
Aggregate revenue out-turn compared to original approved budget	A	A	B	Decline, due to the sharp reduction of grants following the 2013 aid suspension
Comprehensiveness and transparency				
Stock and monitoring of expenditure payment arrears	D+	B	B+	Improvement
Classification of the budget	A	A	A	Stable
Comprehensive-ness of information included in budget documentation	D	A	A	Improvement
Extent of unreported government operations	D+	D+	B+	Improvement
Transparency of inter-governmental fiscal relations	B	A	A	Improvement
Oversight of aggregate fiscal risk from other public-sector entities	D+	C	C+	Improvement
Public access to key fiscal information	C	A	B	The decline is due to delays in publishing the award of large contracts.
Policy-based budgeting				
Orderliness and participation in the annual budget process	B+	B+	A	Improvement
Multi-year perspective in fiscal planning, expenditure policy, and budgeting	C+	C+	B+	Improvement
Accounting, recording, and reporting				
Timeliness and regularity of accounts reconciliation	B+	B+	A	Improvement
Availability of information on resources received by service delivery units	D	D	C	Improvement
Quality and timeliness of in-year budget reports	D+	D+	D+	Stable
Quality and timeliness of annual budget statements	C+	D+	C+	Stable

Source: PEFA evaluations, different years. Accessible at: https://www.pefa.org/country/rwanda.

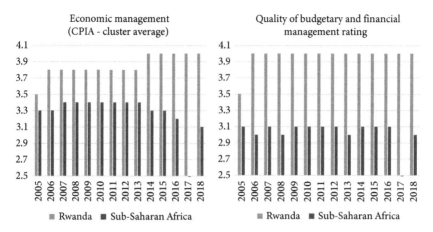

Figure 6.3 Selected CPIA indicators for Rwanda, 2005–2018

Source: World Bank's CPIA assessment (https://www.worldbank.org/en/data/datatopics/cpia, data for 2017).

Two main periods can be identified in the rise of MINECOFIN, initially as a PoE-outlier amidst the wreckage of the early post-genocide era and later as a HPSA in the context of generally rising governance standards. The first, from 1997 to 2005, involved the birth of a high-performing organization. The Ministry's centrality within the state apparatus was extended through its merger with the Ministry of Planning in 1997. This new mandate made MINECOFIN the linchpin of the RPF transformative project, charged with the formulation and the implementation of the government's grand plan, 'Vision 2020'. No mere technical document, Vision 2020 acts as the strategic and symbolic demonstration of the Rwandan elite's commitment to development, 'the only hymn sheet to which everyone needs to abide' (Campioni and Noack 2012: 5). As captured by a Rwandan civil servant, 'I think the task of MINECOFIN drives performance: it has a very sensitive mandate for Rwanda.[3] The Ministry was also made responsible for coordinating the massive external support that flowed into post-genocide Rwanda, a move that in turn incentivized donors to make the Ministry the focus of training and public finance management (PFM) reforms, to staff it with highly paid consultants, and to finance the wages of high-capacity staff that the state could not otherwise afford.

The other main dynamic behind the rise of MINECOFIN is the leadership of its most long-serving minister (1997–2005), Donald Kaberuka. A powerful player within the RPF via his seat on the party's national executive committee (NEC), this allowed Kaberuka to push through some key reforms, including the creation in the late 1990s of autonomous agencies under MINECOFIN such as the Office of the Auditor General and the RRA. His clout was instrumental in overcoming some resistance in cabinet meetings, as these new autonomous agencies were seen by some as a danger to the unity of the state.

---

[3] Interview, 13 June 2018.

Kaberuka also instilled a management style that has set MINECOFIN apart. He surrounded himself with a group of young, educated individuals from the diaspora, which an informant nicknamed the 'Kaberuka boys',[4] and helped their rise through the ranks by working closely with them. He chose his personal assistant from among them, on a rotational basis, for training purposes. His management style was also conducive to learning. He gave leeway to his subordinates to make decisions and did not embarrass them publicly, which differs from the management style that tends to prevail within the Rwandan bureaucracy.

The second period of MINECOFIN's evolution, from 2005, involved the consolidation of MINECOFIN functioning. After the departure of Kaberuka, the top level of the Ministry sought to formalize the gains made under him, issuing procedural manuals, streamlining functions, and undertaking PFM reforms. Reforms were often the result either of a crisis or challenge that the government felt it had to address. For example, the disappointing results of the first Poverty Reduction Strategy Paper (2001–2006) evaluation triggered a wave of reforms in PFM to improve budgeting, planning, and resource mobilization. Reforms were also driven by the need to encourage direct budgetary support by donors' from the mid-2000s onwards (Chemouni 2017, 2019).

The political significance of MINECOFIN's task and its leadership translated into an organizational culture that was particularly conducive to performance. While management based on top-down pressure, performance targets (*imihigo*) and a good work ethic, is shared by other organizations in the state, specific traits can explain why the Ministry performs relatively better than others. First, its staff are relatively empowered. As explained by a former employee, in MINECOFIN 'you have less scrutiny', and the chain of command is more flexible and less hierarchical: 'as an analyst, you can be called to brief the PS [permanent secretary] or the minister'.[5] This management style can be traced back to Kaberuka's time and to MINECOFIN's capacity to attract talent, notably thanks to better wages than the rest of the civil service and a recruitment strategy that targets high-performing graduates. This means that high-ranking officials operating under pressure are less worried about delegating tasks to lower-ranking officials. Employees have also developed some *esprit de corps*: 'there is a general sense of being a team'.[6] This notably comes from the prestige attached to working in the Ministry and being seen as more capable than other bureaucrats. As explained by a MINECOFIN employee: 'if you are from MINECOFIN, they listen to you differently'.[7]

The nature of recruitment and promotion processes within MINECOFIN is central here. Access to high-level jobs, such as director general (DG) and permanent secretary (PS), is often the result of internal promotion, rather than transfer from another ministry. All PSs since the departure of Kaberuka have risen through

---

[4] Interview with senior Rwandan official, 22 July 2017.
[5] Interview, 13 June 2018.
[6] Interview with former MINECOFIN PS, 29 June 2018.
[7] Interview, 29 June 2018.

the ranks. Instances of patronage are limited in the Ministry, mainly because of the importance of its mandate, which requires capable officials, often hired fresh from university. As explained by a former PS, other state organizations 'know [a MINECOFIN employee] will be a good technician, because in MINECOFIN there is really merit-based recruitment, not because you are my cousin'.[8] The stable leadership of the Ministry and its relationship with the top political leadership is another influence on performance. PS and ministers have a rather long tenure in the Ministry. In twenty-five years, only six ministers and six PSs have led the Ministry, with some especially lengthy tenures. For example, the PS Kampeta Syingoza was in post for seven years, 2009–2016, a period of particularly strong performance. In addition, the replacement of the PS is generally not concomitant with the replacement of ministers, ensuring continuity within the bureaucracy.

As a result, MINECOFIN has enjoyed significant autonomy, protected from political interference. For instance, presidential elections do not translate into abnormal peaks of public expenditure (Figure 6.4).

Extraordinary spending around elections time is deemed unnecessary, given the weakness of the opposition, thus enabling MINECOFIN to deliver on its mandate (Chemouni 2019: 31–2).

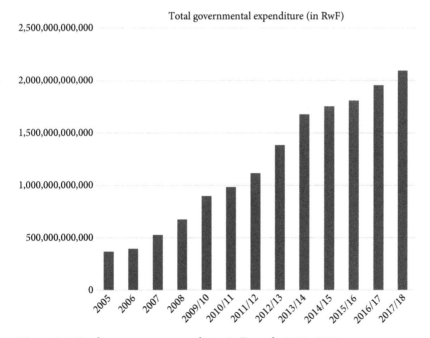

Figure 6.4 Total government expenditure in Rwanda 2005–2018
Source: Annual state budget laws.

---

[8] Interview, 29 June 2018.

The Rwandan Revenue Authority

For most observers, 'the story of taxation in post-genocide Rwanda has been one of remarkable success' (Goodfellow 2014: 319).[9] Following the creation of the RRA, the tax-to-GDP ratio increased markedly, from 10.8 per cent in 1998 to 16.7 per cent in 2017. In the second half of the 2010s, revenue increased by 10 per cent per year on average (Schreiber 2018: 10), although this performance has recently plateaued. As shown in Figure 6.5, the performance is also conspicuously good in comparison to other countries.

The RRA was created by law in 1997 and instituted in 1998. As a semi-autonomous agency of the kind promoted by donors across Africa at the time (Fjeldstad and Moore 2009), RRA was supposed to enhance domestic revenue mobilization by introducing a private-sector ethos and staff motivation. As explained by Donald Kaberuka, then minister of finance, to Schreiber (2018: 2), 'we thought its functions were so critical that [the RRA] had to operate independently—almost on the private-sector model.' This was to be achieved through granting autonomy to RRA in the recruitment of its staff and in the determination of their pay scale.

The creation and subsequent strengthening of the RRA has to be understood as the consequence of the vulnerability of the ruling elite. In the late 1990s, high levels of military expenditure, the decrease of foreign aid following the end of the emergency period, and cutbacks from donors following Rwanda's involvement

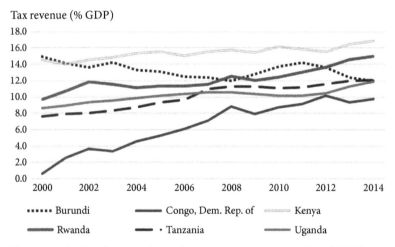

Tax revenue (% GDP)

•••••• Burundi   Congo, Dem. Rep. of   Kenya
       Rwanda   • Tanzania   Uganda

Figure 6.5 Regional comparison of tax revenue, 2000–2014 (% of GDP)
Source: Reproduced from (USAID 2018: 2).

---

[9] This section draws on Chemouni (2020).

in Congo (AfDB 2011: vi), made the need for effective domestic resource mobilization clear to the government. The RRA's mandate is also at the core of the RPF's paradigmatic idea of self-reliance that underpins much of its approach to the rebuilding of the country, itself shaped by a desire to avoid foreign influence (Chemouni and Mugiraneza 2019) and the unreliable flows of aid. This is encapsulated in the RRA's current official 'vision': 'To become a world-class efficient and modern revenue agency, *fully financing national needs* [my emphasis].'

From the beginning, the RRA has benefitted from two factors. First, it has 'been able to count on the personal support of the president, who has played a major role in the campaign to change public attitudes towards paying taxes and corruption' (Fjeldstad and Moore 2009: 6). In addition, it received the strong financial and technical backing of donors, especially the UK Department for International Development (DFID). The RRA has undergone a series of reforms, starting with efforts to improve its internal organization in the early 2000s. The second wave of reform in the mid-2000s focused on revamping the tax system to enable it to join the East African Community's customs union in 2009. This involved lowering tariffs, which provided a strong incentive for the government to widen the tax base to counterbalance the loss of customs revenues. Between 2007 and 2017, the number of registered taxpayers grew more than thirteenfold, from 26,526 to 355,128 (Schreiber 2018: 20).

From an organizational standpoint, the RRA 'has become well known for meritocracy and for extremely low levels of corruption' (Moore 2014: 106). This was made possible partly by its semi-autonomous status and capacity to pay higher salaries than in the rest of the civil service, in order to dissuade staff from undertaking collusive activities with taxpayers. In addition, as in MINECOFIN, senior officials have usually risen through the ranks in an organization that prides itself on hiring mainly young graduates. As explained by a former senior official of MINECOFIN, 'this means that you've got continuity and the culture of professionalism of the institution is preserved.'[10] This also nurtures autonomy, as staff are not parachuted into the RRA by political patrons to enjoy RRA's higher salaries. RRA's career-oriented management, along with its special legal status, also fosters an *esprit de corps*, enhanced by different social activities. As explained by a RRA employee, 'it's obvious that there is a team spirit. We have RRA football and women's volleyball on Friday afternoons. The teams get uniforms every year, so people like to be a part of that.'[11]

The nature of the RRA's leadership is another cause of its strong performance, with successive commissioner generals helping to make RRA's legal autonomy

---

[10] Interviewed in January 2019.
[11] Interview, 25 June 2018.

a lived reality. The first appointee was a Ghanaian, Edward Larbi-Siaw, a move intended to protect the young organization from clientelism. Successive leaders after 2001, James Musoni (2001–2005) and Mary Baine (2006–2011), were among the most powerful RPF cadres at the time. This gave clout to the organization but also ensured that its leadership could implement bold and potentially unpopular changes. For example, Musoni was instrumental in replacing the senior management, many of whom worked in MINECOFIN's old tax department, with younger ones, either hired externally or promoted internally.

The RRA also pioneered performance-driven management, ahead of the wider introduction of local governments' performance contract (*imihgo*) in 2006. From its creation, each of RRA's departments had its own revenue targets that were, thanks to DFID funding, linked to payment bonuses. The performance system was also rolled out at the individual level, as each member of staff has had personal targets to achieve. This has translated into a punitive approach to taxation, with very high penalties for delayed tax returns and no room for clemency. In order to keep their numbers high, RRA officials can also be reluctant to grant tax holidays and customs exemptions, even when provided for by law.

Unlike in MINECOFIN, staff do not feel empowered to take decisions, a problem that creates a bottleneck at the top of the organization, given the general lack of delegation: 'The culture doesn't encourage people to raise issues and they don't have the capacity to present evidence to the leadership to change course of action. You don't escalate failure [i.e. report issues to higher levels].'[12] This results in a range of issues for taxpayers when interacting with the RRA, as bureaucrats are reluctant to take decisions or answer queries, for fear of reprisals from senior officials.

While the effectiveness of the RRA is clear if viewed through the prism of tax collection, it is much less so if analysed through the broader lens of its relationship with the private sector. Recurring complaints from businesses underline difficulties in accessing information on tax and the fast-changing legislation that regularly imposes sudden, and at times not well-conceived, revisions. For many businesspeople interviewed, this results from a lack of preparation of tax reforms, with limited consultation of the relevant stakeholders. The latest Investor Perception Survey prepared by the World Bank (2018) found that tax predictability was the third main constraint to company growth in Rwanda, according to investors.

The relationship with the private sector also suffers from organizational problems within the RRA. The most problematic issue concerns the reliability of its taxpayer database, which does not allow the RRA to fully know who owns what amount of tax arrears (OAG 2015, 2018). For example, the RRA wrongly reported 32bn Rwf, or 4 per cent of its total revenue, in 2014 (OAG 2015: 16).

---

[12] Interview with RRA advisor, July 2018.

The paradox of the glowing numbers for revenue collection and the problematic book-keeping and tax registration practices can partly be explained by the structure of incentives driving the RRA. Its performance is mainly grasped through aggregate macro indicators of revenue mobilization, whilst other less politically salient aspects of performance are largely overlooked. The RRA still has limited financial, human, and technical capacities at the lower levels of the organization which, coupled with a hierarchical management culture focused on narrow targets, creates a lack of feedback loops that hinders organizational learning and improvement.

Lastly, RRA's performance needs to be understood in relation to tax policy-making, elements of which have undermined revenue mobilization. Although the RRA has a significant *de facto* influence over tax policy despite this being the *de jure* domain of MINECOFIN, it has been unable to resist government policy in tax exemptions. In 2016, tax exemptions were estimated at about 3.3 per cent of GDP, equivalent to almost 10 per cent of government expenditure (World Bank 2019: 131), higher than in Kenya, Uganda, or Tanzania (TJN-A and Action Aid 2016). Exemptions result from an attempt by the government to achieve job creation, export promotion, and the attraction of investments. However, they are not targeted enough to be effective (ActionAid 2011, Steenbergen and von Uexkull 2018, TJN-A and Action Aid 2016) and a survey conducted in 2011 found that 98 per cent of investors in Rwanda would have made their investment without these incentives (IMF 2015: 12).

This situation is the result of a poor coordination within the state between agencies with different incentives. Most notably, this places RRA in conflict with the Rwandan Development Board (RDB), whose mandate to attract investment has led it to push for ad hoc deals, without consulting the RRA or MINECOFIN, thus producing inconsistent tax incentives while eroding the tax base. This example, and also the government's reluctance to impose a property tax on urban elites until 2018 (Chemouni 2020), may explain why Rwanda's tax effort, understood as ratio of the actual tax collection to the predicted tax revenue, while generally better than other countries examined in this book, has not significantly improved with the creation of the RRA (Figure 6.6).

Banque Nationale du Rwanda

Assessed on its key missions of financial-sector stability and, to lesser extent, price stability, the Central Bank of Rwanda (BNR) appears to be a high performing institution. Between 1996 and 2008, inflation was at a controlled level of 5.4 per cent (Rutayisire 2010), although this average masks significant price volatility.[13]

---

[13] This section is based on Behuria (2020a).

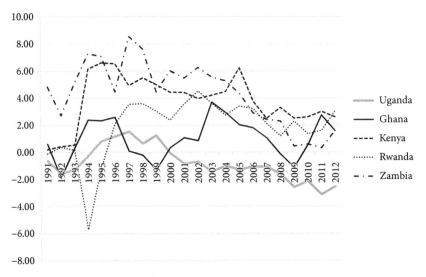

Figure 6.6 Tax effort in our five countries, 1991–2012
Source: Yohou and Goujon (2017).

According to the World Bank (2013a), inflation in Rwanda over the last decade has been lower than other East African countries but above average for sub-Saharan Africa. BNR has thus been largely effective at presenting itself as an effective financial institution on indicators that are prioritized by IFIs. Furthermore, electoral years have not translated into higher inflation, thus indicating that public expenditure is not used for clientelist purposes (Figure 6.7). The BNR's mandate is concerned more with global financial standards than with encouraging structural transformation. This means it has been less effective in promoting a more traditional developmentalist role for central banking, which from a heterodox standpoint (Behuria 2020a), constitutes a significant failing (a debate returned to in Chapter 8).

In terms of financial stability, the BNR has also made tangible progress, overseeing the increase in capital adequacy ratio in the banking system to a level generally higher than in the rest of the region (Behuria 2020a). The BNR successfully decreased the proportion of non-performing loans in the economy, a major issue in the immediate post-genocide period (Figure 6.8). Generally, the BNR is seen as one of the most ardent implementers of the Basel financial regulatory framework on the continent (Behuria 2020b).

Since the genocide, the BNR has presided over the impressive growth of the financial sector in the country. Whereas the sector was extremely shallow before 1994, with only three commercial banks, it has become among the fastest-growing

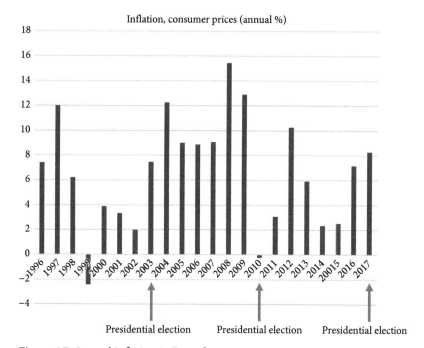

Figure 6.7 Annual inflation in Rwanda, 1996–2017
Source: The World Bank (accessible at https://data.worldbank.org/).

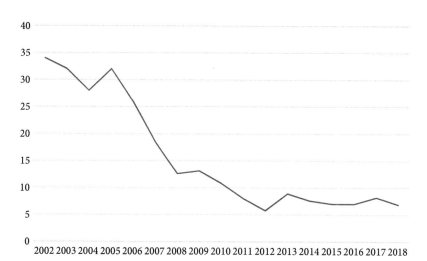

Figure 6.8 Non-performing loans/gross loans in Rwanda, 2002–2018
Source: Behuria (2020a).

economic sectors in the country (Behuria and Goodfellow 2016). In July 2017, there were eleven commercial banks.[14]

Overall, three main dynamics can explain BNR's relatively good performance. The first lies in the fact that the BNR's mandate is directly aligned with the country's economic ambition, articulated in Vision 2020, to diversify the post-genocide economy out of cash-crop revenue by becoming a financial hub and attracting foreign investors. Building the BNR's effectiveness has been perceived as one of the ways to address this vulnerability. It aimed at signalling to foreign investors and IFIs the solidity of the Rwandan economy and, especially, of its financial sector.

This translated into a series of reforms systematically supported by the IFIs, notably through the Poverty Reduction and Growth Facility in 1998 and the 2013 Policy Support Instrument. First of all, the government swiftly embraced the neoliberal agenda of financial liberalization after the genocide. Between 1994 and 2000, in a context of high inflation and financial instability, the BNR implemented some measures from the Structural Adjustment Programme promoted before the genocide by IFIs. In 1996, it fully liberalized interest rates. In 1999, the Rwanda Central Banking Act granted the BNR formal independence in the formulation and implementation of monetary policy and widened its mandate to include financial stability. Francois Kanimba, a former BNR employee and head of the Governance Task Force, which negotiated Rwanda's first structural adjustment programme, was appointed as BNR governor in 2002, a further signal to IFIs of the government's commitment to follow their advice. During his tenure, the financial sector became increasingly aligned with international standards, a trend his successors followed. The BNR's eager adoption of Basel standards epitomizes this (Behuria 2020b), with Rwanda becoming among the most compliant countries in Africa within two years of starting to adopt the reforms. Despite many civil servants and bankers warning that such standards were not appropriate to the country's needs, the will to signal compliance trumped any contextual realities or stakeholders' reservations, in ways that may yet have damaging effects (Behuria 2020b: 138).

The BNR also embarked on strengthening its regulatory authority. The Banking Supervision Department was created in 1999 and has been constantly reinforced since. In the early 2000s, one of BNR's main tasks was the recovery of nonperforming loans (NPLs), an especially pressing issue after the genocide. Public shaming methods were deployed, with the names of all debtors whose case was before court published. Debtors were also refused access to future loans until they had paid back existing ones. These measures led to a dramatic decrease in NPLs.

Inflation control, already a key mandate for BNR, was given a particularly high priority because of the positive signal that price stability sent to investors. An informal objective since the end of the genocide, inflation control became enshrined in

---

[14] As well as four microfinance banks, one development bank, and one cooperative bank.

law in the BNR act of 2007. The BNR's success in delivering on this mandate has been undermined by drought and bad harvests regularly fuelling price volatility, although with MINECOFIN exercising fiscal discipline, it has only rarely suffered from inflation arising from politicized hikes in public expenditure.

The performance of the BNR had been supported by an extremely low turnover of governors: only three were appointed between 2002 and 2020, all of whom had strong technocratic profiles. The BNR seems to be shielded from societal pressures, as epitomized by its capacity to roll out demanding prudential regulations with no opposition from the banking sector. Yet the institution is clearly the implementer of the president's, and the ruling party's, decisions. As Behuria (2020b: 139) notes, rather than the BNR, 'the RPF's economic leadership has been the main driving force behind Basel Implementation.'

Signalling that Rwandan is open for (financial) business is not the only cause of the BNR's good performance. The neoliberal agenda of IFIs has also been followed because it was an effective tool for the RPF to reinforce its power. During the late 1990s when the RPF was seeking to consolidate the new political settlement, businessmen close to the RPF invested in the new licensed commercial banks. However, by the early 2000s, frictions in the RPF developed and some businessmen fell out with Kagame (Reyntjens 2013). In this context, opening the banking sector to foreign capital and sending Rwandan business people to court for the NPLs they received has been used to sideline domestic capitalists (Behuria 2020b).

Assessed by its own neoliberal mandate, the performance of the BNR has been largely successful. However, this form of success has also created tension with the country's developmental project, as it deprives the aspiring developmental state of the ability to use the financial sector for structural transformation (Behuria 2020b). Echoing the case of RRA, the case of the BNR shows the merits of the concentration of power in the ruling party and the top-down pressure to achieve results, but also its limited capacity to nurture social embeddedness, i.e. the capacity of the organization to understand the local constraints of the private sector: 'in Rwanda's ambitious development project, there is little room for BNR and commercial banks to voice criticisms' (Behuria 2020b: 144–5).

Analysing the politics of PoEs in Rwanda

The performance the three organizations analysed in this chapter can be explained by a set of organizational features long identified in the literature on PoEs as drivers of effectiveness (e.g. Grindle 1997, Leonard 2010, Roll 2014). All practised merit-based hiring, which nurtured professionalism. This was eased by their capacity to pay staff better than the rest of the state. In addition, all three organizations have, more than in the rest of the state, tried to encourage internal promotion, which reinforced their autonomy and their staff's *esprit de corps*. These traits were made possible through three main causal factors highlighted in Roll (2014): political economy, organizational function, and organizational leadership.

The political economy of high-performing state agencies

The functioning of the three organizations reflected wider patterns of politics within Rwanda, with the dominant incentives and ideas that characterize its political settlement generally supporting their performance. The concentration of power in the RPF, especially around Paul Kagame, made subverting the organizations' formal rules—for example, replacing merit-based recruitment with clientelism or state capture to accommodate a powerful political opposition—unnecessary. Decisions, once taken, were implemented in a relative straightforward manner. The very few instances when the nature of the settlement somewhat limited performance were due to the internal dynamics of the RPF, such as when the RPF government was initially reluctant to impose a property tax on party elites. Yet, in this case, as with the episode involving bad loans in the banking sector in the late 1990s, the concentration of power in the settlement eventually made the disciplining of the elite possible.

Nonetheless, the dominant nature of the political settlement itself is not sufficient to account for the performance of the three agencies. Whilst dominance provided the space for them to be effective and gave the RPF the enforcement capacities required to implement their programme, it was the systemic vulnerability of the ruling elite, anchored in its ethnic minority status and the genocide, which provided them with the spur to be effective. In this respect, Rwanda's trajectory clearly echoes those of the strong south-east Asian states where the shared experience of vulnerability amongst rulers incentivizes them to solve their collective action problems through building an effective state capable of addressing such a vulnerability (Doner, Ritchie, and Slater 2005, Slater 2010). Similarly, the strengthening of MINECOFIN, the BNR, and the RRA has to be understood as part of a wider attempt to build an effective state able to ensure regime survival through the legitimacy conferred by achieving rapid socio-economic development.

In Rwanda, as a consequence, most of the drivers behind the performance of the state agencies examined here apply to the rest of the state as well. Many traits that explain the performance of MINECOFIN, BNR and RRA are not exceptional: autonomy of the state from society, top-down pressure to deliver development, and target-driven management are all commonplace in Rwanda, whether in relation to agriculture (Ansoms 2009), social protection (Chemouni 2018, Lavers 2016), education (Williams 2017), or the governance of local authorities (Chemouni 2014). Consequently, it seems that a real trajectory of state-building is at play in Rwanda, instead of just the emergence of isolated PoEs operating within an otherwise dysfunctional state. This is supported by the expert surveys that reported high

Which of the following statements best describes the distribution of
performance amongst different parts of government in Rwanda?

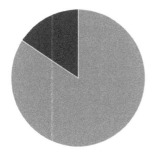

a) Most MDA regularly deliver on their
mandate, with only a few failing to do so.

b) On average, around half of all MDA
regularly deliver on their mandate, whilst the
remainder struggle to do so.

c) Only a few MDA regularly deliver on their
mandate, whilst the majority generally fail to
do so.

Figure 6.9   Expert views on public sector performance in Rwanda
Source: Author's expert survey.

levels of overall effectiveness, with respondents finding it difficult to clearly separate high performers from the norm (Figure 6.9), as well as more widely recognized
performance indicators of effective governance (Figure 6.1).

Why then do some organizations, such as the RRA, MINECOFIN, and the
BNR, stand at least somewhat apart in Rwanda? One reason is the role of ideas. All
three are organizations whose mission strongly fits not only the interests but also
the ideological worldview of the RPF. RRA's extraction of taxes, MINECOFIN'
strengthening of PFM procedures, and BNR's role of reassuring investors to move
the economy away from a risky commodity-based growth, all serve the core RPF's
paradigmatic ideas about self-reliance that underpins much of its approach to the
rebuilding of the country (Chemouni and Mugiraneza 2019: 23).

The other reasons for the particularly high performance of these three agencies
concerns the nature of their policy domain and of the tasks that they perform.
While, for the elite, a performing state *as a whole* is the response to their vulnerability, the RRA, MINECOFIN, and the BNR performed better because they
are the ones at the frontline of this legitimation project. Their mandates, whether
it is implementing the regime's ambitious developmental plan (MINECOFIN),
finding the resources for it (RRA), or signalling that Rwanda is financially stable
(BNR), are especially vital. As a result, they are prioritized by the elite in terms of
resources, political clout, and autonomy. They become lead climbers in the wider
dynamics of state-building, not because they are isolated 'islands' of performance
but as the result of a process of 'state-building prioritization'.

Organizational function

The nature of the tasks performed by these state agencies also seems to have
played an important role (Andrews, Pritchett, and Woolcock 2017, Israel 1987,
Leonard 2010). As emphasized by Evans (1995), performance often requires both

embeddedness and autonomy. The vulnerability of the Rwandan elite, anchored in its elite's minority status, its origins in the diaspora abroad and its limited ties with the rural world, means that the current state might not be sufficiently embedded within society. In the case of the RRA, and to a lesser extent the BNR, this results in inconstant performance: tasks requiring autonomy (extracting tax, imposing prudential regulations) are performed well, whilst those requiring embeddedness (consulting the business sector for formulating tax laws or new regulation), much less so. The capacity to nurture 'institutionalized channels for the continual nego-tiation and renegotiation of goals and policies' (Evans 1995: 12) is limited in Rwanda, since bureaucrats' accountability flows upwards.

Organizations undertaking tasks that are specific, technical, and measurable are more likely to perform well (Israel 1987, Leonard 2010, Roll 2014: 34), which is the case in all three of our cases. In contrast, organizations performing 'transactional' activities, i.e. involving many stakeholders to achieve results, face a more daunting task (Andrews, Pritchett, and Woolcock 2017). Unsurprisingly, the worst perform-ers identified in the Rwanda expert survey were in service delivery (Figure 6.10), which involves the complex coordination of different tasks at different levels of the state, and interactions with the population. In these cases, even if an orga-nization's policy domain makes it a high priority for the elite, the nature of the task might prevent it from becoming a 'best performer'. The case of the energy department in the Rwanda Ministry of Infrastructure exemplifies this (Chemouni and Dye 2020). Increasing electricity production capacity had been identified as vital for Rwanda's developmental project and the organization, as a result, received unfaltering political and financial support. While on paper, the Ministry of Infras-tructure (MININFRA) had good reason to become a PoE, it has been considered a bad performer (Figure 6.10) partly because of the difficulty of the task and its trans-actional nature: negotiating with investors, choosing a technology, conducting feasibility studies, etc. This was compounded by the range of unintended con-sequences of top-down pressure on its staff. Unlike the three HPSAs analysed here, this translated into a high turnover of leadership and the disempowerment of bureaucrats by the ruling party, which undermined the Ministry's performance. Tim Williams (2017) observed a similar dynamic in the Ministry of Education, also one of the worst performers in the state.

Organizational leadership

Organizational leadership played a significant role in the performance of MINECOFIN, the RRA, and the BNR. The respective leaders of these organi-zations had the skills, the expertise, and the political clout to carry out changes necessary for performance to emerge in each organization. They nearly all had a technocratic profile with many of them already having a significant previous

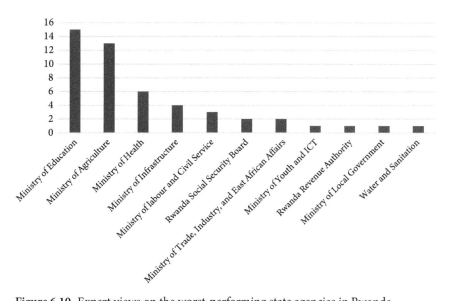

Figure 6.10 Expert views on the worst-performing state agencies in Rwanda (number of mentions)
Source: Expert survey.

experience in their own organizations. In addition, many PoEs' leaders had the profile of a 'technopol' (Domínguez 1997, Joignant 2011), i.e. individuals with both technical and political competences, able to rally political support to their objective. For example, Donald Kaberuka (former minister of finance), James Musoni (former minister of finance and RRA DG), Mary Baine (former RRA DG), Claver Gatete and John Rwangombwa (both former ministers of finance and BNR governors) were all heavyweights in the RPF. Their political clout reinforced their capacity to take bold and potentially unpopular decisions.

Consequently, leadership was an additional condition for HPSAs to emerge. Yet, this factor is only partly independent from political economy dynamics. Leadership conducive to performance in the PoEs was also able to thrive because of the political economy context, in that this allowed idiosyncratic leaders to be selected, empowered to carry out their work without interference, and left in post long enough to develop and deploy their leadership skills. At the same time, the pressure to perform undermined other state organizations, such as the Ministry of Infrastructure (Chemouni and Dye 2020) or the Ministry of Education (Williams 2017), with perceived failures leading to the high turnover of leaders.

Conclusion and policy implications

Overall, the case of PoEs in Rwanda is both exceptional and familiar. It is familiar in that all three state agencies studied here emerged as a result of the interaction of a specific political economy context, a policy domain, organizational leadership, and the nature of the task undertaken. However, it is also exceptional in that these three state agencies are not public organizations that are relatively effective '*despite operating in an environment in which effective public service delivery is not the norm*' (Roll 2014: 24, emphasis added). MINECOFIN, the BNR, and RRA may have initially resembled PoEs, in that they emerged in a post-genocide environment of low state performance, but they are now better defined as relatively high-performing state agencies in a generally functional state. The collective vulnerability of the Rwandan elite has created an incentive to undertake a fairly systematic project of state-building, albeit one that started with those agencies at the forefront of the country's developmental ambitions and of the related need to build legitimacy (both domestically and internationally).

Three main policy implications can be derived from this analysis. First, the Rwandan case indicates that the hope of building a state through islands of effectiveness becoming an archipelago and then a continent is not always warranted. The spillover effects identified here were mainly limited to the rotation of some staff from the RRA and MINECOFIN into the rest of the state, and to some PFM training that MINECOFIN provided to civil servants. Consequently, donors could support PoEs for their own sake, but should not assume that PoE practices will spill over into the rest of the state.

Second, analysis of PoEs reveals the merits, but also the dangers, of a high concentration of power in a settlement. Whilst this can offer the capacity to undertake difficult reforms and impose high levels of performance, it can also generate contradictory incentives and significant blind spots. Organizations operating in such contexts are unlikely to perform well if the task requires some level of embeddedness, especially the bottom-up gathering of information, or cannot easily be grasped by narrow indicators used by the top to assess performance. In addition, while the support and involvement of the ruling party and the presidency offers precious support for PoEs, it can also generate subservience and prevent bureaucrats from fully deploying their technical expertise and innovative capacities (cf. Fukuyama 2013), a phenomenon also conspicuous in other relatively poorly performing organizations in Rwanda, such as the Ministry of Infrastructure (Chemouni and Dye 2020). More generally, the pattern of performance in Rwanda, underpinned by a top-down style of governance, can also create a range of unintended consequences, including the disempowerment of staff, a lack of critical appraisal of policy and an incentive to 'cook' statistics, an issue already identified in the Rwandan case (Chemouni 2014: 251, 2018: 90, Reyntjens 2015). Lessons on some of these failings can be learned from the management style introduced by Kaberuka within MINECOFIN, whereby senior officials were encouraged to take risks and junior officials were relatively empowered.

Finally, the pattern of public-sector performance in Rwanda is a reminder of the extraordinary concentration of power in the ruling party, and especially around the president, and the danger that goes with it. This begs the question of whether the country's performance can survive the inevitable departure of Paul Kagame. This may happen if the norms and practices identified here become sufficiently ingrained in the state to persist and if the wider vulnerability of the elite continues to play its role of incentivizing a state-building project. This is not, however, certain, given the generational shift under way in the RPF, encouraged by the president, that gives rise to younger bureaucrats and politicians who may not have the same memory of the atrocities of the genocide, or the extraordinary challenges of the immediate post-1994 period. In this case, the current state-building dynamics may prove to be short lived, unable to survive the individual that was so pivotal in nurturing them and a historical driver whose power may be diminishing.

References

ActionAid (2011). *The Impact of Tax Incentives in East Africa—Rwanda Case Study Report*. Kigali: ActionAid.

AfDB (2011). 'Domestic Resource Mobilisation for Poverty Reduction in East Africa: Lessons for Tax Policy and Administration—Rwanda Case Study'. Tunis: African Development Bank Group.

Andrews, M., Pritchett, L., and Woolcock, M. J. V. (2017). *Building State Capability: Evidence, Analysis, Action*. First edition. Oxford; New York: Oxford University Press.

Ansoms, A. (2009). 'Re-engineering Rural Society: The Visions and Ambitions of the Rwandan Elite', *African Affairs*, 108(431): 289–309.

Behuria, P. (2016). 'Centralising Rents and Dispersing Power While Pursuing Development? Exploring the Strategic Uses of Military Firms in Rwanda'. *Review of African Political Economy*, 43(150): 630–47.

Behuria, P. (2020a). 'Central Banks as Pockets of Effectiveness in the 21st-century Global Political Economy: An Analysis of the National Bank of Rwanda'. ESID Working Paper. Manchester: Effective States and Inclusive Development Research Centre, University of Manchester.

Behuria, P. (2020b). 'Rwanda: Running without Legs'. In E. Jones (ed) *The Political Economy of Bank Regulation in Developing Countries: Risk and Reputation*. Oxford: Oxford University Press. 126–46.

Behuria, P. and Goodfellow, T. (2016). 'The Political Settlement and "Deals Environment" in Rwanda: Unpacking Two Decades of Economic Growth'. ESID Working Paper 57. Manchester: Effective States and Inclusive Development Research Centre, University of Manchester.

Campioni, M. and Noack, P. (eds) (2012). *Rwanda Fast Forward: Social, Economic, Military and Reconciliation Prospects*. London: Palgrave Macmillan.

Chemouni, B. (2014). 'Explaining the Design of the Rwandan Decentralization: Elite Vulnerability and the Territorial Repartition of Power', *Journal of Eastern African Studies*, 8(2): 246–62.

Chemouni, B. (2017). 'The politics of core public sector reform in Rwanda'. ESID Working Paper 88. Manchester: Effective States and Inclusive Development Research Centre, University of Manchester.

Chemouni, B. (2018). 'The Political Path to Universal Health Coverage: Power, Ideas and Community-based Health Insurance in Rwanda'. *World Development*, 106: 87–98.

Chemouni, B. (2019). 'The Rise of the Economic Technocracy in Rwanda: A Case of Bureaucratic Pocket of Effectiveness or Pocket of Priority?' Pockets of Effectiveness Working Paper 4. Manchester: Effective States and Inclusive Development Research Centre, University of Manchester.

Chemouni, B. (2020). 'Revenue Extraction Is Not Enough: The Ambiguous Effectiveness of the Rwandan Revenue Authority'. ESID Working Paper No. 157. Manchester: Effective States and Inclusive Development Research Centre, University of Manchester.

Chemouni, B. and Dye, B. (2020). 'The Contradictions of the Authoritarian Developmental State: Energy Boom and Policy-making in Rwanda'. FutureDAMS Working Paper 8. Manchester: University of Manchester.

Chemouni, B. and Mugiraneza, A. (2019). 'Ideology and Interests in the Rwandan Patriotic Front: Singing the Struggle in Pregenocide Rwanda', *African Affairs*, 119(474): 115–40.

Domínguez, J. I. (ed.) (1997). *Technopols: Freeing Politics and Markets in Latin America in the 1990s*. University Park, PA: Pennsylvania State University Press.

Doner, R. F., Ritchie, B. K., and Slater, D. (2005). 'Systemic Vulnerability and the Origins of Developmental States: Northeast and Southeast Asia in Comparative Perspective', *International Organization*, 59(02): 327–61.

Evans, P. B. (1995). *Embedded Autonomy: States and Industrial Transformation*. Princeton, NJ: Princeton University Press.

Fjeldstad, O.-H. and Moore, M. (2009). 'Revenue Authorities and Public Authority in Sub-Saharan Africa', *The Journal of Modern African Studies*, 47(1): 1–18.

Fukuyama, F. (2013). 'What Is Governance? Commentary', *Governance*, 26(3): 347–68.

Golooba-Mutebi, F. and Habiyonizeye, Y. (2018). 'Delivering Maternal Health Services in Rwanda: The Role of Politics'. ESID Working Paper 106. Manchester: Effective States and Inclusive Development Research Centre, University of Manchester.

Goodfellow, T. (2014). 'Rwanda's Political Settlement and the Urban Transition: Expropriation, Construction and Taxation in Kigali', *Journal of Eastern African Studies*, 8(2): 311–29.

Grindle, M. S. (1997). 'Divergent Cultures? When Public Organizations Perform Well in Developing Countries'. *World Development*, 25(4): 481–95.

IMF (2015). *Options for Low Income Countries' Effective and Efficient Use of Tax Incentives for Investment*. Washington, DC: IMF.

Israel, A. (1987). *Institutional Development: Incentives to Performance*. Baltimore, MD: Johns Hopkins University Press.

Joignant, A. (2011). 'The Politics of Technopols: Resources, Political Competence and Collective Leadership in Chile, 1990–2010', *Journal of Latin American Studies*, 43(03): 517–46.

Khan, M. (2010). 'Political Settlements and the Governance of Growth-enhancing Institutions. Draft paper'. Research Paper Series on 'Growth-enhancing Governance'. London: SOAS, University of London.

Kimonyo, J. P. (2017). *Rwanda, Demain! Une Longue Marche vers la Transformation*. Paris: Éditions Karthala.

Kimonyo, J. P. (2020). 'La Révolte des Kada Du FPR (1997–1998), Un "moment Critique" dans l'évolution du Rwanda Post-Génocide', *Politique Africaine*, 160(4): 159–86.

Lavers, T. (2016). 'Understanding Elite Commitment to Social Protection: Rwanda's Vision 2020 Umurenge Programme'. ESID Working Paper 68. Manchester: Effective States and Inclusive Development Research Centre, University of Manchester.

Leonard, D. K. (2010). '"Pockets" of Effective Agencies in Weak Governance States: Where Are They Likely and Why Does It Matter?' *Public Administration and Development*, 30(2): 91–101.

Moore, M. (2014). 'Revenue Reform and Statebuilding in Anglophone Africa', *World Development*, 60: 99–112.

OAG (2015). Report of the Auditor General of State Finances for the Year Ended 30 June 2014. Kigali: Office of the Auditor, Republic of Rwanda.

OAG (2018). Report of the Auditor General of State Finances for the Year Ended 20 June 2017. Kigali: Office of the Auditor, Republic of Rwanda.

Reyntjens, F. (2013). *Political Governance in Post-Genocide Rwanda*. Cambridge: Cambridge University Press.

Reyntjens, F. (2020). 'Au source de la gouvernance dans le Rwanda postgenocide', *Politique Africaine*, 160(4): 139–58.

Reyntjens, F. (2015). 'Lies, Damned Lies and Statistics: Poverty Reduction Rwandan-style and How the Aid Community Loves It'. African Arguments, 3 November. Available online: https://africanarguments.org/2015/11/03/lies-damned-lies-and-statistics-poverty-reduction-rwandan-style-and-how-the-aid-community-loves-it/ (accessed 2 May 2019).

Roll, M. (ed.) (2014). *The Politics of Public Sector Performance: Pockets of Effectiveness in Developing Countries*. London and New York: Routledge.

Rutayisire, M. (2010). 'Economic Liberalization, Monetary Policy and Money Demand in Rwanda: 1980–2005'. Working Paper. Nairobi: African Economic Research Consortium.

Schreiber, L. (2018). 'A Foundation for Reconstruction: Building the Rwanda Revenue Authority, 2001–2017'. Princeton, NJ: University of Princeton. Available online: https://successfulsocieties.princeton.edu/publications/foundation-reconstruction-building-rwanda-revenue-authority-2001-2017/ (accessed 27 June 2019).

Slater, D. (2010). *Ordering Power, Contentious Politics and Authoritarian Leviathans in Southeast Asia*. Cambridge: Cambridge University Press.

Steenbergen, V. and von Uexkull, E. (2018). 'Raising the Cost-effectiveness of Rwanda's Tax Incentives'. Working Paper. Kigali: IGC.

TJN-A and Action Aid (2016). *Still Racing toward the Bottom? Corporate Tax Incentives in East Africa*. Nairobi and Johannesbourg: Tax Justice Network—Africa and Action Aid.

USAID (2018). 'Domestic Resource Mobilization Case Study: Rwanda—Leadership in Public Financial Management II (LPFM II)'. Washington, DC: USAID.

Williams, T. P. (2017). 'The Political Economy of Primary Education: Lessons from Rwanda', *World Development*, 96: 550–61.

World Bank (2013a). Rwanda Economic Update, May 2013: Maintaining Momentum with a Special Focus on Rwanda's Pathway Out of Poverty. Washington, DC: World Bank.

World Bank (2013b). Transforming Central Finance Agencies in Poor Countries: A Political Economy Approach. Washington, DC: World Bank.

World Bank (2019). Future Drivers of Growth in Rwanda: Innovation, Integration, Agglomeration, and Competition. Washington, DC: World Bank Group.

World Bank Group (2018). Rwanda Investor Perceptions Survey 2018. Washington, DC: World Bank. Available online: https://openknowledge.worldbank.org/handle/10986/30202 License: CC BY 3.0 IGO.

Yohou, D. H. and Goujon, M. (2017). 'Reassessing Tax Effort in Developing Countries: A Proposal of a Vulnerability-adjusted Tax Effort Index'. Working Paper. Clermont-Ferrand, France: FERDI.

7

The Politics of PoEs in Uganda

Trapped between Neoliberal State-building and the Politics of Survival?

Sam Hickey, Badru Bukenya, and Haggai Matsiko

Introduction

Uganda's lauded record of economic growth and poverty reduction performance over much of the past three decades has often been linked to the performance of certain 'pockets of effectiveness' (PoEs). These include the Budget Directorate within the Ministry of Finance, Planning, and Economic Development (MFPED), the Bank of Uganda (BoU) and, to some extent, the Uganda Revenue Authority (URA). These PoEs and their 'technopol' leaders have loomed large in Uganda's public life since the mid-1990s, with their activities and pronouncements a matter of regular discussion, gossip, and critique that often makes media headlines. The prominence of these unelected technocrats—the permanent secretary at MFPED, the BoU governor, and the commissioner general of the URA—hinges on their close relationships with the president and the international financial institutions (IFIs), and is revealing of the semi-authoritarian, personalized, and transnational logics that underpin political and economic governance in Uganda.

These state agencies have played a central role in Uganda's shifting political economy of development over the past three decades, helping to embed neoliberal economic governance and, from the late 2000s, contesting efforts to move towards a more heterodox approach. They have also been central to the country's shifting politics over this period, first through their association with Uganda's initial politics of renewal in the first years of rule by the National Resistance Movement (NRM), before later becoming mired within the degenerative politics of survival that emerged from the early 2000s onwards and which continues to characterize the country's governance today. This chapter charts the rise and fall of Uganda's premier PoEs from the early 1990s until the late 2010s. Our evidence comes from in-depth case-study investigations of MFPED, BoU, and the URA undertaken between 2016 and 2019, involving between forty and fifty key informant interviews for each organization. These qualitative insights were triangulated with

Sam Hickey, Badru Bukenya, and Haggai Matsiko, *The Politics of PoEs in Uganda*. In: *Pockets of Effectiveness and the Politics of State-building and Development in Africa*. Edited by Sam Hickey, Oxford University Press. © Oxford University Press (2023). DOI: 10.1093/oso/9780192864963.003.0007

systematic analysis of relevant policy documentation and statistical performance data.

The chapter starts with a discussion of Uganda's changing political settlement dynamics since the mid-1980s and how this has shaped public-sector performance. It then introduces the expert survey that we used to help identify high-performing organizations, before summarizing the performance patterns of each PoE in turn. The analysis section argues that the main drivers of their performance over time flow from the country's changing political settlement dynamics, which have directly shaped the relationship between political rulers and senior bureaucrats, although international factors have also played an important role. The conclusion argues for a more balanced approach to state-building in Uganda, involving a shift away from neoliberalism and towards building the capacities required to support a productivist developmental agenda.

Economic governance within Uganda's shifting political settlement

Uganda's trajectory of state-building and development has been closely shaped by the shifting nature of its transnationalized political settlement since independence.[1] The country's political settlement was broadly stable and concentrated during Milton Obote's first period of rule (1964–1970). However, the political equilibrium was undermined by the constitutional changes of 1967 and the onset of militarized and narrowly ethnicized rule that was established in its aftermath (Mutibwa 1992, Reid 2017). The deepening of this mode of rule under Idi Amin (1970–1979) and Obote II (1980–1985) resulted in an economic collapse that was only reversed once the NRM brought stability to most of the country from 1986. For over a decade, Museveni was able to rule without the threat of being overturned by excluded elites within a no-party system and without facing significant demands from within his broadly based coalition. However, Museveni's refusal to allow an NRM successor to stand for the 2001 presidential elections led senior figures to depart the ruling coalition and form opposition parties that would mount serious challenges at the ballot box. This increased dispersal of power invoked an increasingly personalized form of rule by the president, with efforts to pander to demands from an increasingly fractious ruling coalition.

One of the mechanisms through which Uganda's political settlement dynamics have shaped the country's trajectory of economic growth since independence has been through the quality of economic governance. When the NRM came to power in Uganda in 1986, it inherited a state bureaucracy severely undermined by years of political unrest, civil strife, and economic turmoil and amongst

[1] On political settlements, see Chapter 2, this volume. For a fuller discussion of Uganda's political settlement, see Golooba-Mutebi and Hickey (2013), Kjaer (2015), Whitfield et al. (2015).

the worst macroeconomic indicators in sub-Saharan Africa. Graduate economists recruited by the finance ministry earned under $10 per month, and were demoralized to the extent that they stopped turning up for work (Simson and Wabwire 2016).

Within the first decade of NRM rule, however, senior bureaucrats working within the then separate Ministries of Finance and of Planning and Economic Development, reported how their organizations were transformed in ways that enabled them to play a critical role in rejuvenating Uganda's economy (Kuteesa et al. 2010). This transformation involved a new deal between rulers, bureaucrats, and external actors that reflected the broader character of Uganda's transnationalized political settlement at the time. By 1987, President Museveni was forced to adopt structural adjustment reforms targeting the public sector, exchange rate, and trade liberalization, among others (Bukenya and Muhumuza 2017). The full conversion to neoliberal economics arrived in 1992. The then permanent secretary at Planning and Economic Development, Emmanuel Tumusiime-Mutebile, persuaded the president that the reason inflation had reached 200 per cent was weak fiscal discipline, using rhetoric that appealed to the president's strong attachment to 'military discipline' (Mutebile 2010: 42).

This deal was underwritten by high levels of donor assistance. Salary supplements paid by donors helped incentivize staff attendance and removed the need for moonlighting (Mutebile 2010: 43). Expatriate assistants, focused on delivering reforms and training staff, were embedded first within MFPED (Mutebile 2010: 44–5) and later the URA, established under donor influence in 1993. Processes of state-building and public-sector reform in Uganda throughout this period were thus closely entwined with the imperatives of neoliberal logics and the associated agenda of good governance (Harrison 2010, Lie 2018).

However, this combination of strong donor support, presidential commitment, and bureaucratic capacity started to unravel in the mid-2000s, as Uganda's return to multi-party politics institutionalized the ongoing dispersal of power within the political settlement. Frustrated at the incapacity of government to deliver on his campaign promises, Museveni increasingly brought mainstream policy functions within State House and circumvented formal institutional mechanisms to reach out to people directly (Kjaer 2015). This was also a watershed moment in political economy terms. The discovery of commercial quantities of oil, the growing role of Chinese investment and Uganda's graduation from international debt all challenged the neoliberal hegemony of traditional donors (Hickey 2013, Rubongoya 2018). The gap between the façade of formal institutional arrangements in Uganda and their ability to function grew throughout this period (Andrews 2018), particularly in relation to corruption (Tangri and Mwenda 2013; see Figures 7.1 and 7.2). This pattern was also apparent in the trajectory of economic growth over time (see Figure 7.3). Uganda therefore largely upholds a core proposition of political settlements theory (Kelsall 2018, Khan 2010), namely that the level

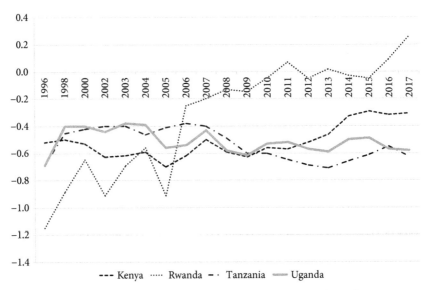

Figure 7.1 Government effectiveness in Uganda, Kenya, Rwanda, and Tanzania, 1996–2017

Source: World Governance Indicators.
Note: −2.5 weak; 2.5 strong.

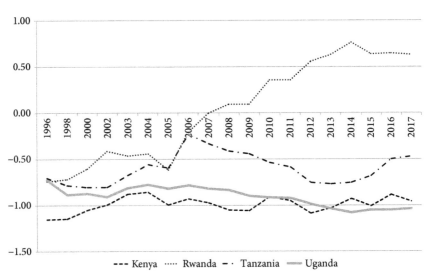

Figure 7.2 Control of corruption within East African countries, 1996–2017

Source: World Governance Indicators.
Note: −2.5 weak; 2.5 strong.

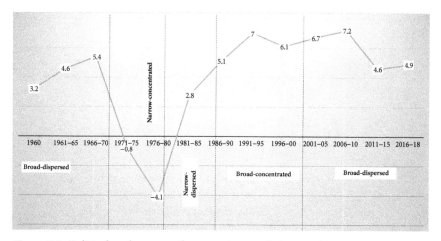

Figure 7.3 Political settlement and economic growth in Uganda, 1960–2018
Source: Adapted from Bukenya and Hickey (2018).
Note: The fall in average real GDP growth rates since the late 2000s also reflects a change in the methodology of calculating GDP (which was applied to 2008/09 onwards, but not used to recalculate previous years).

of commitment to growth-enhancing institutions is likely to be strongest under 'concentrated' political settlements, and that the increased dispersal of power will result in both declining commitment and enforcement capabilities.

The PoE phenomenon in Uganda

In 2017, we undertook an expert survey with thirty-three respondents to identify the highest-performing state agencies in Uganda. The clear majority concurred that 'only a few Ministries, Departments or Agencies (MDAs) regularly deliver on their mandate, whilst the majority generally fail to do so' (Figure 7.4). This underlined the strong sense that high-performing 'MDAs' are an exception rather than the norm in Uganda and that the 'PoE phenomenon' as defined by Michael Roll (see Chapter 1) is an integral part of the country's public-sector landscape.

When asked to specify the ministries which they considered to perform better relative to others, a majority rated the Ministry of Finance highest (Figure 7.5). In terms of regulatory agencies, the central bank (BoU) emerged as the top candidate, with the URA perceived to be the next highest performing, albeit by a much smaller margin (Figure 7.6). Therefore, and although the survey and our own earlier research had alerted us to the presence of other high-performing state agencies in Uganda,[2] these three were chosen for in-depth case-study investigations.

---

[2] The definition of PoEs from Roll (2014) that we use here (see Chapter 2) meant that we could not look at other possibilities identified by our experts, including the army (association with human rights abuses) and Kampala Capital City Authority (not national in character). We did examine the

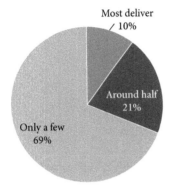

Figure 7.4 Expert views on public sector performance in Uganda
Source: Authors, expert survey.

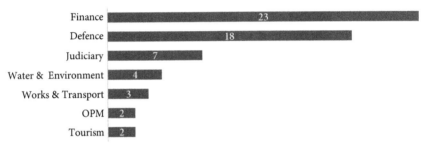

Figure 7.5 Expert ratings of high-performing ministries in Uganda
Source: Authors, expert survey.

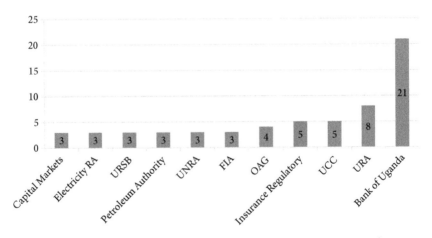

Figure 7.6 Expert ratings of high-performing regulatory agencies in Uganda
Source: Authors, expert survey.

National Water and Sewerage Corporation, with these results reported elsewhere (Bukenya 2020), and had already investigated the petroleum department (Hickey and Izama 2016, 2020).

We now set out the results of our in-depth investigations into how each of MFPED, BoU, and the URA have performed over time in relation to the transationalized political settlement dynamics identified above. In each case, we focus first on charting the effectiveness of their performance against their mandates, before turning to the wider questions concerning the ideological character of these mandates and the implications for Uganda's development trajectory. The summaries represent condensed versions of more detailed case-study papers (Bukenya and Hickey 2019, Hickey forthcoming, Hickey and Matsiko forthcoming).

Charting the performance of Uganda's premier PoEs over time

Ministry of Finance, Planning and Economic Development: Still Uganda's 'super ministry'?

Uganda's Ministry of Finance became transformed during the 1990s, from being an underpowered ministry that was unable to resist the demands of political leaders into a 'super ministry' that dominated other parts of government and offered the main interface with external actors. MFPED's official mandate is 'To mobilize financial resources, regulate their management, and formulate policies that enhance overall economic stability and development'.[3] We focus specifically on MFPED's capacity to effectively manage financial resources through a budgetary process directed towards economic development. A key indicator here is the extent to which supplementary budgets were deployed in relation to the rules governing this, which capped their use at 3 per cent of the overall budget. As Figure 7.7 shows, these rules were followed until 2002/03, after which they were broken each year until 2013/14, at an average of 10.22 per cent pa, with a particularly excessive episode just before the 2011 elections.

For the period before the law on supplementary expenditures was passed in 2001, we use the annual percentage growth in public expenditure as a rough proxy (Figure 7.8). Taken collectively, these figures suggests that after a period of relative stability during the 1990s, a political business cycle then sets in (Block 2002), with spikes occurring around the election years of 2001, 2006, 2011, and 2016. Importantly, Figure 7.9 shows that the gap between the resources allocated to public administration, security, and justice and those actually spent in these sectors widened from the early 2000s onwards; all three are strongly associated with political expenditure in Uganda.

A further source of evidence on MFPED's handling of the budget process comes from Public Expenditure and Financial Accountability (PEFA) assessments, which

---

[3] https://www.finance.go.ug/mofped/our-vision-mission-and-mandate (accessed 26 April 2021).

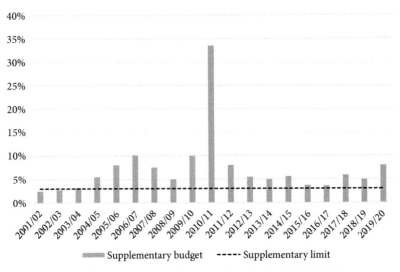

Figure 7.7 Supplementary expenditures in Uganda (%, 2001–2020)

Source: Authors based on the following sources: data for the years 2001–2012 from Bogetic et al. (2015); 2013–14 from Centre for Policy Analysis [nd]); and 2015–2020 from DEG (2020).

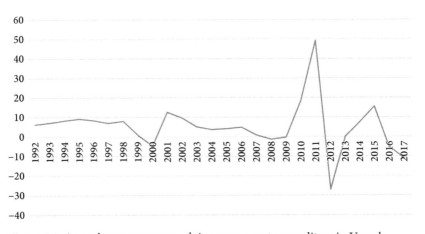

Figure 7.8 Annual percentage growth in government expenditure in Uganda, 1992–2017

Source: Based on World Bank data.
Note: See https://data.worldbank.org/indicator/NE.CON.GOVT.KD.ZG?locations=UG.

have been undertaken four times in Uganda from 2008.[4] The pattern of results is mixed, with aspects of budget management (e.g. on data) being performed at a

---

[4] PEFA started in 2001 as a donor initiative for harmonizing country-level assessment of public financial management (PFM) across 150 countries. It is supported by seven agencies, including the European Commission, International Monetary Fund, World Bank, and the governments of France,

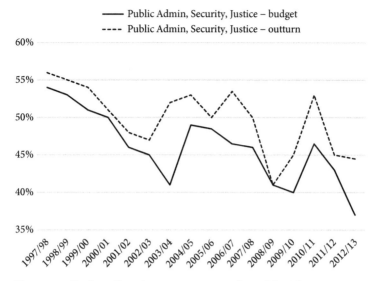

Figure 7.9 Budget allocation versus outturn for Public Administration in Uganda, 1997–2013

Source: IMF (2017: 30). Uganda Fiscal Transparency evaluation. IMF Country Report No. 17/130.

high level throughout the last decade (Table 7.1). However, other indicators also point to a declining level of performance during the late 2000s and early 2010s (e.g. on the 'extent of unreported government operations'), followed by improvements in almost all areas by 2017.

The increasing laxity around budget management and public expenditure from the early to mid-2000s suggests an important breakpoint within the trajectory of MFPED's performance. That the level of supplementary budgets is then reined back in after 2011 and, with PEFA scores improving between 2012 and 2017, indicates a further turning point from around 2012/13 (PEFA 2017). When combined with the qualitative accounts that we gathered on MFPED's performance over time, this suggests three distinct performance periods:

I. a period of *reform and strong performance* from 1992 until the early 2000s;

II. a period of *decline and capture* from the early/mid-2000s until 2012; and

III. a period from 2013 involving *partial reform amidst continued decline*.

Norway, Switzerland, and the United Kingdom (https://www.pefa.org/about/history, accessed 26 April 2021).

Table 7.1 Trends in selected Public Expenditure and Financial Accountability (PEFA) indicators in Uganda, 2008–2017

Indicator	2008	2009	2012	2017	Comments
Classification of the budget	A	A	A	A	No change
Comprehensiveness of information included in budget documentation	A	A	A	A	No change
Extent of unreported government operations	B+	D+	D+	C+	Only 1.9 per cent of central government budget is unreported
Transparency of inter-governmental fiscal relations	D+	D+	D+	C	LGs have sufficient time to prepare their budget after second budget call circular
Public access to key fiscal information	C	B	B	B	No change
Orderliness and participation in the annual budget process	B	C+	C+	A	Impact of PMFA 2015
Multi-year perspective in fiscal planning, expenditure policy and budgeting	B+	C+	C+	B	Medium Term Fiscal Forecast (MTFF) improved and used

Source: PEFA Uganda country reports for the respective years.

The halcyon days of reform: Early 1990s–2002

At that time everyone was reform-minded ... we enjoyed the positive political clout, the political commitment from the president, and the positive technical guidance from our bosses.[5]

It soon became clear that MoFEP had the president's full authority to do whatever was necessary to control inflation. The economic technocrats had taken over.

(Mutebile 2010: 42)

The reform period that began in the early 1990s is spoken of with great fondness and pride by those who worked in the ministry at the time and who considered themselves the bureaucratic vanguard of a wider movement of state-led reform. Emmanuel Tumusiime-Mutebile was a particularly key figure as the first permanent secretary (PS) of the combined Ministry of Finance, Planning and Economic Development[6] from 1992 through until being appointed as governor of the BoU

---

[5] Ex-senior officer within Budget Department, 9 November 2017.

[6] This merger took two rounds (from 1992 to 1996 before a second merger in 1998) and helped to deliver a much more strategic and analytical approach to policymaking during the later years of this period.

from 2001. Mutebile was granted the political authority to enforce strict fiscal discipline. Civil servants knew that 'we enjoyed the political commitment from the president':

> We also had a well-seasoned minister who was very competent, knew the president very well. Mutebile (the PS) was also highly respected, a hardliner, he would tell the president 'over my dead body'. So we technical people were very motivated to work, because we knew if we worked hard and did our work it would be accepted.[7]

Staff appreciated efforts by the ministry's leadership to build a strong organizational culture, noting that they were offered 'clear job specifications and career progression' and that it was 'always clear that promotions were on merit'.[8]

The period of decline: 2003–2012

Many officials involved in the early reform period identify the 2001 elections as the point at which the ministry started to lose this high level of political protection and direction:

> It started changing in 2001 ... I remember going for a meeting and he [the president] was creating a credit scheme ... The president said: 'These are my voters and they don't have access to reliable income. I want money to be able to give out to my citizens.' That is when we knew things had changed.[9]

This change in presidential orientation was reflected within changes to the ministry's leadership. In 2001, Mutebile was moved to the central bank and replaced with a permanent secretary perceived as being less obstructive. The highly regarded minister, Ssendaula, retired in 2005, and 'MFPED has not survived [the] inadequate finance ministers that followed him',[10] none of which possessed his combination of technocratic expertise and political heft. The fact that the average length of a ministerial term has been halved from six to seven years during the first two decades of NRM rule to just over three years from 2005–2019 suggests the growing degree of political interference.

The mid-2000s watershed for Uganda's political economy—which reduced the influence of Western donors and the president's commitment to neoliberal orthodoxy—also had a direct impact in MFPED. One Ugandan advisor to the minister of finance at the time noted that this was 'the moment that we started to push donors away, we had discovered oil and pushed donors to [the] back seat, and

---

[7] Ex-senior officer within the Budget Department, 9 November 2017.
[8] Ex-senior officer within the Budget Department, 9 November 2017.
[9] Ex-senior officer within the Budget Department, 9 November 2017.
[10] Senior government advisor and ex-Ministry of Finance advisor, 6 November 2017.

that took away a little bit of the sanity.[11] With the president increasingly attracted to large infrastructure projects, MFPED was now seen as an obstacle to his ambitions. In 2007, the president shifted responsibility for national development planning away from MFPED to the National Planning Authority and re-enforced parallel processes of economic planning through the Presidential Economic Council. Its hegemony challenged, MFPED also started to experience the internal problems of corruption that had come to typify the public sector in Uganda in the 2000s. Finance officials were heavily implicated in Uganda's mishandled hosting of the Commonwealth Heads of Government Meeting in 2007 and the major theft of donor funds intended to support reconstruction efforts in northern Uganda in 2012. Insiders also note that the previously meritocratic process of appointments and promotions also came under strain during this period.[12]

MFPED's ability to protect the budget process from political interference was severely tested around the 2011 elections, with a massive spike in public expenditure arguably reflecting the wholesale capture of this erstwhile PoE. Under pressure to allocate resources to aid funding of political activities of the ruling party (Abrahamsen and Bareebe 2016), MFPED was forced to approve huge allocations to State House, the Office of the President, and the Ministry of Defence. These are all channels through which the NRM's militarized and monetized strategies of regime survival are funded (Golooba-Mutebi and Hickey 2016; Figure 7.9).

Partial reform amidst continued decline? 2013–2018

The reforms undertaken by MFPED from 2013 were led by the new permanent secretary, a reformist official who 'brought a lot more vigour—he can wade into the murky political waters with some degree of confidence', given his close relationship with the president.[13] Major reforms included the introduction of the Treasury Single Account and the new Public Financial Management Act (PFMA) in 2015, the latter of which included an explicit effort to protect the budget process from political pressure.[14] However, as the 2016 elections approached, the Executive encouraged loyal parliamentarians to table amendments that would loosen the new restrictions on supplementary budgets.[15] On 11 November 2015, parliament passed the PFM Amendment Bill, a mere six months after the original Act, with one senior official admitting that 'we lost that one, the one of supplementaries'.[16] The misuse of the budget for political purposes had, in any case, been re-established through MFPED's agreement to significantly increase the annual

---

[11] Ex-advisor to minister of finance, 29 July 2016.
[12] MFPED commissioner, 6 November 2017.
[13] Leading journalist in Uganda, 10 November 2017.
[14] Interviews with leading officials in Kampala in November 2017, also 19 October 2018.
[15] Interview with senior MFPED official, 18 October 2018.
[16] Interview with senior MFPED official, 29 July 2016.

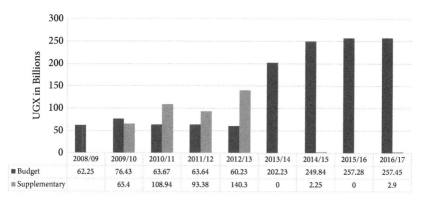

	2008/09	2009/10	2010/11	2011/12	2012/13	2013/14	2014/15	2015/16	2016/17
Budget	62.25	76.43	63.67	63.64	60.23	202.23	249.84	257.28	257.45
Supplementary		65.4	108.94	93.38	140.3	0	2.25	0	2.9

Figure 7.10 State House budget and supplementary budgets in Uganda, 2008–2017

Source: Based on figures from ACFIM (2016) and IMF (2017).

budgetary allocation for State House (Figure 7.10), a move that institutionalized the imperative of political survival within Uganda's budget process.

The Bank of Uganda

> The primary purpose of the Bank is to foster price stability and a sound financial system. Together with other institutions, it also plays a pivotal role as a *centre of excellence* in upholding macroeconomic stability.[17]

> BoU's mandate is financial stability and macro stability, and pretty much we have achieved this. The exceptions were 2011 regarding the macro and Crane Bank with financial stability.[18]

The BoU was established in 1966, with technical and financial support from Britain. Under Idi Amin, the BoU Act was amended to increase the amount that government could borrow and BoU soon became 'a mere service department for the government' (Mutibwa, 2006: 260, Dafe 2019). Nonetheless, staff were paid well and on time and could be characterized as 'a real aristocracy' (Suruma 2014). It was not until just after the inflation crisis of 1992 that BoU was granted formal autonomy. During the 1990s and 2000s BoU was credited with playing a major role in reducing inflation, maintaining macroeconomic stability, and providing the conditions for sustained growth. Appointed BoU governor in 2001, Emmanuel Tumisiime Mutebile became one of the country's most recognizable public figures and was garlanded as African Central Bank Governor of the Year on

---

[17] BoU website, 11 March 2019, emphasis added.
[18] Interview with senior BoU official, 12 March 2019.

several occasions. However, the Bank's performance in terms of both monetary and banking supervision dipped sharply during the late 2000s, only recovering in relation to price stability following the political and economic crisis of 2011/12.

We discuss BoU's performance trajectory in relation to the two main aspects of the Bank's mandate—price and financial stability—before reflecting on the broader developmental implications of BoU's hegemony in the chapter's final section.

The Bank of Uganda and price stability

Uganda's performance on price stability since the early 1990s suggests that BoU has undergone three main performance periods: a period of reform and good performance from 1993 to 1999; a period of capture and failure during 2010–2012; and then a period of recovery from 2013 to date (Figure 7.11).

Although inflation in Uganda is a largely seasonal phenomenon with regards to food production and prices, fiscal indiscipline has also been a key driver. Between 1986 and 1989, borrowing from BoU contributed to 'skyrocketing' levels of inflation (Dafe 2019), with BoU giving money freely to ministers via requests based on revenue predictions rather than actual revenue (Suruma 2014).[19] The fiscal crisis of 1992 led government to agree a Financial Sector Adjustment Program with the IFIs in 1993 to reorient financial policy from financial expansion towards stability (Dafe 2019). This involved BoU taking responsibility for monetary policy and forging a strong working relationship with the newly restrained treasury. Although not appointed as BoU governor until 2001, Mutebile's authority helped consolidate

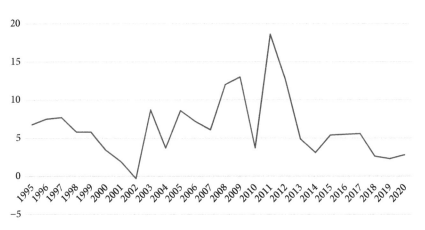

Figure 7.11 Inflation rate in Uganda, 1995–2020 (end-of-period consumer prices)
Source: Based on data from IMF. Available at: https://www.imf.org/external/datamapper/ PCPIPCH@WEO/UGA.

[19] Suruma was deputy governor and director of research at BoU, and also advisor to Minister of Finance Kiyonga, from 1987 to the early 1990s.

these reforms and BoU's autonomy. According to one official who worked at BoU throughout the 1990s and 2000s:

> He has competent staff, they do proper analysis; personality-wise he can be very decisive, once he is convinced, at one time his voice would move the market. He will say no, including to the president.[20]

BoU's Research and Policy directorate was critical here, particularly through its insistence that all decision-making on monetary policy was to be evidence based.[21] The Monetary Policy Committee met regularly and BoU and MFPED officials also established an informal Friday meeting to ensure a joined-up response to the macroeconomic situation.

However, when the deal over fiscal discipline between the president, the economic technocracy, and the IFIs began to unravel in the mid-2000s, BoU's de jure autonomy could not fully protect it. According to one ex-MFPED official who was working in the ministry at the time:

> It was always the case in election year. When he [the president] was withdrawing from taking care of the economy, he asked us, 'Why can't you let inflation go above 5 per cent?'[22]

The massive increase in public expenditures in the run-up to the 2011 elections coincided with other instances of political interference with BoU. This included the apparent complicity of the BoU governor in authorizing an excessive compensatory payment to a politically connected businessman and the purchase of six Russian fighter jets (Hickey and Matsiko 2022). The extent of BoU's role in the 2011 elections became clear in 2014, with the governor admitting that it had reissued old 50,000 Shilling notes in support of the president's election campaign. As one ex-advisor to the Minister of Finance noted:

> Even if it was old bills, it is still new money that is a deviation from the planned money supply route. So it is printing money in a sense. Electoral costs were going through the roof—you have no idea. Not on goods and services, so inflationary.[23]

The flood of money into the economy catalysed a rapid rise of inflation to an average of nearly 19 per cent over 2011, with a peak of 30.5 per cent. This was the first

---

[20] Interview, 9 November 2017.
[21] Interview with ex-BoU official, 9 November 2017.
[22] Ex-senior officer within the Budget Department, 9 November 2017.
[23] Interview, 15 March 2019.

time since 1992 that inflation had reached double figures for inexplicable reasons (see Figure 7.3).[24]

The resulting cost-of-living crisis inspired the popular 'walk-to-work' protests in 2011–12 (Branch and Mampilly 2015). Badly shaken, the government responded rapidly, severely tightening monetary policy, undertaking operational reforms within BoU, and constraining government borrowing through the Public Financial Management Act. The decision 'to push interest rates to the maximum'[25] saw BoU lending rates reaching as high as 30 per cent. Inflation was reduced to single figures by the end of 2012, albeit at a cost to economic activity. Growth rates fell to 3.2 per cent over 2011/12, and have since averaged only 4.1 per cent pa, as compared to an average of over 7 per cent between 2000 and 2007/08 (Figure 7.3).

In the run-up to the 2016 election, BoU undertook a media and lobbying campaign aimed at avoiding a repeat of the political capture it had experienced at the previous poll. BoU and MFPED staff lobbied State House and ministers and issued joint communiqués directed at both the public and the president.[26] The governor gave a series of interviews to the international and national media to proclaim the need to restore central bank autonomy, a point he stressed further in a speech at a conference of central bankers in Uganda on 11 November 2014.[27] One BoU official explained how 'we started tightening monetary policy in 2015 ... explicitly for elections'.[28]

Something worked, with BoU retaining control of macroeconomic stability at the 2016 elections. The IMF's visiting mission just before the 2016 elections reported that 'the pressures were not as bad as last time' and that the government was managing to curtail politically influenced expenditure. Nonetheless, the 2016 elections weighed heavily on the fiscal side and on the real economy, with government freezing expenditure on investment and redirecting public finances to the electoral campaign (ACFIM 2016).

The Bank of Uganda and financial stability

BoU's role in ensuring financial stability involves licensing, monitoring, and disciplining financial institutions. Since BoU was granted autonomy in 1993, we identify three main performance periods regarding this part of its mandate: reform and capacity-building from 1993 to 1998; good performance from 1999 to 2010; and a period of failure from 2011 to date (Figure 7.12). Most indicators of financial soundness suggest that the banking sector operated well within the statutory

---

[24] The smaller spikes in inflation in 2003 and 2008 were due to oil price rises and a mixture of drought and food price rises, respectively.

[25] Interview with senior BoU official, 12 March 2019.

[26] Interview with senior MFPED advisor, 15 March 2019.

[27] e.g. Issac Imaka and Stephen Otage, 'I was misled into funding 2011 polls, says Mutebile', *The Monitor*, 12 November 2014. Available online: https://www.monitor.co.ug/uganda/news/national/i-was-misled-into-funding-2011-polls-says-mutebile-1590724 (accessed 26 April 2021).

[28] Interview, 12 March 2019.

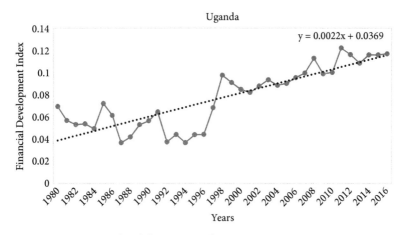

Figure 7.12 Financial stability in Uganda, 1980–2016

Source: IMF online data https://data.imf.org/?sk=F8032E80-B36C-43B1-AC26-493C5B1CD33B.

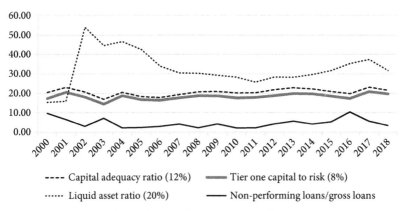

Figure 7.13 Financial soundness indicators in Uganda, 2000–2018

Source: Based on Bank of Uganda data.

requirements over the past two decades (Figure 7.13). Although the spike in the level of non-performing loans around 2016 may relate to the series of bank closures that took place between 2012 and 2017, these closures did not result in any negative systemic effects on the banking system. However, we show below that it is necessary to pay close attention to the process through which central banks handle specific bank closures, rather than focus on aggregate performance indicators.

Officials working in the bank in the late 1980s report that the supervision unit was largely sidelined by the bank's leadership, heavily understaffed, poorly trained, and poorly managed,[29] a view confirmed by the IMF (1991). In 1993, the IFIs led institutional reforms to the BoU and public-sector banks amidst financial liberalization. The supervision unit was elevated to directorate level in 1992 and the Financial Institutions Statute of 1993 increased BoU's capacity in banking supervision (Dafe 2019). Poorly managed banks that had been overlooked were now targeted for closure, as with Teefe Bank in 1993 (Suruma 2014: 51). Further closures of failing banks in 1998–1999 revealed a willingness by BoU to punish institutions despite their high-level political connections, including to the president's brother (Hickey and Matsiko forthcoming).

These bank closures catalysed a new round of reforms and lesson-learning, with the revised BoU Act of 2000 strengthening its powers over all financial institutions (BoU 2002: 6) and the 2004 Financial Institutions Act leading BoU to adopt principles from the Basel accord. From 2005 onwards, the banking sector was relatively free from financial distress (Figure 7.13, IMF 2005). This recovery was helped by changes within the central bank: the supervision department was restructured and successive executive directors with strong credentials were appointed. The new director from 2005, Justine Bagyenda, became renowned as 'the iron lady' of the banking sector for her tough approach to banking supervision, apparently terrifying senior bank executives during inspections.[30]

On the surface, this high-level commitment to banking supervision seemed to continue into the 2010s, with aggregate levels of financial stability remaining sound (BoU 2012). However, in 2012 and 2014, BoU closed two major banks, including the National Bank of Commerce which was owned by the then prime minister and political rival of the president. In 2018, investigations by the Office of the Auditor General and the parliamentary committee on Commissions, Statutory Authorities, and State Enterprises revealed that the closures violated the Financial Institutions Act.[31] Still more controversial was the closure of Crane Bank Limited (CBL), Uganda's third biggest bank. CBL's owner, Sudhir Ruparelia, was renowned as the richest man in Uganda and for having been a strong financial supporter of the NRM government. The BoU took over management of Crane Bank on 20 October 2016, on the (largely justifiable) grounds that it was significantly undercapitalized and posed a systemic risk to the stability of the financial system.

However, the BoU's handling of the closure catalysed a series of investigations from mid-2018, formally by the auditor general and parliament, and less formally at the orders of State House. According to the parliamentary investigation, staff with BoU's supervisory directorate ignored the excesses of some bank operators

---

[29] Interviews, 8 and 9 May 2019.
[30] Interview with ex-commercial bank secretary, 8 February 2019.
[31] A. Mwenda (2013). 'Battle for 2016', *The Independent*, 6 December.

and flouted laws and procedures during all three bank closures between 2012 and 2016 (COSASE 2019: 20). The executive director of supervision, Justine Bagyenda, was heavily criticized for deploying lawyers with vested interests against CBL and for having diluted reports from junior BoU officials that had raised concerns about CBL.[32] Although the banking system and depositors have been protected, the costs to the taxpayer have been growing; in the case of Crane Bank, BoU injected Shs.487 billion to pay depositors and keep the bank afloat ahead of its sale.

The BoU's handling of this crisis was further marred by an internal conflict that pitted the governor against not only Bagyenda but also the deputy governor, who had expected to be promoted to the governorship in 2015. However, at that point President Museveni had just ousted the prime minister and felt unable to remove the governor, given that both hailed from the same influential constituency in Western Uganda.[33] One member of the presidential investigation team attributed BoU's declining performance during the 2012–2016 period to this infighting.[34] The parliamentary investigations were televised live and caused a major stir amongst a public that had previously trusted the BoU as the country's most independent and effective public-sector organization.

The Uganda Revenue Authority

> Even if it [URA] runs smoothly, it will still be tampered with: large businesses go to State House and get tax waivers. These are [the] same companies that have been bankrolling the government. It all ties into [the] longevity of the current system.[35]

The claim that the URA is one of the country's best-performing state agencies sits awkwardly with the fact that Uganda's record on revenue mobilization is comparatively poor. In 2016, Uganda's tax-to-GDP ratio was over five percentage points lower than the average of twenty-one other African countries (Figure 7.14), partly because the informal economy in Uganda is somewhat larger than in most of Africa. Low levels of tax compliance are also historically embedded in Uganda's experience of colonial rule and state collapse, as well as the ongoing discontent with corruption and low-quality service delivery. However, the fact that Uganda's record of revenue generation is worse than countries with similar economic structures, and that this record has been uneven over the past three decades, suggests that other domestic political economy factors are also important here.

---

[32] Ex-director BoU supervision directorate, 16 April 2019.
[33] Interviews with author, July 2016.
[34] Interview, 13 March 2019.
[35] Senior government official, 26 July 2016.

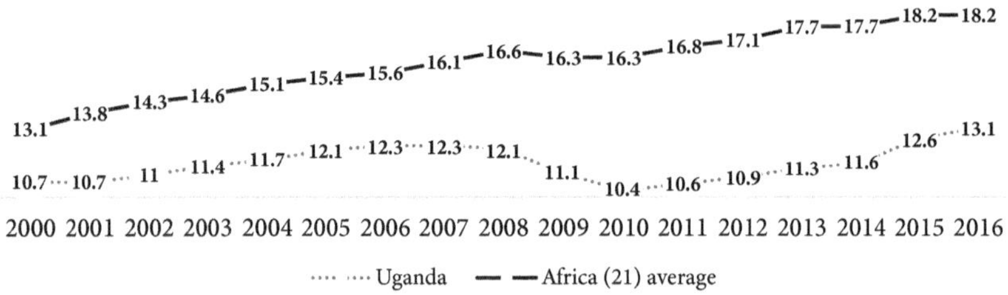

Figure 7.14 Uganda's tax-to-GDP ratio, 2000–2016
Source: Revenue Statistics in Africa 2018 oe.cd/revenue-statistics-in-africa.

Table 7.2 URA leadership 1991 to 2020

Time period	Name	Politically connected/ protected?	Technically competent?
1991–1997	Edward Larbi Siaw (expat)	Yes	Yes
1997–2000	Elly Rwakakooko	Yes	No
2001–2004	Annebrit Aslund (expat)	No	Yes
2004–2015	Allen Kagina	Yes	Yes
2015–2020	Doris Akol	No	Yes

Source: Authors.

Our evidence suggests that the uneven performance of the URA over time is closely linked to whether (a) tax policy *and* tax administration were *both* benefitting from political support at the same time, and (b) the quality and political connectedness of URA's leadership (Table 7.2). Below we discuss both the strong periods of URA performance, from 1991–1997 and 2005–2012, and the weaker periods that occurred in between 1998–2004 and from 2013–2019.

Prior to the NRM taking power in 1986, political instability meant that tax policy had become chaotic and 'tax administration capacity had deteriorated greatly' (Cawley and Zake 2010: 103). Between 1986 and 1991, Uganda's ratio of tax revenue to GDP averaged 5.8 per cent and taxpayer compliance was a major problem. The establishment of the URA as a semi-autonomous authority in 1991 had a significant impact, with the tax-to-GDP ratio rising from 6.8 per cent in 1991/92 to 11.3 per cent in 1996/97 (Cawley and Zake 2010: 120). Tax effort rose significantly during this period, suggesting that both tax policy and administration were being actively and effectively pursued. For example, the 1996 VAT and 1997 Income Tax Acts curtailed both the discretionary award of exemptions to businesses and the removal of exemptions from public servants and parastatals from the income-tax system (Cawley and Zake 2010: 112). Reforms were also implemented enthusiastically on the administration side. URA officials were paid wages significantly above the average for civil servants, in a bid to reduce the incentives for corruption, and all senior positions within the URA were initially filled by experienced expatriates, who were charged with training up Ugandans to replace them (Cawley and Zake 2010: 116).

This reformist impetus tailed off towards the end of the 1990s. From 1996/97 to 2003/04, the URA only managed to meet its revenue target on two occasions and the tax-to-GDP ratio eventually dipped below the level inherited at the start of the period. Tax effort reduced significantly from 1999 and continued to fall during this period, indicating that neither tax policy nor tax administration were being pursued with any commitment or efficacy. This was partly due to the URA's failure to curb evasion and corruption (Cawley and Zake 2010: 120), particularly after the initial salary improvements enjoyed by URA officials tailing off (Kjaer et al. 2017: 20) and a new commissioner general being appointed in 1997 on the basis of political connections rather than technical or leadership capacities (Table 7.2). The move to appoint an expatriate leader (2001–2004) reversed this approach, leaving the URA with a technically competent leader but one who lacked the political connections to do the job properly (Kangave and Katusiimeh 2015: 6). The tax regime also weakened during this period, with the 2001 election seeing the removal of taxes on the informal sector and new tax exemptions for business owners supportive of the president.

The period from 2004 to 2012 is widely referred to as being a highly successful period for the URA, with political commitment, leadership, organizational capacity, and external support all at high levels. The commissioner general throughout this period, Allen Kagina, would later recount that:

> Revenue collections had grown rapidly by 317% in the period. Tax contribution to the National Budget grew from 58.7% to 71.5% ... Public perception made a complete turnaround with various sections of society and leaders calling [the] URA a model public institution.
>
> (Kagina 2015: 3–4, cited in Magumba 2019: 2)

Under Kagina, the entire staff of the URA was fired in 2004, with selective re-hiring leading to a more streamlined organization. The 2006–2010 Modernization Plan established a new set of priorities through a participatory process, and interviews suggest that Kagina's style reflected a 'problem-driven-iterative-adaptive' approach (Andrews et al. 2017). Importantly, Kagina enjoyed a close relationship with the president, giving her considerable clout within and beyond the URA.

Nonetheless, between 2005 and 2015, tax revenues were unresponsive to overall GDP growth: the tax-to-GDP ratio flatlined at 13 per cent for most of the period (Mawejje and Munyambonera 2016). The data on tax effort (Figure 7.15) suggests a partial recovery, at least between 2004 and 2007, followed by continued deterioration. The logical explanation for this apparent discrepancy between the URA's

Figure 7.15 Uganda's tax effort 1991–2012 in comparative perspective
Source: Based on data from Yohou and Goujon (2017).

reputation as a PoE and the country's comparatively weak performance on revenue generation lies in the further politicization of tax policy during this period, which undermined the gains being made on the administrative side. This included the president abolishing the Graduated Tax in 2006, to avoid alienating his rural base. Uganda also eschewed the adoption of exceptional tax handles that enabled other countries in the region to boost their tax-to-GDP ratios (including pay roll, property, and air departure taxes) whilst offering generous exemptions worth around five per cent of GDP.

The late 2010s saw a further decline in political commitment to the URA, alongside panicky measures to generate revenue in response to budgetary shortfalls, rather than a coherent strategy for taxation. The tax-to-GDP ratio improved from around 13 per cent to 14 per cent, with experts suggesting that this reflectsed the short-run effects of these ad hoc policy measures plus Kagina's earlier reforms.[36] The new commissioner general, who served from 2014 to 2020, was considered to be highly competent and a person of integrity. However, she lacked a close relationship with the political leadership, and interviews with close observers suggest a leadership style that tended to stifle other senior managers and a failure to protect the budget for staff training. There is also a growing sense that the URA is being forced to undertake political work on behalf of government. According to one civil society leader, 'if you are critical, they (URA) will come and freeze your assets'.[37]

---

[36] Personal communication with IFI specialist, May 2018.
[37] Interview, 7 November 2011.

Explaining the politics of performance in Uganda

Since being targeted for political protection and international investment in the early 1990s, each of Uganda's premier PoEs have a somewhat different story to tell in terms of their performance trajectories. Some of this can be explained in terms of the particular policy challenge being addressed and the degree of organizational autonomy that characterizes each agency. For example, the more autonomous status granted to BoU, along with its critical role vis-à-vis IFIs and credit markets, enabled it to resist political capture for somewhat longer than MFPED, a more mainstream part of government. The semi-autonomous URA is somewhat different again: its activities are more directly connected to actual voters than those of the treasury or central bank, and the fact that it is a policy taker rather than a policymaker means its performance is shaped by factors beyond its control. The URA's reliance on MFPED to set the policy direction on taxation has created a further dynamic that highlights the limitations of 'agencification' as a strategy for improved performance over time. Importantly, MFPED's tax-policy capabilities were significantly undermined both by the URA's creation, which saw experienced staff leave the ministry for higher-paid positions in the URA, and by the dominance of the budget department within MFPED. This uneven distribution of capabilities within government in turn reflects the nature of Uganda's political settlement, whereby patron–client logics dictating that resources flow downwards to voters in return for political loyalty, rather than the opposite way in the form of a social contract. There is, in other words, a particular politics to each organization and the relationships between them that matters when trying to understand their performance patterns over time, including the good working relationships between the treasury and central bank required to balance fiscal and monetary policy.

However, these factors have been relatively constant over the time period discussed here. This suggests that the more important causal mechanisms that have shaped organizational performance can be located elsewhere, and specifically in the interplay of political settlement dynamics, organizational leadership, and international influence. This section explains the performance patterns identified above in relation to these factors, starting with the most influential.

Uganda's premier PoEs and the country's shifting political settlement

There had been a major expansion of the budget ... this should have led to political support and Museveni realized it hadn't due to the challenge from Besigye (in 2001). Economic policy made in a technocratic and impersonal manner would not work; he realized he had to use patronage and be seen to be associated with it. That is when the political economy really changed in this country ... Realized he had to deliver patronage to political bigwigs or they would desert.[38]

The fact that the president retains the power to appoint the leaders of even autonomous and semi-autonomous organizations such as the URA and BoU, and has been the dominant player in Uganda's political settlement since 1986, is pivotal here. The tripartite deal on economic governance that was struck in the early 1990s between a reformist president, IFIs and senior bureaucrats largely held for the decade within which Uganda's political settlement concentrated power around a dominant leader. There was also a degree of 'systemic vulnerability' (Doner et al. 2005) during this period. The various insurgency movements in the countryside, the need to forge a broad-based settlement with multiple social groups, and a lack of foreign exchange (Rubongoya 2018), all helped to incentivize a degree of state-building, albeit of a highly partial and neoliberalized form.

The increased dispersal of power within Uganda's political settlement from the late 1990s onwards would steadily undermine presidential commitment to even this narrow form of state-building, as highlighted in the quote that opened this section. Indeed, the 1996 elections had already led the president to weaken his commitment to the URA, despite there being no real threat at the ballot box. This threat grew significantly over successive elections in the 2000s. With the costs of maintaining provisioning pacts with elites rising significantly, MFPED and then BoU were subject to growing levels of political interference, culminating in their outright capture around the 2011 elections. The declining influence of international actors such as the World Bank and IMF from the mid-2000s seemed to further weaken the capacity of bureaucrats within core economic agencies to protect themselves from political interference. The neoliberal ideological settlement that helped hold the original deal together became further weakened by the advent of oil and China (Hickey 2013), with Museveni now invoking 'a more state-oriented, populist ideology' (Rubongoya 2018: 105). The dilution of the Public Financial Management Act in the run-up to the 2016 elections and the compromise reached around State House budgetary allocations suggest that the political imperatives of regime survival were continuing to outweigh the technical imperatives of economic governance.

The broad social foundations of Uganda's political settlement also played an important role here. The president has been increasingly unwilling to antagonize those social and economic constituencies upon which he relies to stay in power. This in turn has moderated the executive commitment to building and protecting meritocratic public-sector organizations over time, often in ways that are linked to the increased dispersal of power since the early 2000s. A notable

---

[38] Long-term senior advisor to MFPED and BoU, 6 November 2017.

example concerns the reluctance to impose increased taxation burdens on petty traders in Uganda's informal sector and the willingness to offer exemptions to companies in return for financial and political support. Another growing trend over the 2000s was an increased reliance on making appointments from the president's own ethno-regional base, particularly in senior political and bureaucratic positions (Lindemann 2011), in ways that arguably betrayed a growing insecurity about his grip on power. Insiders within all of our case-study organizations report a growing sense that the balance that had previously been struck between meritocracy and political loyalty in relation to appointments and promotions had been increasingly eroded over the 2000s, with some observers going as far as to argue that:

> There is no meritocracy: they are his people in the army, diplomacy—across the public service, there is no competitive meritocracy, across all institutions.[39]

However, the politics of ethno-regional balancing has also played a more profound role in relation to public-sector performance and state-building in Uganda since the NRM came to power. Viewed over time and also in relation to other political settlements within the region (see Chapter 6 on Rwanda), it is apparent that Museveni has always privileged provisioning pacts with various social constituencies as the best route to holding together a ruling coalition in multi-ethnic Uganda, rather than undertaking the difficult work of building protection pacts that involved a long-term commitment to state-building across the board (Slater 2010, also Chapter 8).

Organizational leadership: The critical (and declining) role of technopols in Uganda's political settlement

> President Museveni does not understand institutional reform, just trusts certain people. He (the BoU governor) balances the political with the interests of the IMF, realigns policy objectives. Mutebile reads his (the president's) mind and will strike a balance between the two. If the two were at conflict it would not work.[40]

Emmanuel Tumusiime-Mutebile was Uganda's archetypal technopol: the country's longest-serving governor and one of its most prominent public figures.[41] An Oxford-educated NRM loyalist who made an early conversion from Marxist to

---

[39] Independent Ugandan MP, 8 November 2017.
[40] Personal advisor to the president, 28 July 2016.
[41] Emmanuel Tumusiime-Mutebile passed away in January 2022. As discussed in Chapter 1, the term technopol refers to actors that transcend the categories of 'technocrats' or 'politicians', by virtue

neoclassical economics, Mutebile provided the linchpin in the original three-way deal between the president, technocrats, and donors that established the basis for PoEs in Uganda's economic policy domain. The public shock concerning the revelations of BoU's mishandling of the banking sector in 2018 was closely related to a sense that a figure that citizens had previously trusted to hold the line had fallen.

Mutebile's close political connections to the president and formidable skills of political management were as important to his success as his technocratic capabilities as an economist and bureaucratic leader. The same holds for successive permanent secretaries at MFPED and certain commissioner generals at the URA, as well as other PoEs in Uganda.[42] The choice of commissioner general for the URA has swung between those appointed largely on the basis of connections and those too disconnected and autonomous to manoeuvre effectively in Uganda's political context (Table 7.2). It is no coincidence that the URA's two best performance periods occurred under commissioner generals who were both highly capable bureaucrats and closely connected to the president. Since Ssendaula, no finance minister has combined both political clout *and* technical capacity and finance ministers have played second fiddle to senior technocrats within MFPED, reinforcing the sense in which PoEs are often associated with less-than-democratic forms of rule.

Organizational factors: Culture and policy type

Our research offers some support for the argument that high-performing public-sector organizations rely as much on the creation of an 'organizational culture' of performance as more material incentives (Grindle 1997). Officials working at MFPED during the 1990s and the URA during the mid-2000s speak fondly of the periods in which they were supported to do their work by the top leadership and empowered to take decisions and risks in pursuit of a wider goal during a period of national recovery. High levels of pay and other perks clearly matter. But they seemed to be secondary to the availability of professional training and the sense that technical skills were respected and being directed towards the patriotic goal of national development. Nurturing this requires creative and flexible forms of leadership, with enough continuity to ensure that a new ethos becomes institutionalized. Whilst such institutionalized cultures of performance may outlast the removal of political support and protection (for example, MFPED staff would still arrive at work at 7 a.m. even after the budget process had been subjected to significant interference), they cannot maintain high levels of performance without political backing.

---

of possessing both the technical and political resources required to drive forward certain policy and organizational agendas (Domínguez 1997, Joignant 2011).

[42] These include the National Water and Sewerage Corporation (Bukenya 2020), the Petroleum Exploration and Production Department (PEPD) (Hickey and Izama 2016, 2020) and arguably also the Kampala Capital City Authority, for a period at least.

Developing organizational cultures of performance, even for limited periods, may be more achievable in agencies that are separate from the mainstream of the public service and which have autonomy over issues of pay and other working conditions. However, this can also lead to more problematic organizational cultures emerging. For example, although the autonomous BoU is renowned for offering the best working conditions within the country's public sector, we found little evidence of an organizational culture that put the institution (or the country) ahead of individual fulfilment, unlike with MFPED during the 1990s. Mutebile, who worked for many yars in Finance before becoming BoU governor, agreed: 'It (BoU) was different, less mission driven than MFPED',[43] perhaps in part because of its greater autonomy as compared to its more politically embedded counterpart.

A further organizational factor that matters for PoEs in Uganda is the nature of the task being undertaken. It is not surprising that the budget department was identified as the highest-performing part of the ministry, as its remit is at least somewhat more bounded and controllable than, say, the directorate of economic affairs or department of debt management. BoU has found it comparatively easier to establish and maintain high levels of performance in relation to the logistical challenge of controlling inflation than it has with the more transactional challenge of maintaining financial stability. The research directorate or monetary policy committee offer far fewer rent-seeking opportunities than banking supervision, where staff interact frequently with banks that are not just secretive and difficult to regulate but also (at times) open to collusive activities. In this respect, the assumption that PoEs are more likely to emerge and be sustained around more logistical tasks (Roll 2014), is largely sustained here.

Transnational influences and the developmental implications of Uganda's premier PoEs

The transnational project of promoting neoliberal principles of economic governance since the late 1980s has directly shaped the nature of the state, in Uganda as elsewhere in Africa (Harrison 2010). All of the PoEs that we identified in Uganda had received considerable international support, both at their inception and beyond. This was mainly from Western donors but also through links to global epistemic communities of professional expertise, including regional and international associations for central bankers and tax administrators. The neoliberal consensus that emerged amongst most of Uganda's political and bureaucratic elite in the early 1990s helped to align MFPED with BoU, to align the economic technocracy as a whole with strong sources of international assistance, ideas, and finance, and to provide ideological coherence within each organization. The IMF, with its offices located within the BoU building, helped forge a powerful

---

[43] Interview, 13 March 2019.

'finance ministry' tendency within Uganda dedicated to maintaining a neoliberal policy direction.

However, this convergence started to fracture after 2006, as Uganda's political economy became geared towards a more fiscally expansive mode of development. MFPED's declining performance from the mid-2000s was influenced by this ideological and institutional challenge to its authority. Inspired by the discovery of oil and Chinese investment, the president authorized the National Planning Authority (NPA) to take on national planning responsibilities, thus removing a significant element of MFPED's responsibility and power (Hickey 2013), and adopt a more interventionist approach. This led to a backlash. The treasury and central bank both sought to curtail the capacity and ambitions of this productivist tendency within government, restricting the flow of high-quality technocrats from MFPED to NPA and opposing major hikes in expenditure. NPA has struggled to establish a new developmentalist project, lacking the decades of international support that MFPED and BoU have benefitted from or alliances with other productivist elements required of a more developmental state (industry, trade, commerce), which were also marginalized within the period of neoliberal hegemony. Even those who helped engineer Uganda's neoliberal reforms concur that there has been a lack of structural transformation and investment in industry (Whitworth and Williamson 2010). The waxing and waning of PoEs in Uganda thus continues to be closely shaped by ideological and institutional imperatives that are embedded not only within Uganda's political settlement but also its insertion within the wider global political economy.

Conclusion and implications

> (Museveni's) style of government puts enormous pressure on him—constantly politicking, going to events—never through institutions, he has personalized everything.[44]

The evidence presented here suggests that state-building in Uganda under Museveni has only ever been a partial project. Investments have been limited to the bureaucratic (and military) enclaves charged with delivering the core economic (and security) functions required to maintain a sense of juridicial statehood in the global order. These PoEs helped to offer the ruling coalition a sense of legitimacy at national and global levels. And they imposed a degree of political and economic stability that enabled the country to achieve impressive growth rates that were also pro-poor for most of the 1990s. However, they have also helped to reproduce a particular political and economic order, one that is both narrowly neoliberal and

---

[44] Long-term senior advisor to MFPED and BoU, 20 November 2018.

militaristic in nature and which has undermined the pursuit of alternative development strategies. Run on the basis of close personal relationships between the president and a handful of select bureaucrats, PoEs also emerge as a profoundly undemocratic mode of governance.

PoEs thus currently represent a highly partial and lopsided strategy for developmental governance in Uganda. Any new effort to build strong public-sector organizations needs to focus much more strongly on the productivist functions that Uganda needs to achieve structural transformation, as required to deliver more jobs and a sustained process of poverty reduction. This can be directed both at alternative centres of power within government (planning, industry, trade) and more productivist and developmental functions within the organizations discussed here. For example, central banks have historically played a much more proactive role in providing development finance to support late developers than they have been encouraged to do under the neoliberal dispensation (Epstein 2005). Current calls for BoU to adopt a more activist approach are growing louder, including with reference to greater support for the Uganda Development Bank. Within MFPED, there are strong grounds for raising the status of the tax-policy function and enabling a more joined-up relationship between tax policy and administration. This is required to drive up the revenue required for more ambitious development interventions and, ideally, longer-term processes of state-building.

This more joined-up approach is arguably a more fruitful one than a return to focusing on specific 'islands' of effectiveness, which has proven to be an increasingly contradictory strategy. For example, the relative decline of the URA in recent years needs to be set against the rise of other newly formed agencies, some of which have been able to offer higher salaries and attract staff away from the URA (including Uganda National Roads Authority, Kampala Capital City Authority, the Petroleum Authority of Uganda, and the Uganda National Oil Company). Maintaining PoEs, including through the payment of relatively generous salaries and allowances, is an expensive business, which undermines other deserving areas of the public sector. However, the prospects of Uganda undertaking a more broad-based project of state-building within the context of its prevailing political settlement dynamics seem remote, with the politics of regime survival continuing to trump all other incentives in relation to the public sector.

References

Abrahamsen, R. and Bareebe, G. (2016). 'Uganda's 2016 Elections: Not Even Faking It Any More', *African Affairs*, 115(461): 751–65.

ACFIM (2016). 'Extended Study on Campaign Financing for Presidential and Members of Parliament Races'. Kampala: Alliance for Campaign Finance Monitoring.

Andrews, M. (2018). 'Overcoming the Limits of Institutional Reform in Uganda', *Development Policy Review*, 36: O159–O182.

Andrews, M., Pritchett, L., and Woolcock, M. (2017). *Building State Capability: Evidence, Analysis, Action*. Oxford: Oxford University Press.

Block, S. A. (2002). 'Political Business Cycles, Democratization, and Economic Reform: The Case of Africa', *Journal of Development Economics*, 67(1): 205–28.

Bogetic, Z., Caputo, E., Piatti-Funfkirchen, M., Valmarana, C., Bartholomew, A., Ekman, B., Moulders, C., Smail, T., Dietrich, S., and Meller, M. (2015). 'Joint Evaluation of Budget Support to Uganda'. Available online at https://ec.europa.eu/international-partnerships/system/files/strategic-evaluation-cooperation-ec-bs-uganda-1344-main-report-201505_en_0.pdf.

BoU (2002). 'The Annual Supervision and Regulatory Report'. Kampala: Bank of Uganda.

BoU (2012). 'The Annual Supervision and Regulatory Report'. Kampala: Bank of Uganda.

Branch, A. and Mampilly, Z. (2015). *Africa Uprising: Popular Protest and Political Change*. London: Zed Books.

Bukenya, B. (2020). 'The Politics of Building Effective Water Utilities in the Global South: A Case of NWSC Uganda'. ESID Working Paper No. 152. Manchester: Effective States and Inclusive Development Research Centre, University of Manchester.

Bukenya, B. and Hickey, S. (2018). 'Dominance and Deals in Africa: How Politics Shapes Uganda's Transition from Growth to Transformation'. In L. Pritchett, K. Sen, and E. Werker (eds), *Deals and Development: The Political Dynamics of Growth Episodes*. Oxford: Oxford University Press. 183–216.

Bukenya, B. and Hickey, S. (2019) 'The Shifting Fortunes of the Economic Technocracy in Uganda: Caught between State-building and Regime Survival?' ESID Working Paper No. 121. Manchester: Effective States and Inclusive Development Research Centre, University of Manchester.

Bukenya, B. and Muhumuza, W. (2017). 'The Politics of Core Public Sector Reform in Uganda: Behind the Façade'. ESID Working Paper 85. Manchester: Effective States and Inclusive Development Research Centre, University of Manchester.

Cawley, G. and Zake, J. (2010). 'Tax Reform'. In F. Kuteesa, E. Tumusiime-Mutebile, A. Whitworth, and T. Williamson (eds), *Uganda's Economic Reforms: Insider Accounts*. Oxford: Oxford University Press. 103–28.

Centre for Policy Analysis [nd]. 'Inclusivity, Fiscal Deficit and Role of Parliament: Perspective from the Proposed Budget for Financial Year 2015/16'. Available online at http://cepa.or.ug/wp-content/uploads/2018/06/274364109-INCLUSIVITY-FISCAL-DEFICIT-AND-ROLE-OF-PARLIAMENT-PERSPECTIVE-FROM-THE-PROPOSED-BUDGET-FOR-FINANCIAL-YEAR-2015-16.pdf.

COSASE (2019). 'COSASE Report on the Special Audit of the Auditor General on Defunct Banks'. Kampala: COSASE.

Dafe, F. (2019). 'The Politics of Finance: How Capital Sways African Central Banks', *Journal of Development Studies*, 55(2): 311–27.

DEG (2020). 'Briefing Paper on Supplementary Expenditures'. Available online at https://www.ldpg.or.ug/wp-content/uploads/2021/04/Briefing-paper-on-Supplementary-Expenditures.pdf.

Domínguez, J. I. (1997). *Technopols: Freeing Politics and Markets in Latin America in the 1990s*. University Park, PA: Penn State Press.

Doner, R., Ritchie, B., and Slater, D. (2005). 'Systemic Vulnerability and the Origins of Developmental States: Northeast and Southeast Asia in Comparative Perspective', *International Organization*, 59(2): 327–61.

Epstein, G. (2005) 'Central Banks as Agents of Development'. Political Economy Research Institute Working Paper 104. Amherst, MA: University of Massachusetts Amherst.

Golooba-Mutebi, F. and Hickey, S. (2013). 'Investigating the Links between Political Settlements and Inclusive Development in Uganda: Towards a Research Agenda'. ESID Working Paper No. 20. Manchester: Effective States and Inclusive Development Research Centre, University of Manchester.

Golooba-Mutebi, F. and Hickey, S. (2016). 'The Master of Institutional Multiplicity? The Shifting Politics of Regime Survival, State-building and Democratisation in Museveni's Uganda', *Journal of Eastern African Studies*, 10(4): 601–18.

Grindle, M. S. (1997). 'Divergent Cultures? When Public Organizations Perform Well in Developing Countries', *World Development*, 25(4): 481–95.

Harrison (2010). *Neoliberal Africa: The Impact of Global Social Engineering*. London: Zed Books.

Hickey, S. (2013). 'Beyond the Poverty Agenda? Insights from the New Politics of Development in Uganda', *World Development*, 43: 194–206.

Hickey, S. (forthcoming). 'The Politics of Taxation in Uganda'. ESID Working Paper. Manchester: Effective States and Inclusive Development Research Centre, University of Manchester.

Hickey, S. and Matsiko, H. (forthcoming). 'The Politics of Central Banking in Uganda: Exploring the Rise and Fall of Uganda's Premier "Pocket of Effectiveness"'. ESID Working Paper. Manchester: Effective States and Inclusive Development Research Centre, University of Manchester.

Hickey, S. and A. Izama. (2016). 'The politics of governing oil in Uganda: Going against the grain?'. African Affairs, 116 (463): 163–185.

Hickey, S. and A. Izama. (2020). 'The politics of governing oil after 'best-practice' reforms: Can 'pockets of effectiveness' survive within Uganda's political settlement?', The Extractive Industries and Society, 7(4): 1200–1210.

IMF (1991). 'Financial Sector Review Report No. 9099-UG'. Washington, DC: International Monetary Fund.

IMF (2005). 'IMF Country Report No. 05/183, Uganda'. June. Washington, DC: International Monetary Fund.

IMF (2017). 'Uganda Fiscal Transparency Evaluation IMF Country Report No. 17/130'. Washington, DC: International Monetary Fund.

Joignant, A. (2011). 'The Politics of Technopols: Resources, Political Competence and Collective Leadership in Chile, 1990–2010', *Journal of Latin American Studies*, 43(3): 517–46.

Kangave, J. and Katusiimeh, M. (2015). 'Tax Bargains: Understanding the Role Played by Public and Private Actors in Influencing Tax Policy Reform in Uganda'. UNRISD Working Paper 2015–2. Available online at www.unrisd.org/kangave-katusiimeh (accessed 27 April 2021).

Kelsall, T. (2018). 'Towards a Universal Political Settlement Concept: A Response to Mushtaq Khan', *African Affairs*, 117(469): 656–69.

Khan, M. (2010). 'Political settlements and the governance of growth-enhancing institutions. Draft paper'. Research Paper Series on 'Growth-enhancing Governance'. London: SOAS, University of London.

Kjær, A. M. (2015). 'Political Settlements and Productive Sector Policies: Understanding Sector Differences in Uganda', *World Development*, 68: 230–41.

Kjær, A. M. and Ulriksen, M. S. with Kangave, J. and Katusiimeh, M. (2017). 'A political economy analysis of domestic resource mobilization in Uganda'. Geneva: UNRISD Working Paper 2017–8.

Kuteesa, F., Tumusiime-Mutebile, E., Whitworth, A., & Williamson, T. (Eds.). (2010). *Uganda's Economic Reforms: Insider Accounts*. Oxford: Oxford University Press.

Lie, J. H. S. (2018). 'Donor-driven State Formation: Friction in the World Bank–Uganda Partnership'. In J. Wiegratz, G. Martiniello, and E. Greco (eds), *Uganda: The Dynamics of Neoliberal Transformation*. London, Zed Books. 43–59.

Lindemann, S. (2011). 'Just Another Change of Guard? Broad-based Politics and Civil War in Museveni's Uganda', *African Affairs*, 110(440): 1–30.

Magumba, M. (2019). 'Tax Administration Reforms: Lessons from Georgia and Uganda'. ICTD African Tax Administration Paper 5. Brighton: ICTD.

Mawejje, J. and Munyambonera, E. Z. (2016). 'Tax Revenue Effects of Sectoral Growth and Public Expenditure in Uganda'. EPRC Research Series 125. Makerere: Economic Policy Research Centre.

Mutebile, E. T. (2010). 'Institutional and Political Dimensions of Economic Reform'. In F. Kuteesa, E. Tumusiime-Mutebile, A. Whitworth, and T. Williamson (eds), *Uganda's Economic Reforms: Insider Accounts*. Oxford: Oxford University Press. 35–51.

Mutibwa, P. (1992). *Uganda since Independence: A Story of Unfulfilled Hopes*. London: C. Hurst & Co.

Mutibwa, P. (2006). *The Bank of Uganda (1966–2006): A Historical Perspective*. Kampala: BoU.

PEFA (2017). 'Uganda Public Expenditure and Financial Accountability (PEFA) Assessment 2016'. Washington, DC: PEFA.

Reid, R. (2017). *A History of Modern Uganda*. Cambridge: Cambridge University Press.

Roll, M. (ed.) (2014). *The Politics of Public Sector Performance: Pockets of Effectiveness in Developing Countries*. London: Routledge.

Rubongoya, J. (2018). 'Movement Legacy and Neoliberalism as Political Settlement in Uganda's Political Economy'. In J. Wiegratz, G. Martiniello, and E. Greco (eds), *The Dynamics of Neoliberalism in Uganda*. London: Zed Books. 95–110.

Simson, R. and Wabwire, M. (2016). 'The Capabilities of Finance Ministries: Uganda'. London: Overseas Development Institute.

Slater, D. (2010). *Ordering Power: Contentious Politics and Authoritarian Leviathans in Southeast Asia*. New York: Cambridge University Press.

Suruma, E. (2014). *Advancing the Ugandan Economy: A Personal Account*. Washington, DC: Brookings Institution Press.

Tangri, R. and Mwenda, A. (2013). *The Politics of Elite Corruption in Africa: Uganda in Comparative African Perspective*. London: Routledge.

Whitfield, L., Therkildsen, O., Buur, L., and Kjær, A.-M. (2015). *The Politics of African Industrial Policy: A Comparative Perspective*. Cambridge: Cambridge University Press.

Whitworth, A. and Williamson, T. (2010). 'Overview of Ugandan Economic Reform since 1986'. In F. Kuteesa, E. Tumusiime-Mutebile, A. Whitworth, and T. Williamson (eds), *Uganda's Economic Reforms: Insider Accounts*. Oxford: Oxford University Press. 1–34.

Yohou, H. D. and Goujon, M. (2017). 'Reassessing Tax Effort in Developing Countries: A Proposal of a Vulnerability-adjusted Tax Effort Index', Ferdi Working Paper No. 186. Clermont-Ferrand: Foundation for Studies and Research on International Development.

PART III
PATTERNS AND WAYS FORWARD

8

Comparative Analysis

PoEs and the Politics of State-building and Development in Africa

Sam Hickey

Introduction and overview of main findings

Why do some parts of government perform much better than others in developing countries? This question has gained increased importance during the early decades of the twenty-first century as issues of state capacity and performance have returned to the forefront of development theory and practice (Acemoglu and Robinson 2019, Centeno et al. 2017). A series of material and ideological shifts are behind this move, including successive economic and health crises that require an organized public response, the decline of neoliberal policy doctrines, and the related rise of alternative geopolitical powers and narratives, all of which have helped bring the state back into focus. Within this context, scholars and policy actors alike have made a renewed effort to explore why capacity levels vary so much *within* as well as *between* states (Bersch et al. 2017, Centeno et al. 2017) and, in particular, what lessons can be learned from studying how high-performing state agencies or PoEs become able to deliver on certain developmental objectives within difficult governance contexts (McDonnell 2020, Roll 2014).

This volume offers the first systematic examination of the political conditions under which such PoEs emerge and become sustained within developing-country contexts. In doing so it speaks to the now widespread recognition that 'politics matters' when it comes to explaining why some countries develop faster than others, not simply in terms of institutions but in terms of the forms of elite bargaining and ruling coalitions that shape which institutions emerge and how they actually function (Acemoglu and Robinson 2012, 2019, Kelsall et al. 2022, North, Wallis, and Weingast 2009). This recognition has changed how we understand state capacity and performance and here we seek answers to the question of which *types* of power relations and politics enable states (or parts thereof) to deliver on their mandates. Examining the politics of PoEs has gained strategic relevance in light of the need to move beyond the 'institutional mono-cropping' (Evans 2004) approach to promoting 'good governance' in developing countries (Grindle 2007). Might PoEs

Sam Hickey, *Comparative Analysis*. In: *Pockets of Effectiveness and the Politics of State-building and Development in Africa.* Edited by Sam Hickey, Oxford University Press. © Oxford University Press (2023). DOI: 10.1093/oso/9780192864963.003.0008

form the vanguard of a more realistic governance agenda (World Bank 2017) that enables states to deliver development?

This chapter offers a comparative analysis of the answers to these questions delivered by our case-study chapters on Ghana, Kenya, Rwanda, Uganda, and Zambia, and discusses the theoretical and strategic implications that flow from this. The remainder of this introduction sets out the volume's key contribution and headline findings. Turning to questions of theory and intellectual debate, the chapter then argues that the emergence and performance of PoEs is shaped by particular types of political settlement and explores the wider implications that this has for the politics of state-building in contemporary Africa. It then examines the organizational aspects of PoEs, with a particular focus on the mandate, functions, and leadership of high-performing agencies. The final substantive section argues that transnational actors and agendas have been central to improving the capacity of certain state agencies to deliver, but only in terms of achieving neoliberal policy objectives whilst undermining the capacity of the state in Africa to deliver on alternative development agendas. The conclusion discusses some of the strategic implications that flow from this analysis.

Contributions and key findings

This volume has tried to start filling in what Merilee Grindle has identified as the 'missing middle' within the broader field of governance and development, between theoretical literature on the long-run political drivers of development on the one hand and the emerging new governance agenda around 'thinking and working politically' on the other (Grindle 2017, also her foreword to this volume). We do this by reframing PoEs not as 'islands' divorced from a wider sea of neopatrimonialism (Mkandawire 2015), but as state agencies that are embedded within particular relations of power at both national and transnational levels (Jessop 2008). The 'power domains' framework set out in Chapter 2 distinguishes between different configurations of political and social power—or political settlements—in an echo of Centeno et al.'s (2017) emphasis on political coalitions and social forces as being critical to shaping state capacity and performance. Political settlements analysis offers a coherent framework for analysing the balance of forces within a given polity in ways that can be differentiated both across country contexts and within the same country over time. This then provides the platform for understanding how this configuration of power shapes the emergence and deployment of state capacity, especially when aligned with an understanding of the *transnational* forces that operate both within and outside the state (Jessop 2008, 2016), and particularly within sub-Saharan Africa (Hagman and Peclard 2010). In order to overcome the exoticism of certain approaches to the African state, we move beyond the language of neopatrimonialism and integrate insights from the historical literature on state-building and the bureaucracy (Grindle 2012). This enables us to place the contemporary state in Africa in comparative conversation with long-term processes of political development in other world regions, whilst recognizing the extent to which it is embedded within a highly transnationalized context that has, over the past three decades that our investigations have focused most closely on, been characterized by the rise and at least partial decline of neoliberal hegemony.

In a bid to bring a more systematic methodological approach to the study of PoEs, we then applied this framework to five countries in sub-Saharan Africa, each with broadly similar experiences of the world historical moment from around 1990 until 2020 but which are characterized by different types of political settlement. Our ability to focus on the political conditions that shape PoEs was further enhanced by our decision to focus on the same types of state agency in each country, namely budget departments within ministries of finance, central banks, and revenue authorities.

Key findings

The headline findings from our research—most of which offer strong support for the propositions set out in Chapter 2—can be summarized as follows:

Politics is the defining factor that shapes the performance of PoEs and their ability to maintain this over time. *The distribution of political power within a political settlement* plays a particularly important role in shaping both the emergence of PoEs and their performance over time. The durable relationships between rulers and senior bureaucrats are more likely to be sustained where power is concentrated rather than dispersed (offering support for Proposition 1a). As the cases of Ghana, Kenya, Uganda, and Zambia show, the growing dispersal of power, both within ruling coalitions and between opposing coalitions competing for power, can directly limit the autonomy and effectiveness of public-sector organizations in ways that undermines their capacity to deliver on their mandate (Proposition 1b). PoEs can emerge in contexts where the power is dispersed, but this requires other conditions to be present and PoEs are also likely to endure for shorter periods in such contexts. This in turn tends to reinforce the sense that PoEs represent a less than democratic mode of governance.

The social foundations of the political settlement also matter, particularly in terms of whether the investment in PoEs forms part of a *wider project of state-building*. A comparison of the politics of PoEs in Uganda and Rwanda shows that concentrating power around the same leader over time is insufficient; there also needs to be a perception amongst ruling elites that the social foundations of their political settlement poses a threat to which investing in a wider state-building effort is a logical response (Proposition 2a). Without this sense of 'systemic vulnerability', PoEs can fall prey to the whims of presidential caprice (Proposition 2b).

Organizational leadership forms the key causal mechanism that links the political settlement and broader political economy dynamics to organizational performance. All cases involved technically competent and politically connected leaders (Proposition 4b). These technopols were rewarded with the lengthy tenures required to build cultures of organizational performance and had the political authority required to navigate difficult contexts.

Organizational mandate and function matter but are insufficient: our case-study organizations had legally enforceable mandates in areas of core state functioning (Proposition 4a), were often protected by formal organizational autonomy, and performed policy tasks that were more logistical than transactional in character (Proposition 4c). Nonetheless, this was not enough to protect them from capture in certain political conditions.

International support is essential but also insufficient and problematic: we did not identify any PoEs that had emerged and flourished *without* high levels of external support (Proposition 5). However, the specific nature of this support has profoundly (mis)shaped the pattern of state-building in Africa. This legacy, along with other factors, has foreclosed the possibility of African governments developing the capacity to move beyond neoliberalism and pursue the more productivist pathways that global political economy trends since the mid-2000s may have otherwise enabled.

Ideas clearly matter: this is true not only in terms of the profound influence of neoliberal thinking over economic governance organizations but also in other respects. Home-grown notions of 'self-reliance' encouraged rulers to build the capacity of revenue authorities in Kenya and Rwanda and bureaucrats are also influenced by the norms of professionalism inculcated via regional and global epistemic communities (Proposition 3).

In practical terms, PoEs can effectively deliver certain forms of development but are no panacea: high-functioning bureaucratic enclaves can help secure economic (and sometimes political) stability through delivering core tasks that are largely logistical in nature. However, we found little evidence that PoEs can play an important role in delivering on the more difficult policy challenges involved in securing inclusive development (Pritchett and Woolcock 2004), and some evidence of negative spillovers whereby the high levels of financial and human resources required to run PoEs are subtracted from the broader public service. Any effort to support PoEs in Africa by external actors must involve a much more balanced approach that moves beyond neoliberal agencies of constraint and supports the capacities of those state agencies required to pursue more ambitious forms of structural transformation and deliver social provisioning.

Caveats

Inevitably, our study suffers from certain limitations. Conceptually, our predominant concern has been to identify the *political* conditions under which high-performing state agencies emerge and are sustained, rather than what McDonnell (2020: 10–11) terms the 'social foundations of doing bureaucracy' as a 'cultural practice'. Methodologically, and although we stand by the research design set out in Chapter 2–including with regards the choice of country cases, state agencies, and performance indicators–these choices inevitably limit the reach of our findings. We have sought to overcome the Africanist bias of our country cases by drawing out the strong parallels with similar work on Latin America (Geddes 1990, Grindle 1997, Hout 2014) and East Asia (Evans 1995), and in her closing commentary in this volume (Chapter 9), Julia Strauss explores the links between our findings and existing scholarship on PoEs and state-building in East Asia, including her own path-breaking work on China's trajectory during the late 1920s and 1930s (Strauss 2008).

Our focus on state agencies operating in the domain of economic governance reflects the relative dearth of PoEs in other parts of the state in Africa, a direct outcome of the ideological priorities established during the era of structural adjustment (Mkandawire 2014). This limits the reach of our findings beyond this policy domain whilst at the same time enhancing the rigour of this comparative analysis, a trade-off discussed by Michael Roll in Chapter 10. In addition, the focus on state agencies that are central to basic state functioning has also enabled deeper insights into the often competing logics of state-building and political survival. By echoing studies of how bureaucratic enclaves around the treasury and revenue have provided the building-blocks of the modern state (e.g. Grindle 2012), this has helped to avoid the exoticism of many studies of the state in Africa and enabled a conversation around processes of political development across space and time.

A final challenge concerns our decision to assess the effectiveness of these agencies in terms of whether or not they delivered on their respective mandates. Whilst this is clearly the fairest way to assess organizational capacity and performance, it risks overlooking the ways in which the mandates of African state agencies operating within the economic realm were, via programmes of debt-related conditionality, re-engineered towards a particular agenda of austerity and neoliberal economics (e.g. Mkandawire 2014). We have approached this problem by first assessing each agency's performance in accordance with its mandate before then critically addressing the wider implications that have flowed from this exercise of state engineering in many African countries over the past three decades (see the penultimate section of this chapter). The following sections now offer a comparative analysis of how political, organizational, and transnational drivers shaped PoEs and broader processes of state-building and development in our case-study countries over the past three decades.

PoEs, political settlements, and the politics of state-building

That politics is the critical driver of PoEs (Roll 2014), and of broader investments in state capacity and state performance (Centeno et al. 2017), is now widely accepted. Our contribution here has been to show in a systematic way how different kinds of politics—framed here in terms of political settlements—create different possibilities for the emergence of PoEs, their sustainability over time, and whether or not they form part of a wider project of state-building. Here we examine the influence of the key dimensions of any political settlement, namely the distribution of political power and the social foundations of power, before discussing the implications of our findings for the wider trajectory of state-building in Africa.

How the distribution of political power shapes PoEs

The degree of power concentration around a country's political leadership directly shapes whether PoEs become established and if their performance will be sustained over time. Our findings resonate with the existing literature on both PoEs and state-building more broadly in Africa (Roll 2014), Latin America (Geddes 1990), and ex-Soviet contexts (Hout 2013), much of which also associates PoEs with more concentrated forms of political leadership and elite cohesion. The key causal mechanisms that emerge from our cases include the longer-term time-horizons that this offers to rulers and the capacity to formulate and enforce politically difficult reforms that might otherwise have been blocked. Lengthy periods of stable rule offer favourable conditions for building durable relations between rulers and the leaders of state agencies, who in turn are able to undertake organizational reform and build performance cultures. Bureaucratic agents also receive direction from a more limited range of political principals than tends to be the case where power is more dispersed. These causal mechanisms are all apparent in the onset of impressive periods of PoE formation and performance in Ghana during the mid-1980s, Uganda from the early 1990s, and Rwanda in the early 2000s. The fact that these periods all involved the establishment of new political settlements following periods of major instability emphasizes the importance of discussing state performance in relation to underlying processes of state formation (Centeno et al. 2017).

As power became more dispersed in Ghana during the 1990s and Uganda during the 2000s—as argued in Chapter 3 by Abdul-Gafaru Abdulai and Chapter 7 by Badru Bukenya, Haggai Matsiko, and Sam Hickey respectively—all of these mechanisms were weakened, with a corresponding drop-off in the performance of our state agencies. In Kenya, Matt Tyce showed in Chapter 4 how the incentives to use the fiscal levers of the state to retain and attract votes, and to avoid antagonizing both voters and party financiers through revenue raising, proved too strong, as did the lure of using public-sector appointments for the purposes of patronage and partisan rewards even within critical state agencies. All three cases plus Zambia, as Caesar Cheelo and Marja Hinfelaar show in Chapter 5, highlight that this is not simply about power being dispersed *between* factions competing for power but also that the dispersal of power *within* governing coalitions can significantly undermine the autonomy and effectiveness of state agencies.[1]

Nonetheless, PoEs can still emerge in dispersed political settlements, albeit for shorter periods of time and only, it seems, where other conditions hold. In Ghana, Kenya and Zambia, this occurred via the formation of technocratic coalitions of politicians, bureaucrats, and external actors with similar ideas around economic governance. Importantly, this was amidst the favourable economic conditions that most of many African countries experienced during the early/mid-2000s, and arguably at the high point of neoliberalism's disciplinary powers, as discussed below. In most cases, these short-lived periods of high performance often barely stretched to the five-year timeframe suggested by Roll (2014) as being definitive of attaining the status of PoE. Nonetheless, they delivered improvements in the quality of economic governance and arguably helped establish certain norms of bureaucratic performance in core state agencies that might, under more favourable political conditions, be reactivated. In all types of political settlement, and unlike McDonnell (2020), we found that executive support was a necessary (if not sufficient) condition for PoEs to maintain high levels of performance over time and that the removal of this led to a decline in organizational performance.

This analysis tends to reinforce the sense that PoEs represent a less than democratic mode of governance. Thandika Mkandawire warned against this problem in relation to the granting of central bank independence in the 1990s, of which he noted: 'It is as if attempts were being made to create "authoritarian enclaves" à la Pinochet over which democratic rule has no control' (1999: 338). The longest periods of high performance that we identified—in Ghana, Rwanda, and Uganda—occurred under leaders with a strong military background. As in 1940s Brazil (Geddes 1990), some bureaucrats in post-colonial Africa seem to have craved the certainty and continuity that military and/or authoritarian leaders claim to offer (Abernethy 1971). Although this association between PoEs and undemocratic and militarized forms of rule raises normative concerns, it is important not to overstate the contemporary relevance of connections between variables that differ significantly across time and place. We also find evidence from Rwanda that there are downsides to public bureaucracies adopting a top-down and

---

[1] 'This point is echoed in David Waldner's study (1999) of Syria, Turkey, South Korea, and Taiwan, which argues that "elite cohesion" was a necessary condition for the expansion of state capacities for development, whereas elite disunity and factionalism produced broad cross-class coalitions, which were ultimately not conducive to the building of developmental states' (vom Hau 2012: 11).

militarized approach to governance: as Benjamin Chemouni reports in Chapter 6, where civil servants feel unable to take risks or delegate tasks to junior officials for fear of reprisals, they are unlikely to identify and deliver the kinds of creative solutions and leadership required for cultures of organizational performance to flourish (see next section).

In terms of the difficulties that the dispersal of power within political settlements seems to create for PoEs, the point here is not to bemoan the onset of democracy as an obstacle to the performance of state agencies in Africa. It certainly does not follow that we can expect the current era of democratic backsliding to offer a boost to PoEs: the cases of Uganda and Zambia reveal that the authoritarian tendencies of leaders in increasingly dispersed settlements characterized by high levels of elite factionalism is a recipe for the decline and capture of even core state agencies. Rather, the tensions between democratization and bureaucratic governance have long been noted in the literature on state-building and help justify the comparative and historical framing adopted here. Subjecting poorly institutionalized, low capacity state institutions to the forces of open political competition, itself often trammelled through personalized rather than programmatic political parties, is a recipe for intensifying rather than displacing patronage politics (Grindle 2012, Shefter 1994). This is as clear from the United States of America in the late nineteenth century as from contemporary Africa (Levy 2014). Our findings underline the extent to which African leaders have, particularly over the past three decades, faced an almost insuperable challenge to maintain high standards of public-sector performance amidst not only the third wave of democratization (Centeno et al. 2017: 2), but also the neoliberal onslaught on state capacity (see below). As discussed further below, we identify only one case, namely Ghana, where the tensions between democratization and state-building seem to have been held in creative as well as destructive tension.

The political sociology of PoEs in Africa: How a political settlement's social foundations shape public-sector performance

The concentration of political power is not the only political settlement variable that shapes public-sector performance: the social foundation of a given political settlement—which defines the social groups that a governing coalition has to take into account—matters too. Our case studies suggest three main routes through which this occurs: through the influence that social forces have over state agencies within the economic realm, via the social politics of appointments and promotion within state agencies and, most profoundly, through whether governing coalitions perceive the social foundations of the settlement to pose a threat that amounts to 'systemic vulnerability' (Doner et al. 2005). We discuss each of these in turn before discussing the wider implications for the politics of state-building in Africa.

The need for governing coalitions to be responsive to certain social forces influences the performance of our state agencies in both general and specific ways. At a general level, the broad-based nature of all of our settlements has tended to incentivize governments to dispense high levels of public spending, as in Zambia where the necessity of building inclusive ruling coalitions across multiple social groups has proved costly. Whilst high levels of public spending can of course have positive developmental outcomes, the politicized use of public funds identified here can prevent core state agencies from delivering on their particular mandates, including the obligation of ministries of finance to fulfil legally enshrined commitments on public financial management and, in extremis, of central banks to maintain price stability. More directly, most governments studied here have been highly reluctant to formulate and implement tax policies that would affect those specific groups on whose support it relied, whether through votes or political financing. This has directly undermined the capacity of revenue authorities to deliver on their mandate, even where they seemed to be operating as PoEs in most other respects, as in Kenya, Uganda, and Zambia during the mid- to late-2000s.

This more direct type of influence that social actors can exert over state performance can even be felt by the 'bureaucratic aristocrats' operating within central banks. Despite their *de jure* autonomy, some central bankers we interviewed were well aware of how their decision-making on rates of interest and foreign currency exchange had uneven effects on different economic groups, and were much warier of antagonizing the thousands of traders who could bring a capital city to a standstill than they were of the smaller manufacturing class located beyond the capital. The capacity of banking supervision departments within central banks is also deployed selectively. Banks owned by political opponents or domestic capitalists becoming wealthy enough to gain autonomy from the ruling coalition are generally treated much more harshly.

The second type of link between a settlement's social foundations and the performance of state agencies concerns the influence over patterns of appointment and promotion. Here we found some evidence to support the most prevalent thesis in the literature discussed in Chapter 1, which holds that a politics of ethnicity generally undermines the development of a bureaucratic ethos and sense of meritocracy within state agencies. Kenya presents the most obvious example here, whereby the ethnicized politics of factionalism *within* Kenya's ruling coalitions, particularly in the past decade, has proved particularly damaging to PoE performance (also Tyce 2020). In Ghana, each electoral turnover is accompanied by the mass displacement of senior bureaucrats on the basis of partisan loyalties that are to some extent shaped by ethno-regional considerations.

However, and as proposed in Chapter 1, we also found important instances where ethnicity played a positive role in shaping higher levels of bureaucratic performance. In both Kenya and Uganda, the halcyon periods for their respective economic technocracies was directly shaped by a politics of patronage that managed to fuse a bureaucratic ethos dedicated to delivering in the national interest with ethnic loyalty. In Kenya, Kibaki's appointment of highly trained economists drawn largely from his own ethnic group to key positions echoes Kenyatta's approach to appointing senior bureaucrats, which John Lonsdale (1994) characterized has termed a form of 'moral' as opposed to 'tribal' ethnicity. Museveni's early appointments to key PoEs similarly combined the logics of political loyalty, ethno-regional links, and professional merit. We did not find a fuller fusion of bureaucratic ethos and commitment to the national interest with ethnic self-identification, as per Werbner's (2004) characterization of the Kalangala in Botswana. However, these findings suggest that the general dismissal of ethnic politics as an enemy of public-sector performance needs to be nuanced and that contemporary studies of PoEs could usefully incorporate a stronger focus on social identity. Our evidence indicates that it is where political settlement dynamics shift, often in terms of a greater dispersal of power within a ruling coalition and/or a narrowing of the social foundation, that the politics of ethnicity becomes directly damaging to public-sector performance, as with the growing level of ethno-regional factionalism that has further undermined the performance of Uganda's central bank over the past few years. The sweet spot where a politics of patronage manages to combine both loyalty and merit—which Grindle (2012) identifies as critical to the early stages of building civil-service systems in the developed as well as developing world—is difficult to sustain over time.

The third and most powerful way in which the social foundation of a political settlement shapes state performance is via the level of 'systemic vulnerability' that it imparts. To recap, Doner et al. (2005) suggest that elites invest in state-building and economic upgrading when they face three vulnerabilities, two of which concern economic scarcity (including due to national insecurity), whilst the third concerns a credible threat that any deterioration in the living standards of popular sectors could trigger unmanageable unrest (Doner et al. 2005: 328). The resulting 'systemic vulnerability' incentivizes leaders to build bureaucracies, forge coalitions, and invest in development to secure survival. As discussed in Chapters 1 and 2, there are similarities here to Slater's (2010) proposition that, in the absence of an external security threat, only where 'contentious politics from below' threatens the privileges of elites will they accept the centralization of power required for the governing coalition to undertake a process of state-building via 'protection pacts'. Where the social configuration offers no such threat, rulers can rely on distributing state resources to other powerful actors in the form of personalized 'provisioning' pacts that ultimately undermine processes of institutional development.

This distinction emerges most clearly from a comparison of Rwanda and Uganda over time. When the National Resistance Movement (NRM) took power in Uganda in 1986 it faced both an economic and a security crisis following nearly two decades of ethno-regionally fuelled civil conflict that was directly shaped by the 'divide-and-rule' nature of British colonial rule. It dealt with the security crisis by either crushing rebel groups through military means or co-opting the leadership of Uganda's many ethno-regional groupings within a broad and largely inclusive governing coalition (Golooba-Mutebi 2008, Lindemann 2011). This involved extending the strategic coalition that the NRM had forged between the small ethnic group of its leaders, based in western Uganda, and the country's largest single group, the Baganda. Notwithstanding the prolonged unrest generated in the north by the Lords Resistance Army, these strategies quelled the security threat to the governing coalition, thus reducing the incentives for the NRM to forge a protection pact with ethno-regional elites already satisfied with provisioning pacts. The economic crisis, meanwhile, could be dealt with through a selective strategy of protecting small number of bureaucratic enclaves within the economic technocracy, an approach that persuaded the IFIs to bankroll Uganda's war-ravaged economy (Chapter 7). The swiftness with which the NRM undermined the newly autonomous Uganda Revenue Authority from 1997, only four years after it had been established, underlines the limited extent to which Museveni felt able or willing to invest in a broader state-building project once confronted with even the mildest threat during the 1996 elections.

In contrast, the social foundations of the political settlement (and the economic circumstances) that faced the RPF in the 1990s Rwanda catalysed a sense of systemic vulnerability that incentivized an apparent effort towards state-building (Chapter 6, also Mann and Berry 2016). Confronted by a majority Hutu population in the aftermath of the 1994 genocide, and in the context of immense political, security, and economic challenges, a minority Tutsi government seems to have calculated that building an effective state that promised to deliver development impartially to all citizens offered a means to achieve their survival and wider stability. Only in Rwanda do we identify a sustained effort to build state capacity beyond key bureaucratic enclaves and of political elites using PoEs as a platform from which to extend capacity and a bureaucratic ethos outwards to the broader reaches of the state apparatus (e.g. by seconding staff from high-performing to weaker agencies and ministries to help drive up performance there). For this reason, Benjamin Chemouni suggests in Chapter 6 that the term 'high-performing state agencies' is arguably more appropriate for Rwanda than PoEs, given Roll's (2014) definition of the latter as 'high-performing organizations in otherwise dysfunctional contexts'.

The level of strategic intentionality behind this 'project' in Rwanda should not be overstated and there is no guarantee that this approach will outlast the country's current leader. Efforts to build state capacity in Rwanda have been driven less by a grand masterplan than by a somewhat haphazard process of identifying priorities in relation to specific policy challenges and external agendas as they arise. Notwithstanding the difficult relationship between political competition and state-building highlighted above, we find little evidence that Rwanda's state-building project has been enhanced by the imposition of restrictions on democratic rights and closing of political space that critics of the RPF have long railed against (e.g. Reyntjens 2013). As discussed elsewhere (Hickey and Sen 2023), more intellectual and political work is required to locate debates around state capacity and actual processes of state-building within a progressive political project.

From PoEs to the politics of state-building in Africa

Our focus on high-performing state agencies offers only one of several routes through which to explore the wider politics of state-building in sub-Saharan Africa (Mkandawire 2017, Seekings 2017). Nonetheless, our findings are suggestive of at least two distinctive pathways through which state-building may take place in sub-Saharan Africa at the current juncture. The first is via the broad-concentrated settlement route that Rwanda seems to be taking and which has a family resemblance to historical processes of state-building and development in other world regions (Doner et al. 2005, Slater 2010). However, this trajectory is highly contested and recent survey work to map out different types of political settlement in the developing world highlights that the concentrated-broad type is a waning phenomenon (Schulz and Kelsall 2021, Kelsall et al 2023). What is of greater relevance for the much wider range of countries where power is dispersed and the social foundations broad, as in four of our five cases, is how to manage the tensions between state-building and democratization.

Of the countries examined here, Ghana has the most promising trajectory in this regard. Although even the most important state agencies are offered little protection from the demands of political competition at key points in the electoral cycle, Abdul-Gafaru Abdulai shows in Chapter 3 that the country continues to score nearly as highly as Rwanda on general governance indicators and has not succumbed to either the democratic backsliding or governance crises witnessed in our other cases. The reasons for this are likely to have multiple roots, including the sense that Ghana can cope with large-scale turnovers of even senior civil servants after elections because of its unusually strong human capital base. However, we would argue that the main reason is because of the ways in which the configuration of power and social foundations that characterize Ghana's political settlement have been channelled through particular institutional reforms and arrangements. Politically, Ghana has found a way of institutionalizing intra-elite competition within a loosely programmatic form of two-party politics that could otherwise have become trammelled through more nakedly personalized and/or ethnicized vehicles (as in Kenya, Uganda, and Zambia). All parties in Ghana have to generate nationwide support that cuts across ethno-regional groups. Meanwhile, the alternation of power on a regular basis between two competing blocs has offered the main competing coalitions a sufficient stake in the system to avoid stretching the rules to breaking point.

Just as important in terms of the bureaucratic dimensions of state-building is that, although public resources are frequently misdirected for political purposes in Ghana (e.g. Abdulai and Hickey 2016), this nearly always occurs *directly through the state system* as opposed to the more personalized routes increasingly deployed in Uganda, Kenya, and Zambia.[2] It is difficult to characterize this as happening on a fully programmatic basis, but it is possible to view redistributive politics in Ghana as being more in line with pork-barrel politics than with mass clientelism (Kitschelt 2007, cf. van de Walle 2014).[3] This continued provision of goods via the state bureaucracy at least holds the promise of building state capacity, including via the learning-by-doing route (Skopcol 1992), even if only as a by-product of a political strategy (Grzymala-Busse, 2008) that has been forced to play itself out through certain institutional channels. The politics of patronage and clientelism therefore seems to have taken a different turn in Ghana than in most other broadly based and dispersed settlements, suggesting that a more democratic route to state-building may still be viable in contemporary Africa.

The organizational politics of being a PoE

Politics, then, is the defining force that shapes the performance of the state agencies examined here, albeit within a transnational context (see next section). However, the mechanisms and channels through which politics shapes the performance of our state agencies occurred through 'organizational-level' factors within the domain of economic governance (McDonnell 2017, Roll 2014). Our case studies suggest that organizational leadership, organizational cultures, the mandate and legal status of the state agencies involved, and the nature of the particular policy challenges that they were confronted with were the most important organizational level factors at play.

---

[2] Examples here would include the establishment of parallel processes of both economic decision-making and social provisioning via the respective State Houses of Uganda and Zambia, constituency development funds in Kenya, and the public–private collusion around agricultural subsidies in Zambia.

[3] Van de Walle (2014) argues that the kinds of 'mass clientelism' that have intensified and become more widespread in countries like Ghana under democratization are compatible with state-building, although only in favourable economic conditions given the costly nature of this form of governance. On the current state of clientelism in Ghana, see Abdulai (2020) and Nathan (2019).

Organizational leadership, performance cultures, and the importance of technopols

Organizational leadership is the key mechanism through which political settlement dynamics shape organizational performance in the cases studied here. All of our high-performing cases involved organizational leaders who were not just technically competent, but also politically loyal and connected enough to be rewarded with lengthy tenures, and empowered to run their organization relatively free from political pressures. Conversely, weaker performance periods were often heralded by decisions to appoint leaders that lacked either political connections and/or technical expertise, as well as to shorten terms of appointment, as with finance ministers in Ghana and Uganda's increasingly factionalized settlements. Lengthy tenures enabled organizational leaders to invest in building high-quality bureaucratic cadres and cultures of performance (McDonnell 2020), particularly through providing training opportunities for staff, ensuring that appointment and promotion processes were strongly guided by meritocratic principles, establishing performance-related bonus schemes and encouraging staff to take responsibilities and risks. Such organizational cultures in turn help to breed new leaders, with many of our highest-performing agencies benefitting from a tradition of appointing leaders from within.

The term technopol captures the particular blend of political savvy and technical competence that characterized our leaders, whether as politicians with technocratic expertise and/or technocrats able to operate politically (Domínguez 1997, Joignant 2011). This includes presidents such as Kenya's Kibaki, an economist trained at Makerere and the London School of Economics, and Zambia's lawyerly Mwanawasa; finance ministers that blended expertise with considerable political authority (e.g. Botchwey in Ghana, Magande in Zambia, Ssendaula in Uganda, Kabureka in Rwanda), and bureaucratic leaders with highly developed political management skills such as the many permanent secretaries, central bank governors, and commissioner generals of revenue authorities discussed in our case-study chapters. These technopols were critical to stitching together reform-oriented coalitions of national and international actors that in turn provided the relational basis for PoEs to emerge and flourish.

Organizational mandate, autonomy, and function

What a state agency actually does, and how this is codified in terms of official mandate and legal status, also matters (Roll 2014). The fact that our case-study organizations were all located within the economic domain is obviously significant here: this domain includes a number of organizations with legally enforceable mandates that often have some degree of autonomous status, and which are often charged with delivering policy tasks of a logistical nature that are critical to state-functioning. If PoEs are to emerge anywhere within the state in Africa it would surely be here, particularly given the level of international interest and support on offer to the 'agencies of constraint' within this domain (see next section). Indeed, the fuller autonomy granted to central banks and their embedding within the transnational networks of disciplinary neoliberalism (Mkandawire 1999) generally enabled them to remain focused on their organizational mandate for longer than our other state agencies. However, even these favourable conditions needed political-technocratic coalitions to continually mobilize in defence of the *de facto* as well as *de jure* autonomy of these agencies. A clear majority of our fifteen case-study organizations experienced significant fluctuations in performance levels despite their mandates and status remaining constant throughout; and, as noted earlier, the quality of such agencies in low- and middle-income countries spans the full range of (under)performance (McDonnell 2020: 18–19).

'Policy function' also seems to be a defining characteristic of the kinds of PoEs we've examined here, whereby the highest levels of organizational performance emerge in relation to 'logistical' policy functions that can be largely performed by relatively small groups of highly trained experts. Typical examples from our sample include managing an effective budget process and developing effective forms of macroeconomic policy. This is distinct from more 'transactional' policy challenges that require longer governance chains and multiple face-to-face inter-actions, not only within organizations but also between organizations and their clients (Pritchett and Woolcock 2004).[4] This distinction is also apparent within our case-study organizations; for example, central banks generally performed better in relation to their price stability mandate than their financial stability mandate, not least because the task of banking supervision is a transactional affair that is more personalized, less easy to audit, and more open to malfeasance. This seems to support Roll's (2014) finding that PoEs are generally associated with a somewhat limited range of policy functions. However, there is historical evidence that key bureaucratic enclaves have been able to form a range of more transactional policy functions—including disciplining firms, investing in technological upgrading, and negotiating and monitoring performance standards—when sufficiently equipped with both the political support and 'embedded autonomy' required to do so (Evans 1995). Our findings may therefore be reflecting the limits of our particular sample of state agencies, and the ideological constraints that they have been operating under in the particular historical period studied here, rather than the limits of PoEs per se. In their respective closing chapters to this volume, Julia

---

[4] Wilson (2000) draws similar distinctions between four types of government agencies, those involved in Craft (roughly transactional), Procedural (roughly logistical), Coping and Production tasks.

Strauss and Michael Roll both urge the field of PoE studies to be extended into the domain of social provisioning.

The transnational politics of state performance and state-building in Africa

Transnational ideas and actors have played an important role in shaping state performance in Africa over the past three decades and beyond. As noted in Chapter 1, contemporary PoEs seem to reproduce the distant and unaccountable bureaucratic elite that was, much more than any rational bureaucratic order, the hallmark of colonial administration (at least within metropolitan centres). Some of the state agencies examined here were established during the colonial period, with their mandates correspondingly skewed more towards the needs of empire than national development, as with central banks. Although the early decades of independence saw the state in Africa re-geared towards the imperatives of national development, the imposition of 'disciplinary neoliberalism' (Gill 1995) via programmes of structural adjustment from the 1980s offered IFIs significant influence over economic governance in Africa in ways that would profoundly affect the shape of the state (Harrison 2010). Indeed, the project of neoliberal economic governance promoted by IFIs directly drove the emergence of the PoE phenomenon over the 1990s by undermining broader-based state capacities and then privileging only certain state agencies with the capacities and mandates to deliver on a heavily conscribed policy agenda. Our research did not identify any PoEs that had emerged and been sustained *without* transnational support, including those beyond the economic technocracy (Bukenya 2020). Nor were we able to identify high-performing state agencies within the economic domain beyond those required to embed the new policy orthodoxy and thus grant states in Africa legitimacy within the neoliberal economic order (Mkandawire 2014).[5] This trend of state restructuring (Brenner 2004), which helped secure the hegemony of treasuries and central banks vis-à-vis spending departments and those of planning and industry (Jessop 2013), was also apparent in transitional economies (Phillips et al. 2006) and the Global North, in the context of financial capitalism's growing dominance within post-industrializing contexts. Here we discuss our findings on how the rise and then fall of disciplinary neoliberalism has shaped not only state capacity and performance in our African cases but also their wider developmental trajectories and, in some cases, their political settlements.

---

[5] As noted in other work on the bureaucracy in Africa during this period (Bierschenk and Olivier de Sardan 2014), the priorities of the 'developmental configuration' helped hollow out the public service, creating unequal pay rates and working conditions in ways that sucked the best talent into specific enclaves charged with delivering a specifically neoliberal project of development.

Our investigations of finance ministries, central banks, and revenue author-ities offer in-depth case studies of how this project of state restructuring became embodied in transnational policy coalitions, involving presidents, finance ministers, and senior economic technocrats as well as IFIs and external consul-tants.[6] External interventions are always filtered through national-level political dynamics and involve room for African political agency (Whitfield 2009), and in some cases there was a direct alignment between external agendas and the polit-ical imperatives of rulers to secure both economic and political stability in the face of soaring inflation, as in Ghana in the 1980s and Uganda in the early 1990s. Nonetheless, the effort to secure hegemony for a new policy agenda involved a concerted international effort to re-orientate finance ministries and central banks away from broader objectives of economic development and nation-building to the narrower issues of stabilization and debt (Mkandawire 1999), and to establish new-look revenue authorities (Fjeldstad and Moore 2009). Financial and technical assistance was obviously central here, but so was the active inculcation of a shared ideology amongst donors and key technocrats that in turn helped develop a uni-fied sense of purpose both within key state agencies within the economic domain. This also involved a wider effort by IFIs to inculcate a narrow form of economics within broader epistemic institutions and networks (Mkandawire 2014).[7]

This process did not go uncontested and ideas derived from national politi-cal contexts were also relevant for our PoEs during this period. In both Kenya and Rwanda, leaders mobilized home-grown discourses of 'self-reliance' to bol-ster support for a focus on fiscal prudence and domestic revenue mobilization. In both cases governments have also directly challenged IMF advice on monetary policy in ways that helped improve performance levels of their respective central banks and treasuries (e.g. see Matt Tyce on Kenya in Chapter 4). Interestingly, Caesar Cheelo and Marja Hinfelaar show how the economic technocracy in Zam-bia enjoyed its most effective performance period from the mid-2000s, after the country had graduated from debt conditionality, reduced its dependence on aid, and was largely calling the shots during in its dealings with development agen-cies (Chapter 5). As McDonnell (2020: 19) notes, 'Exposure to global forces and capitalist interests may be one pathway to greater organizational effectiveness, but empirical patterns suggest it is neither necessary nor sufficient.'

---

[6] Indeed, this epistemic community has played an influential role in documenting their role during this historical period (e.g. Kuteesa et al. 2010 on Uganda).

[7] The embedding of certain norms around budget-setting and macroeconomic stability within the rules of regional bodies such as the East African Community has offered further support for this agenda. More broadly, the professional norms and policy ideas adopted by those working for revenue authorities and central banks in Africa are increasingly set by professional associations at regional and international levels, and which have become more prominent in recent years. This embedding of eco-nomic technocrats within supra-national networks and epistemic communities has offered a sense of professional pride and belonging as well as a means of securing protection from political interference, whilst at the same time embedding the neoliberal project within the most powerful sites of the state.

Indeed, the hold of disciplinary neoliberalism over all of our countries began to slip from the mid-2000s onwards. Tensions between governments and IFIs increased as countries graduated from debt, reduced their dependence on aid and started to benefit from both rising commodity price rises and new financial flows from China, even before the global financial crisis dealt a further blow to the neoliberal model. These trends, along with ongoing processes of democratization, heightened the ambitions of leaders in countries like Uganda and Zambia to engage in more ambitious and transformative development agendas. In particular, the failure of the technocratic-neoliberal mode of governance to deliver more inclusive forms of growth in Zambia helped generate momentum for a shift in that country's governing coalition from the largely neoliberal MMD to the populist Patriotic Front in 2011. What Ilene Grabel terms the 'productive incoherence' of this interregnum period provided 'developing countries with more room to maneuver than they enjoyed in the stultifying neoliberal era' (2017: xv). This was apparent in several of our cases, including around major infrastructure investments that challenged the fiscal conservatism of the neoliberal order and catalysed a new round of 'palace wars' (Mkandawire 2014), between 'new productivists' and a re-energized planning tendency (Chimhowu et al. 2019, Hickey 2013) on the one hand, and the older 'Finance Ministry' tendency (Kanbur 2001) on the other.

However, what is striking from our cases is the limited extent to which this moment has led to a new era of state restructuring involving a shift of power between state agencies and the corresponding emergence of alternative development agendas. Our evidence suggests that this is partly because of the enduring hold of neoliberal ideas and institutional legacies—and the absence of any alternative international push for an alternative project of state-building—but also because of the nature of the governing coalitions in power in our countries during this period. The case of Zambia, which seemed well positioned to take advantage of the new openings offered by the resource commodity boom and new flows of finance from China, helps illustrate these trends. From 2011, the ruling Patriotic Front did flirt with the idea of mounting a fuller resource nationalist challenge to neoliberal orthodoxy (Chapter 5). This never came to fruition in part because political power was insufficiently concentrated around the leadership of the Patriotic Front's ruling coalition within Zambia's increasingly fractured political settlement (Caramento, Hinfelaar, and Cheelo, forthcoming). Moreover, the social foundations of Zambia's political settlement had long lacked the autonomous capitalist class capable of redirecting state policy. In Jepson's systematic (2020) study of which countries were able to diverge from neoliberal orthodoxy as a result of the geopolitical and geoeconomic openings of the mid-2000s, he argues that the presence of such a social force was a key requirement.

This dynamic is somewhat specific to Zambia, where the privatization of mines in the late 1990s, several years before the commodity supercycle commenced, ruled out the possibility of domestic firms and state-owned enterprises playing a fuller role in capturing the benefits of the resource boom. However, the absence of domestic capitalists holds across our cases and has already been identified as a critical constraint on the emergence of industrial policy across sub-Saharan Africa (Whitfield et al. 2015). Rather, Jepson (2020) suggests that in countries that combined the lack of an autonomous capitalist and a history of donor dependency, it was 'state managers' who defined how countries responded to the openings of the mid-2000s.[8] Indeed, leaders of finance ministries and central banks often fought back against any threat to the orthodoxy and took active steps to curtail the rise of alternative centres of state power that might challenge their hegemony (see Hickey 2013). Although by now even IFIs had accepted discourses of 'structural transformation' (Lin 2010) and of the need to invest in higher levels of counter-cyclical social spending (ILO and IMF 2012), this was not accompanied by the same commitment to building the capacity of those state agencies required to deliver on these new agendas. This would have been no mean feat given the extent of neoliberal state engineering: as Mkandawire (2014: 188) notes, 'There simply were no national planners, no industrial economists, no urban economists, no transport economists, no health economists' for politicians or donors to engage with by the time this new era of more heterodox possibilities emerged. Nor has Chinese investment been accompanied by a project of institutional reform aimed at reshaping the state in Africa into a form that is capable of taking advantage of this opportunity in a systematic manner, with little direct support flowing to more productivist state agencies. This is a significant problem, given the extent to which

> a long-term shift in hegemony requires not only a new 'hegemonic project', but also the reorganization of the state system towards underwriting a more durable shift in the balance of forces.
>
> (Jessop 2016: 68)

As a result, and although heavily discredited and weakened, the global neoliberal order retains a powerful hold on the ideational and incentive structure that confronts low- and middle-income countries. Emily Jones (2020) points out in her study of central banking that low- and middle-income governments retain a belief in the value of global financial governance standards despite these not forming part of a wider package of debt-related conditionality. Such 'institutional isomorphism', which the IMF itself has often discouraged in low- and middle-income countries (Jones 2020), retains its attraction because of the promise of credibility within financial markets but perhaps also as a form of learned practice reproduced within organizational cultures. Any move by central banks to adopt a more active developmental role once has been confined to a focus on 'financial inclusion' that bears little comparison with the move towards more muscular and state directed forms of development finance employed by some rising powers (Grabel 2017).

---

[8] As discussed in Chapter 1, this is an echo of Fred Block's (1981) effort to insert a political logic into critical (Marxist) analysis of the state (also Poulantzas 1978),

Overall, then, the earlier period of 'state restructuring' that heralded the displacement of statist-led Keynesianism by post-Fordism and neoliberal economics (Brenner 2004) has yet to be reversed or replaced by a new project of state restructuring around a more productivist economic project. The now widespread calls for African states to adopt industrial policy in pursuit of structural transformation, a process that has historically been critical to enabling sustained levels of poverty reduction, look set to go unanswered.

Concluding thoughts and strategic implications

This book has engaged with longstanding debates over state capacity and development that have been resurgent during the first decades of the twenty-first century, this time with the role of politics and power relations to the fore. Drawing on critical political theory and political settlements analysis, it has proposed a new way of conceptualizing and investigating pockets of bureaucratic effectiveness, one that reframes PoEs as being firmly embedded within both the transnationalized realities of negotiated statehood in contemporary Africa and longer-run processes of state-building, as opposed to operating as *deus ex machina* imported from some ungraspable Weberian future (Mkandawire 2015). We hope that this contribution helps advances this specific field of inquiry and also helps close the gap between theories of long-run development and the more immediate concerns of devising institutional fixes for pressing development problems discussed in Merilee Grindle's Foreword to this volume. We leave any judgement on this to our readers and to the leading experts whose critical commentary chapters close this volume. In this brief conclusion, we emphasize the central messages for development theory and practice that emerge from our study.

Africa's high-performing bureaucratic enclaves offer a fascinating window onto how the politics of state-building, democratization, and regime survival are currently unfolding in Africa, in relation to broader processes of capitalist development and international development interventions. Tracking their ups and downs over the past three decades from a political settlements perspective helps reveal the specific configurations of power under which high-performing enclaves are both more likely to emerge and to form part of a state-building process. To recap, we argue that although PoEs can emerge in any type of political settlement, they are more likely to be sustained overtime where power is concentrated around a governing coalition. However, this is only likely to form part of a wider process of state-building where governing elites perceive that the social foundations of their settlement generates a systemic threat to their hold on power and the settlement itself. In the absence of such a threat, then PoEs may well flourish for a time but will remain vulnerable to the caprice of their patron (Grindle 2012) and are highly unlikely to form part of a wider state-building project. An alternative pathway to achieving improved levels of governance is illustrated here by Ghana, where the historical difficulties that intense political competition can cause for state-building and bureaucratic performance seems to have been at least partially offset by two factors: a well-institutionalized party system that can channel political competition and a tendency for redistributive politics to be channelled through the bureaucratic structures of the state rather than more personalized vehicles.

The interplay of institutional forms with underlying structures of power is therefore critical here. However, PoEs also reveal the critical role that agency plays in this process (Leftwich 2010), primarily in the form of coalitions involving politicians and bureaucrats (in technopol mode) that are embedded within the wider transnational flow of ideas, finance, and expertise. The particular type of 'economic governance PoE' examined here emerges as a highly negotiated form of governance that has been critical to the transnational politics of negotiating statehood in Africa, sending signals to the international community that countries are willing to be good citizens of the global liberal economic order (Hagmann and Peclard 2010). They reveal something of the different trajectories of rule and governance that are possible for countries with different types of political settlement in the contemporary era, and of the nature and limits of the developmental projects they represent and enable.

At their best, PoEs could be said to operate as bulwarks against the most damaging tactics of political survival, preserving a space in which the public interest can be protected through the nurturing of a bureaucratic ethos (McDonnell 2020) and enabling some form of development to flourish. However, our PoEs have generally thrived in a 'greyer' middle-ground of 'developmental patronage', enabled as much by their embeddedness within informal political and personal relationships as with any project of rules-based state-building. PoEs seem to operate at the intersection of multiple logics of political rule, involving patronage as well as meritocracy, and to carry echoes of the elite bureaucratic caste introduced by colonial rule. Moreover, there is a strong sense in which this expert-led form of governance, built on close and often collusive relationships between rulers and senior bureaucrats, will always suffer from a democratic deficit. The extent to which economic governance has been ceded to state agencies, such as central banks that lack clear lines of political or popular oversight and accountability, has been increasingly recognized in a post-financial crisis world, with growing pressures in the Global North as well as Global South for central banks to be subjected to greater political oversight. How these tensions between democracy, technocracy and the politics of regime survival play out gained increased significance in light of the coronavirus pandemic, with treasuries and revenue authorities in particular set to play a critical role in overcoming the economic and social damage wrought by economic slowdowns and lockdowns introduced in many parts of Africa during 2020.

From a strategic perspective, support for PoEs can form part of a broad governance strategy whilst clearly not offering a panacea. High-functioning enclaves can perform important governance tasks that matter for maintaining economic and political stability, and which are largely logistical in nature. Such organizations benefit from leaders with political as well as technical skills and lengthy tenures, highly trained staff, positive organizational cultures, and exposure to international norms, expertise, and protection. All of these offer important points for intervention, particularly in organizations that share family resemblances to the state agencies identified here in terms of their mandate and function, including within the domains of governance (e.g. auditor generals, inspectorates of government), regulation (e.g. investment boards, certification, research), and perhaps smaller units within social services (e.g. drugs delivery units).

The case for further extending the autonomy of public-sector organizations from political oversight and direction is more difficult to make, not least given the growing concerns around the lack of public accountability associated with autonomous state agencies. Indeed, the benefits that accrue from granting state agencies such as revenue authorities semi-autonomous status are debatable (Dom 2019). Our evidence suggests that whilst this autonomy has offered revenue authorities all the trappings of being PoEs—including better-paid and trained staff, high-level leadership, and some sense of bureaucratic ethos—this has not necessarily resulted in improved performance. Given that the majority of state agencies are 'policy-takers' rather than policymakers, it is not clear that creating further degrees of separation between policy and administrative functions as opposed to a more integrated approach would offer the best way forward.[9] In particular, we find a good deal of evidence that improved mechanisms of coordination across state agencies is critical to improved performance, and there are good reasons to focus support on building 'networks of excellence'.

We found little evidence of PoEs playing an important role in delivering on the more difficult policy challenges involved in securing inclusive development (Pritchett and Woolcock 2004) and some negative spillovers, whereby PoEs hoover up the best staff and can also offer powerful tools that ruling elites can use to maintain themselves in power. Only where very particular conditions hold did we see positive spillovers from PoEs in ways that raised standards elsewhere, undermining any optimism that PoEs may (in the short term at least) provide the building-blocks of a wider state-building strategy.

Finally, it is imperative that a more balanced and joined-up approach is adopted to the challenge of building high-performing state agencies. Support needs to be extended beyond the 'agencies of restraint' that were deemed necessary for the neoliberal project of development to become embedded within Africa and elsewhere, and which have since acted as bulwarks against the possibility of pursuing alternative developmental projects that recent political economy trends may have otherwise enabled (Jepson 2020). Ensuring sustainable forms of structural

---

[9] We plan to pursue these debates further in dedicated collections on central banks and revenue authorities respectively.

transformation and higher levels of domestic revenue mobilization arguably constitute the most critical economic development and governance challenges facing African countries today. This, in turn, signals where the locus of state power needs to be shifted towards in order to help underpin the new balance of forces and relationships required for these projects to take hold.

References

Abdulai, A.-G. (2020). 'Competitive Clientelism, Donors and the Politics of Social Protection Uptake in Ghana', *Critical Social Policy*, 41(2): 270–93.

Abdulai, A.-G., and S. Hickey. 2016. 'The Politics of Development under Competitive Clientelism: Insights from Ghana's Education Sector'. *African Affairs*, 115(458): 44–72.

Abernethy, D. B. (1971). 'Bureaucracy and Economic Development in Africa', *African Review*, 1(1): 93–107.

Acemoglu, D. and Robinson, J. (2012). *Why Nations Fail: The Origins of Power, Prosperity and Poverty*. London: Profile Books.

Acemoglu, D. and Robinson, J. (2019). *The Narrow Corridor*. London: Penguin Press.

Berman, B. (2004). 'Ethnicity, Bureaucracy and Democracy: The Politics of Trust'. In B. Berman, D. Eyoh, and W. Kymlicka (eds), *Ethnicity and Democracy in Africa*: Oxford: James Currey. 39–53.

Bersch, K., Praça, S., and Taylor, M. M. (2017). 'Bureaucratic Capacity and Political Autonomy within National States: Mapping the Archipelago of Excellence in Brazil'. In M. A. Centeno, A. Kohli, and D. J. Yashar (eds). *States in the Developing World*. Cambridge, MA: Cambridge University Press. 157–83.

Bierschenk, T. and J.-P. Olivier de Sardan (eds) (2014). *States at Work: Dynamics of African Bureaucracies*. Leiden: Brill.

Block, F. (1981). 'Beyond Relative Autonomy: State Managers as Historical Subjects', *New Political Science*, 2(3): 33–49.

Brenner, N. (2004) *New State Spaces: Urban Governance and the Rescaling of Statehood*. New York and Oxford: Oxford University Press.

Bukenya, B. (2020). 'The Politics of Building Effective Water Utilities in the Global South: A Case of NWSC Uganda'. ESID Working Paper 152. Manchester: Effective States and Inclusive Development Research Centre, University of Manchester.

Caramento, A., Hinfelaar, M., and Cheelo, C. (forthcoming) 'Asymmetries of Power and Capacity: the Zambia Revenue Authority (ZRA) as an Instrument of Resource Nationalism', *Journal of Southern African Studies*.

Centeno, M. A., Kohli, A., and Yashar, D. J. (2017). *States in the Developing World*. Cambridge: Cambridge University Press.

Chimhowu, A., Hulme, D., and Munro, L. (2019). 'The "New" National Development Planning and Global Development Goals: Processes and Partnerships', *World Development*, 120: 76–89.

Dom, R. (2019) 'Semi-autonomous Revenue Authorities in Sub-Saharan Africa: Silver Bullet or White Elephant', *The Journal of Development Studies*, 55(7): 1418–35.

Domínguez, J. I. (1997). *Technopols: Freeing Politics and Markets in Latin America in the 1990s*. University Park, PA: Penn State Press.

Doner, R., Bryan, F., Ritchie, K., and Slater, D. (2005). 'Systemic Vulnerability and the Origins of Developmental States: Northeast and Southeast Asia in Comparative Perspective', *International Organization*, 59(2): 327–61.

Evans, P. (1995). *Embedded Autonomy: States and Industrial Transformation*. Princeton, NJ: Princeton University Press.

Evans, P. (2004). 'Development as Institutional Change: The Pitfalls of Monocropping and the Potentials of Deliberation', *Studies in Comparative International Development*, 38: 30–52.

Fjeldstad, O.-H. and Moore, M. (2009). 'Revenue Authorities and Public Authority in Sub-Saharan Africa', *The Journal of Modern African Studies*, 47(1): 1–18.

Geddes, B. (1990). 'Building "State" Autonomy in Brazil, 1930–1964'. *Comparative Politics*, 22(2): 217–35.

Gill S. (1995) 'Globalisation, Market Civilisation, and Disciplinary Neoliberalism', *Millennium*, 24(3): 399–423.

Golooba-Mutebi, F. (2008). 'Collapse, War and Reconstruction in Uganda: An Analytical Narrative on State Making'. Working Paper No. 27, Crisis States Research Centre. London: London School of Economics and Political Science.

Grabel, I. (2017). *When Things Don't Fall Apart: Global Financial Governance and Developmental Finance in an Age of Productive Incoherence*. Cambridge, MA: MIT Press.

Grindle, M. (1997). 'Divergent Cultures? When Public Organisations Perform Well in Developing Countries', *World Development*, 25(4): 481–95.

Grindle, M. S. (2007). 'Good Enough Governance Revisited', *Development Policy Review*, 25(5): 553–74.

Grindle, M. S. (2012). *Jobs for the Boys: Patronage and the State in Comparative Perspective*. Cambridge, MA: Harvard University Press.

Grindle, M. S. (2017). 'Good Governance, RIP: A Critique and an Alternative', *Governance*, 30(1): 17–22.

Grzymala-Busse A. (2008). 'Beyond Clientelism: Incumbent State Capture and State Formation', *Comparative Political Studies*, 41(4–5): 638–73.

Hagmann, T. and Peclard, D. (2010). 'Negotiating Statehood: Dynamics of Power and Domination in Africa', *Development and Change*, 41(4): 539–62.

Harrison, G. (2010). *Neoliberal Africa: The Impact of Global Social Engineering*. London: Zed Books.

Hertog, S. (2014). 'Defying the Resource Curse: Explaining Successful State-owned Enterprises in Rentier States'. In M. Roll (ed.), *The Politics of Public Sector Performance: Pockets of Effectiveness in Developing Countries*. Oxford: Routledge. 173–93.

Hickey, S. (2013). 'Beyond the Poverty Agenda? Insights from the New Politics of Development in Uganda', *World Development*, 43: 194–206.

Hickey, S. and Sen, K. (2023). *Pathways to Development: From Politics to Power*. Oxford: Oxford University Press.

Hout, W. (2013). 'Neopatrimonialism and Development: Pockets of Effectiveness as Drivers of Change', *Revue Internationale de Politique Comparée*, 20(3): 79–96.

Hout, W. (2014). '"Confidence in our Own Abilities": Suriname's State Oil Company as a Pocket of Effectiveness'. In M. Roll (ed.), *The Politics of Public Sector Performance: Pockets of Effectiveness in Developing Countries*. Oxford and New York: Routledge. 147–72.

ILO and IMF (2012). 'Towards Effective and Fiscally Sustainable Social Protection Floors'. Preliminary report prepared for the meeting of the G20 Labour and Employment Ministers in Guadalajara, Mexico, 17–18 May. Geneva and Washington, DC: ILO and IMF.

Jepson, N. (2020) *In China's Wake: How the Commodity Book Transformed Development Strategies in the Global South*. New York: Columbia University Press.

Jessop, B. (2008). *State Power: A Strategic and Relational Approach*. Cambridge: Polity Press.

Jessop, B. (2013). 'Finance-dominated Accumulation and Post-democratic Capitalism'. In S. Fadda and P. Tridico (eds), *Institutions and Economic Development after the Financial Crisis*. London: Routledge. 83–105.

Jessop, B. (2016). *The State: Past, Present, Future*. Cambridge: Polity Press.

Joignant, A. (2011). 'The Politics of Technopols: Resources, Political Competence and Collective Leadership in Chile, 1990–2010', *Journal of Latin American Studies*, 43(3): 517–46.

Jones, E. (ed.) (2020). *The Political Economy of Bank Regulation in Developing Countries: Risk and Reputation*. Oxford: Oxford University Press.

Kanbur, R. (2001). 'Economic Policy, Distribution and Poverty: The Nature of Disagreements', *World Development*, 29(6): 1083–94.

Kelsall, T., N. Shulz, M. vom Hau, W. Ferguson, S. Hickey and B. Levy. (2022). *Political Settlements and Development: Theory, Evidence, Implications*. Oxford: Oxford University Press.

Kuteesa, F., Tumusiime-Mutebile, E., Whitworth, A., and Williamson, T. (eds) (2010). *Uganda's Economic Reforms: Insider Accounts*. Oxford: Oxford University Press

Leftwich, A. (2010). 'Beyond Institutions: Rethinking the Role of Leaders, Elites and Coalitions in the Industrial Formation of Developmental States and Strategies', *Forum for Development Studies*, 37(1): 93–111.

Levy, B. (2014). *Working with the Grain: Integrating Governance and Growth in Development Strategies*. New York: Oxford University Press.

Lin, J. (2010). *New Structural Economics*. Washington, DC: World Bank.

Lindemann, S. (2011). 'Just Another Change of Guard? Broad-based Politics and Civil War in Museveni's Uganda', *African Affairs*, 110(440): 1–30.

Lonsdale, J. (1994). 'Moral Ethnicity and Political Tribalism'. In P. Kaarsholm and J. Hultin (eds), *Inventions and Boundaries: Historical and Anthropological Approaches to the Study of Ethnicity*. Roskilde University. 131–50.

Mann, L. and Berry, M. (2016). 'Understanding the Political Motivations That Shape Rwanda's Emergent Developmental State', *New Political Economy*, 21(1): 119–44.

McDonnell, E. M. (2017). 'The Patchwork Leviathan: How Pockets of Bureaucratic Governance Flourish within Institutionally Diverse Developing States', *American Sociological Review*, 82(3): 476–510.

McDonnell, E. M. (2020). *Patchwork Leviathan: Pockets of Bureaucratic Effectiveness in Developing States*. Princeton, NJ: Princeton University Press.

Mkandawire, T. (1999). 'The Political Economy of Financial Sector Reform', *Journal of International Development*, 11(3): 321–42.

Mkandawire, T. (2014). 'The Spread of Economic Doctrines and Policymaking in Postcolonial Africa', *African Studies Review*, 57(1): 171–98.

Mkandawire, T. (2015). 'Neopatrimonialism and the Political Economy of Economic Performance in Africa: Critical Reflections', *World Politics*, 67(3): 563–612.

Mkandawire, T. (2017). 'State Capacity, History, Structure, and Political Contestation in Africa'. In M. A. Centeno, A. Kohli, and D. J. Yashar (eds) (2017). *States in the Developing World*. Cambridge, MA: Cambridge University Press. 184–216.

Nathan, N. L. (2019). *Electoral Politics and Africa's Urban Transition: Class and Ethnicity in Ghana*. New York: Cambridge University Press.

North, D. C., Wallis, J. J., Webb, S. B., and Weingast, B. R. (2009). *In the Shadow of Violence: Politics, Economics, and the Problems of Development*. New York: Cambridge University Press.

Phillips, R., Henderson, J., Andor, L., and Hulme, D. (2006). 'Usurping Social Policy: Neoliberalism and Economic Governance in Hungary', *Journal of Social Policy*, 35(4): 585–606.

Poulantzas, N. (1978). *State, Power, Socialism*. London: Verso.

Pritchett, L. and Woolcock, M. (2004). 'Solutions When the Solution Is the Problem: Arraying the Disarray in Development', *World Development*, 32(2): 191–212.

Reyntjens, F. (2013). *Political Governance in Post-genocide Rwanda*. Cambridge: Cambridge University Press.

Roll, M. (ed.) (2014). *The Politics of Public Sector Performance: Pockets of Effectiveness in Developing Countries*. Oxford: Routledge.

Schulz, N. and Kelsall, T. (2021). 'The Political Settlements Dataset: An introduction with Illustrative Applications'. ESID Working Paper No. 165. Manchester: Effective States and Inclusive Development Research Centre, University of Manchester.

Seekings, J. (2017). 'State Capacity and the Construction of Pro-poor Welfare States in the "Developing" World'. In M. A. Centeno, A. Kohli, and D. J. Yashar (eds), *States in the Developing World*. Cambridge, MA: Cambridge University Press. 363–79.

Shefter, M. (1994). *Political Parties and the State: The American Historical Experience*. Princeton, NJ: Princeton University Press.

Skocpol, T. 1992. *Protecting Soldiers and Mothers: The Political Origins of Social Policy in the United States*. Cambridge, MA: Harvard University Press.

Slater, D. (2010). *Ordering Power: Contentious Politics and Authoritarian Leviathans in Southeast Asia*. New York: Cambridge University Press.

Strauss, J. C. (2008). *Strong Institutions in Weak Polities: State Building in Republican China, 1927–1940*. Oxford: Oxford University Press.

Tyce, M. (2020). 'Unrealistic Expectations, Frustrated Progress and an Uncertain Future? The Political Economy of Oil in Kenya', *The Extractive Industries and Society*, 7(2): 729–37.

Van de Walle, N. (2014). 'The Democratization of Clientelism in Sub-Saharan Africa'. In D. Abente Brun and L. Diamond (eds), *Clientelism, Social Policy and the Quality of Democracy*. Baltimore, MD: Johns Hopkins University Press. 230–52.

Vom Hau, M. (2012). 'State Capacity and Inclusive Development: New Challenges and Directions'. Effective States and Inclusive Development Research Centre Working Paper No. 2. Manchester: Effective States and Inclusive Development.

Werbner, R. (2004). *Reasonable Radicals and Citizenship in Botswana: The Public Anthropology of Kalanga Elites*. Bloomington, IN: Indiana University Press.

Whitfield, L. (2009). *The Politics of Aid: African Strategies for Dealing with Donors*. Oxford: Oxford University Press.

Whitfield, L., Therkildsen, O., Buur, L., and Kjær, A. M. (2015). *The Politics of African Industrial Policy: A Comparative Perspective*. Cambridge: Cambridge University Press.

Wilson, J. (2000). *Bureaucracy: What Government Agencies Do and Why They Do It*. New York: Basic Books.

World Bank (2017). *World Development Report 2017: Governance and the Law*. Washington, DC: World Bank. Available online: http://www.worldbank.org/en/publication/wdr2017 (accessed 6 June 2019).

9

Pockets of Effectiveness

Afterwords and New Beginnings

Julia C. Strauss

This volume is a welcome intervention into the ever-growing literature on what are now called 'pockets of effectiveness', or PoEs. Rather than simply extrapolating the conditions for the rise and fall of PoEs as best guesses from a particular case study or set of case studies, it combines the analytical concept of 'political settlements' with granular detail from case studies to discern broader patterns in the emergence and decline of PoEs. First, the PoEs are identified as those most cited by practitioners themselves in five sub-Saharan African countries: Kenya, Rwanda, Zambia, Uganda, and Ghana. These high-prestige, high-performing PoEs are unsurprisingly almost uniformly located in the economic technocracy, including ministries of finance, central banks, and semi-autonomous revenue agencies (SARAs). Chapters specific to each country then apply the notion of political settlements as 'concentrated' in which a dominant power constellation of political elites provides the potential conditions for either longer-term horizons, or 'dispersed' horizons, which increasepolitical pressures to dispense short-term patronage. Concentrated political settlements are especially likely to adopt the longer-term horizons necessary for PoEs when they perceive themselves to be existentially vulnerable, but may permit the emergence of PoEs as part of patronage based regime survival. These two axes: concentrated vs. dispersed political settlements and systematic vulnerability vs. the use of PoEs for patronage, provide much greater analytical rigour to questions of PoE variation both between cases and within cases over time. While it is often been remarked that PoEs are heavily concentrated in the econ-technocracy managing finance and tax, there is little that systematically engages the all important questions of how and why *particular* organizations within the same broad field emerge as PoEs in some countries and not others. There is even less on variation in what we might call 'degrees of PoE-ness' between different organizations within the same country (with the same broad political settlement). And although it has long been understood that PoEs are prone to erosion over time because they attract attacks and jealousy from elsewhere in the political system, until now no one has specified the *general* range of

Julia C. Strauss, *Pockets of Effectiveness*. In: *Pockets of Effectiveness and the Politics of State-building and Development in Africa*. Edited by Sam Hickey, Oxford University Press. © Oxford University Press (2023).
DOI: 10.1093/oso/9780192864963.003.0009

conditions under which one can expect the maintenance, decline, or, more rarely, the revival of PoEs after a period of decline.

The notion of 'political settlements'—and what it does to explain variation in country, case, and change over time—is the volume's core and offers a clear and convincing picture, not just as a series of static snapshots, but more of an unfolding reel. Thus the propositions suggested in Chapter 2: that PoEs emerge where power is concentrated rather than dispersed, where there is system vulnerability, where elites dominate but PoEs are part of patronage-based survival, and there is alignment between paradigmatic ideas and the centrality of policy domain are borne out in the both the broad-brush and micro details laid out in the meat of the substantive chapters. Cases at opposite ends of the spectrum: Kenya and Rwanda, prove these points. Kenya's increasingly dispersed political settlement and fractious electoral politics map almost perfectly onto the performance of its PoEs: organizations that had stable and embedded leaderships continued to enjoy positive performance despite a gradual dispersion of the wider political settlement, until the wider political settlement became so fractious that all previous PoEs were substantially weakened. Ghana follows a similar pattern to Kenya, with clear evidence that the dispersal of power both between competing elite factions and within ruling coalitions, tends to undermine the performance of PoEs, albeit within the context of higher levels of state performance overall. In stark contrast to this pattern, Rwanda's highly concentrated (and minority) political settlement, amplified by the regime's systemic vulnerability, has led to the usual suspects in the Ministry of Finance and Economic Planning, the Rwanda Revenue Authority, and the National Bank of Rwanda not only emerging as high performers, but as 'higher performers within a generally functional state' (Chapter 6). This forms part of the constellation of minority capture of the state after the extraordinary event of genocide that committed the political leadership to a programme of strong state-building with long-term horizons. Quite incredibly, the cohesiveness of the authoritarian political settlement in Rwanda has even permitted a willingness to learn from rather than punish mistakes within PoEs. The examples of Zambia and Uganda fall between these extremes, with Zambia leaning more towards a Kenya/Ghana-style increasingly dispersed political settlement—and demonstrating just how difficult it is to get even economic technocracy 'right'—while Uganda illustrates how even under strongmen like Museveni political settlements may become more dispersed with damaging consequences for PoEs.

For these reasons, this volume comes in with an important intervention in terms of both its analytical framework and the solidity of its data. It provides a strong evidentiary base for and explanation of systematic variation both between cases and over time. What emerges is a complex, shifting kaleidoscope of interactions between technical domain, organizational leadership, and the wider political settlement. Indeed, the nearly constant flux demonstrated in all of these cases suggests that relative degrees of 'PoE-ness' are hard won, changeable, and highly contingent on factors beyond the control of the PoE itself. Either in sub-Saharan Africa or beyond it, creating a PoE is hard work. Most are doomed to failure. Maintaining one over time is harder work. And reversing the decline of a PoE might be most difficult and fraught of all. But it is perhaps here that we should pause and think through what it means—both within the framing of a political settlement but beyond a given political settlement—to create, maintain, and with luck even revive a PoE in decline. This is a question of real importance for both sub-Saharan Africa and states in other regions of the developing world.

Some three decades ago, when PoE had not yet been invented as a concept, and the idea of SARAs was just beginning to get purchase, I rewrote my dissertation on a time and place as far geographically and temporally removed from contemporary sub-Saharan Africa as one could imagine: China in the late 1920s and 1930s. As is often the way with dissertation research, I went to the field fully expecting to write on one subject (China's civil service and examination systems), and came out with the material to write quite another (on how closely linked the effectiveness and efficiency of *particular* state organizations were to their own civil service and examination systems; notably in the salt tax and general tax divisions of the Ministry of Finance, but also the Ministry of Foreign Affairs). Indeed, in the weak but reintegrating Republican Chinese state of the 1930s, there was almost perfect alignment between those parts of the state that we would now consider to be PoEs and systems of recruitment and promotion that were separate from the rest of the Republican Chinese state: Customs, Salt Tax, the highest performing sections of the Ministry of Finance, the national post office, and the Ministry of Foreign Affairs. Based on this data (minus case studies for Customs and the post office), I argued that for these unusual successes, there were two strategies that were simultaneously deployed: 1) rigorous policies of *insulation* that quite literally screened off the institution from a wider environment of nepotism and patronage in combination with 2) equally rigorous policies of *goal achievement* that demonstrated the ongoing importance of the organization to its wider political masters—as without conscientious diplomats and an ever increasing stream of revenue pouring into the central government's coffers, the regime's own internal and external security, which was always precarious, might well fall (Strauss 1998, especially pp. 66–79). This combination of strategies of internal insulation, to get that all-important breathing space and autonomy from nepotism and patronage, and clearly demonstrable goal achievement, in providing services that were absolutely core to the functioning of the state, were unusual in China at the time. Indeed, the only sectors of the state that were even more crucial were those that had to do with the military and internal security (the two were deeply intertwined at the time), and were of course far too sensitive to get solid documentation on— either in the late 1980s when I was engaged in the original research collection, or at any time since then.

Indeed, so 'captured' was I by my sources (and their vociferous insistence on rigorous civil-service insulation from a wider, patronage-riven political and economic environment) that first as a graduate student and then as junior faculty writing up a first monograph, I simply did not appreciate what is, in effect, the founding principle of this volume: that organizations are *never* divorced from their surrounding environments, and that surrounding environments are far from uniform. Political settlements suggest a great deal for the matrices within which PoEs emerge (or do not emerge), but their constellations fluctuate, and fluctuate in ways that are either unpredictable or beyond the control of the would-be PoE. Thus, in the wildly different time and place of Republican China, my own charting of the rise and eventual decline of the Sino-foreign Salt Inspectorate, an anomalous organization whose life span between 1913 and 1949 was, with various name changes, more or less the lifespan of the Republic of China on the mainland of China itself, I noted the following elements without ever developing them into a coherent analytical framework that took account of this all-important wider political environment.

In retrospect, the Sino-foreign Salt Inspectorate was *tolerated* but not loved by a Nationalist government that was persuaded to reconstitute it after abolishing it in 1927–1928, on the grounds that only the salt tax would be a steady supply of tax funds that the weak central government so desperately needed (Strauss 1998: 84–90). Simultaneously, it was *hated*, and subjected to repeated attacks by nationalists outside the top ranks of the government (Strauss 1998: 91–6), who frequently criticized it on the grounds of its foreign presence as an affront to national sovereignty and pride. For a brief period in the mid-1930s, the Salt Inspectorate was admired and *emulated* by technocrats elsewhere in the government, notably when it provided a model for newly formed divisions within the Ministry of Finance (Strauss 1998: 131–3). And finally the Salt Inspectorate was ultimately *undone* by forces beyond its or anyone's control, namely the mass de-institutionalization and fourfold expansion that was set in train by the outbreak of the Sino-Japanese War (Strauss 1998: 97–104). Despite the chaos of the Republican period, which included its offices being repeatedly robbed at gunpoint by marauding warlord soldiers, being abolished and re-instated by the Nationalist government in 1927-1928, and the loss of many of its most productive salt works over the course of the Sino-Japanese War, its political safety lay in its insistence that it was merely 'technocratic'—an impersonal bureaucratic organization that would serve its political masters uncomplainingly and well. (This mattered, because the weak central governments of the time always needed more funds.). It surely helped that its trumpeting of its impersonal and 'fair' civil-service system resonated positively within the cultural predisposition of Chinese elites towards examinations as a mechanism that delivered well deserved meritocracy. But cultural predisposition only gets one so far: weaker organizations that did not provide core services to the central state in Republican China were allowed no such insulation or indulgence.

The Salt Inspectorate (and Customs, and the post office) was allowed to do its work relatively unmolested by political incursions in day-to-day workings because 1) it accepted the political leadership of the Nationalist government, which meant accepting its political appointees at the top, and 2) because it delivered the goods. Despite griping over the political appointees who were imposed from above, what ultimately weakened it was not political interference per se, but being over-whelmed by exactly the same forces that weakened and did in the government as a whole: uncontrolled inflation in combination with uncontrolled recruitment—both of which were of a piece with a weak government's capacity to respond to foreign invasion and civil war. The case of China suggests that even cohesive political settlements can and do change, sometimes dramatically, in response to either internal or external shocks that overwhelm its pre-sets and its capacities. Just because a coalition appears to be stable does not mean that it will remain so.

PoEs as a realm of the techno-pols: Being 'seen', policy domain, and questions of capacity

The great inescapable in this volume is that the PoEs that provide all its won-derfully rich data and case-study work are, without exception, to be found in the economic-technocratic wings of the state, particularly in finance, tax, and central banks. This leads to a serious question: do the technopols truly rule the realm of PoE-world or is this simply a matter of perception? Certainly, in sub-Saharan Africa as elsewhere, PoEs *appear* to be heavily concentrated in the realm of finance and econ-technocracy. But is it really the case that the PoEs that seem to work well enough to emerge and have enough prestige that they are consistently identified as such are inevitably to be found in what the authors call the 'logistical' elements of the state? What, exactly *are* the 'logistical' parts of the state? There are, I think, several analytically separable elements with a direct bearing on this question: 1) how state bureaucracies are defined in terms of their effectiveness and efficiency (which translate into 'excellence'), 2) relative degrees of policy agreement in terms of a) what should be done and b) how it should be implemented, 3) how open or closed the organization is to the rest of society in its policy domain and 4) the degree to which organizational goals are, in at least rough terms, aligned with organizational capacity. When these elements all come together, they are not only a product or a consequence of political settlements, important as political settle-ments and the wider political context might be. Rather these factors in turn affect the way in which aspiring PoEs are 'seen' by the wider state of which they are a part. (Scott, 1998) Ultimately these are the conditions with which leaders of PoE work when they need to generate support for the establishment of a PoE, to head off the withdrawal of that support, or be part of the renegotiation of the political settlement in ways that will permit the revival of a PoE.

If we consider what state bureaucracies are and do, their first imperative is to demonstrate both loyalty *and* competence as they deliver on the core needs of the state. When considered in any kind of longer historical frame of state making, it is clear that apart from the obvious core importance of the military and internal security, these 'core needs' have *always* revolved around tax extraction, banking and credit (to raise loans), and managing relations with foreign powers. It was only much later—in the late nineteenth and twentieth century—that the state began to take on provision of infrastructure (first railroads, then roads, sanitation, lighting, and electricity), before moving into more contemporary and 'softer' concerns of public health, social welfare, and the environment. Amounts of revenue collected against administrative costs expended, kilometres of roads tarmacked, metres of pipes laid for clean water or electrical lines put up—these were activities that were all easily measurable, inherently divisible and readily managed by technological expertise. And indeed in the early twentieth century, this was the genius of the Weberian formulation of legal-rational bureaucracy: a formula of strict hierarchy, depersonalization, and rule orientation seemed to best attract and retain both loyalty and competence in a world in which state functions *were* in fact largely reducible to activities that could be de-personalized around uniform rules, standards, and measures. This Weberian model was, in theory, exported to different degrees and with different variations in effectiveness around the world through colonial bureaucracies. One variant of this model was what would now be called SARAs: agencies initially staffed at the top by Westerners with 'expertise' and large numbers of local staff that were imposed on the Qing and the Ottoman empires for the collection of customs and salt taxes from the mid nineteenth through the early twentieth century to, in effect, guarantee the loans made to these empires (often to finance domestic military modernization initiatives). Nor should the impact of these early hybrid institutions—imposed as they were by Western creditors in noxious semi-colonial conditions of dominance—be discounted. They often provided the core personnel, training, and models for central finance and tax until at least the middle of the twentieth century for these countries. While different in form, patterns of foreign influence in the earliest 'modern' banks were often similar. Iran's entire modern banking system had been given over to Rothschild concession in the late nineteenth century, the Imperial Ottoman Bank of the late nineteenth century was a Franco-British partnership, and was still a going concern into the 1970s, the place where one still cashed one's American Express traveller's cheques in Istanbul.

Thus tax and the econ-technocracy are unusual in several respects. First they are readily 'seen as core to its survival'. Their policy domains have historically been and continue to be unusually amenable to Weberian criteria of hierarchy, depersonalization, and expertise. Their daily workings are readily broken down into statistics and charts that can be easily 'read' by the higher levels of the state. Because they deal in cold hard numbers, it is relatively straightforward to determine both high performance and its converse, incompetence or outright malfeasance. Finally, tax and econ-technocracies, while enormously important politically and for the state as a whole generally possess much more straightforward decision-making with short time lags between cause and effect (monthly, quarterly, annually) than is the case in many policy domains with longer lags between policy implementation and effect, such as education. As long as there are enough statisticians on hand to do the counting and fill in the reports, these short lags between cause and effect correct things going awry, and, in combination with agreed upon goals and largely agreed upon means, tend to dampen down politically raised temperatures in terms of internal workings. The goals are almost always agreed, and there is typically substantial agreement in terms of how to achieve those goals. In short, the policy domain of econ-techs lends itself much more to classic Weberian markers of well-functioning state institutions (hierarchy, depersonalization, remoteness from populations, and technocratic expertise) than do most of the other policy domains with which the state might concern itself. This does not by any means suggest that all, or most, econ-tech organizations of this sort are going to become PoEs; only that the criteria by which 'PoE-ness' is determined are most likely to be found in the kinds of organizations that most clearly have conformed to the ideal type of Weberian legal-rational bureaucracy in the first place.

Seen in this light, the technopol domain is characterized by features that are relatively unusual among the multitude of policy arenas for state action: measurable and divisible tasks, relative agreement about goals and strategies to achieve them, and short time lags between performance and outcomes. But there may well be an even wider category that the econ-tech domain fits within: namely being part of a relatively closed system. If open systems are characterized by multiple points of access and exchange with the surrounding environment, closed systems have relatively fewer points of access and feedback. The bureaucratic organizations of the state are *predicated* on being fairly closed: indeed, a certain amount of 'closedness' is necessary to maintain organizational discipline and coherence. It therefore stands to reason that the more closed the policy domain (for example, deciding on fiscal policy or the budget), or the more rule-bound the interaction with society (as, for example, tax assessment), the easier it will be to resist demands from clients and different elements in society to behave in particularlistic ways. Insofar as an organization either decides on policies but does not interact with society directly, or keeps its distance from society by administering policies handed down from the hierarchy by uniform rules, it is relatively closed. This provides organizational coherence. It is also in principle impervious to feedback from the societies in which it operates—except when matters come to a point of affecting the political settlement itself.

Finally, successful PoEs are all characterized by something that is itself a product of the interaction between the wider political settlement, the PoE leadership, and the resources at the disposal of that leadership: relative alignment between the organization's capacity and its goals. Establishing clear goals that are reasonably *achievable* is the first step in setting in train a virtuous cycle of goal achievement, internal morale, and external prestige. This is not easy even within an econ-tech policy environment. The developing world is littered with examples of would-be PoEs in tax regimes, central banks, and economic development units that fail—not because of lack of talent or will, but because the organization's stated goals were far beyond its capacity to achieve. One historical example, again from Republican China, is a familiar one (Strauss 1998: 126–38). The Sino-foreign Salt Inspectorate was deemed to be so successful that its personnel systems of separate civil-service salaries and progression, as well as its techniques of assessing tax, were deemed to be a model for the Ministry of Finance, which established a new division of Consolidated Tax in the mid-1930s. The Consolidated Tax Administration assessed business taxes on factories, and in particular on cigarettes and alcohol, before expanding to cotton yarn, matches, and other consumer products, like firecrackers. And here the story was a decidedly mixed one. Consolidated Tax was staffed by young, motivated techocrats, who did an excellent job when the tax was within their reasonable capacity. Therefore the Consolidated Tax Administration did an impressive job at raising taxes from the 'modern' industrial sector in and around Shanghai, which was served by good transport links and where the taxable physical plants were large and immobile. The taxes collected on cigarettes, alcohol, matches, and cotton yarn produced by factories in this region went up sharply. Consolidated Tax even did reasonably well when its inspectors went to other urban areas to assess taxes on the factories that its inspectors could locate. But the Consolidated Tax Administration did infinitely less well in taxing the numerous small-scale operations that permeated the market towns of China, particularly locally rolled cigarettes and the alcohol produced by small distillers. These were numerous, dispersed, and small scale. Here the tax 'take' relative to amount of effort expended was unfavourable (cigarettes, for example, were often rolled by hand in people's homes and were then sold in local markets far from the eyes of tax inspectors). The Ministry of Finance understood very well that *if* it could capture even a reasonable proportion of the locally made cigarettes and alcohol distilled that it could put the government on a much stronger financial footing. But to do so in any kind of systemic way required organizational capacity that was far beyond its resource base in trained personnel. The Ministry of Finance's decision to form another division for Direct Tax based on the Salt Inspectorate model was a dramatic failure from the outset. Its personnel were, like those in the Division of Consolidated Tax, young, well trained, and keen. But the technical capacity and resource base to impose a direct income tax was far beyond the ability of even the most committed and elite new division. Lacking payroll reporting or measures to enforce the creation of a national income-tax system, the only sector that could be taxed were civil servants themselves. Unsurprisingly, this caused huge resentment among the people the state most needed, and the policy was quietly shelved amid the rising inflation of the early 1940s. The limits to the success of Consolidated Tax—in its failure to truly tap what is now called the informal economy—are replicated by today's states in sub-Saharan Africa in their efforts to systematically reach—indeed enclose—the open informal economy in one that is regularized, monitored, and 'seen' by the bureaucratic state.

Into the future: PoEs beyond the economic technocracy

Given all this, are the features described in this volume and suggested above pre-conditions for what we might call 'PoE-ness'? Is it only the elements that we see in the policy domains of econ-techs that have even a fighting chance of becoming a PoE? After all, relatively closed systems, amenability to Weberian ideal-type criteria of hierarchy, rule boundedness, and bureaucratic expertise, short elapsed time between policy implementation and evidence of effectiveness, agreed upon goals and means of achieving those goals, divisibility into standard categories of measurement and analysis, and relative alignment between goals and organizational capacity are relatively rare. Apart from the important, but still restricted realm of econ-techs, there are almost *no* state organizations that enjoy all of these favourable characteristics. Is, as a matter of definition, PoE-ness to forever be equated with those finance, tax, and central banking and regulatory institutions that manage to negotiate their political settlements well? Is PoE-ness in necessary opposition to the responsive, democratic, and service-provision sectors of the state in developing countries?

Here there are no conclusive answers, but a developing world in which the crucial sectors of public health, education, social services, anti-poverty, basic incomes, infrastructure, agricultural extension, and the environment (just to cite several) are forever consigned to be non-PoEs is a deeply impoverished one indeed. Many—if not most—of the activities of states in the developing world are to be found in exactly the policy areas that are deeply engaged with society, that attempt to alter human behaviour (from planting crops differently, to recycling, to reducing water use), or that despite their technical basis fundamentally transform natural and human environments (e.g. road building, opening mines, conducting anti-malaria campaigns) for everyday people whose lives are thus altered. And here it seems that *if* the skills that make for successful econ-tech leadership—the ability to become credible and 'visible' within the political settlement to maintain insulation—can be replicated down to the bottom of the organizational hierarchy, to the interface of state agents with human and natural environments, there is reason to believe that they might, in aggregate become micro-PoEs. The ability of the grassroots agricultural extension workers, park rangers, public-health workers, teachers and principals in state schools, and foremen building roads to not only apply impersonal rules but to make those rules approachable, comprehensible, understandable, and responsive through discussion and negotiation—in short what is often called *embeddedness*—is as determinative of success as the factors that enable distance, counting, and negotiation with important actors in the political settlement is for the econ-tech leadership. How such combinations of approachability, comprehensibility, and responsiveness might be replicated in different policy areas at scale is, of course, an important question that is unlikely to be resolved by one technique or method. But in the same way that econ-tech leaders have to spend much of their time balancing between managing internal operations and the external political settlement, grassroots civil servants, agricultural extension workers, elementary school teachers, health-care workers, and foremen managing road building have to spend much of their time balancing between the policies they are expected to implement, and individuals or groups in society with minds of and interests of their own. In both cases embeddedness and positive reputation is both a cause and consequence of being persuasive. For the econ-techs, the embeddedness is in the political settlement at the top; for the grassroots representatives of the state, the embeddedness is with relevant client groups or local social eco-system. How these two differing vantage points of embeddedness intersect, disconnect, or work at cross purposes is not only a question for future work on PoEs, but for conceptualization of the state in the developing world writ large.

References

Scott, J. C. (1998). *Seeing Like a State: How Certain Schemes to Improve the Human Condition Have Failed.* New Haven: Yale University Press.

Strauss, J. C. (1998). *Strong Institutions in Weak Polities: State Building in Republican China, 1927–1940.* Oxford: Oxford University Press.

10

From Pockets of Effectiveness to Topographies of State Performance?

Michael Roll

Introduction

While research on pockets of effectiveness (PoEs) has been around for a while, more systematic research, knowledge accumulation, and theoretical consolidation has only taken off in the past few years (see McDonnell and Vilaça 2021 for a recent overview). This volume is an important step in that direction. It advances existing work by systematically investigating the link between political context and bureaucratic performance, by presenting a new theoretical framework in conjunction with a comparative research design, and by linking PoE research to broader debates about the politics of state-building.

Based on a critical assessment of the book's contributions to the field as well as its limitations and remaining open questions, this critical commentary suggests some future directions that PoE research could take. The many opportunities that exist for future research reflect both the relatively early stage that the field is still in in terms of knowledge accumulation, and the continuing practical importance of building state capacity for sustainable development in many parts of the world.

Contributions and limitations

Four contributions make this book stand out. The first one is its theoretical framework. The 'power domains framework' allows Hickey and his team to systematically link political context, defined in terms of political settlements, to bureaucratic organizational performance and thereby go beyond earlier discussions about this interaction. Together with the second main contribution, the theoretically informed research design, this makes the book the most systematic comparative study of PoEs and political context to date. The case studies of state agencies themselves are the third main contribution. They are among the most empirically rich and robust examinations of state agencies in Africa, where research on bureaucracies is generally scarce (Bierschenk and Olivier de Sardan 2014a). The level of detail they provide—both in these chapters and even more

Michael Roll, *From Pockets of Effectiveness to Topographies of State Performance?*. In: *Pockets of Effectiveness and the Politics of State-building and Development in Africa*. Edited by Sam Hickey, Oxford University Press. © Oxford University Press (2023). DOI: 10.1093/oso/9780192864963.003.0010

so in the original working papers[1]—along with the systematic presentation of the material allows readers (and the occasional critical commenter) to crosscheck the book's conclusions. The volume's fourth main contribution is that it links the discussion about PoE to broader debates about the politics of state-building in the developing world in general and in Africa in particular.

The volume's limitations are mostly the result of the authors' clearly defined analytical focus and the relatively early stage that the field of PoE research is still in. These limitations should therefore be regarded as inspirations for future researchers to build on and go beyond the book's contributions. I begin with a discussion of the reframing of PoEs that the authors suggest, then move on to their power domains framework, the distinction between PoEs emergence and persistence, the role of ideas for PoEs, and to the generalizability of the book's findings. In my suggestions for future directions of PoE research, I discuss theoretical framework, methodology, and moving from a PoE focus to a broader perspective on 'topographies of state performance'.

Framing PoEs

In Chapter 1, Hickey and Pruce contend that the framing of high-performing state agencies in weak governance states as 'islands' suggests two things. It first suggests a neopatrimonial framing of the public sector, with PoEs as the Weberian rational bureaucracy anomaly in it and, second, that PoEs are disconnected from their political and institutional context. Alternatively, they argue, PoEs should be seen as outcomes of their political context and that—depending on the context—they can be both attempts at more comprehensive state building and/or tools of a broader strategy of patronage politics, particularly of the regulated kind.

Especially in the literature on the state in Africa, the concept of neopatrimonialism has played an important but ambivalent role and has rightly been criticized (Mkandawire 2015, Pitcher, Moran, and Johnston 2009, Therkildsen 2005). Early studies of PoEs have however mostly focused on organizations in Latin America (Daland 1981, Evans 1992, 1995, Geddes 1990, 1994, Grindle 1997, Schneider 1991, Tendler 1997, Willis 1995). And while PoE studies with a focus on Africa have referred to the literature on neopatrimonialism, they have not all accepted or adopted a neopatrimonial lens (Leonard 1991, Roll 2014). However, because neopatrimonialism is so prominent in the literature on the state in Africa and because it is tempting to frame PoE studies along these lines, Hickey and Pruce are right to point this out and suggest an alternative framing for PoE studies.

Have PoEs been conceptualized as disconnected from their political context in the literature so far? It seems that just as the 'islands' metaphor has not been

---

[1] The original working papers are available at https://www.effective-states.org/publications.

widely used in the PoE literature, many authors have indeed looked at how PoEs are embedded in their respective political contexts (Geddes 1990, Leonard 1991, Schneider 1991, Tendler 1997, the contributions in Roll 2014). The main issue may not be that these earlier studies assumed a disconnect—they rather prioritized the analysis of historically specific processes in individual countries in great detail instead of categorizing political contexts in more abstract theoretical terms for comparative analytical purposes. These studies analysed the specific relations and dynamics between individuals or networks at the micro and meso level rather than at higher levels of abstraction. It is this theoretically guided systematic comparative approach to studying how different political macro-contexts shape the formation and performance of PoEs that makes this book a truly novel contribution.

The power domains framework

The 'power domains' framework that Hickey and Mohan suggest for analysing how the political context shapes PoEs is a combination of a political settlements and a policy domains approach. This framework has a lot going for it: it does not use political regimes as a starting point, it considers different ways in which social and political power can be organized, it acknowledges the importance of distinguishing policy domains, and it appreciates complexity by including a wide variety of additional factors. The framework provides a useful heuristic and has allowed Hickey and his team to develop a strong comparative research design.[2]

Its analytical potential, however, is less obvious. While the political settlements part is well defined and improved by adding the 'systemic vulnerability' dimension to it, the policy-domain side remains underspecified. The idea itself is intriguing but, at the same time, it is not clear what the boundaries of policy domains are, what the key criteria are to distinguish them, how coherent policy domains are in terms of the interests, orientations, and ideas that dominate within them, and which domains there are. Answers to these questions have implication for how generalizable the authors' findings are for PoEs in policy domains other than the 'economic technocracy' policy domain they are focusing on as I discuss below. In fact, I refer to the authors' policy domain as 'financial technocracy' because the economic policy domain is much larger than what the case studies cover. Overall, the policy-domain concept holds a lot of promise for PoE studies but could have been spelled out more clearly given its centrality to the framework.

Partly inspired by the PoE literature, Hickey and Mohan also add several other factors to the policy-domain part of the framework such as ideas, actors,

---

[2] Focusing on the regulation of extractive industries and taxation in Uganda and Tanzania, Kjær, Therkildsen, Buur, and Wendelboe Hansen (2021) have also recently used a political settlements framework to study PoE.

governance arrangements, organizational factors, policy types, and transnational influences. While this openness to complexity and to a wide range of factors has advantages, it makes the framework harder to pin down. It is often not clear if a causal hierarchy is assumed between these factors, if they are expected to interact with and moderate each other in certain ways, or whether there are typical trajectories in which they are likely to play out. Because so many options are possible, it is hard to come up with a figure that summarizes the framework in more detail than the one provided by the authors. The propositions formulated in Chapter 2 are helpful but not all of them are clearly linked to the framework. Proposition pairs 1–2 are clearly deduced from the framework but the links of propositions 3, 4a, and especially 4b to the framework are less straightforward. A more concise and coherent framework would have helped to drive home the authors' key contributions and to assess their analytical use. The power domains framework therefore is a good starting point, but one that future researchers should continue to work on.

PoE emergence and persistence

For analytical purposes, the distinction between the emergence and the persistence of PoEs is crucial. Previous studies have shown that explanations for how PoEs emerge differ from explanations for how they persist (McDonnell 2020, Roll 2014). One of this volume's key findings is that political context is critical for the persistence of PoEs but not for their emergence. As the editor discusses in Chapter 8, PoEs established under more concentrated forms of political leadership following periods of conflict or instability may be particularly durable. But the case studies show that PoEs also emerged in political settlements that were theoretically deemed unfavourable like in Kenya's narrow-dispersed settlement under Kibaki or in Zambia's highly competitive political context under Mwanawasa. The conclusion from this is that PoE *emergence* is not primarily explained by a country's political settlement but by either highly motivated political leaders or by 'merely willing or inattentive' political leaders (McDonnell 2020: 8) in combination with senior bureaucrats with political management skills or 'technopols' (Domínguez 1997, Joignant 2011), political framing, and organizational factors. While it might be possible to identify typical trajectories of PoE emergence, these processes generally are contingent enough to occur under very different political circumstances.

The same is not true for PoE *persistence*. Political settlements seem to go a long way to explain why PoEs persist or why they disintegrate. This finding significantly improves our understanding of PoE dynamics and should be taken into account and investigated in more detail in future studies. This conclusion that political context is crucial for PoE persistence but not emergence suggests a reformulation of one of Hickey's and Pruce's central claims in Chapter 1. The case studies suggest that PoEs are not direct outcomes of political structures but rather contingent phenomena that can emerge in a variety of contexts but whose persistence is enabled and made more likely by favourable political settlements. In short: politics is enabling and sustaining but not driving PoEs.

Ideas and PoEs

One of the book's innovations is that it includes the role of ideas in the study of PoEs. However, partly because the authors do not spell out how precisely ideas fit into their power domains framework, this contribution is empirically insightful but conceptually and analytically incomplete. Future work on PoEs should help to overcome this and the data presented in the case studies suggest an important differentiation that should be considered in these efforts. While ideas are presented as important for PoE emergence and persistence in the case studies, they include two very different understandings of ideas. These are, first, an instrumental understanding of ideas as a strategic framing device to convince political leaders to take action and, second, a normative understanding of ideas as strongly held norms and beliefs that motivate behaviour.[3] This differentiation is important for understanding both the emergence and the persistence of PoEs.

When political settlements turn unfavourable for PoEs, the likeliness that they will persist drops. But the case studies show that ideas in the form of strongly held norms and beliefs can mediate this process, at least for certain periods of time. Presidents Kibaki and Mwanawasa tried to protect their financial technocracy PoEs because they held strong professional norms and beliefs about the central importance of these organizations' tasks for state performance.

Under the same conditions, ideas as strategic framing devices are quickly disposed of and do not mediate between unfavourable political settlements and protection and support for PoEs. Ugandan president Museveni did not hold strong beliefs with regards to public management and monetary policy. By framing these tasks in terms of the military discipline in which he did believe, his advisors convinced him of the usefulness of creating PoEs in this domain. But this only worked as long as the political settlement remained favourable, and the president thought that PoEs might win him votes. Protection and support for these PoEs vanished as soon as the president's position weakened, and he realized these effective agencies did not generate the expected political returns which was the main function he expected these organizations to perform (in addition to legitimacy amongst

---

[3] McDonnell's (2020) discussion of bureaucratic ethos and the 'dual habitus' of PoE founding cadres is relevant here although she focuses on the lived experience of bureaucratic practices while the normative understanding of ideas as discussed here is more about how development happens, and which policy domains should be prioritized for that.

international financial institutions). Instead, using these very state agencies and their financial power as part of his patronage strategy to fight for political survival became the top priority and sacrificing PoEs was not considered too high a price to pay for that.

While ideas as strategic framing devices may be instrumentally useful for certain periods of time, strongly held norms and beliefs are probably more powerful and more enduring motivating factors. Future PoE studies should clearly distinguish and examine these different understandings and effects of ideas.

Generalizability

How much can we learn from the book about PoEs in general? The answer to that question depends on how domain-specific PoEs in the financial technocracy are. As the authors point out, there are good reasons to believe that financial technocracy PoEs are very domain-specific which would make this a book about 'pockets of financial technocracy effectiveness' (or PoFTE) as a specific subtype of PoE. Because of the early stage that the field of PoE research is in, this both advances and limits the book's contribution. It advances it by providing new knowledge about a particular subtype of PoE but it limits the generalizability of the findings for PoEs in other policy domains. A discussion of which aspects may apply to PoEs more generally and which ones may be more domain-specific, however, is missing.

The authors decided to focus on financial technocracy PoEs in the first place because the expert surveys they conducted on organizational performance in each of the countries showed that PoEs were more prominent in this domain than in others. The fact that other PoE studies also focus on financial technocracy PoEs or see the most potential in them seems to corroborate that (e.g. Johnson 2015, Strauss 1998, Willis 1995). In the remainder of this section, I discuss three reasons why this may not actually be the case.

The first reason is the importance of *relative* effectiveness (Roll 2014: 25, 36). While PoEs must provide the public goods or services they are mandated to provide, their effectiveness is 'relative to the context they operate in and relative to other public organizations in the same context' (Roll 2014: 36), especially in the same policy domain. Some state agencies and even whole policy domains have a systematic advantage over others because the nature of their tasks is logistical. They can achieve 'core effectiveness' (Roll 2014: 201) much easier than agencies with transactional tasks because they only operate at headquarters in a highly centralized manner, have a limited and highly specified number of tasks, and only interact with a comparatively small number of organizations and individuals. State agencies or policy domains with tasks that are transactional such as health and education must overcome far more challenges to achieve 'scale effectiveness' (Roll 2014: 201) because they have a broader variety of tasks, have countrywide networks of offices with thousands of officials to lead and coordinate, and because they have daily interactions with a broad variety of actors at all levels. The authors discuss this distinction in Chapters 1 and 8 but, given the importance of this point, I repeat the argument here and suggest options for dealing with the problem. If these two types of effectiveness are systematically different and if achieving core effectiveness is much easier than achieving scale effectiveness, then state agencies that operate in these two fields cannot be compared to each other without taking this into account. There are two options for resolving this. The first one is to develop a truly relative context-specific understanding and operationalization of effectiveness to find out if PoEs are more frequent in certain policy domains than in others. The second option is to restrict the concept of PoEs to tasks that are broadly logistical where core effectiveness is attainable and to develop a new conceptual framework and terminology for more complex transactional tasks that aim for scale effectiveness and which cannot be undertaken by narrowly bounded organizations.[4]

The second reason why PoE may not be more frequent in the financial technocracy domain than in others is epistemological. Partly due to the nature of their task, certain state agencies and agencies in certain policy domains are more visible than others and are more likely to be perceived as 'effective' bureaucracies.[5] They might be perceived as more effective than others because they confirm existing stereotypes and norms and expectations of what 'effective bureaucracies' look like. Just as certain norms and expectations are linked to what is called 'hegemonic masculinity' (Connell and Messerschmidt 2005), for example, there might also be a 'hegemonic (neoliberal) PoEs'. It is likely that this model of a hegemonic PoE features number-crunching men in dark suits with laptops and leather briefcases in high-rise office buildings rather than nurses and teachers in run-down rural health centres and schools. The analogy of this image of a hegemonic PoE with a private corporation is probably not coincidental. A study in Denmark has shown that perceived organizational performance declines when respondents are informed that an organization is a public instead of a private organization (Hvidman and Andersen 2015). If existing norms and expectations influence the results of perception-based surveys about organizational performance to such a degree even in strong-governance contexts irrespective of actual organizational performance, the results of PoE-identification surveys should be assessed even more carefully. Depending on how well these surveys are developed and conducted, their results may at least in part be methodological artefacts. While the PoE-identification surveys that have been conducted as part of the case studies presented in this book are among the more systematic efforts to do so,

---

[4] Thanks to Sam Hickey for questioning whether the first option would resolve the problem and for suggesting the second option as an alternative.

[5] Julia C. Strauss makes a similar point in her critical commentary in this book.

this possibility cannot be ruled out. To evaluate that, more information about the respondents would be necessary such as their professions and disciplinary background, their fields of expertise and observation regarding agency performance, their understanding of 'effectiveness', their exposure to international development policy debates, and, perhaps, their gender.

Beyond these epistemological and methodological challenges, however, governance surveys and PoE-identification assessments in weak governance contexts have *not* consistently found that financial or economic technocracy agencies are perceived to be most effective (McDonnell 2020: 12–19, Pogoson and Roll 2014: 100, Portes and Smith 2012). The surveys conducted for this book also identified PoEs outside of the economic technocracy domain such as Uganda's National Water and Sewerage Corporation (Bukenya 2020) and Zambia's Seed Control and Certification Institute. What that says about the validity of PoE-identification surveys and the role of stereotypes is an important question that clearly requires more research.

The third point is more speculative and accepts that PoEs could be more frequent in the financial policy domain—but only for certain periods of time. In the book's conclusion, and referring to Mkandawire (2014), Hickey argues that the higher frequency of PoEs in what he calls the economic technocracy domain might have to do with the shifting prioritization from 'spending ministries' to 'agencies of constraint' in the era of structural adjustment. This is an important qualification and might hint at a more general point. There might be a temporal pattern in the sense of historical periods during which certain policy domains are prioritized which is why PoEs are more likely to exist in these domains during these phases. The 1960s and early 1970s might have been the era in which comparatively many PoEs existed in the agricultural domain (Leonard 1991), the late 1970s and 1980s the era of industrial policy PoEs (Johnson 1982), and since then the era of financial technocracy. The rise of neoliberalism and global financialization probably drove this latest shift (see Chapter 8, also Jones 2020).[6] In other words: if such an empirical pattern exists—and it is far from certain that it does—it might suggest that PoEs are more frequent in those policy domains that are regarded as priority domains for development by powerful actors in the respective historical periods. If that were true, this book's findings would not only be policy-domain specific but also historically specific. But whether such a temporal pattern exists is an open question that can only be answered by more high-quality data and systemic comparative research. The same is true for a better assessment of how domain- and time-specific and therefore how generalizable the findings of this book are for PoEs beyond the financial technocracy domain.

---

[6] Since the late 1990s, however, there has been another global trend that is often overlooked. Since then, pro-poor welfare-state services and programmes have been massively expanded in the developing world (Seekings 2017). I discuss this in more detail below.

Suggestions for future PoE research

This book advances the understanding of how politics and PoE are linked by answering many important questions. As with any good book, however, it raises even more questions. Future PoE researchers, therefore, can explore many different options for building on and going beyond the book's contributions.[7] Below, I suggest some directions that future PoE research could take. These suggestions are, of course, not exhaustive and are shaped by my own understanding of the field. The first two points follow directly from the critical discussion of the book. The third point suggests adopting a broader perspective and research design and move from PoE research to an understanding of 'topographies of state performance' into which PoEs could then be embedded.

Theoretical framework

The power domains framework and its components, political settlements and policy domains, are important innovations for PoE research and future researchers should apply and further elaborate them. Considering the multitude of additional factors that have been integrated into this framework in the book, there are two broad options: either to integrate all these elements in a more coherent way or to work with more parsimonious models. Both strategies would allow us to test emanating hypotheses in more systematic ways.

On the link between PoEs and state capacity, this book confirms previous findings that there is little evidence that PoEs build more general state capacity beyond the confines of the respective state agencies. By including the case of Rwanda, the book also shows that the mode of comprehensive state capacity-building there did not rely on individual PoEs and was driven by other factors than those that explain PoE emergence and persistence. For a better understanding of the links between state capacity and PoEs, however, a more systematic comparative study of historical and current episodes of state (capacity) building and the role of PoEs in these processes would be worthwhile.

Methodology

PoE research could be improved significantly with better methodology. One way is to develop more sophisticated ways of identifying PoEs. Perception- and experience-based surveys will continue to play an important role. But to produce more nuanced insights, especially about similarities and differences across policy

---

[7] For more suggestions for future PoE research, see McDonnell and Vilaça 2021.

domains, a more reflective approach is necessary which takes existing stereotypes (Hvidman and Andersen 2015) into account. Alternative and more objective ways of identifying PoEs and measuring their autonomy and performance are another promising way to go if the necessary data are available or can be generated (see, for example, Bersch, Praça, and Taylor 2017).

An important methodological challenge is to define and operationalize PoEs in policy domains that are transactional (scale effectiveness) rather than logistical (core effectiveness). Finding the best performers in policy domains such as education and health is possible but perhaps more challenging than in financial and economic policy. Comparing the relative effectiveness of these agencies to each other across policy domains, however, requires new ways of understanding, measuring, and analysing effectiveness.

Topographies of state performance, or: The bureaucratic performance continuum perspective

The biggest strength of PoE research is also its greatest weakness: its focus on extreme cases. While studying changes in bureaucratic organizational performance over longer periods of time—as this volume does—goes some way to mitigate this problem, the focus remains on agencies that have been at the extreme end of a country's bureaucratic performance continuum for at least five years. While PoE studies improve our understanding of how they work, we often know very little about the broader universe of bureaucratic performance and how bureaucracies are distributed across that performance continuum. Inspired by Catherine Boone's metaphor (2003), I refer to these universes or bureaucratic performance continua as the 'topographies of state performance'.[8] We may know—or think we know— the agencies at the extreme ends, the best and the worst performers. But the real problem lies in the middle. What is the middle range of bureaucratic performance, how do agencies differ within that range, and what makes them improve or deteriorate from that middle section of the continuum? When Bersch et al. (2017) used objective indicators to measure the 'autonomous state capacity' of state agencies in Brazil, they discovered 'the absence of a clear dichotomy between a few islands of excellence and a broader morass of terrible agencies' and instead 'a very large set of agencies of middling, reasonable but not outstanding, capacity' (Bersch et al. 2017: 178). While Brazil's relatively strong state capacity may partly explain this, similar patterns might very well also exist in countries with lower state capacity.

---

[8] In her book *Political Topographies of the African State: Territorial Authority and Institutional Choice* (2003), Boone uses the metaphor 'political topography' to refer to the highly uneven power that central states have within national spaces, primarily because the bargaining power of regional elites and the political economies of regions differ which shapes centre–provincial relations in varying ways.

To improve the understanding of state performance, particularly in the developing world, it may therefore be necessary to complement the study of PoEs with a better understanding of the topographies of state performance within and across policy domains. From a researcher's point of view, this perspective would allow for a better comparative understanding of bureaucratic performance including PoEs, especially if changes in the topography of state performance would be observed over longer periods of time.[9] And for practitioners and citizens it would be important to know if moderate performance improvements in particular agencies may contribute considerably more to sustainable development and well-being than a few top performers in other policy domains—although the mechanisms that explain moderate and extreme PoE-level improvements are likely to differ.

This bureaucratic performance continuum, or topography of state performance perspective, seems to be most promising for studying two types of performance variation: variation *within* policy domains and variation *across* policy domains. The first step for studying varying bureaucratic performance *within* policy domains is to define the domain boundaries. Next, the bureaucratic performance of state agencies within this domain could be measured and compared. This could be done at the country level or across countries. It would be interesting to see if there are common patterns regarding the better- or worse-performing agencies, the middle range of organizations, and the major changes of agencies across the performance continuum over time. Studies of the topography of state performance within policy domains could first focus on domains that have so far been neglected in PoE research, especially those in more transactional domains such as social and industrial policy.[10]

For studying the variation of bureaucratic performance *across* policy domains, defining domain boundaries is equally important. It would then be possible to compare entire domain-specific topographies of state performance to each other (e.g. financial policy and education) to see if certain topographical patterns appear to be domain-specific (e.g. many organizations in the middle and few extreme cases or a more even distribution). Another approach would be to take agencies from different policy domains and directly compare their performance to each other. However, this would require new ways of measuring and analysing domain-specific *relative* effectiveness as discussed above. It would then be possible to show if PoEs really are more frequent in certain policy domains or whether this is an epistemological or methodological artefact. Again, this could be done at

---

[9] The World Bank Bureaucracy Lab's new dataset Worldwide Bureaucracy Indicators (WWBI) so far mostly focuses on the personnel and wage dimensions of the public sector.

[10] While they do not work with PoE frameworks, there are important contributions that could be used as starting points for this, such as the work on pro-poor welfare states in the developing world (Seekings 2017) and the study on the politics of industrial policy in Africa by Whitfield, Therkildsen, Buur, and Kjær (2015).

country level or across countries, although this would increase the complexity and methodological challenges even more.

Finally, if a better understanding of the full topography of state performance is the goal, one might rightly ask if state agencies are the best unit of analysis. Some of the most impressive social development achievements in the developing world in recent years were not primarily driven by state agencies. Instead, they came in the form of new legislation on taxation, land rights, universal health care, and others and were driven by diverse groups of actors such as 'development entrepreneurs' (Faustino and Booth 2014, Sidel and Faustino 2019) or 'professional movements' (Harris 2017). Other achievements came in the form of dedicated programmes developed and lobbied for by coalitions of progressive politicians, social movements, and trade unions such as Bolsa Familia in Brazil. Overall, the progress with pro-poor welfare-state-building in the developing world at the national level (Seekings 2017) and to varying degrees at the subnational level (Singh 2016) in recent years, and especially in Latin America often in conjunction with more inclusionary forms of policymaking (Kapiszewski, Levitsky, and Yashar 2021), is a little studied but important part of the modern topography of state performance in the Global South. Many countries that were previously deemed too poor in resources and bureaucratic capacity have increased public spending in education and health and have introduced social assistance programmes such as old-age and disability pension programmes, universal health care, and child and family support programmes. This has also been the case in many African countries, partly because cash-transfer programmes do not require a large bureaucracy but can be organized using new technologies and private-sector administrative capacity. In his review of the construction of pro-poor welfare states in the developing world, Seekings (2017) distinguishes between developmental and welfare state capacity and concludes: 'Even where states lacked capacity to perform many other functions, including especially developmental ones, capacity was rarely if ever a significant constraint on building inclusive welfare states' (Seekings 2017: 379). Whether these observations alleviate Hickey's concern that PoEs seem to be less frequent in more social-service-oriented policy domains remains to be seen. But what they certainly do is to question the centrality of PoEs and the use of state agencies as the exclusive or dominant unit of analysis for state capacity and as drivers of sustainable development more generally. Instead, they provide additional support for the idea of moving from a focus on PoEs to a broader topographies-of-state-performance perspective in which PoEs could then be embedded.

Such a broader perspective might also help PoE studies to contribute to building a robust research programme that can be linked more systematically to other programmes. This would be in line with the resurgence of subnational comparative research (Giraudy, Moncada, and Snyder 2019) and a growing interest in the role of bureaucracy for development in the social sciences (Andrews,

Pritchett, and Woolcock 2017, Besley, Burgess, Khan, and Xu 2021, Bierschenk and Olivier de Sardan 2014b, Pepinsky, Pierskalla, and Sacks 2017). Related research programmes beyond the one on state capacity already discussed in this book (Centeno, Kohli, and Yashar with Mistree 2017) include those on institutions and institutional change more generally (Bersch 2019, Brinks, Levitsky, and Murillo 2020, Cheeseman 2018, Tapscott 2021), and on state–society embeddedness, interaction, and coproduction (Evans 1995 and 1997, Evans, Huber, and Stephens 2017). A systematic discussion of the implications of PoE research findings and a topographies-of-state-performance perspective for development policy is also necessary, especially considering more recent political and adaptive approaches to development assistance (Roll 2021).

Whichever direction PoE researchers take, this book's fresh theoretical framework, novel findings, and fascinating empirical details will continue to inspire and provoke future studies of PoEs and the politics of state performance. Work on PoEs can no longer be considered 'marginal monologues' (Roll 2014: 26) and has entered a phase in which a community-wide discussion is ongoing that others in the state capacity, governance, and development field are increasingly paying attention to. This book is an important step in this direction.

References

Andrews, M., Pritchett, L., and Woolcock, M. (2017). *Building State Capability: Evidence, Analysis, Action*. Oxford: Oxford University Press.

Bersch, K. (2019). *When Democracies Deliver: Governance Reform in Latin America*. Cambridge: Cambridge University Press.

Bersch, K., Praça, S., and Taylor M. M. (2017). 'Bureaucratic Capacity and Political Autonomy within National States: Mapping the Archipelago of Excellence in Brazil'. In M. A. Centeno, A. Kohli, and D. J. Yashar (eds), *States in the Developing World*. Cambridge: Cambridge University Press. 157–83.

Besley, T. J., Burgess, R., Khan, A., and Xu, G. (2021). 'Bureaucracy and Development'. NBER Working Paper 29163. Cambridge, MA: National Bureau of Economic Research.

Bierschenk, T. and Olivier de Sardan, J.-P. (2014a). 'Studying the Dynamics of African Bureaucracies. An Introduction to States at Work'. In T. Bierschenk and J.-P. Olivier de Sardan (eds), *States at Work: Dynamics of African Bureaucracies*. Leiden: Brill. 3–33.

Bierschenk, T. and Olivier de Sardan, J.-P. (eds) (2014b). *States at Work: Dynamics of African Bureaucracies*. Leiden: Brill.

Boone, C. (2003). *Political Topographies of the African State: Territorial Authority and Institutional Choice*. Cambridge: Cambridge University Press.

Brinks, D. M., Levitsky, S., and Murillo, M. V. (eds) (2020). *The Politics of Institutional Weakness in Latin America*. Cambridge: Cambridge University Press.

Bukenya, B. (2020). 'The Politics of Building Effective Water Utilities in the Global South: A Case of NWSC Uganda'. ESID Working Paper No. 152. Manchester: Effective States and Inclusive Development Research Centre, University of Manchester.

Cheeseman, N. (ed.) (2018). *Institutions and Democracy in Africa: How the Rules of the Game Shape Political Developments*. Cambridge: Cambridge University Press.

Centeno, M. A., Kohli, A., and Yashar, D. J. with Mistree, D. (eds) (2017). *States in the Developing World*. Cambridge: Cambridge University Press.

Connell, R. W. and Messerschmidt, J. (2005). 'Hegemonic Masculinity: Rethinking the Concept', *Gender and Society*, 19: 829–59.

Daland, R. (1981). *Exploring Brazilian Bureaucracy: Performance and Pathology*. Washington, DC: University Press of America.

Domínguez, J. I. (1997). *Technopols: Freeing Politics and Markets in Latin America in the 1990s*. University Park, PA: Penn State Press.

Evans, P. (1992). 'The State as Problem and Solution: Predation, Embedded Autonomy, and Structural Change'. In S. Haggard (ed.), *The Politics of Economic Adjustment: International Constraints, Distributive Conflicts, and the State*. Princeton, NJ: Princeton University Press. 140–81.

Evans, P. (1995). *Embedded Autonomy: States and Industrial Transformation*. Princeton, NJ: Princeton University Press.

Evans, P. (1997). *State–Society Synergy: Government and Social Capital in Development*. Berkeley, CA: University of California at Berkeley.

Evans, P., Huber, E., and Stephens, J. D. (2017). 'The Political Foundations of State Effectiveness'. In M. A. Centeno, A. Kohli, and D. J. Yashar (eds), *States in the Developing World*. Cambridge: Cambridge University Press. 380–408.

Faustino, J. and Booth, D. (2014). 'Development Entrepreneurship: How Donors and Leaders Can Foster Institutional Change'. Working Politically in Practice Series—Case Study No. 2. San Francisco, CA and London: The Asia Foundation and the Overseas Development Institute.

Geddes, B. (1990). 'Building "State" Autonomy in Brazil, 1930–1964', *Comparative Politics*, 22(2): 217–35.

Geddes, B. (1994). *Politician's Dilemma: Building State Capacity in Latin America*. Berkeley, CA: University of California Press.

Giraudy, A., Moncada, E., and Snyder, R. (eds) (2019). *Inside Countries: Subnational Research in Comparative Politics*. Cambridge: Cambridge University Press.

Grindle, M. (1997). 'Divergent Cultures? When Public Organisations Perform Well in Developing Countries', *World Development*, 25(4): 481–95.

Harris, J. (2017). *Achieving Access: Professional Movements and the Politics of Health Universalism*. Ithaca, NY: Cornell University Press.

Hvidman, U. and Andersen, S. C. (2015). 'Perceptions of Public and Private Performance: Evidence from a Survey Experiment', *Public Administration Review*, 76(1): 111–20.

Johnson, C. A. (1982). *MITI and the Japanese Miracle: The Growth of Industrial Policy 1925–1975*. Stanford, CA: Stanford University Press.

Johnson, M. C. (2015). 'Donor Requirements and Pockets of Effectiveness in Senegal's Bureaucracy', *Development Policy Review*, 33(6): 783–804.

Joignant, A. (2011). 'The Politics of Technopols: Resources, Political Competence and Collective Leadership in Chile, 1990–2010', *Journal of Latin American Studies*, 43(3): 517–46.

Jones, E. (ed.) (2020). *The Political Economy of Bank Regulation in Developing Countries: Risk and Reputation*. Oxford: Oxford University Press.

Kapiszewski, D., Levitsky, S., and Yashar, D. J. (2021). *The Inclusionary Turn in Latin American Democracies*. Cambridge: Cambridge University Press.

Kjær, A. M., Therkildsen, O., Buur, L., and Wendelboe Hansen, M. (2021). 'When "Pockets of Effectiveness" Matter Politically: Extractive Industry Regulation and Taxation in Uganda and Tanzania', *The Extractive Industries and Society*, 8(1): 294–302.

Leonard, D. K. (1991). *African Successes: Four Public Managers of Kenyan Rural Development*. Berkeley, CA: University of California Press.

McDonnell, E. M. (2020). *Patchwork Leviathan: Pockets of Bureaucratic Effectiveness in Developing States*. Princeton, NJ: Princeton University Press.

McDonnell, E. M. and Vilaça, L. (2021). 'Pockets of Effectiveness and Islands of Integrity: Variation in Quality of Government within Central State Administrations'. In A. Bågenholm, M. Bauer, M. Grimes, and B. Rothstein (eds), *The Oxford Handbook of the Quality of Government*. Oxford: Oxford University Press. 662–83.

Mkandawire, T. (2014). 'The Spread of Economic Doctrines and Policymaking in Postcolonial Africa', *African Studies Review*, 57(1): 171–98.

Mkandawire, T. (2015). 'Neopatrimonialism and the Political Economy of Economic Performance in Africa: Critical Reflections', *World Politics*, 67(3): 563–612.

Pepinsky, T. B., Pierskalla, J. H., and Sacks, A. (2017). 'Bureaucracy and Service Delivery', *Annual Review of Political Science*, 20: 249–68.

Pitcher, A., Moran, M. H., and Johnston, M. (2009). 'Rethinking Patrimonialism and Neopatrimonialism in Africa', *African Studies Review*, 52: 125–56.

Pogoson, A. I. and Roll, M. (2014). 'Turning Nigeria's Drug Sector around: The National Agency for Food and Drug Administration and Control (NAFDAC)'. In M. Roll (ed.), *The Politics of Public Sector Performance: Pockets of Effectiveness in Developing Countries*. Abingdon: Routledge. 97–127.

Portes, A. and Smith, L. D. (eds) (2012). *Institutions Count: Their Role and Significance in Latin American Development*. Berkeley, CA: University of California Press.

Roll, M. (ed.) (2014). *The Politics of Public Sector Performance: Pockets of Effectiveness in Developing Countries*. Abingdon: Routledge.

Roll, M. (2021). 'Institutional Change through Development Assistance: The Comparative Advantages of Political and Adaptive Approaches'. DIE Discussion Paper 28/2021. Bonn: German Development Institute/Deutsches Institut für Entwicklungspolitik.

Schneider, B. R. (1991). *Politics within the State: Elite Bureaucrats and Industrial Policy in Authoritarian Brazil*. Pittsburgh, PA: University of Pittsburgh Press.

Seekings, J. (2017). 'State Capacity and the Construction of Pro-Poor Welfare States in the "Developing" World'. In M. A. Centeno, A. Kohli, and D. J. Yashar (eds) (2017). *States in the Developing World*. Cambridge: Cambridge University Press. 363–79.

Sidel, J. T. and Faustino, J. (2019). *Thinking and Working Politically in Development: Coalitions for Change in the Philippines*. Pasig City: The Asia Foundation.

Singh, P. (2016). *How Solidarity Works for Welfare: Subnationalism and Social Development in India*. Cambridge: Cambridge University Press.

Strauss, J. C. (1998). *Strong Institutions in Weak Polities: State Building in Republican China, 1927–1940*. Oxford: Oxford University Press.

Tapscott, R. (2021). *Arbitrary States: Social Control and Modern Authoritarianism in Museveni's Uganda*. Oxford: Oxford University Press.

Tendler, J. (1997). *Good Government in the Tropics*. Baltimore, MD: Johns Hopkins University Press.

Therkildsen, O. (2005). 'Understanding Public Management through Neopatrimonialism: A Paradigm for All African Seasons?' In U. Engel and G. R. Olsen (eds), *The African Exception*. Aldershot: Ashgate. 35–52.

Whitfield, L., Therkildsen, O., Buur, L., and Kjær, A. M. (2015). *The Politics of African Industrial Policy: A Comparative Perspective*. Cambridge: Cambridge University Press.

Willis, E. (1995). 'Explaining Bureaucratic Independence in Brazil: The Experience of the National Economic Development Bank', *Journal of Latin American Studies*, 27: 625–61.

Pockets of Effectiveness: Expert Survey (v_1)

Introduction

The aim of this survey is to advance understanding of public sector performance in (insert country name) and to inform efforts to promote bureaucratic capacity and developmental governance in (insert country name). We are asking experts to share their perceptions of the effectiveness of a variety of bureaucratic organizations and regulatory authorities. By 'effective', we refer to the capacity of these public sector organizations to *regularly achieve mandated functions* and to *perform at a higher level than other ministries /departments/ agencies in a similar area of government.*

This survey is intended to perform two roles. The first is to gain a clearer sense of the incidence and spread of high-performing organizations within the (insert country name) public sector. The second is to identify some specific organizations for in-depth case study research. We are particularly interested in sectors of governance that have a major role in promoting development, including those concerned with economic growth and macroeconomic stability; the regulation of key sectors (e.g. natural resource governance, agriculture, health, education) and the delivery of public services and infrastructure. Given that there is no index of high-performing organizations within the public sector in (insert country name), the expert opinions of informed observers such as you are critical to this project.

Confidentiality: please be assured that all responses will be treated as confidential, and that no sources will be named in any of the project's outputs.

Part A: General survey of government ministries/departments/agencies

A1. How would you describe the performance of different parts of the Government over the past five years, in terms of how effective they have generally been at regularly achieving their mandated functions? (e.g. in terms of policy-making, implementation of public policies and programmes/service delivery and monitoring and evaluation of policies/programmes/ service delivery)?

A2. Which of the following statements best describes the distribution of performance amongst different parts of government in (insert country name)?

Most ministries/departments/agencies regularly deliver on their mandate, with only a few failing to do so.

On average, around half of all ministries/departments/agencies regularly deliver on their mandate, whilst the remainder struggle to do so.

Only a few ministries/departments/agencies regularly deliver on their mandate, whilst the majority generally fail to do so.

A3. Can you identify any particular sectors of government that tend to have more higher-performing units than other sectors? Why, in your view, do these sectors have more high performers?

A4. Can you identify any particular sectors of government that tend to have lower numbers of higher-performing units than others? Why, in your view, do these sectors have fewer high performers?

A5. In your experience and knowledge, are there any ministries, departments, or agencies that stand out as examples of highly effective government administration? By highly-effective, we refer to the capacity to <u>regularly achieve mandated functions</u> and to <u>perform at a higher level than other ministries/departments/agencies in a similar area of government</u>. Please identify sub-units where appropriate, e.g. specific departments within ministries.

If it would help to jog your memory, here is a list of the <u>Ministries and Pubic Service Organizations</u>. Are there any Ministries or groups within a Ministry from this list that have a reputation for being highly effective in achieving their mandated functions? If so, please identify sub-units here appropriate, e.g. specific departments within ministries.

Add list here.

A6. Which ministries/departments/agencies would you judge to be currently the most powerful, with regards to having the greatest influence over (a) the direction of government policy and (b) the performance of government? Has this altered significantly over the past five–ten years?

A7. Can you identify any ministries/departments/agencies that used to be high-performing but which have become less effective in achieving their mandate in recent years? Which ones?

A8. Similarly, have any ministries/departments/agencies significantly improved their performance in recent years? Which ones?

Part B: General survey of regulatory agencies

B1. How would you describe the performance of different regulatory authorities over the past five years, in terms of how effective they have generally been at <u>regularly achieving their mandated functions</u>?

B2. Which of the following statements best describes the distribution of performance amongst different regulatory authorities in (insert country name)?

Most regulatory authorities regularly deliver on their mandate, with only a few failing to do so.

On average, around half of all regulatory authorities regularly deliver on their mandate, whilst the remainder struggle to do so.

Only a few regulatory authorities regularly deliver on their mandate, whilst the majority generally fail to do so.

B3. Can you identify any particular sectors that tend to have more/higher-performing regulatory agencies as compared to other sectors?

B4. Can you identify any particular sectors that tend to have fewer/no high-performing regulatory agencies as compared to other sectors?

B5. In your experience and knowledge are there any regulatory authorities that stand out as examples of being highly effective in <u>regularly achieving their mandated functions</u> and in <u>performing at a higher level than other regulatory authorities in similar</u>

<u>areas of governance?</u> Please identify sub-units where appropriate, e.g. specific units within regulatory authorities.

Here is a list of <u>regulatory authorities</u> by sector: are there any here that have a reputation for being highly effective in discharging their mandated functions? Please identify sub-units here appropriate, e.g. specific units within these authorities.

Add list here.

B6. Have there been any significant changes in the capacity of regulatory authorities to deliver on their mandates in the past ten years? E.g. have any started to decline from previously high levels of performance? Which ones?

B7. Similarly, have any regulatory authorities significantly improved their performance over this timeframe? Which ones?

Part C: Agency details

For each of those identified as a high-performing MDA and/or regulatory authority:

C1. On a scale of 1–10 (1 = low, 10 = high), how effective would you judge this agency to be in terms of the capacity to deliver on its mandated functions?

C2. On what basis would you consider this to be a high-performing agency/authority? Are there any indicators of its ability to deliver on its mandate? (Probe for data sources that we can follow-up on here).

C3. Can you identify any particular instances/cases where the unit/agency/authority in question performed its roles effectively? (Probe for examples that we can follow-up in more depth on).

C4. What reasons would you identify for this success? (Probe for the possible role of politics, e.g. to what extent has this agency managed to avoid some of the problems that are often noted as holding back other public sector agencies from doing their jobs effectively, including political interference around appointment processes etc.)

C5. Who would you advise we talk to further about gaining a clearer understanding of the performance of this unit?

Part D: Validity check (to be undertaken with respondents once certain agencies have been mentioned regularly with initial respondents)

D1. Please offer your opinion on some other organizations that have been suggested as high-performing agencies. I would very much appreciate your expert view on whether you agree or disagree, and the reasons why. [Insert any previously nominated organizations not mentioned by R. Repeat Qs.]

D2. Would you be interested in/available to attend a workshop that we plan to hold with key informants and stakeholders to discuss the results of this survey and to assist in the final identification of cases for follow-up research?

Index